SPANISH THE EASY WAY

BOOK 2

by

CHRISTOPHER KENDRIS

B.S., M.S., Columbia University
M.A., Ph.D., Northwestern University
Diplômé, Faculté des Lettres, Sorbonne

Department of Foreign Languages
The Albany Academy
Albany, New York

BARRON'S EDUCATIONAL SERIES, INC.
Woodbury, New York • London • Toronto • Sydney

All inquiries should be addressed to:
Barron's Educational Series, Inc.
113 Crossways Park Drive
Woodbury, New York 11797

Library of Congress Catalog Card No. 82-20788

International Standard Book No. 0-8120-2636-5

Library of Congress Cataloging in Publication Data

Kendris, Christopher.
  Spanish the easy way, book 2.

  (Easy way)
  Continues: Spanish the easy way, book 1 / by Ruth J.
Silverstein, Allen Pomerantz, Heywood Wald.
  Includes index.
  1. Spanish language—Self-instruction. I. Silver-
stein, Ruth J.   Spanish the easy way, book 1.
II. Title. III. Series.
PC4112.5.K46 1983   468.2'421   82-20788
ISBN 0-8120-2636-5

PRINTED IN THE UNITED STATES OF AMERICA
4567   695   9876543

To all my students at The Albany Academy,
Albany, New York

CONTENTS

PART I: GRAMMAR AND VOCABULARY

PART II: FIVE PRACTICE TESTS

This is the second of two books. Book 2 is intended for you if you have begun to study Spanish either in school, in college, at home on your own, or with a private tutor.

Book 2 in this new EASY WAY series is a continuation of Spanish 1, with an emphasis on intermediate and advanced language, including a complete and thorough review of beginning Spanish.

If I have inadvertently omitted any points in Spanish grammar, vocabulary, and idiomatic expressions you think are important, please write to me, care of the publisher of this book, so that I may include them in the next edition.

ABOUT THE AUTHOR

Christopher Kendris is at present a teacher of Spanish language and literature at The Albany Academy, Albany, New York. He is also a teacher of French. His credentials are as follows.

Dr. Kendris earned his B.S. and M.S. degrees at Columbia University in the City of New York, where he held a New York State scholarship, and his M.A. and Ph.D. degrees at Northwestern University in Evanston, Illinois. He also earned two diplomas with *Mention très Honorable* at the Université de Paris (en Sorbonne), Faculté des Lettres, Ecole Supérieure de Préparation et de Perfectionnement des Professeurs de Français à l'Etranger, and at the Institut de Phonétique, Paris.

He has taught at the College of The University of Chicago as visiting summer lecturer and at Northwestern University, where he held a Teaching Assistantship and Tutorial Fellowship for four years. He has also taught at Colby College, Duke University, Rutgers—the State University of New Jersey, and the State University of New York at Albany. He was Chairman of the Foreign Languages Department at Farmingdale High School, Farmingdale, New York, where he was also a teacher of Spanish and French.

He is the author of numerous school and college books, workbooks, dictionaries, and other language aids. Among his most popular works are *201, 301,* and *501 Spanish Verbs Fully Conjugated in All the Tenses* (latter one, second edition, with special features); *201, 301,* and *501 French Verbs Fully Conjugated in All the Tenses* (latter one, second edition, with special features); *French Now!* (Level One textbook and workbook); *How to Prepare for College Board Achievement Tests: Spanish,* fourth edition; *How to Prepare for College Board Achievement Tests: French,* third edition; *French Composition, a Practical Guide; French the Easy Way, Books 1 and 2;* and two workbooks, *Beginning to Write in Spanish* and *Beginning to Write in French*—all of which have been issued by this publisher. He also wrote the English version of Maurice Grevisse's *Le français correct,* published under the title *Correct French,* also issued by this publisher.

Dr. Kendris is listed in *Contemporary Authors* and *Directory of American Scholars.*

INTRODUCTION

This book is intended for you if you have at least some knowledge of the basic elements of the Spanish language. You can improve what you may already know of Spanish grammar if you study this book twenty minutes each day, starting at the beginning.

You can review by yourself what you have studied, what you have not studied too thoroughly in the past, or what you have forgotten from your Spanish 1, 2, and 3 classes, because this book contains all the fundamentals generally presented in those three levels.

The main points in Spanish grammar in this book are arranged in a § decimal system for quick and easy reference. If you want to review Spanish pronouns (of which there are several different kinds), for example, the Index in the back tells you in what § (section) you can find them, with examples that illustrate them both in Spanish and English.

Do you feel you need to refresh your memory of direct and indirect object pronouns? Turn to the Index, and look up the § number for the entry **pronouns.** There, I refer you to several sections, for example, §25. (f) & (g), §56.5, §66.7–§66.16, and others. Double object pronouns and their position? In the Index I refer you to §66.43–§66.53. The Index is very useful and informative. Use it.

Maybe you do not know a noun from a pronoun, a possessive adjective from a possessive pronoun. In that case, look up the different parts of speech in the Index, or look up a particular Spanish word. For example, you may not know when to use the verb *jugar* and when to use *tocar*, both of which mean *to play*. In that case, look up the entry **jugar** in the Index, and read about it in §37.1; look up the entry **tocar** in the Index, and read about its use in §37.2. In addition to these, I include in the Index many key words in Spanish that are usually troublesome for English-speaking students learning the Spanish language.

You say you can't unhook Spanish verbs yet?! Look up the entry **verbs** in the Index, and it will send you to different sections of this book where you can get a better picture of what they are all about. See, for example, §68.12–§68.64, where you will find an in-depth analysis of Spanish verb tenses and moods as related to English verb tenses and moods, with abundant examples in Spanish and English.

Do you want to review the correct sequence of verb tenses when the subjunctive is required? In the Index, the entry **sequence of tenses** sends you to §67.101–§67.110, where this is explained clearly with examples in Spanish and English. Do you know how to handle a verb form in a *si* ("if") clause? The entry **si clauses** in the Index sends you to §67.111, where this is explained with examples.

When I give you examples in Spanish, I frequently give you the English translation. Nevertheless, there is a Spanish-English Vocabulary in the back of the book for your use.

Browse through the Index. You may stumble on something that will arouse your curiosity. The Index has been compiled to help you find efficiently and quicky what you need to know. If you study this book every day, you should score high on the grammar section of standardized tests given to students in schools, to students entering college, and to graduate students who are preparing to take placement, proficiency, qualifying, and validating tests in Spanish.

If I have inadvertently omitted any point in Spanish grammar that you think is important, please write to me, care of the publisher of this book, so that I may include it in the next edition.

Christopher Kendris

ABBREVIATIONS

adj.	adjective	***i.e.***	that is to say	**part.**	participle
adv.	adverb, adverbial	**imper.**	imperative	**perf.**	perfect
ant.	anterior	**imperf.**	imperfect	**pers.**	person
art.	article	**indef.**	indefinite	**pl.**	plural
aux.	auxiliary	**indic.**	indicative	**plup.**	pluperfect
cond.	conditional	**indir.**	indirect	**poss.**	possessive
conj.	conjunction	**inf.**	infinitive	**prep.**	preposition
def.	definite	**interj.**	interjection	**pres.**	present
dem. *or* **demons.**	demonstrative	**interrog.**	interrogative	**pret.**	preterit
dir.	direct	**introd.**	introduction	**pron.**	pronoun
disj.	disjunctive	**m.** *or* **masc.**	masculine	**refl.**	reflexive
e.g.	for example	**n.**	noun	**rel.**	relative
f. *or* **fem.**	feminine	**obj.**	object	**s.** *or* **sing.**	singular
ff	and the following	**p.**	page	**subj.**	subjunctive
fut.	future	**par.**	paragraph	**v.**	verb

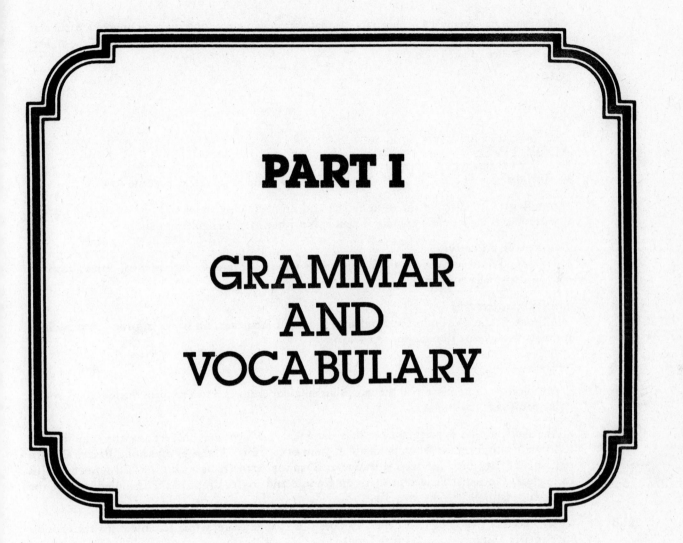

PART I

GRAMMAR
AND
VOCABULARY

GRAMMAR AND VOCABULARY

A § decimal system has been used in this book so that you may quickly find the reference to a particular point of grammar when you use the Index. For example, if you look up the entry **adjectives** in the Index, you will find the reference given as §1.

§1.   ADJECTIVES

§1.1   **Definition:** An adjective is a word that describes a noun or pronoun in some way.

§1.2   **Agreement:** An adjective agrees in gender and number with the noun or pronoun it describes. **Gender** means masculine, feminine or neuter. **Number** means singular or plural.

§1.3   **Descriptive adjectives**

A descriptive adjective is a word that describes a noun or pronoun: **casa blanca, chicas bonitas, chicos altos;** Ella es **bonita.**

§1.4   **Limiting adjectives**

A limiting adjective limits the number of the noun: **una casa, un libro, algunos muchachos, muchas veces, dos libros, pocos amigos**

§1.5   **Gender**

§1.6   An adjective that ends in **o** in the masculine singular changes **o** to **a** to form the feminine: **rojo / roja, pequeño / pequeña**

§1.7   An adjective that expresses a person's nationality, which ends in a consonant, requires the addition of **a** to form the feminine singular: **Juan es español / María es española; Pierre Cardin es francés / Simone Signoret es francesa; El señor Armstrong es inglés / La señora Smith es inglesa.** Note that the accent mark on **francés** and **inglés** drops in the feminine because the stress falls naturally on the vowel **e.**

§1.8   An adjective that ends in **e** generally does not change to form the feminine: **un muchacho inteligente / una muchacha inteligente**

§1.9   An adjective that ends in a consonant generally does not change to form the feminine: **una pregunta difícil / un libro difícil; un chico feliz / una chica feliz**—except for an adjective of nationality, as stated above in §1.7, and adjectives that end in **-án, -ón, -ín, -or** (**trabajador / trabajadora,** industrious).

§1.10   **Position** (See also §1.65)

§1.11   Normally, a descriptive adjective is placed after the noun it describes: **una casa amarilla; un libro interesante**

§1.12   Two descriptive adjectives, **bueno** and **malo,** are sometimes placed in front of the noun. When placed in front of a masculine singular noun, the **o** drops: **un buen amigo; un mal alumno.** See §1.18 below.

§1.13   A limiting adjective is generally placed in front of the noun: **algunos estudiantes; mucho dinero; muchos libros; cada año; tres horas; pocos alumnos; varias cosas**

§1.14   In an interrogative sentence, the predicate adjective precedes the subject when it is a noun: **¿Es bonita María? ¿Es inteligente la profesora?**

§1.15   Some adjectives have a different meaning depending on their position:

un nuevo sombrero / a new (different, another) hat
un sombrero nuevo / a new (brand new) hat

un gran hombre / a great man
un hombre grande / a large, big man

una gran mujer / a great woman
una mujer grande / a large, big woman

la pobre niña / the poor girl (unfortunate, unlucky)
la niña pobre / the poor girl (poor, not rich)

§1.16   **As nouns**

§1.17   At times, an adjective is used as a noun if it is preceded by an article or a demonstrative adjective: **el viejo** / the old man; **aquel viejo** / that old man; **la joven** / the young lady; **estos jóvenes** / these young men; **este ciego** / this blind man.

§1.18   **Shortened forms (apocopation of adjectives)**

§1.19   Certain masculine singular adjectives drop the final **o** when in front of a masculine singular noun:

§1.20
alguno: algún día	**primero: el primer año**
bueno: un buen amigo	**tercero: el tercer mes**
malo: mal tiempo	**uno: un dólar**
ninguno: ningún libro	

NOTE that when **alguno** and **ninguno** are shortened, an accent mark is required on the **u**.

§1.21   **Santo** shortens to **San** before a masculine singular saint: **San Francisco, San José**; but remains **Santo** in front of **Do-** or **To-**: **Santo Domingo, Santo Tomás**.

§1.22   **Grande** shortens to **gran** when in front of any singular noun, whether masc. or fem.: **un gran hombre** / a great (famous) man; **una gran mujer** / a great (famous) woman. See also §1.15 above.

§1.23   **Ciento** shortens to **cien** when in front of any plural noun, whether masc. or fem.: **cien libros** / one (a) hundred books; **cien sillas** / one (a) hundred chairs.

§1.24   **Ciento** shortens to **cien** when in front of a number greater than itself: **cien mil** / one hundred thousand; **cien millones** / one hundred million.

§1.25   **Ciento** remains **ciento** when combined with any other number which is smaller than itself: **ciento tres dólares**.

§1.26   NOTE that in English we say *one* hundred or *a* hundred, but in Spanish no word is used in front of **ciento** or **cien** to express *one* or *a*; it is merely **ciento** or **cien**. For an explanation of when to use **ciento** or **cien**, see §1.23—§1.25 above.

§1.27   **Cualquiera** and **cualesquiera** lose the final **a** in front of a noun: **cualquier hombre, cualquier día,** but if after the noun, the final **a** remains: **un libro cualquiera**.

§1.28   **Plural of adjectives**

§1.29   Like nouns, to form the plural of an adjective, add **s** if the adj. ends in a vowel: **blanco / blancos; blanca / blancas**.

§1.30   If an adj. ends in a consonant, add **es** to form the plural: **español / españoles; difícil / difíciles.** NOTE that the accent on **difícil** remains in the plural in order to keep the stress there: **difíciles.**

§1.31   Some adjectives drop the accent mark in the plural because it is not needed to indicate the stress. The stress falls naturally on the same vowel in the plural: **cortés / corteses; alemán / alemanes.**

§1.32   Some adjectives add the accent mark in the plural because the stress needs to be kept on the vowel that was stressed in the singular where no accent mark was needed. In the singular, the stress falls naturally on that vowel: **joven / jóvenes.**

§1.33   An adjective that ends in **z** changes **z** to **c** and adds **es** to form the plural: **feliz / felices.** Here, there is no need to add an accent mark because the stress falls naturally on the vowel **i,** as it does in the singular.

§1.34   If an adjective describes or modifies two or more nouns that are all masculine, naturally the masculine plural is used: **Roberto y Felipe están cansados.**

§1.35   If an adjective describes or modifies two or more nouns that are all feminine, naturally the feminine plural is used: **Elena y Marta están cansadas.**

§1.36   If an adjective describes or modifies two or more nouns of different genders, the masculine plural is used: **Pablo y Juanita están cansados; María, Elena, Marta, y Roberto están cansados.**

§1.37   **Comparatives and Superlatives** (See also **§1.66** and **§1.67**)

§1.38   **Comparatives**

§1.39   Of equality: **tan . . . como** (as . . . as)
    María es tan alta como Elena / Mary is as tall as Helen.

§1.40   Of a lesser degree: **menos . . . que** (less . . . than)
    María es menos alta que Anita / Mary is less tall than Anita.

§1.41   Of a higher degree: **más . . . que** (more . . . than)
    María es más alta que Isabel / Mary is taller than Elizabeth.

§1.42   **Superlatives**

§1.43   To express the superlative degree, use the comparative forms given above in §1.38 with the appropriate definite article:

§1.44   **With a proper noun: Anita es la más alta** / Anita is the tallest.
    Roberto es el más alto / Robert is the tallest.
    Anita y Roberto son los más altos / Anita and Robert are the tallest.
    Marta y María son las más inteligentes / Martha and Mary are the most intelligent.

§1.45   **With a common noun: La muchacha más alta de la clase es Anita** / The tallest girl in the class is Anita.
    El muchacho más alto de la clase es Roberto / The tallest boy in the class is Robert.

§1.46   NOTE that after a superlative in Spanish, *in* is expressed by **de,** not **en.**

When two or more superlative adjectives describe the same noun, **más** or **menos** is used only once in front of the first adjective: **Aquella mujer es la más pobre y vieja.**

§1.47   **Absolute superlative:** adjectives ending in **-ísimo, -ísima, -ísimos, -ísimas**

§1.48 To express an adj. in a very high degree, drop the final vowel (if there is one) and add the appropriate ending among the following, depending on the correct agreement: **-ísimo, -ísima, -ísimos, -ísimas: María está contentísima** / Mary is very (extremely) happy; **Los muchachos están contentísimos.** These forms may be used instead of **muy** + adj. **(muy contenta / muy contentos); una casa grandísima / una casa muy grande.**

§1.49 Never use **muy** in front of **mucho.** Say: **muchísimo. Muchísimas gracias** / many thanks; thank you very, very much.

§1.50 Irregular comparatives and superlatives

ADJECTIVE	COMPARATIVE	SUPERLATIVE
bueno (good)	**mejor** (better)	**el mejor** (best)
malo (bad)	**peor** (worse)	**el peor** (worst)
grande (large)	**más grande** (larger)	**el más grande** (largest)
	mayor (greater, older)	**el mayor** (greatest, oldest)
pequeño (small)	**más pequeño** (smaller)	**el más pequeño** (smallest)
	menor (smaller, younger)	**el menor** (smallest, youngest)

§1.51 NOTE, of course, that you must be careful to make the correct agreement in gender and number. See **§1.2** above.

NOTE also that in English, the superlative is sometimes expressed with definite article *the* and sometimes it is not. See **§1.43.**

§1.52 **Más que** (more than) or **menos que** (less than) becomes **más de, menos de** + a number:

El Señor Gómez tiene más de cincuenta años.
Mi hermano tiene más de cien dólares.
BUT: **No tengo más que dos dólares** / I have only two dollars.
In this example, the meaning is *only,* expressed by **no** in front of the verb; in this case, you must keep **que** to express *only.*

§1.53 **Tanto, tanta, tantos, tantas** + noun + **como:** as much (as many) . . . as

Tengo tanto dinero como usted / I have as much money as you.
Tengo tantos libros como usted / I have as many books as you.
Tengo tanta paciencia como usted / I have as much patience as you.
Tengo tantas plumas como usted / I have as many pens as you.

§1.54 **Demonstrative adjectives**
A demonstrative adjective is used to point out someone or something. Like other adjectives, a demonstrative adjective agrees in gender and number with the noun it modifies. The demonstrative adjectives are:

ENGLISH MEANING	MASCULINE	FEMININE
this (*here*)	**este libro**	**esta pluma**
these (*here*)	**estos libros**	**estas plumas**
that (*there*)	**ese libro**	**esa pluma**
those (*there*)	**esos libros**	**esas plumas**
that (*farther away or out of sight*)	**aquel libro**	**aquella pluma**
those (*farther away or out of sight*)	**aquellos libros**	**aquellas plumas**

§1.55 If there is more than one noun, a demonstrative adjective is ordinarily used in front of each noun: **este hombre y esta mujer** / this man and (this) woman

§1.56 The demonstrative adjectives are used to form the demonstrative pronouns. See **§66.54 ff.**

§1.57 **Possessive adjectives**
A possessive adjective is a word that shows possession and it agrees in gender and number

with the noun, not with the possessor. A short form of a possessive adjective is placed in front of the noun. If there is more than one noun stated, a possessive adjective is needed in front of each noun: **mi madre y mi padre** / my mother and (my) father

§1.58   There are two forms for the possessive adjectives: the short form and the long form. **The short form is placed in front of the noun.** The short forms are:

ENGLISH MEANING	BEFORE A SINGULAR NOUN	BEFORE A PLURAL NOUN
1. my	mi amigo, mi amiga	mis amigos, mis amigas
2. your	tu amigo, tu amiga	tus amigos, tus amigas
3. your, his, her, its	su amigo, su amiga	sus amigos, sus amigas
1. our	nuestro amigo nuestra amiga	nuestros amigos nuestras amigas
2. your	vuestro amigo vuestra amiga	vuestros amigos vuestras amigas
3. your, their	su amigo, su amiga	sus amigos, sus amigas

§1.59   In order to clarify the meanings of **su** or **sus**, when there might be ambiguity, do the following: Replace **su** or **sus** with the definite article + the noun and add **de Ud., de él, de ella, de Uds., de ellos, de ellas:**

su libro OR **el libro de Ud., el libro de él, el libro de ella; el libro de Uds., el libro de ellos, el libro de ellas**

sus libros OR **los libros de Ud., los libros de él, los libros de ella; los libros de Uds., los libros de ellos, los libros de ellas**

§1.60   **The long form is placed after the noun.** The long forms are:

ENGLISH MEANING	AFTER A SINGULAR NOUN	AFTER A PLURAL NOUN
1. my; (of) mine	mío, mía	míos, mías
2. your; (of) yours	tuyo, tuya	tuyos, tuyas
3. your, his, her, its; (of yours, of his, of hers, of its)	suyo, suya	suyos, suyas
1. our; (of) ours	nuestro, nuestra	nuestros, nuestras
2. your; (of) yours	vuestro, vuestra	vuestros, vuestras
3. your, their; (of yours, of theirs)	suyo, suya	suyos, suyas

Examples: **amigo mío** / my friend; **un amigo mío** / a friend of mine

§1.61   The long forms are used primarily:

(a) In direct address, that is to say, when you are talking directly to someone or when writing a letter to someone:

¡Hola, amigo mío! ¿Qué tal? / Hello, my friend! How are things? **Queridos amigos míos** / My dear friends

(b) When you want to express *of mine, of yours, of his, of hers,* etc. See **§1.60.**

(c) With the verb **ser: Estos libros son míos** / These books are mine.

(d) In the expression: **¡Dios mío!** / My heavens! My God!

§1.62   In order to clarify the meanings of **suyo, suya, suyos, suyas** (since they are third person singular or plural), do the same as for **su** and **sus** in **§1.59** above: **dos amigos suyos** can be clarified as: **dos amigos de Ud., dos amigos de él, dos amigos de ella, dos amigos de Uds., dos amigos de ellos, dos amigos de ellas** / two friends of yours, of his, of hers, *etc.*

§1.63   The long forms of the possessive adjectives are used to serve as possessive pronouns. See **§66.63** and **§66.64ff.**

§1.64   A possessive adjective is ordinarily not used when referring to an article of clothing being worn or to parts of the body, particularly when a reflexive verb is used: **Me lavo las manos antes de comer** / I wash my hands before eating.

§1.65   **Two or more descriptive adjectives** (See also **§1.10** and **§51.**)
Two or more descriptive adjectives of equal importance are placed after the noun. If there are two, they are joined by **y** (or **e**). If there are more than two, the last two are connected by **y** (or **e**):

un hombre alto y hermoso / a tall, handsome man

una mujer alta, hermosa e inteligente / a tall, beautiful and intelligent woman

§1.66   **Cuanto más (menos) . . . tanto más (menos)** / the more (the less) . . . the more (less) (See also **§1.37ff**)

A proportion or ratio is expressed by **cuanto más (menos) . . . tanto más (menos)** / the more (the less) . . . the more (less):

Cuanto más dinero tengo, tanto más necesito / The more money I have, the more I need.

Cuanto menos dinero tengo, tanto menos necesito / The less money I have the less I need.

§1.67   **Comparison between two clauses** (See also **§1.37ff**)

(a) Use **de lo que** to express *than* when comparing two clauses with different verbs if an adjective or adverb is the comparison:

Esta frase es más fácil de lo que Ud. cree / This sentence is easier than you think.

Paula trabaja mejor de lo que Ud. cree / Paula works better than you think.

(b) Use the appropriate form of **de lo que, de los que, de la que, de las que** when comparing two clauses with the same verbs if a noun is the comparison:

Tengo más dinero de lo que Ud. tiene / I have more money than you have.

María tiene más libros de los que Ud. tiene / Mary has more books than you have.

Roberto tiene más amigas de las que tiene Juan / Robert has more girl friends than John has.

§2.   ADVERBS

§2.1   **Definition:** An adverb is a word that modifies a verb, an adjective or another adverb.

§2.2   **Regular formation:** An adverb is regularly formed by adding the ending **mente** to the fem. sing. form of an adj.:

lento, lenta / **lentamente**: slow / slowly; **rápido, rápida** / **rápidamente**: rapid / rapidly

If the form of the adj. is the same for the fem. sing. and masc. sing. **(fácil, feliz),** add **mente** to that form. See **§1.9.**

    fácil (easy) / **fácilmente** (easily)
    feliz (happy) / **felizmente** (happily)

NOTE that an accent mark on an adjective remains when changed to an adverb. And note that the Spanish ending **mente** is equivalent to the ending **-ly** in English.

§2.3   An adverb remains invariable; that is to say, it does not agree in gender and number and therefore does not change in form.

§2.4   There are many adverbs that do not end in **mente**. Some common ones are:

abajo / below	**bien** / well	**hoy** / today	**siempre** / always	**aquí** / here
arriba / above	**mal** / badly	**mañana** / tomorrow	**nunca** / never	**allí** / there

§2.5   The adverbial ending **ísimo**
Never use **muy** in front of **mucho**. Say **muchísimo: Elena trabaja muchísimo** / Helen works a great deal; Helen works very, very much.

§2.6   **Regular comparison of adverbs**
An adverb is compared regularly as an adjective. (See **§1.38–§1.41**).

María corre tan rápidamente como Elena / Mary runs as rapidly as Helen.

María corre menos rápidamente que Anita / Mary runs less rapidly than Anita.

María corre más rápidamente que Isabel / Mary runs more rapidly than Elizabeth.

§2.7   **Irregular comparative adverbs**
mucho, poco / much, little: **Roberto trabaja mucho; Felipe trabaja poco.**

bien, mal / well, badly: **Juan trabaja bien; Lucas trabaja mal.**

más, menos / more, less: **Carlota trabaja más que Casandra; Elena trabaja menos que Marta.**

mejor, peor / better, worse: **Paula trabaja mejor que Anita; Isabel trabaja peor que Elena.**

§2.8   **Con, sin** + noun (See also idioms with **con** and with **sin** in **§53**.)
At times, an adverb can be formed by using the prep. **con** (with) or **sin** (without) + a noun:

con cuidado / carefully	**con dificultad** / with difficulty
sin cuidado / carelessly	**sin dificultad** / without difficulty

§2.9   The adverb **recientemente** (recently) becomes **recién** before a past participle: **los recién llegados** / the ones recently arrived; the recently arrived (ones)

§2.10   **Interrogative adverbs**
Some common interrogative adverbs are: **¿cómo?** / how? **¿cuándo?** / when? **¿por qué?** / why? **¿para qué?** / why? **¿dónde?** / where? **¿adónde?** / where to? (to where)?

§2.11   **Adverbs replaced by adjectives**
An adverb may sometimes be replaced by an adjective whose agreement is with the subject, especially if the verb is one of motion:

Las muchachas van y vienen silenciosas / The girls come and go silently.

§3.   **ANTONYMS** (see also **§14**.)
One very good way to increase your Spanish vocabulary is to think of an antonym (opposite meaning) or synonym (similar meaning) for every word in Spanish that you already know. Of course, there is no antonym or synonym for all words in the Spanish language—nor in English. If you plan to achieve a high score on the next standardized Spanish test that you take, you must increase your vocabulary. Study the following antonyms. There are many ways to study new vocabulary. You have to find the best way that suits you. One way is to see a picture in your mind of the word when you see the Spanish word. When you hear or read the Spanish word, you will see the picture first and that will reveal the meaning to you. You can also take a few

minutes and write the new Spanish word as many times as you need to at the same time as you pronounce it aloud and try to see a picture either of the word or of a situation where that word would be used. You can also examine the Spanish word very carefully and make one or two observations; for example, is there another word within the new word that you already know? Is the new word based on another word? Is it a word that sounds special and reveals the meaning by its sound? Take the simple adjective **bello / bella** (beautiful), which I am sure you already know. Have you ever stopped to wonder what the antonym of it is? Picture in your mind **una dama bella;** next to it, picture the opposite: **una dama fea.** I am sure you now know what **feo / fea** means without my telling you in English what the meaning is. To my ear, the word **fea** sounds ugly.

But for the sake of expediency, here are some antonyms that you ought to become acquainted with. As you study them, follow my suggestions given above.

I will occasionally guide you by suggesting what to see in the word and how to remember its meaning. Remember that the best way to learn vocabulary is the way that suits you best. You might think of other ways that come more naturally to you.

aburrirse / to be bored; **divertirse** / to have a good time

aceptar / to accept; **ofrecer** / to offer

acordarse de / to remember; **olvidar, olvidarse de** / to forget (Does **acordarse de** remind you of **recordar,** which means *to remember, to remind*? When you remember something or someone, don't you *record* it in your mind? As for **olvidar** and **olvidarse de,** you might think of the English words *oblivion, oblivious.*)

admitir / to admit; **negar** / to deny

agradecido, agradecida / thankful; **ingrato, ingrata** / thankless (You might think of *grateful* and associate it with **agradecido.** As for **ingrato,** you might think of *ungrateful* or *ungracious*; there is also the word *ingrate* in English.)

alejarse de / to go away from; **acercarse a** / to approach (In **acercarse a,** do you see the word **cerca** / near, close by? In **alejarse de,** do you see the word **lejos** / far? See a picture of a person coming close to you (**acercarse a**) and then that person goes away from you (**alejarse de.**)

amar / to love; **odiar** / to hate

ancho, ancha / wide; **estrecho, estrecha** / narrow

antipático, antipática / unpleasant; **simpático, simpática** / nice (people)

aplicado, aplicada / industrious; **flojo, floja** / lazy

apresurarse a / to hasten, to hurry; **tardar en** / to delay (Here, you have the cognate *tardy* and as for **apresurarse a,** you can picture a person who is hurrying because he or she is *pressed* for time.)

atrevido, atrevida / bold, daring; **tímido, tímida** / timid, shy

aumentar / to augment, to increase; **disminuir** / to diminish, to decrease

ausente / absent; **presente** / present

claro, clara / light; **oscuro, oscura** / dark

cobarde / cowardly; **valiente** / valiant, brave

cómico, cómica / comic, funny; **trágico, trágica** / tragic

costoso, costosa / costly, expensive; **barato, barata** / cheap, inexpensive

culpable / guilty, culpable; **inocente** / innocent

dar / to give; **recibir** / to receive

débil / weak, debilitated; **fuerte** / strong

delgado, delgada / thin; **gordo, gorda** / stout, fat

derrota / defeat; **victoria** / victory

descansar / to rest; **cansar** / to tire, **cansarse** / to get tired

descubrir / to uncover; **cubrir** / to cover (Here is another word with the prefix **des,** which usually makes the word opposite in meaning.)

descuido / carelessness; **esmero** / meticulousness

desgraciado, desgraciada / unfortunate; **afortunado, afortunada** / fortunate

destruir / to destroy; **crear** / to create

desvanecerse / to disappear; **aparecer** / to appear (Here, you might think of *vanish* to remind you of the meaning of **desvanecerse;** for the meaning of **aparecer,** isn't it an obvious cognate?)

distinto, distinta / different; **semejante** / similar

elogiar / to praise; **censurar** / to criticize (Here, you might see a picture of a clergyman reading a eulogy in praise of someone; do I need to suggest to you what word to think of in English for the Spanish **censurar?** Are you developing ways to remember the meanings of Spanish words, following my advice and suggestions given above in the short introduction to §3.?)

este / east; **oeste** / west

fatigado, fatigada / tired; **descansado, descansada** / rested (Here, in **descansado,** do you see the Spanish word **cansar** within that word? See the entry **descansar** above.)

feo, fea / ugly; **bello, bella** / beautiful

gastar / to spend (money); **ahorrar** / to save (money) (You might see a picture of a person *hoarding* money for **ahorrar;** you might see an opposite picture of a person *wasting* money to remind you of **gastar.**)

gigante / giant; **enano** / dwarf

hablador, habladora / talkative; **taciturno, taciturna** / silent, taciturn

hembra / female; **macho** / male

ida / going; **vuelta** / return

ignorar / not to know; **saber** / to know

interesante / interesting; **aburrido, aburrida** / boring

inútil / useless; **útil** / useful

juntar / to join; **separar** / to separate

lejano / distant; **cercano** / nearby (Do these two words remind you of **alejarse de** and **acercarse a** given above?)

lentitud / slowness; **rapidez** / speed

libertad / liberty; **esclavitud** / slavery

luz / light; **sombra** / shadow

llegada / arrival; **partida** / departure

llenar / to fill; **vaciar** / to empty (Think of *vacate.*)

maldecir / to curse; **bendecir** / to bless (Think of *malediction* and *benediction.*)

menor / younger; **mayor** / older (Think of *minor* and *major.*)

mentira / lie, falsehood; **verdad** / truth (Think of *veracity.*)

meridional / southern; **septentrional** / northern

negar / to deny; **otorgar** / to grant

orgulloso / proud; **humilde** / humble

oriental / eastern; **occidental** / western

peligro / danger; **seguridad** / safety

perder / to lose; **ganar** / to win

porvenir / future; **pasado** / past

puesta del sol / sunset; **salida del sol** / sunrise

recto / straight; **tortuoso** / winding

riqueza / wealth; **pobreza** / poverty

romper / to break; **componer** / to repair (Here, in *romper,* you can see a picture in your mind of something *ruptured* in the sense that it is broken. In *componer,* you can see something that is put (*poner*) together in the sense that it is repaired.)

seco / dry; **mojado** / wet

separar / to separate; **juntar** / to join

sucio / dirty; **limpio** / clean

tonto / foolish; **listo** / clever

tranquilo / tranquil, peaceful; **turbulento** / restless, turbulent

§4. ARTICLES

§4.1 Definite article

§4.2 There are four forms of the definite article (the) in Spanish. They are as follows:

	Singular	Plural
Masculine	**el**	**los**
Feminine	**la**	**las**

EXAMPLES:
el libro (the book); **los libros** (the books)
la pluma (the pen); **las plumas** (the pens)

§4.3 A definite article agrees in gender and number with the noun it modifies. If you do not know or do not remember what is meant by gender and number, see §1.2 and §1.5ff. (If you do not know or do not remember what the abbreviation **ff** means, see the list of abbreviations on p. ix.)

§4.4 If a noun is masculine singular, you must use the masculine singular form of *the,* which is **el.** If a noun is masculine plural, you must use the masculine plural form of *the,* which is **los.** If a noun is feminine singular, you must use the feminine singular form of *the,* which is **la.** If a noun is feminine plural, you must use the feminine plural form of *the,* which is **las.** See §4.2 above.

§4.5 How do you know if a noun is masculine or feminine? See farther on in §5., which is the beginning of the topic **Nouns.**

§4.6 If a feminine singular noun begins with stressed **a** or **ha,** use **el,** not **la.** This is done in order to avoid slurring the **a** in **la** with the stressed **a** or **ha** at the beginning of the noun that follows. Actually, that is what happened; the two vowel sounds **a** were not pronounced distinctly because they were slurred and **el** replaced **la.** For example, **hambre** (hunger) is a feminine noun but in the singular it is stated as **el hambre.** NOTE: **Tengo mucha hambre.** And NOTE:

el agua / the water; but **las aguas** / the waters
el hacha / the axe; but **las hachas** / the axes

However, if the def. art. is in front of an adj. that precedes the noun, this is not observed: **la alta montaña** / the high (tall) mountain, **la árida llanura** / the arid (dry) prairie.

§4.7 Contraction of the definite article **el**

§4.8 When the preposition **a** or **de** is in front of the definite article **el,** it contracts as follows:
a + **el** changes to **al**
de + **el** changes to **del**
EXAMPLES:
Voy al parque / I am going to the park.
Vengo del parque / I am coming from the park.
But if the def. art. **el** is part of a denomination or title of a work, there is no contraction: **Los cuadros de El Greco.**

§4.9 **The definite article is used:**
   (a) In front of each noun even if there is more than one noun stated, as in a series, which is not always done in English: **Tengo el libro, el cuaderno, y la pluma** / I have the book, notebook, and pen. See §4.18(c).
   (b) With a noun when you make a general statement: **Me gusta el café** / I like coffee; **La leche es buena para la salud** / Milk is good for health.
   (c) With a noun of weight or measure: **un dólar la libra; un peso la libra** / one dollar a pound (per pound).
   (d) In front of a noun indicating a profession, rank, title followed by the name of the person: **El profesor Gómez es inteligente** / Professor Gomez is intelligent; **La señora García es muy amable** / Mrs. García is very nice; **El doctor Torres está enfermo** / Dr. Torres is sick.

But in direct address (when talking directly to the person and you mention the rank, profession, *etc.*), do not use the definite article: **Buenas noches, señor Gómez** / Good evening, Mr. Gomez.

(e) With the name of a language: **Estudio el español** / I study Spanish.

For examples of when you do not use the definite article with the name of a language, see **§4.10(b)** farther on.

(f) With the name of a subject matter: **Estudio la historia** / I study history. See **§4.10(c).**

(g) With the days of the week, when in English we use *on:* **Voy al cine el sábado** / I am going to the movies on Saturday.

(h) With parts of the body or articles of clothing, especially if the possessor is clearly stated: **Me pongo el sombrero** / I put on my hat; **Me lavo la cara todas las mañanas** / I wash my face every morning.

(i) With common expressions, for example: **a la escuela** / to school; **en la iglesia** / in church; **en la clase** / in class; **la semana pasada** / last week; **la semana próxima** / next week.

(j) With the seasons of the year: **en la primavera** / in spring; **en el verano** / in summer; **en el otoño** / in autumn; **en el invierno** / in winter.

(k) To show possession with the preposition **de** + a common noun: **el libro del alumno** / the pupil's book; **los libros de los alumnos** / the pupils' books; **los niños de las mujeres** / the women's children.

Note that when a proper noun is used, the definite article is not needed with **de** to show possession: **el libro de Juan** / John's book; **el libro de María** / Mary's book; **los libros de Juan y de María** / John's and Mary's books. See **§4.10(d)** below.

(l) With names of some cities, countries and continents: **la Argentina, el Brasil, el Canadá, los Estados Unidos, la Habana, la América del Norte, la América Central, la América del Sur.** See **§4.10(h).**

(m) With a proper noun modified by an adjective: **el pequeño José** / Little Joseph.

(n) With a noun in apposition with a pronoun: **Nosotros los norteamericanos** / We North Americans.

(o) With an infinitive used as a noun, especially when it begins a sentence: **El estudiar es bueno** / Studying is good. There are some exceptions: **Ver es creer** / Seeing is believing; and other proverbs. But you do not normally use the definite article with an infinitive if it does not begin a sentence: **Es bueno estudiar** / It is good to study. See §4.10(e) below. This is a general rule.

(p) When telling time: **Es la una** / It is one o'clock; **Son las dos** / It is two o'clock.

§4.10   **The definite article is not used:**

(a) In direct address with the rank, profession, title of the person to whom you are talking or writing: **Buenos días, señora Molina** / Good morning, Mrs. Molina.

(b) After the verb **hablar** when the name of a language is right after a form of **hablar**: **Hablo español** / I speak Spanish. See §4.9(e) above.

(c) After the prepositions **en** and **de** with the name of a language or a subject matter: **Estoy escribiendo en inglés** / I am writing in English; **La señora Johnson es profesora de inglés** / Mrs. Johnson is a teacher of English; **El señor Gómez es profesor de historia** / Mr. Gomez is a teacher of history. See §4.9(f) above.

(d) With a proper noun to show possession when using **de: los libros de Marta** / Martha's books. See §4.9(k) above.

(e) With an infinitive if the infinitive does not begin the sentence: **Es bueno trabajar** / It is good to work. **Me gusta viajar** / I like to travel. See §4.9(o). This is a general rule.

(f) With a noun in apposition with a noun: **Madrid, capital de España, es una ciudad interesante** / Madrid, capital of Spain, is an interesting city.

(g) With a numeral that denotes the order of succession of a monarch: **Carlos V (Quinto)** / Charles the Fifth.

' (h) With names of some countries and continents: **España** / Spain; **Francia** / France; **México** / Mexico; **Europa** / Europe; **Asia** / Asia; **África** / Africa.

§4.11 **The neuter article lo** (See also idioms with **lo** in **§53.15**)

The neuter article **lo** has idiomatic uses, generally speaking.

It is used:

(a) With a masculine singular form of an adjective that is used as a noun: **lo bueno** / the good; **lo malo** / the bad; **lo simpático** / what(ever) is kind.

(b) With a past participle: **lo dicho y lo escrito** / what has been said and what has been written.

(c) With an adjective or adverb + **que**, meaning *how*: **Veo lo fácil que es** / I see how easy it is.

§4.12 **Indefinite article**

§4.13 In Spanish, there are four forms of the indefinite article (a, an, some, a few). They are as follows:

	Singular	Plural
Masculine	**un**	**unos**
Feminine	**una**	**unas**

EXAMPLES:

un libro (a book); **unos libros** (some books, a few books)

una naranja (an orange); **unas naranjas** (some oranges, a few oranges)

§4.14 An indefinite article agrees in gender and number with the noun it modifies. If you do not know or do not remember what is meant by gender and number, see §1.2 and §1.5ff. (If you do not know or do not remember what the abbreviation **ff** means, see the list of abbreviations on p. ix.)

§4.15 If a noun is masculine singular, you must use the masculine singular form of *a, an* which is **un.** If a noun is masculine plural, you must use the masculine plural form of *some, a few* which is **unos.**

If a noun is feminine singular, you must use the feminine singular form of *a, an* which is **una.** If a noun is feminine plural, you must use the feminine plural form of *some, a few* which is **unas.** See §4.13 above.

§4.16 How do you know if a noun is masculine or feminine? See farther on in §5., which is the beginning of the topic **Nouns.**

§4.17 The plural of the indefinite article indicates an indefinite number: **unas treinta personas** / some thirty persons.

§4.18 **The indefinite article is used:**

(a) When you want to say *a* or *an*. It is also used as a numeral to mean *one*: **un libro** / a book or one book; **una pluma** / a pen or one pen. If you want to make it clear that you mean *one*, you may use **solamente** (*only*) in front of **un** or **una**: **Tengo solamente un libro** / I have (only) one book.

(b) With a modified noun of nationality, profession, rank, or religion: **El doctor Gómez es un médico excelente** / Dr. Gomez is an excellent doctor.

(c) In front of each noun in a series, which we do not always do in English: **Tengo un libro, un cuaderno, y una pluma** / I have a book, notebook, and pen. This use is the same for the definite article in a series of nouns. See §4.9(a) above.

(d) In the plural when an indefinite number is indicated: **Tengo unos dólares** / I have some (a few) dollars.

§4.19   **The indefinite article is not used:**

(a) With **cien** and **mil: cien libros** / a (one) hundred books; **mil dólares** / a (one) thousand dollars.

(b) **cierto, cierta** and **tal: cierto lugar** / a certain place; **cierta persona** / a certain person; **tal hombre** / such a man; **tal caso** / such a case

(c) With **otro, otra: otro libro** / another book; **otra pluma** / another pen.

(d) With an unmodified noun of nationality, profession, rank, or religion: **Mi hijo es dentista** / My son is a dentist; **Soy mexicano** / I am Mexican; **Es profesora** / She is a teacher. However, when the subject is qualified, the indef. art. is used. See §4.18(b).

(e) When you use **Qué** in an exclamation: **¡Qué hombre!** / What a man! **¡Qué lástima!** / What a pity!

(f) With some negations, particularly with the verb **tener**, or in an interrogative statement before an unmodified noun object: **¿Tiene Ud. libro?** / Do you have a book? **No tengo libro** / I don't have a book.

(g) With a noun in apposition: **Martí, gran político y más grande poeta...** / Martí, a great politician and greatest poet...

§5.   NOUNS

§5.1   A noun is a word that refers to a person (**Roberto, Elena, el muchacho, la muchacha**), a thing (**el libro, la pluma**), a place (**la casa, la escuela, el parque**), a quality (**la excelencia, la honra**).

§5.2   In Spanish, a noun is either masculine or feminine. When you learn a noun in Spanish, you must learn it with the article (see §4.ff), for example: **el libro, la pluma; el muchacho, la muchacha; el hombre, la mujer.**

§5.3   A noun that refers to a male person or animal is masculine in gender, naturally: **el hombre, el toro, el tío, el padre.** A noun that refers to a female person or animal is feminine in gender, naturally: **la mujer, la chica, la tía, la vaca, la madre.** This is easy to understand. What is not so easy to understand for us English-speaking persons is that a noun referring to a thing, a place, or a quality also has a gender. You must learn the gender of a noun when you learn the word by using the article with it.

§5.4   Generally speaking, a noun that ends in **o** is masculine: **el libro.**

§5.5   Generally speaking, a noun that ends in **a** is feminine; also a noun that ends in **ción, sión, dad, tad, tud, umbre: la casa, la lección, la ilusión, la ciudad, la dificultad, la nacionalidad, la solicitud, la costumbre.**

§5.6   Generally speaking, a noun that ends in **nte** refers to a person and the gender is masculine or feminine, depending on whether it refers to a male or female person:

el estudiante / la estudiante; el presidente / la presidente

§5.7   Generally speaking, it is difficult to tell the gender of a noun that ends in **e**. Some are feminine, some are masculine. You must learn the gender of the noun when you learn the word with the definite or indefinite article.

MASCULINE	FEMININE
el aire / air	**la calle** / street
el arte / art	**la clase** / class
el baile / dance	**la fe** / faith
el bosque / forest	**la fuente** / fountain
el coche / car	**la gente** / people
el parque / park	**la leche** / milk

§5.8   **Irregular gender of nouns**

§5.9   Feminine nouns that end in **o**. Three common ones are:
la mano / hand; **la radio** (**la radio** is the radiotelephonic broadcast that we listen to; **el radio** is the object, the apparatus) / radio; **la foto** / photo (actually, this word is a shortened form of **la fotografía**)

§5.10   Masculine nouns that end in **a**. Four common ones are:

el día / day; **el clima** / climate; **el drama** / drama; **el mapa** / map

§5.11   Nouns that end in **ista**
These nouns are generally masculine or feminine, depending on whether they refer to male or female persons:

el dentista, la dentista / dentist; **el novelista, la novelista** / novelist

§5.12   **Plural of nouns**
To form the plural of a noun that ends in a vowel, add **s**:

el chico / **los chicos**; **la chica** / **las chicas**; **el libro** / **los libros**
la dentista / **las dentistas**; **el coche** / **los coches**; **la clase** / **las clases**

§5.13   To form the plural of a noun that ends in a consonant, add **es**:

el profesor / **los profesores**; **la flor** / **las flores**; **la ciudad** / **las ciudades**

§5.14   A noun that ends in **z** changes **z** to **c** before adding **es**:

el lápiz / **los lápices**; **la luz** / **las luces**

§5.15   Sometimes a masculine plural noun refers to both male and female persons:

los padres / the parents, the mother and father
los tíos / the aunt and uncle, the aunts and uncles
los niños / the children, the little boy and little girl, the little boys and little girls
los hijos / the children, the son and daughter, the sons and daughters

§5.16   Generally, a noun that ends in **ión** drops the accent mark in the plural. The accent mark is not needed in the plural because the stress naturally falls on the syllable that contained the accent mark in the singular. This happens because another syllable is added when the noun is made plural: **la lección** / **las lecciones**; **la ilusión** / **las ilusiones**

§5.17   Generally, a noun that ends in **és** drops the accent mark in the plural. The accent mark is not needed in the plural because the stress naturally falls on the syllable that contained the accent mark in the singular. This happens because another syllable is added when the noun is made plural: **el francés** / the Frenchman; **los franceses** / the Frenchmen

§5.18   Sometimes the accent mark is kept in the plural in order to keep the stress where it is in the singular. This generally happens when there are two vowels together and one of them is strong and the other weak: **el país** / **los países**

§5.19   Some nouns have a plural ending but they are regarded as singular because they are compound nouns; that is to say, the single word is made of two words which combine into one: **el tocadiscos** / the record player; **los tocadiscos** / the record players; **el paraguas** / the umbrella; **los paraguas** / the umbrellas; **el abrelatas** / the can opener; **los abrelatas** / the can openers; **el sacapuntas** / the pencil sharpener.

§5.20   Generally speaking, a noun that ends in **s** in the singular with no stress on that final syllable remains the same in the plural: **el lunes / los lunes; el martes / los martes**

§5.21   Generally speaking, a noun that ends in **s** in the singular with the stress on that syllable (usually it is a word of one syllable) requires the addition of **es** to form the plural: **el mes / los meses**

§5.22   Some nouns that contain no accent mark in the singular require an accent mark in the plural in order to preserve the stress where it fell naturally in the singular: **el joven** / the young man: **los jóvenes** / the young men

§5.23   **Nouns that change meaning according to gender**
Some nouns have one meaning when masculine and another meaning when feminine. Here are two common examples:

NOUN	MASCULINE GENDER MEANING	FEMININE GENDER MEANING
capital	capital (money)	capital (city)
cura	priest	cure

§5.24   **Nouns used as adjectives**
It is common in English to use a noun as an adjective: *a history class, a silk tie, a gold watch.* When this is done in Spanish, the preposition **de** is usually placed in front of the noun that is used as an adjective and both are placed after the noun that is being described:

una clase de historia / a history class (a class of history); **una corbata de seda** / a silk tie (a tie of silk); **un reloj de oro** / a gold watch (a watch of gold)

Also note that the preposition **para** (*for*) is used in order to indicate that something is intended for something: **una taza para café** / a coffee cup (a cup for coffee). However, if the cup is filled with coffee, we say in Spanish: **una taza de café** / a cup of coffee

§5.25   Nouns ending in **ito** or **illo**
Generally speaking, the ending **ito** or **illo** can be added to a noun to form the diminutive form of a noun. This makes the noun take on the meaning of little or small in size:

un vaso / a glass (drinking); **un vasito** / a little drinking glass; **una casa** / a house; **una casita** / a little house; **un cigarro** / a cigar; **un cigarillo** / a cigarette

To form the diminutive in Spanish, ordinarily drop the final vowel of the noun and add **ito** or **illo: una casa / una casita.** If the final letter of the noun is a consonant, merely add **ito** or **illo: papel** / paper; **papelito** *or* **papelillo** / small bit of paper

At other times, these diminutive endings give a favorable quality to the noun, even a term of endearment:

una chica / a girl; **una chiquita** / a cute little girl. Here, note that before dropping the final vowel **a** to add **ita,** you must change **c** to **q** in order to preserve the hard sound of *K* in **chica; un perro** / a dog; **un perrito** / a darling little dog; **una abuela** / a grandmother; **abuelita** / "dear old granny"

In English, we do something similar to this: drop / droplet; doll / dolly *or* dollie; pig / piggy *or* piggie or piglet; bath / bathinette; book / booklet; John / Johnny; Ann / Annie.

§6. DATES, DAYS, MONTHS, SEASONS

§6.1 Dates

You ought to know the following expressions:

(a) **¿Cuál es la fecha?** / What's the date?
¿Cuál es la fecha de hoy? / What's the date today?

(b) **Es el primero de junio** / It is June first.
Es el dos de mayo / It is May second.

NOTE that when stating the date, in Spanish we use **el primero,** which is an ordinal number, for the first day of any month. To state all other dates, use the cardinal numbers: **Hoy es el dos de enero, el tres de febrero, el cuatro de marzo,** *etc.*

(c) **¿A cuántos estamos hoy?** / What's the date today?
Estamos a cinco de abril / It's April 5th.

(d) When stating a date, the English word (preposition) *on* is expressed in Spanish by using the definite article **el** in front of the date: **María nació** *el* **cuatro de julio** / Mary was born *on* the fourth of July.

(e) When stating the year, in Spanish we use thousand and hundreds:

el año mil novecientos ochenta y dos / the year 1982

This is very different from English, which is usually stated as nineteen eighty or nineteen hundred eighty. In Spanish we must state **mil** (one thousand) + **novecientos** (nine hundred): **mil novecientos setenta y nueve** (1979), **mil novecientos ochenta y uno** (1981).

(f) To sum it up: **Hoy es lunes, el primero de marzo, mil novecientos ochenta y dos** / Today is Monday, March first, 1982.

§6.2 Days

(a) The days of the week, which are all masculine, are:

domingo / Sunday; **lunes** / Monday; **martes** / Tuesday; **miércoles** / Wednesday, **jueves** / Thursday; **viernes** / Friday, **sábado** / Saturday

(b) In Spanish, the days of the week are ordinarily not capitalized. In newspapers, magazines, business letters, and elsewhere, you sometimes see them capitalized.

(c) When stating the day of the week in English we may use *on,* but in Spanish we use **el** or **los** in front of the day of the week:

el lunes / on Monday; **los lunes** / on Mondays, *etc.*

(d) NOTE that the days of the week whose last letter is **s** do not change in the plural: **el martes** / **los martes; el miércoles** / **los miércoles.** But: **el sábado** / **los sábados; el domingo** / **los domingos**

(e) **¿Qué día es?** / What day is it?
¿Qué día es hoy? / What day is it today?
Hoy es lunes / Today is Monday.

§6.3 Months

(a) The months of the year, which are all masculine, are:

enero / January; **febrero** / February; **marzo** / March; **abril** / April, **mayo** / May; **junio** / June; **julio** / July; **agosto** / August; **septiembre** / September; **octubre** / October; **noviembre** / November; **diciembre** / December

(b) In Spanish, the months of the year are ordinarily not capitalized. In newspapers, magazines, business letters, and elsewhere, you sometimes see them capitalized.

      (c)   To say *in* + the name of the month, use **en: en enero** / in January; or: **en el mes de enero** / in the month of January

      (d)   The plural of **el mes** is **los meses.**

§6.4   Seasons

      (a)   The seasons of the year (**las estaciones del año**) are:

         la primavera / spring; **el verano** / summer; **el otoño** / autumn, fall; **el invierno** / winter

      (b)   In Spanish, the seasons of the year are not capitalized.

      (c)   The definite article usually precedes a season of the year:

         ¿En qué estación hace frío? / In what season is it cold?
         Generalmente, hace frío en el invierno / Generally, it is cold in winter.

§7.   CONJUNCTIONS, CONJUNCTIVE LOCUTIONS, AND CORRELATIVE CONJUNCTIONS

§7.1   **Definition:** A conjunction is a word that connects words, phrases, clauses or sentences, *e.g.,* and, but, or, because / **y, pero, o, porque.**

§7.2   Certain conjunctions that introduce a clause require the subjunctive mood of the verb in that clause. See Subjunctive in §67.33ff farther on to know what those conjunctions are.

§7.3   Here are some conjunctions that you certainly ought to know before you take the next standardized test in Spanish. Some require the subjunctive and they are discussed under the entry **Subjunctive** in §67.33ff farther on in this section.

      (a)   **a fin de que** / so that, in order that
         a menos que / unless
         antes (de) que / before
         apenas . . . cuando / hardly, scarcely . . . when
         así que / as soon as, after
         aun / even, still
         aunque / although
         como / as, since, how
         como si / as if
         con tal (de) que / provided that
         cuando / when
         de manera que / so that
         de modo que / so that, in such a way that
         después (de) que / after
         e / and (See the entry **y** and **e** in the General Index)
         en cuanto / as soon as
         hasta que / until
         luego que / as soon as, after
         mas / but
         mas que / even if, however much
         mientras / while
         mientras que / while, so long as, as long as
         ni / neither, nor (**ni . . . ni** / neither . . . nor)
         ni siquiera / not even
         ni sólo . . . (sino) también / not only . . . but also
         o / or (**o . . . o** / either . . . or)
         o sea . . . o sea / either . . . or
         para que / in order that, so that
         pero / but

por cuanto / inasmuch as
porque / because
pues que / since
puesto que / although, since, inasmuch as, as long as
que / that, because
según que / according as
si / if, whether
sin embargo / nevertheless, notwithstanding, however (in whatever way)
sin que / without
sino / but, but rather
sino que / but that, but rather that
siquiera / though, although, whether, or
tan pronto como / as soon as
u / or (See the entry **o** and **u** in the General Index)
y / and
ya . . . ya / now . . . now
ya que / since, seeing that

§7.4   And here are some that maybe you are not too familiar with. You ought to get acquainted with them because they are often used in the reading comprehension passages on standardized tests in Spanish. Some of them require the subjunctive form of the verb in the clause that they introduce and they are discussed under the entry **Subjunctive** in §67.33.

(b) **a condición de que** / on condition that
a pesar de que / in spite of
así . . . como / both . . . and *or* as well . . . as
aun cuando / even if
caso que / in case that
como que / it seems that, apparently
como quiera que / although, since
con la condición de que / on condition that
con que / so then, and so, then
conque / and so, well then, so then, now then
dado caso que / supposing that
dado que / supposing that
de condición que / so as to
de suerte que / so that, in such a manner as
del mismo modo que / in the same way that
desde que / since
empero / yet, however, notwithstanding
en caso de que / in case, in case that
en razón de que / for the reason that, because of
entretanto que / meanwhile, while
lo mismo que / as well as, the same as
lo mismo . . . que . . . / both . . . and . . . *or* as well . . . as
más bien que / rather than
mientras tanto / meanwhile, in the meantime
no bien . . . cuando / no sooner . . . than
no obstante / in spite of the fact that (notwithstanding)
por más que / no matter how, however much
por razón de que / because of, for the reason that
salvo que / unless
siempre que / whenever, provided that
supuesto que / since, allowing that, granting that
tan luego como / therefore
tanto . . . como / both . . . and *or* as well . . . as

§8.   TRICKY WORDS

NOTE well the English meanings of the following Spanish words. They often appear in the reading comprehension passages on standardized tests in Spanish.

actual *adj.* present, of the present time, of the present day

el anciano, la anciana old (man or woman)

antiguo, antigua *adj.* former, old, ancient

la apología eulogy, defense

la arena sand

asistir a *v.* to attend, to be present at

atender *v.* to attend to, to take care of

el auditorio audience

el bachiller, la bachillera graduate of a secondary school; *also means* babbler

el bagaje beast of burden, military equipment

la bala bullet, shot, bale, ball

bizarro, bizarra *adj.* brave, gallant, generous

el campo field, country(side), military camp

el carbón coal, charcoal, carbon

el cargo duty, post, responsibility, burden, load

la carta letter (to mail)

el collar necklace

colorado, colorada *adj.* red, ruddy

la complexión temperament, constitution

la conferencia lecture

la confianza confidence, trust

la confidencia secret, trust

constipado, constipada *adj.* sick with a head cold or common cold

la consulta conference

convenir *v.* to agree, to fit, to suit, to be suitable

la chanza joke, fun

de *prep.* from, of

dé *irreg. v. form: imper., 3rd pers., s. and 1st & 3rd pers. s., pres. subj. of* **dar**

la decepción disappointment

el delito crime

la desgracia misfortune

el desmayo fainting

diario, diaria *adj.* daily; **el diario** diary, journal, daily newspaper

disfrutar *v.* to enjoy

divisar *v.* to perceive indistinctly

el dormitorio bedroom, dormitory

el editor publisher

embarazada *adj.* pregnant

emocionante *adj.* touching (causing an emotion)

esperar *v.* to hope, to expect, to wait for

el éxito success, outcome

la fábrica factory

hay *idiomatic form* there is, there are

el idioma language

ignorar *v.* not to know, to be unaware

intoxicar *v.* to poison, to intoxicate

el labrador farmer

largo, larga *adj.* long

la lectura reading

la librería bookstore

la maleta valise, suitcase

el mantel tablecloth

mayor *adj.* greater, older

la mesura moderation

la pala shovel

el palo stick, pole

el pan bread

pasar *v.* to happen, to pass

el pastel pie; **la pintura al pastel** pastel painting

pinchar *v.* to puncture, to prick, to pierce

realizar *v.* to achieve (to realize, in the sense of achieving something: He realized his dreams, *i.e.*, his dreams came true)

recordar *v.* to remember

el resfriado common cold (illness)

restar *v.* to deduct, to subtract

sano, sana *adj.* healthy

soportar *v.* to tolerate, to bear, to endure, to support

suceder *v.* to happen, to come about, to succeed (follow)

el suceso event, happening

la tabla board, plank, table of contents

la tinta ink, tint

la trampa trap, snare, cheat, trick

tu *poss. adj., 2nd pers. s., fam.* your

tú *persl. subj. pron., 2nd pers. s., fam.* you

el vaso drinking glass

§9.   INTERROGATIVES (See also §1.14, §2.10, §11., and §61.)

Here are a few common interrogatives that you should be aware of when preparing to take the next standardized Spanish test. NOTE the required accent mark on these words when used in a question:

¿qué . . . ? what . . . ? (See also §61.)

¿cuándo . . . ? when . . . ?

¿dónde . . . ? where . . . ?

¿por qué . . . ? why . . . ?

¿para qué . . . ? why . . . ? what for . . . ? for what purpose . . . ?

¿cuánto . . . ?
¿cuánta . . . ?
¿cuántos . . .? } how much . . . ? how many . . . ?
¿cuántas . . . ?
¿cómo . . . ? how . . . ?
¿cuál . . . ? which, which one . . . ? (See also **§61**.)
¿cuáles . . . ? which, which ones . . . ? (See also **§61**.)
¿quién . . . ? ¿quiénes . . . ? who . . . ?
¿a quién . . . ? ¿a quiénes . . . ? whom . . . ? to whom . . . ?
¿de quién . . . ? of whom, from whom, by whom, whose . . . ? (**¿De quién es este lápiz?** / Whose is this pencil?)

§10. **EXCLAMATORY ¡Qué . . . !** and **¡Tal . . . !**

In English, when we exclaim *What a class! What a student! What an idea!* or *Such an idea!* we use the indefinite article *a* or *an.* In Spanish, however, we do not use the indefinite article:

¡Qué clase! ¡Qué alumno! ¡Qué alumna! ¡Qué idea! or **¡Tal idea!**

§10.1 If an adjective is used to describe the noun, we generally use **más** in front of the adjective, or **tan,** in order to intensify the exclamation:

¡Qué chica tan bonita! / What a pretty girl!
¡Qué libro más interesante! / What an interesting book!

§10.2 When we use **¡Qué!** + an adjective, the meaning in English is *How . . . !*

¡Qué difícil es! / How difficult it is!

§11. **¿Para qué . . . ?** and **¿Por qué . . . ?** (See also the entries **para** and **por** in the General Index)

Both of these interrogatives mean *why* but they are not used interchangeably. If by *why* you mean *for what reason,* use **¿por qué . . . ?** If by *why* you mean *for what purpose (what for?)* use **¿para qué . . . ?**

Juanita, ¿Por qué lloras? / Jeanie, why [for what reason] are you crying?
Mamá, ¿para qué tenemos uñas? / Mom, why [what for, for what purpose] do we have fingernails?
¿Para qué sirven los anteojos? / What [why, what for, for what purpose] are eyeglasses used for?

§12. **CAPITALIZATION, PUNCTUATION MARKS, AND DIVISION OF WORDS INTO SYLLABLES**

§12.1 Generally speaking, do not capitalize days of the week, months of the year, languages, nationalities, and religions:

domingo, lunes, martes, *etc.;* **enero, febrero, marzo,** *etc.;* **español, francés, inglés,** *etc.;* **Roberto es español, María es española, Pierre es francés; Elena es católica.**

§12.2 **Common punctuation marks in Spanish are as follows:**

apóstrofo / apostrophe '
comillas / quotation marks " "
paréntesis / parentheses ( )
principio de interrogación / beginning question mark ¿
fin de interrogación / final question mark ?
punto / period .
coma / comma ,
punto y coma / semicolon ;
dos puntos / colon :
puntos suspensivos / suspension points . . .

§12.3   It is good to know how to divide a word into syllables (not only in Spanish but also in English) because it helps you to pronounce the word correctly and to spell it correctly. The general rules to follow when dividing Spanish words into syllables are:

§12.4

(a) A syllable must contain a vowel.

(b) A syllable may contain only one vowel and no consonant: **e / so (eso).**

(c) If you are dealing with single separate consonants, each consonant remains with the vowel that follows it: **mu / cho (mucho), ca / ba / llo (caballo), pe / ro (pero), pe / rro (perro).** Did you notice that the consonants **ch, ll,** and **rr** are considered as one consonant sound and are not separated?

(d) If you are dealing with two consonants that come together (other than **ch, ll,** or **rr** as stated in (c) above), the two consonants are separated; the first remains with the preceding syllable and the second remains with the following syllable when they are split:

her / ma / no (hermano), at / las (atlas), ter / cer (tercer)

But if the second of the two consonants that come together is **l** or **r,** do not separate them:

ha / blo (hablo), a / pren / do (aprendo), li / bro (libro)

(e) If you are dealing with three consonants that come together, the first two remain with the preceding vowel and the third consonant remains with the vowel that follows it:

ins / ti / tu / to (instituto)

But if the third of the three consonants is **l** or **r,** do not separate that third consonant from the second; it remains with the second consonant:

com / pren / der (comprender), sas / tre (sastre), sal / dré (saldré)

(f) Two vowels that are together are generally separated if they are strong vowels. The strong vowels are: **a, e, o:**

a / e / ro / pla / no (aeroplano), o / a / sis (oasis), re / a / li / dad (realidad)

But if you are dealing with a weak vowel (**i, u**) it ordinarily remains in the same syllable with its neighboring vowel, especially if that other vowel is a strong vowel:

trein / ta (treinta), ru / bio (rubio), hue / vo (huevo)

(g) The letter **y** is considered to be a consonant when a vowel follows it. Keep it with the vowel that follows it:

a / yer (ayer), a / yu / dar (ayudar)

(h) If a vowel contains a written accent mark, it becomes strong enough (because of the stress required by the accent mark) to remain in its own syllable:

Ma / rí / a (María), re / ú / ne (reúne), dí / a (día)

(i) There are other considerations that must be made regarding syllabification of Spanish words, but those stated above are the basic essential ones that you need to know to help you pronounce and write Spanish words correctly.

§13.   COGNATES

Another good way to increase your vocabulary is to become aware of cognates. A cognate is a word whose origin is the same as another word in other languages. There are many cognates in Spanish and English. Their spelling is sometimes identical or very similar in both languages. Most of the time, the meaning is the same or similar; sometimes they appear to be related because of the similar or identical spelling but they are not true cognates. Those are described as "false cognates"—for example, the Spanish word **actual** means *present-day*, not *actual*; the English word *actual* is expressed in Spanish as **real, verdadero, efectivo,** or **existente.** Also, the Spanish word **pan** means *bread*, not *pan*. The English word *pan* is **cacerola, cazuela,** or **sartén** in Spanish.

You ought to get into the habit of looking for cognates on standardized tests in Spanish and, if you must guess the meaning of a Spanish word if it appears to be a cognate, then guess. There are not that many "false cognates" which would be in your way. As a matter of fact, there are many more true cognates than false ones. Here is how you can recognize a true cognate:

Generally speaking, Spanish words that have certain endings have equivalent endings in English. For example:

Spanish ending of a word	Equivalent English ending of a word
-ario	-ary
-ción	-tion
-dad	-ty
-fía	-phy
-ia	-y
-ía	-y
-io	-y
-ista	-ist
-mente	-ly
-orio	-ory
-oso	-ous

There are others, but the above seem to be the most common. Also note that Spanish words that begin with **es** are generally equivalent to an English word that begins with *s*. Just drop the **e** in the beginning of the Spanish word and you have a close equivalent to the spelling of an English word; for example, **especial** / special; **estudiante** / student.

Here are examples to illustrate true cognates whose spellings are identical or similar:

actor / actor
admiración / admiration
atención / attention
autoridad / authority
central / central
civilización / civilization
color / color
correctamente / correctly
chocolate / chocolate
dentista / dentist
doctor / doctor
dormitorio / dormitory, bedroom
escena / scene
estúpido / stupid
famoso / famous
farmacia / pharmacy
finalmente / finally
fotografía / photography
generoso / generous
geografía / geography
historia / history
hotel / hotel
idea / idea
invitación / invitation
manual / manual
nación / nation
naturalmente / naturally
necesario / necessary
necesidad / necessity
novelista / novelist
piano / piano
posibilidad / possibility

> **radio** / radio
> **realidad** / reality
> **remedio** / remedy
> **sección** / section
> **sociedad** / society
> **universidad** / university
> **violín** / violin
> **vocabulario** / vocabulary

Finally, consult the Comprehensive Index under the entry **vocabulary** to find references to other sections in this Grammar Part for other kinds of vocabulary that you ought to know.

§14.   MORE ANTONYMS (see also §3.)

You ought to know the following antonyms to prepare yourself for the next standardized test in Spanish:

> **alegre** / happy; **triste** / sad
> **algo** / something; **nada** / nothing
> **alguien** / someone; **nadie** / no one
> **alguno (algún)** / some; **ninguno (ningún)** / none; see §1.19 and §1.20
> **amigo, amiga** / friend; **enemigo, enemiga** / enemy
> **antes (de)** / before; **después (de)** / after
> **antiguo, antigua** / ancient, old; **moderno, moderna** / modern
> **aparecer** / to appear; **desaparecer** / to disappear
> **aprisa** / quickly; **despacio** / slowly
> **aquí** / here; **allí** / there
> **arriba** / above, upstairs; **abajo** / below, downstairs
> **bajo, baja** / low, short; **alto, alta** / high, tall
> **bien** / well; **mal** / badly, poorly
> **blanco, blanca** / white; **negro, negra** / black
> **bueno (buen), buena** / good; **malo (mal)** / bad; see §1.19 and §1.20
> **caballero** / gentleman; **dama** / lady
> **caliente** / hot; **frío** / cold
> **caro, cara** / expensive; **barato, barata** / cheap
> **cerca (de)** / near; **lejos (de)** / far
> **cerrar** / to close; **abrir** / to open
> **cielo** / sky; **tierra** / earth, ground
> **comprar** / to buy; **vender** / to sell
> **común** / common; **raro, rara** / rare
> **con** / with; **sin** / without
> **contra** / against; **con** / with
> **corto, corta** / short; **largo, larga** / long
> **chico** / boy; **chica** / girl
> **dar** / to give; **recibir** / to receive
> **dejar caer** / to drop; **recoger** / to pick up
> **delante de** / in front of; **detrás de** / in back of
> **dentro** / inside; **fuera** / outside
> **despertarse** / to wake up; **dormirse** / to fall asleep
> **dulce** / sweet; **amargo** / bitter
> **duro, dura** / hard; **suave, blando, blanda** / soft
> **empezar** / to begin, to start; **terminar, acabar** / to end
> **encender** / to light; **apagar** / to extinguish
> **encima (de)** / on top; **debajo (de)** / under
> **entrada** / entrance; **salida** / exit
> **esta noche** / tonight, this evening; **anoche** / last night, yesterday evening

este / east; **oeste** / west

estúpido, estúpida / stupid; **inteligente** / intelligent

éxito / success; **fracaso** / failure

fácil / easy; **difícil** / difficult

feliz / happy; **triste** / sad

feo, fea / ugly; **hermoso, hermosa** / beautiful

fin / end; **principio** / beginning

flaco, flaca / thin; **gordo, gorda** / fat

grande (gran) / large, big; **pequeño, pequeña** / small, little; see **§1.15** and **§1.22**

guerra / war; **paz** / peace

hablar / to talk, to speak; **callarse** / to keep silent

hombre / man; **mujer** / woman

ida / departure; **vuelta** / return (**ida y vuelta** / round trip)

ir / to go; **venir** / to come

joven / young; **viejo, vieja** / old

jugar / to play; **trabajar** / to work

juventud / youth; **vejez** / old age

levantarse / to get up; **sentarse** / to sit down

limpio, limpia / clean; **sucio, sucia** / dirty

lleno, llena / full; **vacío, vacía** / empty

llorar / to cry, to weep; **reír** / to laugh

madre / mother; **padre** / father

mañana / tomorrow; **ayer** / yesterday

marido / husband; **esposa** / wife

más / more; **menos** / less

mejor / better; **peor** / worse

menor / younger; **mayor** / older

mentir / to lie; **decir la verdad** / to tell the truth

meter / to put in; **sacar** / to take out

mismo, misma / same; **diferente** / different

morir / to die; **vivir** / to live

muchacho / boy; **muchacha** / girl

mucho, mucha / much; **poco, poca** / little

nacer / to be born; **morir** / to die

natural / natural; **innatural** / unnatural

necesario / necessary; **innecesario** / unnecessary

noche / night; **día** / day

obeso, obesa / obese, fat; **delgado, delgada** / thin

obscuro, obscura / dark; **claro, clara** / light

odio / hate, hatred; **amor** / love

perder / to lose; **hallar** / to find

perezoso, perezosa / lazy; **diligente** / diligent

permitir / to permit; **prohibir** / to prohibit

pesado, pesada / heavy; **ligero, ligera** / light

ponerse / to put on (clothing); **quitarse** / to take off (clothing)

posible / possible; **imposible** / impossible

pregunta / question; **respuesta, contestación** / answer

preguntar / to ask; **contestar** / to answer

presente / present; **ausente** / absent

prestar / to lend; **pedir prestado** / to borrow

primero (primer), primera / first; **último, última** / last; see **§1.19** and **§1.20**

princesa / princess; **príncipe** / prince

quedarse / to remain; **irse** / to leave, to go away

quizá(s) / maybe, perhaps; **seguro, cierto** / sure, certain

rey / king; **reina** / queen
rico, rica / rich; **pobre** / poor
rubio, rubia / blond; **moreno, morena** / brunette
ruido / noise; **silencio** / silence
sabio, sabia / wise; **tonto, tonta** / foolish
salir (de) / to leave (from); **entrar (en)** / to enter (in, into)
sí / yes; **no** / no
siempre / always; **nunca** / never
sobrino / nephew; **sobrina** / niece
subir / to go up; **bajar** / to go down
sur / south; **norte** / north
temprano / early; **tarde** / late
tío / uncle; **tía** / aunt
tomar / to take; **dar** / to give
unir / to unite; **desunir** / to disunite
usual / usual; **extraño, raro** / unusual
verano / summer; **invierno** / winter
vida / life; **muerte** / death
virtud / virtue; **vicio** / vice
y / and, plus; **menos** / minus, less
zorro / fox; **zorra** / vixen, she-fox

§15. ACABAR DE + INF. (See also idioms with DE in §53.7)

The Spanish idiomatic expression **acabar de + inf.** is expressed in English as *to have just +* past participle. This is a very common expression which you surely will find on any standardized test in Spanish.

§15.1 In the present indicative:

María acaba de llegar / Mary has just arrived.
Acabo de comer / I have just eaten.
Acabamos de terminar la lección / We have just finished the lesson.

§15.2 In the imperfect indicative:

María acababa de llegar / Mary had just arrived.
Acababa de comer / I had just eaten.
Acabábamos de terminar la lección / We had just finished the lesson.
NOTE:

§15.3
(a) When you use **acabar** in the present tense, it indicates that the action of the main verb (+ inf.) has just occurred now in the present. In English, we express this by using *have just +* the past participle of the main verb: **Acabo de llegar** / I have just arrived. (See the other examples above under **present indicative.**)

§15.4
(b) When you use **acabar** in the imperfect indicative, it indicates that the action of the main verb (+ inf.) had occurred at some time in the past when another action occurred in the past. In English, we express this by using *had just +* the past participle of the main verb: **Acabábamos de entrar en la casa cuando el teléfono sonó** / We had just entered the house when the telephone rang. (See the other examples above under **imperfect indicative.**)

§15.5
NOTE also that when **acabar** is used in the imperfect indicative + the inf. of the main verb being expressed, the verb in the other clause is usually in the preterit.

§16. AHÍ, ALLÍ, ALLÁ

These three adverbs all mean *there* but they have special uses:

(a) **ahí** means *there*, not too far away from the person who says it: **El libro que Ud. quiere está ahí sobre esa mesa** / The book that you want is *there* on *that* table.

(b) **allí** means *there*, farther away from the person who says it, or even at a remote distance: **¿Quiere Ud. ir a Chicago? Sí, porque mi padre trabaja allí** / Do you want to go to Chicago? Yes, because my father works there.

(c) **allá** means *there*, generally used with a verb of motion: **Me gustaría mucho ir allá** / I would like very much to go there; **Bueno, ¡vaya allá!** / Good, go there!

§17. AQUÍ AND ACÁ

These two adverbs both mean *here* but they have special uses:

(a) **aquí** means *here*, a place close to the person who says it: **Aquí se habla español** / Spanish is spoken here.

(b) **acá** means *here*, a place close to the person who says it, but it is used with a verb of motion: **Señor Gómez, venga acá, por favor!** / Mr. Gomez, come here, please!

§18. CAMPO, PAÍS, PATRIA, NACIÓN

The first three nouns (**el campo, el país, la patria**) all mean *country*. However, note the following:

(a) **campo** means *country* in the sense of countryside, where you find farmlands, as opposite to life in a city: **en el campo** / in the country; **Vamos a pasar el fin de semana en el campo** / We are going to spend the weekend in the country; **Voy al campo este verano** / I am going to the country this summer.

(b) **país** means *country* in the meaning of a *nation*: **¿En qué país nació Ud.?** / In what country were you born?

(c) **patria** means *country* in the sense of *native land*: **El soldado defendió a su patria** / The soldier defended his country.

(d) **nación** means *country* in the sense of *nation*: **Las Naciones Unidas** / the United Nations; **La Sociedad de las Naciones** / The League of Nations.

§19. CONOCER AND SABER (See also §47.)

These two verbs mean *to know* but they are used in a distinct sense:

(a) Generally speaking, **conocer** means to know in the sense of *being acquainted* with a person, a place, or a thing: **¿Conoce Ud. a María?** / Do you know Mary? **¿Conoce Ud. bien los Estados Unidos?** / Do you know the United States well? **¿Conoce Ud. este libro?** / Do you know (Are you acquainted with) this book?

In the preterit tense, **conocer** means *met* in the sense of *first met, first became acquainted with someone*: **¿Conoce Ud. a Elena?** / Do you know Helen? **Sí, (yo) la conocí anoche en casa de un amigo mío** / Yes, I met her [for the first time] last night at the home of one of my friends.

(b) Generally speaking, **saber** means to know a fact, to know something thoroughly: **¿Sabe Ud. qué hora es?** / Do you know what time it is? **¿Sabe Ud. la lección?** / Do you know the lesson?

When you use **saber + inf.**, it means *to know how*: **¿Sabe Ud. nadar?** / Do you know how to swim? **Sí, (yo) sé nadar** / Yes, I know how to swim.

In the preterit tense, **saber** means *found out*: **¿Lo sabe Ud.?** / Do you know it? **Sí, lo supe ayer** / Yes, I found it out yesterday.

§20. DEBER, DEBER DE AND TENER QUE

§20.1   Generally speaking, use **deber** when you want to express a moral obligation, something you ought to do but you may or may not do it: **Debo estudiar esta noche pero estoy cansado y no me siento bien** / I ought to study tonight but I am tired and I do not feel well.

§20.2   Generally speaking, **deber de + inf.** is used to express a supposition, something that is probable: **La señora Gómez debe de estar enferma porque sale de casa raramente** / Mrs. Gomez must be sick (is probably sick) because she goes out of the house rarely.

§20.3   Generally speaking, use **tener que** when you want to say that you *have to* do something: **No puedo salir esta noche porque tengo que estudiar** / I cannot go out tonight because I have to study.

§21. DEJAR, SALIR, AND SALIR DE

§21.1   These verbs mean *to leave*, but notice the difference in use:

§21.2   Use **dejar** when you leave someone or when you leave something behind you: **El alumno dejó sus libros en la sala de clase** / The pupil left his books in the classroom.

   Dejar also means *to let* or *to allow* or *to let go*: **Déjelo!** / Let it! (Leave it!)

§21.3   Use **salir de** when you mean *to leave* in the sense of *to go out of* (a place): **El alumno salió de la sala de clase** / The pupil left the classroom; **¿Dónde está su madre? Mi madre salió** / Where is your mother? My mother went out.

§22. DEJAR DE + INF. AND DEJAR CAER

§22.1   Use **dejar de + inf.** when you mean *to stop* or *to fail to:* **Los alumnos dejaron de hablar cuando la profesora entró en la sala de clase** / The students stopped talking when the teacher came into the classroom.

   ¡No deje Ud. de llamarme! / Don't fail to call me!
   Dejar caer means *to drop:* **Luis dejó caer sus libros** / Louis dropped his books.

§23. IR, IRSE

§23.1   Use **ir** when you simply mean *to go:* **Voy al cine** / I am going to the movies.

§23.2   Use **irse** when you mean *to leave* in the sense of *to go away:* **Mis padres se fueron al campo para visitar a mis abuelos** / My parents left for (went away to) the country to visit my grandparents.

§24. GASTAR AND PASAR

§24.1   These two verbs mean *to spend*, but notice the difference in use:

§24.2   Use **gastar** when you spend money: **No me gusta gastar mucho dinero** / I do not like to spend much money.

§24.3   Use **pasar** when you spend time: **Me gustaría pasar un año en España** / I would like to spend a year in Spain.

§25. GUSTAR

   (a) Essentially, the verb **gustar** means *to be pleasing to* . . .
   (b) In English, we say, for example, *I like ice cream*. In Spanish, we say **Me gusta el helado;** that is to say, "Ice cream is pleasing to me" [To me ice cream is pleasing].

(c) In English, the thing that you like is the direct object. In Spanish, the thing that you like is the subject. Also, in Spanish, the person who likes the thing is the indirect object: to me, to you, *etc.*: **A Roberto le gusta el helado** / Robert likes ice cream; in other words, "To Robert, ice cream is pleasing to him."

(d) In Spanish, therefore, the verb **gustar** is used in the third person, either in the singular or plural, when you talk about something that you like—something that is pleasing to you. Therefore, the verb form must agree with the subject; if the thing liked is singular, the verb is third person singular; if the thing liked is plural, the verb **gustar** is third person plural: **Me gusta el café** / I like coffee; **Me gustan el café y la leche** / I like coffee and milk ["Coffee and milk are pleasing to me".]

(e) When you mention the person or the persons who like something, you must use the preposition **a** in front of the person; you must also use the indirect object pronoun of the noun which is the person:

A los muchachos y a las muchachas les gusta jugar / Boys and girls like to play; that is to say, "To play is pleasing to them, to boys and girls".

(f) Review the indirect object pronouns which are given in §66.14–§66.20. They are: **me, te, le; nos, os, les.**

(g) Other examples:
Me gusta leer / I like to read.
Te gusta leer / You (*familiar*) like to read.
A Felipe le gusta el helado / Philip likes ice cream.
Al chico le gusta la leche / The boy likes milk.
A Carlota le gusta bailar / Charlotte likes to dance.
A las chicas les gustó el libro / The girls liked the book.
Nos gustó el cuento / We liked the story.
¿Le gusta a Ud. el español? / Do you like Spanish?
A Pedro y a Ana les gustó la película / Peter and Anna liked the film.
A mi amigo le gustaron los chocolates / My friend liked the chocolates; that is to say, the chocolates were pleasing [pleased] to him (to my friend).

§26. HABER, HABER DE + INF., AND TENER

§26.1   The verb **haber** (to have) is used as an auxiliary verb (or helping verb) in order to form the seven compound tenses, which are as follows:

Compound Tenses	Example (in the 1st person sing.)
Present Perfect (or Perfect) Indicative	**he hablado** (I have spoken)
Pluperfect (or Past Perfect) Indicative	**había hablado** (I had spoken)
Preterit Perfect (or Past Anterior)	**hube hablado** (I had spoken)
Future Perfect (or Future Anterior)	**habré hablado** (I will have spoken)
Conditional Perfect	**habría hablado** (I would have spoken)
Present Perfect (or Past) Subjunctive	**haya hablado** (I may have spoken)
Pluperfect (or Past Perfect) Subjunctive	**hubiera hablado** *or* **hubiese hablado** (I might have spoken)

For an explanation of the formation of these tenses, see the names of these tenses in the General Index.

§26.2   The verb **haber** is also used to form the Perfect (or Past) Infinitive: **haber hablado** (to have spoken). As you can see, this is formed by using the infinitive form of haber + the past participle of the main verb.

§26.3   The verb **haber** is also used to form the Perfect Participle: **habiendo hablado** (having spoken). As you can see, this is formed by using the present participle of **haber** + the past participle of the main verb.

§26.4   The verb **haber + de + inf.** is equivalent to the English use of "to be supposed to . . ." or "to be to . . .". EXAMPLES:

> **María ha de traer un pastel, yo he de traer el helado, y mis amigos han de traer sus discos** / Mary is supposed to bring a pie, I am supposed to bring the ice cream, and my friends are to bring their records.

§26.5   The verb **tener** is used to mean *to have* in the sense of *to possess* or *to hold:* **Tengo un perro y un gato** / I have a dog and a cat; **Tengo un lápiz en la mano** / I have (am holding) a pencil in my hand.

     In the preterit tense, **tener** can mean *received:* **Ayer mi padre tuvo un cheque** / Yesterday my father received a check.

§27.   HAY AND HAY QUE + INF.

§27.1   The word **hay** is not a verb. You might regard it as an impersonal irregular form of **haber**. Actually, the word is composed of **ha** + the archaic **y,** meaning *there*. It is generally regarded as an adverbial expression because it points out that something or someone "is there". Its English equivalent is *There is . . .* or *There are . . . ,* for example:

> **Hay muchos libros en la mesa** / There are many books on the table; **Hay una mosca en la sopa** / There is a fly in the soup; **Hay veinte alumnos en esta clase** / There are twenty students in this class.

§27.2   **Hay que + inf.** is an impersonal expression that denotes an obligation and it is commonly translated into English as: *One must . . .* or *It is necessary to . . .* EXAMPLES:

> **Hay que estudiar para aprender** / It is necessary to study in order to learn; **Hay que comer para vivir** / One must eat in order to live.

§28.   ¿CUÁNTO TIEMPO HACE QUE + PRESENT TENSE . . . ? (See also §53.5)

(a) Use this formula when you want to ask *How long* + *the present perfect tense* in English: **¿Cuánto tiempo hace que Ud. estudia español?** / How long have you been studying Spanish?

> **¿Cuánto tiempo hace que Ud. espera el autobús?** / How long have you been waiting for the bus?

(b) When this formula is used, you generally expect the person to tell you how long a time it has been, *e.g.,* one year, two months, a few minutes.

(c) This is used when the action began at some time in the past and continues up to the present moment. That is why you must use the present tense of the verb—the action of studying, waiting, *etc.* is still going on at the present.

§29.   HACE + LENGTH OF TIME + QUE + PRESENT TENSE (See also §53.13)

(a) This formula is the usual answer to the question in **§28.** above.

(b) Since the question is asked in terms of *how long,* the usual answer is in terms of time: a year, two years, a few days, months, minutes, *etc.*:

> **Hace tres años que estudio español** / I have been studying Spanish for three years.

> **Hace veinte minutos que espero el autobús** / I have been waiting for the bus for twenty minutes.

(c) The same formula is used if you want to ask *how many weeks, how many months, how many minutes,* etc.:

> **¿Cuántos años hace que Ud. estudia español?** / How many years have you been studying Spanish?

¿**Cuántas horas hace que Ud. mira la televisión?** / How many hours have you been watching television?

§30. **¿DESDE CUÁNDO + PRESENT TENSE . . . ?**

This is another way of asking *How long (since when) + the present perfect tense* in English, as given above in §28.

¿**Desde cuándo estudia Ud. español?** / How long have you been studying Spanish?

§31. **PRESENT TENSE + DESDE HACE + LENGTH OF TIME**

This formula is the usual answer to the question in §30. above. It is similar to the expression given in §29. above.

Estudio español desde hace tres años / I have been studying Spanish for three years.

§32. **¿CUÁNTO TIEMPO HACÍA QUE + IMPERFECT TENSE**

(a) This formula is the same as the one given in §28., except that the tense of the verb is different. If the action of the verb began in the past and ended in the past, use the imperfect tense.

(b) This formula is equivalent to the English: *How long + past perfect tense:*

¿**Cuánto tiempo hacía que Ud. hablaba cuando entré en la sala de clase?** / How long had you been talking when I entered into the classroom?

(c) Note that the action of talking in this example began in the past and ended in the past when I entered the classroom.

§33. **HACÍA + LENGTH OF TIME + QUE + IMPERFECT TENSE**

(a) This formula is the usual answer to the question as stated in §32.(b) above.

(b) It is the same as the one given in §29., except that the tense of the verb is different. The imperfect tense of the verb is used here because the action began in the past and ended in the past; it is not going on at the present moment, as is the case with the expression given in §29. above.

Hacía una hora que yo hablaba cuando Ud. entró en la sala de clase / I had been talking for one hour when you entered the classroom.

§34. **¿DESDE CUÁNDO + IMPERFECT TENSE . . . ?**

(a) This formula is the same as the one given in §30., except that the tense of the verb is different.

(b) This is another way of asking the question stated in §32. above.

¿**Desde cuándo hablaba Ud. cuando yo entré en la sala de clase?** / How long had you been talking when I entered into the classroom?

§35. **IMPERFECT TENSE + DESDE HACÍA + LENGTH OF TIME**

(a) This formula is the same as the one given in §31., except that the tense of the verb is different.

(b) This is another way of answering the question stated in §33. above.

(Yo) hablaba desde hacía una hora cuando Ud. entró en la sala de clase / I had been talking for one hour when you entered into the classroom.

§36. HORA, TIEMPO, AND VEZ

These three words all mean *time;* however, note the differences:

§36.1   **La hora** refers to the time (the hour) of the day: **¿A qué hora vamos al baile?** / At what time are we going to the dance? **Vamos al baile a las nueve** / We are going to the dance at nine o'clock.

¿Qué hora es? / What time is it? **Es la una** / It is one o'clock; **Son las dos** / It is two o'clock.

§36.2   **El tiempo** refers to a vague or indefinite duration of time; in other words, time in general: **No puedo ir contigo porque no tengo tiempo** / I cannot go with you because I don't have time.

As you know, **tiempo** is also used to express the weather: **¿Qué tiempo hace hoy?** / What's the weather like today? **Hace buen tiempo** / The weather is fine.

§36.3   **La vez** means *time* in the sense of segmented time, different times, *e.g., the first time* / **la primera vez;** *this time* / **esta vez;** *many times* / **muchas veces;** *two times* or *twice* / **dos veces;** *again* or *another time* / **otra vez.**

§37. JUGAR AND TOCAR

§37.1   Both these verbs mean *to play* but they have different uses. **Jugar a** is used to play a sport, a game:

¿Juega Ud. al tenis? / Do you play tennis? **Me gusta jugar a la pelota** / I like to play ball.

§37.2   The verb **tocar** is used to play a musical instrument: **Carmen toca muy bien el piano** / Carmen plays the piano very well.

The verb **tocar** has other meanings, too; it is commonly used as follows: *to be one's turn,* in which case it takes an indirect object: **¿A quién le toca?** / Whose turn is it? **Le toca a Juan** / It is John's turn; *to knock on a door:* **tocar a la puerta; Alguien toca a la puerta** / Someone is knocking on (at) the door.

Essentially, **tocar** means *to touch.*

§38. LLEGAR A SER, HACERSE AND PONERSE

These three verbs mean *to become.* Note the difference in use:

§38.1   Use **llegar a ser + a noun,** *e.g., to become a doctor, to become a teacher;* in other words, the noun indicates the goal that you are striving for: **Quiero llegar a ser doctor** / I want to become a doctor. **Hacerse** is used similarly: **Juan se hizo abogado** / John became a lawyer.

§38.2   Use **ponerse + an adj.,** *e.g., to become pale, to become sick;* in other words, the adj. indicates the state or condition (physical or mental) that you have become:

Cuando vi el accidente, me puse pálido / When I saw the accident, I became pale; **Mi madre se puso triste al oír la noticia desgraciada** / My mother became sad upon hearing the unfortunate news.

§39. LLEVAR AND TOMAR

These two verbs mean *to take* but note the difference in use:

§39.1   **Llevar** means *to take* in the sense of carry or transport from place to place: **José llevó la silla de la cocina al comedor** / Joseph took the chair from the kitchen to the dining room.

The verb **llevar** is also used when you *take someone somewhere:* **Pedro llevó a María al baile anoche** / Peter took Mary to the dance last night.

As you probably know, **llevar** also means *to wear*: **María, ¿por qué llevas la falda nueva?** / Mary, why are you wearing your new skirt?

§39.2   **Tomar** means *to take* in the sense of grab or catch: **La profesora tomó el libro y comenzó a leer a la clase** / The teacher took the book and began to read to the class; **Mi amigo tomó el tren esta mañana a las siete** / My friend took the train this morning at seven o'clock.

§40.   MEDIO AND MITAD

Both these words mean *half* but note the difference in use:

§40.1   **Medio** is an adj. and it agrees with the noun it modifies: **Necesito media docena de huevos** / I need half a dozen eggs; **Llegaremos en media hora** / We will arrive in a half hour (in half an hour); **Son las dos y media y ya tengo mucha hambre** / It is two thirty and already I am very hungry.

Medio is also used as an adverb: **Los hombres viejos corrieron rápidamente y ahora están medio muertos** / The old men ran fast and now they are half dead.

§40.2   **Mitad** is a fem. noun: **El alumno estudió la mitad de la lección** / The pupil studied half (of) the lesson.

§41.   PEDIR AND PREGUNTAR

Both these verbs mean *to ask* but note the difference:

§41.1   **Pedir** means *to ask for something* or *to request*: **El alumno pidió un lápiz al profesor** / The pupil asked the teacher for a pencil.

§41.2   **Preguntar** means *to inquire, to ask a question*: **La alumna preguntó a la profesora cómo estaba** / The pupil asked the teacher how she was. See also **§52.19.**

§42.   PENSAR DE AND PENSAR EN

Both these verbs mean *to think of* but note the difference:

§42.1   **Pensar** is used with the prep. **de** when you ask someone what he/she thinks of someone or something, when you ask for someone's opinion: **¿Qué piensa Ud. de este libro?** / What do you think of this book? **Pienso que es bueno** / I think that it is good.

§42.2   **Pensar** is used with the prep. **en** when you ask someone what or whom he/she is thinking about: **Miguel, no hablas mucho; ¿en qué piensas?** / Michael, you are not talking much; of what are you thinking? (what are you thinking of?) **Pienso en las vacaciones de verano** / I'm thinking of summer vacation.

§43.   DICHO, DICHOSO, DICHA

§43.1   The word **dicho** is the past part. (irregular) of **decir**: **¿Ha dicho Ud. la verdad?** / Have you told the truth?

§43.2   The word **dicho** is also used with the neuter article **lo** and has a special meaning: **Lo dicho y lo escrito** / what has been said and what has been written.

§43.3   The word **dicho** is also used in the following expression: **dicho y hecho** / no sooner said than done.

§43.4   The word **dichoso** is an adj. and it means fortunate, happy, lucky: **una vida dichosa** / a happy life.

§43.5   The word **dicha** is a fem. noun and it means happiness, good fortune.

§44.   PERO AND SINO

These two words are conjunctions and they both mean *but*. Note the difference in use:

§44.1   **Me gustaría venir a tu casa esta noche pero no puedo** / I would like to come to your house tonight but I can't.

§44.2   Use **sino** to mean *but rather, but on the contrary*: **Pedro no es pequeño sino alto** / Peter is not short but tall; **Mi automóvil no es amarillo sino blanco** / My car is not yellow but white.

§44.3   Note that when you use **sino** the first part of the sentence is negative. Also note that **sino** may be followed by an inf.: **Pablo no quiere alquilar el automóvil sino comprarlo** / Paul does not want to rent the car but to buy it.

§44.4   If a clause follows **sino**, use **sino que**: **Pablo no alquiló el automóvil sino que lo compró** / Paul did not rent the car but bought it.

§44.5   Remember that a clause contains a subject and verb form.

§44.6   And note finally that **sino** is used instead of **pero** when you make a clear contrast between a negative thought in the first part of the sentence and a positive thought in the second part. If no contrast is made or intended, use **pero**: **María no conoce al niño pero le habla** / Mary does not know the child but talks to him.

§45.   PERO AND MAS

These two words are conjunctions and they both mean *but*. In plays and poems an author may sometimes use **mas** instead of **pero**. In conversation and informal writing, **pero** is used. Note that **mas** with no accent mark means *but* and **más** (with the accent mark) means *more*.

§46.   POCO AND PEQUEÑO

These two words mean *little* but note the difference in use:

§46.1   **Poco** means *little* in terms of quantity: **Tenemos poco trabajo hoy** / We have little work today.

§46.2   **Pequeño** means *little* in terms of size; in other words, *small*: **Mi casa es pequeña** / My house is small.

§47.   PODER AND SABER (See also §19.)

Both these verbs mean *can* but the difference in use is as follows:

§47.1   **Poder** means *can* in the sense of *ability*: **No puedo ayudarlo; lo siento** / I cannot (am unable to) help you; I'm sorry.

§47.2   **Saber** means *can* in the sense of *to know how*: **Este niño no sabe contar** / This child can't (does not know how to) count.

§47.3   In the preterit tense **poder** has the special meaning of *succeeded*: **Después de algunos minutos, Juan pudo abrir la puerta** / After a few minutes, John succeeded in opening the door.

§47.4   In the preterit tense, **saber** has the special meaning of *found out:* **Lo supe ayer** / I found it out yesterday. See also §19.(b).

§48.   SER AND ESTAR

These two verbs mean *to be* but note the differences in use:

§48.1   Generally speaking, use **ser** when you want to express *to be*.

§48.2   Use **estar** when *to be* is used in the following ways:

§48.3   (a)   Health: **¿Cómo está Ud.?** / How are you?

           Estoy bien / I am well.
           Estoy enfermo (enferma) / I am sick.

§48.4   (b)   Location: persons, places, things

      (1) **Estoy en la sala de clase** / I am in the classroom.
      (2) **La escuela está lejos** / The school is far.
      (3) **Barcelona está en España** / Barcelona is (located) in Spain.
      (4) **Los libros están en la mesa** / The books are on the table..

§48.5   (c)   State or condition: persons

      (1) **Estoy contento (contenta)** / I am happy.
      (2) **Los alumnos están cansados (Las alumnas están cansadas)** / The students are tired.
      (3) **María está triste hoy** / Mary is sad today.
      (4) **Estoy listo (lista)** / I am ready.
      (5) **Estoy pálido (pálida)** / I am pale.
      (6) **Estoy ocupado (ocupada)** / I am busy.
      (7) **Estoy seguro (segura)** / I am sure.
      (8) **Este hombre está vivo** / This man is alive.
      (9) **Ese hombre está muerto** / That man is dead.
    (10) **Este hombre está borracho** / This man is drunk.

§48.6   (d)   State or condition: things and places

      (1) **La ventana está abierta** / The window is open.
      (2) **La taza está llena** / The cup is full.
      (3) **El té está caliente** / The tea is hot.
      (4) **La limonada está fría** / The lemonade is cold.
      (5) **La biblioteca está cerrada los domingos** / The library is closed on Sundays.

§48.7   (e)   To form the progressive present of a verb, use the present tense of **estar** + the present participle of the main verb:

       Estoy estudiando en mi cuarto y no puedo salir esta noche / I am studying in my room and I cannot go out tonight.

§48.8   (f)   To form the progressive past of a verb, use the imperfect tense of **estar** + the present participle of the main verb:

       Mi hermano estaba leyendo cuando (yo) entré en el cuarto / My brother was reading when I entered (came into) the room.

§49.   VOLVER AND DEVOLVER

These two verbs mean *to return* but note the difference:

§49.1   **Volver** means *to return* in the sense of *to come back:* **Voy a volver a casa** / I am going to return home. A synonym of **volver** is **regresar**: **Los muchachos regresaron a las ocho de la noche** / The boys came back (returned) at eight o'clock.

§49.2   **Devolver** means *to return* in the sense of *to give back:* **Voy a devolver el libro a la biblioteca** / I am going to return the book to the library.

§50.   O AND U

These two words, which are conjunctions, mean *or*. Use **o** normally but when a word that is right after **o** begins with **o** or **ho**, use **u** instead of **o**: **muchachos u hombres** / boys or men; **septiembre u octubre** / September or October.

§51.   Y AND E

These two words, which are conjunctions, mean *and*. Use **y** normally but when a word that is right after **y** begins with **i** or **hi**, use **e** instead of **y**: **María es bonita e inteligente** / Mary is pretty and intelligent; **Fernando e Isabel; padre e hijo** / father and son; **madre e hija** / mother and daughter.

However, if **y** is followed by a word that begins with **hie**, keep **y**: **flores y hierba** / flowers and grass. (See also §1.65.)

§52.   PARA AND POR (See also §5.24 and §11. and idioms with **para** in §53.20 and with **por** in §53.22.)

These two prepositions are generally translated into English as *for*. Observe the variations in translation and the differences between the two:

§52.1   Use **para** when you mean:

§52.2   Destination: **Mañana salgo para Madrid** / Tomorrow I am leaving for Madrid.

§52.3   Intended for: **Este vaso es para María y ese vaso es para José** / This glass is for Mary and that glass is for Joseph.

   Esta taza es para café; es una taza para café / This cup is for coffee; it is a coffee cup.

§52.4   Purpose (in order to): **Estudio para llegar a ser médico** / I am studying in order to become a doctor.

§52.5   A comparison of some sort: **Para ser norteamericano, habla español muy bien** / For an American, he speaks Spanish very well.

§52.6   At some point in future time: **Esta lección es para mañana** / This lesson is for tomorrow.

§52.7   Use **por** when you mean:

§52.8   A length of time: **Me quedé en casa por tres días** / I stayed at home for three days.

§52.9   In exchange for: **¿Cuánto dinero me dará Ud. por mi trabajo?** / How much money will you give me for my work?

§52.10   To send for: **Vamos a enviar por el médico** / We are going to send for the doctor.

§52.11   By: **Este libro fue escrito por dos autores** / This book was written by two authors; **Quiero enviar esta carta por avión** / I want to send this letter by air mail.

§52.12 For the sake of, as an obligation, on someone's behalf: **Quiero hacerlo por usted** / I want to do it for you.

§52.13 Through: **Dimos un paseo por el parque** / We took a walk through the park.

§52.14 Along, by the edge of: **Anduvimos por la playa** / We walked along the beach.

§52.15 To fight for: **Luché por mi amigo** / I fought for my friend.

§52.16 Out of, because of + noun: **No quisieron hacerlo por miedo** / They refused to do it out of (for) fear.

§52.17 *per*, when expressing frequency: **Los alumnos asisten a la escuela cinco días por semana** / Students attend school five days a (per) week.

§52.18 to go for someone or something: **Mi madre fue por Carmen** / My mother went for (went to get) Carmen; **Mi madre fue por pan** / My mother went for (went to get) bread.

§52.19 to ask about, to inquire about, using **preguntar por**: **Pregunto por el médico** / I am asking for the doctor.

§53. IDIOMS, INCLUDING VERBAL, IDIOMATIC, COMMON, AND USEFUL EXPRESSIONS (ARRANGED ALPHABETICALLY BY KEY WORD)

§53.1 with **a** (See also the entry **a** in the General Index and prepositional phrases with **a** in §62.3)
a beneficio de / for the benefit of
a bordo / on board
a caballo / on horseback
a cada instante / at every moment, at every turn
a casa / home (Use with a verb of motion; use **a casa** if you are going *to* the house; use **en casa** if you are *in* the house: **Salgo de la escuela y voy a casa** / I'm leaving school and I'm going home; **Me quedo en casa esta noche** / I'm staying home tonight.)
a causa de / because of, on account of
a derecha / to (on, at) the right
a eso de / about, around (**Llegaremos a Madrid a eso de las tres de la tarde** / We will arrive in Madrid at about 3 o'clock in the afternoon.)
a fines de / about the end of, around the end of (**Estaremos en Madrid a fines de la semana** / We will be in Madrid around the end of the week.)
a fondo / thoroughly
a fuerza de / by dint of (**A fuerza de trabajar, tuvo éxito** / By dint of working, he was successful.)
a mano / by hand
a mediados de / around the middle of (**Estaremos en Málaga a mediados de julio** / We will be in Málaga around the middle of July.)
a menudo / often, frequently
a mi parecer / in my opinion
a pesar de / in spite of
a pie / on foot
a pierna suelta / without a care
a principios de / around the beginning of (**Estaremos en México a principios de la semana que viene** / We will be in Mexico around the beginning of next week.)
a saltos / by leaps and bounds
a solas / alone
a su parecer / in your (his, her, their) opinion
a tiempo / on time
a toda brida / at top speed
a través de / across, through

a veces / at times, sometimes
conforme a / in accordance with
estar a punto de / to be about to (**Estoy a punto de salir** / I am about to leave.)
frente a / in front of
junto a / beside, next to
poco a poco / little by little
ser aficionado a / to be a fan of
uno a uno / one by one

§53.2   with **a la**
a la derecha / to (on, at) the right
a la española / in the Spanish style
a la francesa / in the French style
a la italiana / in the Italian style
a la izquierda / to (on, at) the left
a la larga / in the long run
a la madrugada / at an early hour, at daybreak
a la semana / a week, per week
a la vez / at the same time

§53.3   with **al** (See also §4.7 and §4.8)
al + inf. / on, upon + pres. part. (**Al entrar en la cocina, comenzó a comer** / Upon entering into the kitchen, he began to eat.)
al aire libre / outdoors, in the open air
al amanecer / at daybreak, at dawn
al anochecer / at nightfall, at dusk
al cabo / finally, at last
al cabo de / at the end of
al contrario / on the contrary
al día / current, up to date
al día siguiente / on the following day, on the next day
al fin / at last, finally
al lado de / next to, beside
al menos / at least
al mes / a month, per month
al parecer / apparently
al por mayor / wholesale
al por menor / retail (sales)
al pronto / at first
al través de / across, through
echar al correo / to mail, to post a letter

§53.4   with **con** (See also **con** in the General Index)
con anterioridad / beforehand
con anterioridad a / prior to
con arreglo a / in accordance with
con frecuencia / frequently
con los brazos abiertos / with open arms
con motivo de / on the occasion of
con mucho gusto / gladly, willingly, with much pleasure
con permiso / excuse me, with your permission
con rumbo a / in the direction of
con voz sorda / in a low (muffled) voice
ser amable con / to be kind to

§53.5   with **cuanto, cuanta, cuantos, cuantas** (See also these entries in the General Index)
cuanto antes / as soon as possible
¿Cuánto cuesta? / How much is it? How much does it cost?
cuanto más . . . tanto más . . . / the more . . . the more . . . (**Cuanto más estudio tanto más aprendo** / The more I study the more I learn.)
¿Cuántos años tiene Ud.? / How old are you?
unos cuantos libros / a few books
unas cuantas flores / a few flowers

§53.6   with **dar** and **darse**
dar a / to face (**El comedor da al jardín** / The dining room faces the garden.)
dar con algo / to find something, to come upon something (**Esta mañana di con dinero en la calle** / This morning I found money in the street.)
dar con alguien / to meet someone, to run into someone, to come across someone, to find someone (**Anoche, di con mi amiga Elena en el cine** / Last night I met my friend Helen at the movies.)
dar contra / to hit against
dar cuerda al reloj / to wind a watch
dar de beber a / to give something to drink to
dar de comer a / to feed, to give something to eat to (**Me gusta dar de comer a los pájaros en el parque** / I like to feed the birds in the park.)
dar en / to hit against, to strike against
dar en el blanco / to hit the target, to hit it right
dar gritos / to shout
dar la bienvenida / to welcome
dar la hora / to strike the hour
dar la mano a alguien / to shake hands with someone
dar las buenas noches a alguien / to say good evening (good night) to someone
dar las gracias a alguien / to thank someone
dar los buenos días a alguien / to say good morning (hello) to someone
dar por + past part. / to consider (**Lo doy por perdido** / I consider it lost.)
dar recuerdos a / to give one's regards (best wishes) to
dar un abrazo / to embrace
dar un paseo / to take a walk
dar un paseo a caballo / to go horseback riding
dar un paseo en automóvil (en coche) / to go for a drive
dar un paseo en bicicleta / to ride a bicycle
dar una vuelta / to go for a short walk, to go for a stroll
dar unas palmadas / to clap one's hands
dar voces / to shout
darse cuenta de / to realize, to be aware of, to take into account
darse la mano / to shake hands with each other
darse por + past part. / to consider oneself (**Me doy por insultado** / I consider myself insulted.)
darse prisa / to hurry

§53.7   with **de** (See also the entry **de** in the General Index and prepositional phrases with **de** in §62.3)
abrir de par en par / to open wide
acabar de + inf. / to have just + past part. (**María acaba de llegar** / Mary has just arrived; **María acababa de llegar** / Mary had just arrived.) See also §15.–§15.5.
acerca de / about, concerning
alrededor de / around (**alrededor de la casa** / around the house)
antes de / before
aparte de / aside from
billete de ida y vuelta / round-trip ticket

cerca de / near, close to
de abajo / down, below
de acuerdo / in agreement, in accord
de ahora en adelante / from now on
de algún modo / someway
de alguna manera / someway
de antemano / ahead of time
de aquí en adelante / from now on
de arriba / upstairs
de arriba abajo / from top to bottom
de ayer en ocho días / a week from yesterday
de balde / free, gratis
de broma / jokingly
de buena gana / willingly
de común acuerdo / by mutual accord, by mutual agreement
de cuando en cuando / from time to time
de día / by day, in the daytime
de día en día / from day to day
de esa manera / in that way
de ese modo / in that way
de esta manera / in this way
de este modo / in this way
de hoy en adelante / from today on, from now on
de hoy en ocho días / a week from today
de la mañana / in the morning (Use this when a specific time is mentioned: **Tomo el desayuno a las ocho de la mañana** / I have breakfast at 8 o'clock in the morning.)
de la noche / in the evening (Use this when a specific time is mentioned: **Mi amigo llega a las nueve de la noche** / My friend is arriving at 9 o'clock in the evening.)
de la tarde / in the afternoon (Use this when a specific time is mentioned: **Regreso a casa a las cuatro de la tarde** / I am returning home at 4 o'clock in the afternoon.)
de madrugada / at dawn, at daybreak
de mal humor / in bad humor, in a bad mood
de mala gana / unwillingly
de memoria / by heart (memorized)
de moda / in fashion
de nada / you're welcome
de ningún modo / no way, in no way, by no means; see §1.19 and §1.20
de ninguna manera / no way, in no way, by no means
de noche / by night, at night, during the night
de nuevo / again
de otra manera / in another way
de otro modo / otherwise
de pie / standing
de prisa / in a hurry
de pronto / suddenly
de repente / all of a sudden
de rodillas / kneeling, on one's knees
de todos modos / anyway, in any case, at any rate
de uno en uno / one by one
de veras / really, truly
de vez en cuando / from time to time
dentro de poco / soon, shortly, within a short time
echar de menos / to miss
en lo alto de / at the top of

en lugar de / in place of, instead of
enfrente de / opposite
estar de acuerdo / to agree
fuera de sí / beside oneself, aghast
ir de compras / to go shopping
la mayor parte de / the greater part of, the majority of
no hay de qué / you're welcome, don't mention it
un billete de ida y vuelta / round-trip ticket
un poco de / a little (of): **un poco de azúcar** / a little sugar

§53.8   with **decir**
decirle al oído / to whisper in one's ears
dicho y hecho / no sooner said than done
Es decir / That is to say . . .
querer decir / to mean   ¿**Qué quiere decir este muchacho?** / What does this boy mean?

§53.9   with **día, días**
al día / current, up to date
al romper el día / at daybreak
algún día / someday; see §1.19 and §1.20
de día en día / day by day
día por día / day by day
estar al día / to be up to date
hoy día / nowadays
ocho días / a week
poner al día / to bring up to date
por día / by the day, per day
quince días / two weeks
un día de éstos / one of these days

§53.10   with **en**; see also §1.45, §1.46, and §4.10(c)
abrir de par en par / to open wide
de ayer en ocho días / a week from yesterday
de casa en casa / from house to house
de cuando en cuando / from time to time
de día en día / from day to day
de hoy en adelante / from today on
de hoy en ocho días / a week from today
de uno en uno / one by one
de vez en cuando / from time to time
en alto / high, high up, up high, on high
en balde / in vain
en bicicleta / by bicycle
en broma / jokingly, in fun
en cambio / on the other hand
en casa / at home (Use **en casa** if you are *in* the house; use **a casa** with a verb of motion, if you are going *to* the house: **Me quedo en casa esta noche** / I am staying home tonight; **Salgo de la escuela y voy a casa** / I'm leaving school and I'm going home.)
en casa de / at the house of (**María está en casa de Elena** / Mary is at Helen's house.)
en caso de / in case of
en coche / by car
en contra de / against
en cuanto / as soon as
en cuanto a / as for, with regard to, in regard to

en efecto / as a matter of fact, in fact
en el mes próximo pasado / in the month just past, this past month
en este momento / at this moment
en lo alto de / on top of it, at the top of, up
en lugar de / in place of, instead of
en marcha / under way, on the way
en medio de / in the middle of
en ninguna parte / nowhere
en punto / sharp, exactly (telling time: **Son las dos en punto** / It is two o'clock sharp.)
en seguida / immediately, at once
en suma / in short, in a word
en todas partes / everywhere
en vano / in vain
en vez de / instead of
en voz alta / in a loud voice
en voz baja / in a low voice

§53.11   with **estar** (See also §48.ff and other references under **estar** in the General Index)
está bien / all right, okay
estar a punto de + inf. / to be about + inf. (**Estoy a punto de salir** / I am about to go out.)
estar a sus anchas / to be comfortable
estar conforme con / to be in agreement with
estar de acuerdo / to agree
estar de acuerdo con / to be in agreement with
estar de boga / to be in fashion, to be fashionable
estar de buenas / to be in a good mood
estar de pie / to be standing
estar de vuelta / to be back
estar en boga / to be in fashion, to be fashionable
estar para + inf. / to be about to (**Estoy para salir** / I am about to go out.)
estar por / to be in favor of
no estar para bromas / not to be in the mood for jokes

§53.12   with **haber** (See also §26.–§26.4 and other references under **haber** in the General Index)
ha habido . . . / there has been . . . , there have been . . .
había . . . / there was . . . , there were . . .
habrá . . . / there will be . . .
habría . . . / there would be . . .
hubo . . . / there was . . . , there were . . .

§53.13   with **hacer** and **hacerse** (See also §29. and other references under the entries **hacer** and **weather expressions** in the General Index)
hace poco / a little while ago
hace un año / a year ago
Hace un mes que partió el señor Molina / Mr. Molina left one month ago.
hace una hora / an hour ago
hacer caso de / to pay attention to
hacer daño a algo / to harm something
hacer daño a alguien / to harm someone
hacer de / to act as (**El señor González siempre hace de jefe** / Mr. González always acts as a boss.)
hacer el baúl / to pack one's trunk
hacer el favor de + inf. / please (**Haga Ud. el favor de entrar** / Please come in.)
hacer el papel de / to play the role of
hacer falta / to be wanting, lacking, needed

hacer la maleta / to pack one's suitcase
hacer pedazos / to smash, to break, to tear into pieces
hacer un viaje / to take a trip
hacer una broma / to play a joke
hacer una pregunta / to ask a question
hacer una visita / to pay a visit
hacerle falta / to need (**A Juan le hace falta un lápiz** / John needs a pencil.)
hacerse / to become (**Elena se hizo dentista** / Helen became a dentist.)
hacerse daño / to hurt oneself, to harm oneself
hacerse tarde / to be getting late (**Vámonos; se hace tarde** / Let's leave; it's getting late.)

§53.14   with **hasta**
hasta ahora / until now
hasta aquí / until now, up to here
hasta después / see you later, until later
hasta entonces / see you then, see you later, up to that time, until that time
hasta la vista / see you again
hasta luego / see you later, until later
hasta mañana / see you tomorrow, until tomorrow
hasta más no poder / to the utmost
hasta no más / to the utmost

§53.15   with **lo** (See also §4.11 and §66.12)
a lo largo de / along
a lo lejos / in the distance
a lo más / at most
a lo mejor / probably
a lo menos / at least
en lo alto / on top of, at the top of, up
lo bueno / what is good, the good part; **¡Lo bueno que es!** / How good it is! **¡Lo bien que está escrito!** / How well it is written!
lo de + inf., adv., or noun / "that matter of . . .", "that business of . . ."
lo escrito / what is written
lo malo / what is bad, the bad part
lo más pronto posible / as soon as possible
lo mejor / what is best, the best part
lo primero debo que decir / the first thing I must say
lo simpático / whatever is kind
por lo común / generally, commonly, usually
por lo contrario / on the contrary
por lo general / generally, usually
por lo menos / at least
por lo pronto / in the meantime, for the time being
por lo tanto / consequently
por lo visto / apparently
¡Ya lo creo! / I should certainly think so!

§53.16   with **luego**
desde luego / naturally, of course, immediately
hasta luego / see you later, so long
luego luego / right away
luego que / as soon as, after

§53.17   with **mañana**
ayer por la mañana / yesterday morning

de la mañana / in the morning (Use this when a specific time is mentioned: **Voy a tomar el tren a las seis de la mañana** / I am going to take the train at six o'clock in the morning.)

mañana por la mañana / tomorrow morning

mañana por la noche / tomorrow night

mañana por la tarde / tomorrow afternoon

pasado mañana / the day after tomorrow

por la mañana / in the morning (Use this when no exact time is mentioned: **El señor Pardo llega por la mañana** / Mr. Pardo is arriving in the morning.)

por la mañana temprano / early in the morning

§53.18 with **mismo**

ahora mismo / right now

al mismo tiempo / at the same time

allá mismo / right there

aquí mismo / right here

así mismo / the same, the same thing

el mismo de siempre / the same old thing

eso mismo / that very thing

hoy mismo / this very day

lo mismo / the same, the same thing

lo mismo da / it makes no difference, it amounts to the same thing

lo mismo de siempre / the same old story

lo mismo que / the same as, as well as

por lo mismo / for the same reason

§53.19 with **no**

Creo que no / I don't think so, I think not

No cabe duda / No doubt about it

No es verdad / It isn't so, It isn't true; **¿No es verdad?** / Isn't that so?

No hay de qué / You're welcome

No hay remedio / There's no way, It cannot be helped

No importa / It doesn't matter

No + verb + más que + amount of money (**No tengo más que un dólar** / I have only one dollar)

no obstante / notwithstanding (in spite of), nevertheless

todavía no / not yet

ya no / no longer

§53.20 with **para** (See also **para** and **por** in **§52.–§52.18** and the entry **para** in the General Index)

estar para / to be about to, to be at the point of (**El autobús está para salir** / The bus is about to leave.)

no estar para bromas / not to be in the mood for jokes

no ser para tanto / not to be so important

para con (see **§62.15**)

para eso / for that matter

para mí / for my part

para que / in order that, so that

para ser / in spite of being (**Para ser tan viejo, él es muy ágil** / In spite of being so old, he is very agile.)

para siempre / forever

un vaso para agua / a water glass; **una taza para café** / a coffee cup; **una taza para té** / a tea cup

§53.21 with **poco** (See also the entry **poco** in the General Index)

a poco / in a short while, presently

dentro de poco / in a short while, in a little while

en pocos días / in a few days

poco a poco / little by little

poco antes / shortly before

poco después / shortly after

por poco / nearly, almost

tener poco que hacer / to have little to do

un poco de / a little (of); **Quisiera un poco de azúcar** / I would like a little sugar.

y por si eso fuera poco / and as if that were not enough

§53.22   with **por** (See also **para** and **por** in **§52.–§52.18** and the entry **por** in the General Index)

acabar por + inf. / to end up by + pres. part. (**Mi padre acabó por comprarlo** / My father finally ended up by buying it.)

al por mayor / wholesale

al por menor / retail (sales)

ayer por la mañana / yesterday morning

ayer por la noche / yesterday evening

ayer por la tarde / yesterday afternoon

estar por / to be in favor of

mañana por la mañana / tomorrow morning

mañana por la noche / tomorrow night, tomorrow evening

mañana por la tarde / tomorrow afternoon

por ahí / over there

por ahora / for just now, for the present

por allá / over there

por aquí / this way, around here

por avión / by air mail

por consiguiente / consequently

por desgracia / unfortunately

por Dios / for God's sake

por ejemplo / for example

por el contrario / on the contrary; or, **por lo contrario**

por escrito / in writing

por eso / for that reason, therefore

por favor / please (**Entre, por favor** / Come in, please.)

por fin / at last, finally

por hora / by the hour, per hour

por la mañana / in the morning (Use this when no exact time is mentioned: **Me quedo en casa por la mañana** / I'm staying home in the morning.)

por la mañana temprano / early in the morning

por la noche / in the evening (Use this when no exact time is mentioned: **Me gusta mirar la televisión por la noche** / I like to watch television in the evening.)

por la noche temprano / early in the evening

por la tarde / in the afternoon (Use this when no exact time is mentioned: **Tengo tres clases por la tarde** / I have three classes in the afternoon.)

por la tarde temprano / early in the afternoon

por lo común / commonly, generally, usually

por lo contrario / on the contrary; or, **por el contrario**

por lo general / generally, usually

por lo menos / at least

por lo pronto / in the meantime, for the time being

por lo tanto / consequently, therefore

por lo visto / apparently

por mi cuenta / in my way of thinking

por mi parte / as for me, as far as I am concerned
por nada / you're welcome
por poco / nearly, almost
por regla general / as a general rule
por semana / by the week, per week
por si acaso / in case
por supuesto / of course
por teléfono / by phone
por todas partes / everywhere
por valor de / worth

§53.23 with **pronto**
al pronto / at first
de pronto / suddenly
lo más pronto posible / as soon as possible
por de pronto / for the time being
por el pronto or **por lo pronto** / in the meantime, for the time being
tan pronto como / as soon as

§53.24 with **que** (See also conjunctions with **que** in §7.3 and §7.4 as well as the entry **que** in the General Index)
Creo que no / I don't think so, I think not.
Creo que sí / I think so.
el año que viene / next year
la semana que viene / next week
¡Qué le vaya bien! / Good luck!
¡Qué lo pase Ud. bien! / Good luck! (I wish you a good outcome!)

§53.25 with **ser** (See also §48.ff and other references under the entry **ser** in the General Index)
Debe de ser . . . / It is probably . . .
Debe ser . . . / It ought to be . . .
Es de lamentar / It's too bad.
Es de mi agrado / It's to my liking.
Es hora de . . . / It is time to . . .
Es lástima or **Es una lástima** / It's a pity; It's too bad.
Es que . . . / The fact is . . .
para ser / in spite of being (**Para ser tan viejo, él es muy ágil** / In spite of being so old, he is very nimble.)
sea lo que sea / whatever it may be
ser aficionado a / to be a fan of (**Soy aficionado al béisbol** / I'm a baseball fan.)
ser amable con / to be kind to (**Mi profesora de español es amable conmigo** / My Spanish teacher is kind to me.)
ser todo oídos / to be all ears (**Te escucho; soy todo oídos** / I'm listening to you; I'm all ears.)
si no fuera por . . . / if it were not for . . .

§53.26 with **sin** (See also **sin** in the General Index)
sin aliento / out of breath
sin cuento / endless
sin cuidado / carelessly
sin duda / without a doubt, undoubtedly
sin ejemplo / unparalleled, nothing like it
sin embargo / nevertheless, however
sin falta / without fail
sin fondo / bottomless
sin novedad / nothing new, same as usual

§53.27   with **tener** (See also **tener** in the General Index)

¿Cuántos años tienes? ¿Cuántos años tiene Ud.? / How old are you? **Tengo diez y seis años** / I am sixteen years old.

¿Qué tienes? ¿Qué tiene Ud.? / What's the matter? What's the matter with you? **No tengo nada** / There's nothing wrong; There's nothing the matter (with me).

tener algo que hacer / to have something to do

tener calor / to feel (to be) warm (persons)

tener cuidado / to be careful

tener dolor de cabeza / to have a headache

tener dolor de estómago / to have a stomach ache

tener éxito / to be successful

tener frío / to feel (to be) cold (persons)

tener ganas de + inf. / to feel like + pres. part. (**Tengo ganas de tomar un helado** / I feel like having an ice cream.)

tener gusto en + inf. / to be glad + inf. (**Tengo mucho gusto en conocerle** / I am very glad to meet you.)

tener hambre / to feel (to be) hungry

tener la bondad de / please, please be good enough to . . . (**Tenga la bondad de cerrar la puerta** / Please close the door.)

tener la culpa de algo / to take the blame for something, to be to blame for something (**Tengo la culpa de eso** / I am to blame for that.)

tener lugar / to take place (**El accidente tuvo lugar anoche** / The accident took place last night.)

tener miedo de / to be afraid of

tener mucha sed / to feel (to be) very thirsty (persons)

tener mucho calor / to feel (to be) very warm (persons)

tener mucho frío / to feel (to be) very cold (persons)

tener mucho que hacer / to have a lot to do

tener poco que hacer / to have little to do

tener prisa / to be in a hurry

tener que + inf. / to have + inf. (**Tengo que estudiar** / I have to study.)

tener que ver con / to have to do with (**No tengo nada que ver con él** / I have nothing to do with him.)

tener razón / to be right (**Usted tiene razón** / You are right.); **no tener razón** / to be wrong (**Usted no tiene razón** / You are wrong.)

tener sed / to feel (to be) thirsty (persons)

tener sueño / to feel (to be) sleepy

tener suerte / to be lucky

tener vergüenza de / to be ashamed of

§53.28   with **todo, toda, todos, todas**

a todo / at most

a todo correr / at full speed

ante todo / first of all, in the first place

así y todo / in spite of everything

con todo / all in all, still, however, nevertheless

de todos modos / anyway, in any case, at any rate

del todo / completely, entirely

en un todo / in all its parts

en todo y por todo / in each and every way

ir a todo correr / to run by leaps and bounds

jugar el todo por todo / to risk everything

por todo / throughout

sobre todo / above all, especially

toda la familia / the whole family

todas las noches / every night
todas las semanas / every week
todo aquel que / whoever
todo aquello que / whatever
todo el mundo / everybody
todo el que / everybody who
todos cuantos / all those that
todos los años / every year
todos los días / every day
todos los que / all who, all those who

§53.29   with **vez** and **veces** (See also the entries **vez** and **veces** in the General Index)
a la vez / at the same time (**Carlos come y habla a la vez** / Charles eats and talks at the same
  time.)
a veces / sometimes, at times
alguna vez / sometime
algunas veces / sometimes
cada vez / each time
cada vez más / more and more (each time)
de vez en cuando / from time to time
dos veces / twice, two times
en vez de / instead of
las más veces / most of the time
muchas veces / many times
otra vez / again, another time, once more
raras veces / few times, rarely
repetidas veces / repeatedly, over and over again
tal vez / perhaps
una vez / once, one time
una vez más / once more, one more time
unas veces / sometimes
varias veces / several times

§53.30   with **y** (See also **y** in the General Index)
dicho y hecho / no sooner said than done
mañana y pasado / tomorrow and the following day
sano y salvo / safe and sound
un billete de ida y vuelta / round-trip ticket
¿y bien? / and then? and so? so what?
y eso que / even though
y por si eso fuera poco . . . / and as if that were not enough . . .

§53.31   with **ya**
¡Hazlo ya! Hágalo ya! / Do it now!
no ya . . . sino / not only . . . but also
¡pues ya! / of course! certainly!
si ya . . . / if only . . .
ya . . . ya . . . / now . . . now . . .
ya . . . ya / whether . . . or; as well . . . as
¡Ya lo creo! / I should certainly think so! Of course!
Ya lo veré / I'll see to it.
ya no / no longer
Ya pasó / It's all over now.
ya que / since, as long as, seeing that . . .
¡Ya se ve! / Yes, indeed!
¡Ya voy! / I'm coming! I'll be there in a second!

§54. **PROVERBS**

Here are a few common proverbs in Spanish that you ought to be familiar with in case you come across them in the reading selections on the next standardized test in Spanish. They also contain some essential Spanish vocabulary which you ought to look up in the back pages of this book.

§54.1 **A Dios rogando y con el mazo dando** / Put your faith in God and keep your powder dry. OR: Praise the Lord and pass the ammunition.

§54.2 **Anda despacio que tengo prisa** / Make haste slowly.

§54.3 **Cuando el gato va a sus devociones, bailan los ratones** / When the cat is away, the mice will play.

§54.4 **Dicho y hecho** / No sooner said than done.

§54.5 **Dime con quien andas y te diré quien eres** / Tell me who your friends are and I will tell you who you are.

§54.6 **La práctica hace maestro al novicio** / Practice makes perfect.

§54.7 **El que mucho abarca poco aprieta** / Do not bite off more than you can chew.

§54.8 **El que no se aventura no cruza la mar** / Nothing ventured, nothing gained.

§54.9 **El tiempo da buen consejo** / Time will tell.

§54.10 **Más vale pájaro en mano que ciento volando** / A bird in the hand is worth two in the bush.

§54.11 **Más vale tarde que nunca** / Better late than never.

§54.12 **Mientras hay vida hay esperanza** / Where there is life there is hope.

§54.13 **Mucho ruido y pocas nueces** / Much ado about nothing.

§54.14 **Perro que ladra no muerde** / A barking dog does not bite.

§54.15 **Piedra movediza, el moho no la cobija** / A rolling stone gathers no moss.

§54.16 **Quien canta su mal espanta** / When you sing you drive away your grief.

§54.17 **Quien siembra vientos recoge tempestades** / If you sow the wind, you will reap the whirlwind.

§54.18 **Si a Roma fueres, haz como vieres** / When in Rome do as the Romans do. [Note that it is not uncommon to use the future subjunctive in proverbs, as in *fueres* (ir or ser) and *vieres* (*ver*).] See **§68.64.**

§54.19 **Tal madre, tal hija** / Like mother, like daughter.

§54.20 **Tal padre, tal hijo** / Like father, like son.

§55. **INDEFINITE AND NEGATIVE WORDS COMMONLY USED** (See also the specific word, *e.g.*, **no, pero, sino, sin,** *etc.* in the General Index and idioms in **§53.ff**)

algo / something, anything (with **sin,** use **nada; sin nada** / without anything)
alguien / anybody, anyone, someone, somebody (with **sin,** use **nadie; sin nadie** / without anyone)

alguno, alguna, algunos, algunas / some, any (See also **§1.20**)

jamás / ever, never, not ever

nada / nothing (**sin nada** / without anything); after **sin, nada** is used instead of **algo; Ella no quiere nada** / She does not want anything.

nadie / nobody, no one, not anyone, not anybody (**sin nadie** / without anybody): after **sin, nadie** is used instead of **alguien**

ni / neither, nor

ni . . . ni / neither . . . nor

ni siquiera / not even

ninguno, ninguna / no one, none, not any, not anybody (See also **§1.20**)

nunca / never, not ever, ever

o / or

o . . . o / either . . . or

siempre / always

también / also, too

tampoco / neither; **ni yo tampoco** / nor I either

unos cuantos, unas cuantas / a few, some, several

§56. INFINITIVES

§56.1 **Definition:** In English, an infinitive is identified as a verb with the preposition *to* in front of it: *to talk, to eat, to live.* In Spanish, an infinitive is identified by its ending: those that end in **-ar, -er, -ir,** for example, **hablar** (to talk, to speak), **comer** (to eat), **vivir** (to live).

§56.2 **Negation:** To make an infinitive negative, place **no** in front of it: **No entrar** / Do not enter; **No fumar** / Do not smoke or No smoking; **No estacionar** / Do not park or No Parking.

§56.3 **As a verbal noun:** In Spanish, an infinitive may be used as a noun. This means that an infinitive may be used as a subject, a direct object, a predicate noun, or object of a preposition. A verbal noun is a verb used as a noun. Examples:

§56.4 **As a subject: Ser o no ser es la cuestión** / To be or not to be is the question. In this sentence, the subject is **ser** and **no ser.**

Other examples:

El estudiar es bueno or **Estudiar es bueno** / Studying (to study) is good. Here, when the infinitive is a subject and it begins the sentence, you may use the definite article **el** in front of the inf. or you may omit it.

But if the sentence does not begin with the infinitive, do not (as a general rule) use the def. art. **el** in front of it: **Es bueno estudiar** / It is good to study. See also **§4.9(o)** and **§4.10(e).**

§56.5 **As a direct object: No deseo comer** / I do not want to eat. Here, the inf. **comer** is used as a noun and it functions as the direct object of the verb **deseo.**

§56.6 **As a predicate noun: Ver es creer** / Seeing is believing (To see is to believe). Here, the inf. **ver** is used as a noun and it functions as the subject. The inf. **creer** is used as a noun and it functions as the predicate noun because the verb is a form of **ser,** which takes a predicate noun or predicate adjective.

Do you know what these grammatical terms mean? A predicate noun is a noun which has the same referent as the subject; in other words, the predicate noun and the subject are pretty much the same thing; for example, in English: He is a father. A predicate adjective is an adjective which is attributive to the subject; in other words, the predicate adjective describes the subject in some way; for example, in English: She is pretty; She is tall. A predicate adjective is also known as an attribute complement because, as an adjective, it is attributive to the subject and it complements (describes) it in some way.

One last comment: In English, we can use an infinitive as a verbal noun, as in the above examples. In English, we can also use a gerund as a noun. A gerund in English looks like a present participle (ends in *-ing,* like *seeing, believing*) and it is used as a noun. But in Spanish, we do not use gerunds as nouns; we use only infinitives as nouns, as in the above examples. The Spanish word **gerundio** is normally translated into English as *gerund.* In a word, when we use a gerund as a noun in English its equivalent use is the infinitive in Spanish: Seeing is believing / **Ver es creer.** See also §58.1.

§56.7 **As object of a preposition: después de llegar** / after arriving. Here, the infinitive (verbal noun) **llegar** is object of the prep. **de.** In English, the word *arriving* in this example is a present participle, not a gerund. In English, present participles and gerunds both end in *-ing* but there is a distinct difference in their use. The point here is that in Spanish, only an infinitive can be used as a verbal noun, not a present participle and not a gerund in the English sense of these two terms. See also §58.1.

§56.8 In Spanish, an infinitive is ordinarily used after such verbs as, **dejar, hacer, mandar,** and **permitir** with no preposition needed: **Luis dejó caer sus libros** / Louis dropped his books; **Mi madre me hizo leerlo** / My mother made me read it; **Mi padre me mandó comerlo** / My father ordered me to eat it; **Mi profesor me permitió hacerlo** / My teacher permitted me to do it. Note that when **dejar** is followed by the prep. **de** it means *to stop* or *to cease:* **Luis dejó de trabajar** / Louis stopped working.

§56.9 The verb **pensar** is directly followed by an infinitive with no preposition required in front of the infinitive when its meaning is *to intend:* **Pienso ir a Chile** / I intend to go to Chile.

§56.10 Ordinarily, the infinitive form of a verb is used right after a preposition: **Antes de estudiar, Rita telefoneó a su amiga Beatriz** / Before studying, Rita telephoned her friend Beatrice; **El alumno salió de la sala de clase sin decir nada** / The pupil left the classroom without saying anything. Here, note **de estudiar** and **sin decir.**

§56.11 The infinitive form of a verb is ordinarily used after certain verbs of perception, such as **ver** and **oír: Las vi salir** / I saw them go out; **Las oí cantar** / I heard them singing.

§56.12 After **al,** a verb is used in the infinitive form: **Al entrar en la escuela, Dorotea fue a su clase de español** / Upon entering the school, Dorothy went to her Spanish class. See §58.13.

§56.13 The Perfect Infinitive (also known as the Past Infinitive) is formed by using **haber** in its inf. form + the past participle of the main verb: **haber hablado** (to have spoken), **haber comido** (to have eaten), **haber escrito** (to have written).

§57. NUMBERS

§57.1 Cardinal numbers: zero to one hundred million

0 cero	62 sesenta y dos, *etc.*
1 uno, una (see §1.18ff)	**70 setenta**
2 dos	71 setenta y uno, setenta y una
3 tres	72 setenta y dos, *etc.*
4 cuatro	**80 ochenta**
5 cinco	81 ochenta y uno, ochenta y una
6 seis	82 ochenta y dos, *etc.*
7 siete	**90 noventa**
8 ocho	91 noventa y uno, noventa y una
9 nueve	92 noventa y dos, *etc.*
10 diez	**100 ciento (cien)** (see
11 once	**§1.23–§1.26 and §4.19a)**
12 doce	101 ciento uno, ciento una
13 trece	102 ciento dos, *etc.*
14 catorce	**200 doscientos, doscientas**
15 quince	300 trescientos, trescientas
16 dieciséis	400 cuatrocientos, cuatrocientas
17 diecisiete	500 quinientos, quinientas
18 dieciocho	600 seiscientos, seiscientas
19 diecinueve	700 setecientos, setecientas
20 veinte	800 ochocientos, ochocientas
21 veintiuno	900 novecientos, novecientas
22 veintidós	**1,000 mil** (see **§4.19a**)
23 veintitrés	2,000 dos mil
24 veinticuatro	3,000 tres mil, *etc.*
25 veinticinco	100,000 cien mil
26 veintiséis	200,000 doscientos mil, doscientas mil
27 veintisiete	300,000 trescientos mil, trescientas mil, *etc.*
28 veintiocho	
29 veintinueve	
30 treinta	**1,000,000 un millón (de + noun)**
31 treinta y uno, treinta y una	2,000,000 dos millones (de + noun)
32 treinta y dos, *etc.*	3,000,000 tres millones (de + noun), *etc.*
40 cuarenta	
41 cuarenta y uno, cuarenta y una	100,000,000 cien millones (de + noun)
42 cuarenta y dos, *etc.*	
50 cincuenta	Approximate numbers
51 cincuenta y uno, cincuenta y una	
52 cincuenta y dos, *etc.*	**unos veinte libros** / about (some) twenty books
60 sesenta	**unas treinta personas** / about (some) thirty persons
61 sesenta y uno, sesenta y una	

§57.2 Simple arithmetical expressions

dos **y** dos son cuatro	$2 + 2 = 4$
diez **menos** cinco son cinco	$10 - 5 = 5$
tres **por** cinco son quince	$3 \times 5 = 15$
diez **dividido por** dos son cinco	$10 \div 2 = 5$

§57.3 **Ordinal numbers: first to tenth**

primero, primer, primera (see §1.20, §6.1)	first	1st
segundo, segunda	second	2nd
tercero, tercer, tercera (see §1.20)	third	3rd
cuarto, cuarta	fourth	4th
quinto, quinta	fifth	5th
sexto, sexta	sixth	6th
séptimo, séptima	seventh	7th
octavo, octava	eighth	8th
noveno, novena	ninth	9th
décimo, décima	tenth	10th

§57.4 NOTE that beyond 10th the cardinal numbers are used instead of the ordinal numbers, but when there is a noun involved, the cardinal number is placed after the noun: **el día 15** (**el día quince** / the fifteenth day).

§57.5 NOTE also that in titles of monarchs, *etc.* the definite article is not used between the person's name and the number, but it is in English: **Alfonso XIII** (**Alfonso Trece** / Alfonso the Thirteenth).

§57.6 AND NOTE that **noveno** (9th) changes to **nono** in such titles: **Luis IX** (**Luis Nono** / Louis the Ninth).

§58. PARTICIPLES

§58.1 **Present participle:** A present participle is a verb form which, in English, ends in *-ing*; for example, *singing, eating, receiving.* In Spanish, a present participle is regularly formed as follows:

drop the **ar** of an **-ar** ending verb, like **cantar,** and add **-ando: cantando** / singing
drop the **er** of an **-er** ending verb, like **comer,** and add **-iendo: comiendo** / eating
drop the **ir** of an **-ir** ending verb, like **recibir,** and add **-iendo: recibiendo** / receiving

In English, a gerund also ends in *-ing* but there is a distinct difference in use between a gerund and a present participle in English. In brief, it is this: In English, when a present participle is used as a noun it is called a gerund; for example: *Reading is good.* As a present participle in English: The boy fell asleep *while reading.*

In the first example (*Reading is good*), *reading* is a gerund because it is the subject of the verb *is.* In Spanish, however, we must not use the present participle form as a noun to serve as a subject; we must use the infinitive form of the verb in Spanish: **Leer es bueno.** See also §56., §56.1, §56.3, §56.4, §56.6, and §56.7.

§58.2 **Common irregular present participles are as follows.** You ought to know them so that you may be able to recognize them if they are on the next standardized Spanish test that you take.

Infinitive	Present Participle
caer / to fall	**cayendo** / falling
conseguir / to attain, to achieve	**consiguiendo** / attaining, achieving
construir / to construct	**construyendo** / constructing
corregir / to correct	**corrigiendo** / correcting
creer / to believe	**creyendo** / believing
decir / to say, to tell	**diciendo** / saying, telling
despedirse / to say good-bye	**despidiéndose** / saying good-bye
destruir / to destroy	**destruyendo** / destroying
divertirse / to enjoy oneself	**divirtiéndose** / enjoying oneself
dormir / to sleep	**durmiendo** / sleeping
huir / to flee	**huyendo** / fleeing

ir / to go	**yendo** / going
leer / to read	**leyendo** / reading
mentir / to lie (tell a falsehood)	**mintiendo** / lying
morir / to die	**muriendo** / dying
oír / to hear	**oyendo** / hearing
pedir / to ask (for), to request	**pidiendo** / asking (for), requesting
poder / to be able	**pudiendo** / being able
reír / to laugh	**riendo** / laughing
repetir / to repeat	**repitiendo** / repeating
seguir / to follow	**siguiendo** / following
sentir / to feel	**sintiendo** / feeling
servir / to serve	**sirviendo** / serving
traer / to bring	**trayendo** / bringing
venir / to come	**viniendo** / coming
vestir / to dress	**vistiendo** / dressing

§58.3   **Uses of the present participle**

§58.4   **To form the progressive tenses:**

§58.5   The **Progressive Present** is formed by using **estar** in the present tense plus the present participle of the main verb you are using; *e.g.,* **Estoy hablando** (*I am talking*), *i.e., I am* (in the act of) *talking* (right now).

§58.6   The **Progressive Past** is formed by using **estar** in the imperfect indicative plus the present participle of the main verb you are using; *e.g.,* **Estaba hablando** (*I was talking*), *i.e., I was* (in the act of) *talking* (then, at some point in the past).

§58.7   The progressive forms are generally used when you want to emphasize what you are saying; if you don't want to do that, then just use the simple present or the imperfect, *e.g.,* say **Hablo,** rather than **Estoy hablando;** or **Hablaba,** rather than **Estaba hablando.** See also **Imperfect Indicative** in the General Index.

§58.8   In brief, the Progressive Present is used to describe with intensification what is happening or going on at present. The Progressive Past is used to describe with intensification what was happening, what was going on at some point in the past.

§58.9   Instead of using **estar,** as noted above, to form these two progressive tenses, sometimes **ir** is used: **Va hablando** / *He (she) keeps right on talking;* **Iba hablando** / *He (she) kept right on talking.* NOTE that they do not have the exact same meaning as **Está hablando** and **Estaba hablando,** as explained above in **§58.5–§58.7.**

§58.10   Also, at times **andar, continuar, seguir** and **venir** are used as helping verbs in the present or imperfect indicative tenses plus the present participle to express the progressive forms: **Los muchachos andaban cantando** / The boys were walking along singing; **La maestra seguía leyendo a la clase** / The teacher kept right on reading to the class.

§58.11   To express vividly an action that occurred (preterit + present participle): **El niño entró llorando en la casa** / The little boy came crying into the house.

§58.12   To express the English use of *by* + present participle in Spanish, we use the gerund form, which has the same ending as a present participle explained above in §58.1: **Trabajando, se gana dinero** / By working, one earns (a person earns) money; **Estudiando mucho, Pepe recibió buenas notas** / By studying hard, Joe received good grades.

NOTE here that no preposition is used in front of the present participle (the Spanish gerund) even though it is expressed in English as *by* + *present participle.*

§58.13 NOTE, too, that in Spanish we use **al + infinitive** (not + present participle) to express *on* or *upon* + *present participle* in English: **Al entrar en la casa, el niño comenzó a llorar** / Upon entering the house, the little boy began to cry. See **§56.12.**

§58.14 To form the Perfect Participle: **habiendo hablado** / having talked.

§58.15 Finally, note that the only preposition that may be used in front of the Spanish gerund (English present participle) is **en** which gives the meaning of *after* + present participle in English: **En corriendo rápidamente, el viejo cayó y murió** / After running rapidly, the old man fell and died.

§58.16 **Past participle:** A past participle is a verb form which, in English, usually ends in *-ed*: for example, *worked, talked, arrived,* as in *I have worked, I have talked, I have arrived.* There are many irregular past participles in English; for example: *gone, sung,* as in *She has gone, We have sung.* In Spanish, a past participle is regularly formed as follows:

drop the **ar** of an **-ar** ending verb, like **trabajar,** and add **-ado: trabajado** / worked
drop the **er** of an **-er** ending verb, like **comer,** and add **-ido: comido** / eaten
drop the **ir** of an **-ir** ending verb, like **recibir,** and add **-ido: recibido** / received

§58.17 **Common irregular past participles are as follows.** You ought to know them so that you may be able to recognize them when you see them on the next standardized Spanish test that you take.

Infinitive	Past Participle
abrir / to open	**abierto** / opened
caer / to fall	**caído** / fallen
creer / to believe	**creído** / believed
cubrir / to cover	**cubierto** / covered
decir / to say, to tell	**dicho** / said, told
descubrir / to discover	**descubierto** / discovered
deshacer / to undo	**deshecho** / undone
devolver / to return (something)	**devuelto** / returned (something)
escribir / to write	**escrito** / written
hacer / to do, to make	**hecho** / done, made
imponer / to impose	**impuesto** / imposed
imprimir / to print	**impreso** / printed
ir / to go	**ido** / gone
leer / to read	**leído** / read
morir / to die	**muerto** / died
oír / to hear	**oído** / heard
poner / to put	**puesto** / put
rehacer / to redo, to remake	**rehecho** / redone, remade
reír / to laugh	**reído** / laughed
resolver / to resolve, to solve	**resuelto** / resolved, solved
romper / to break	**roto** / broken
traer / to bring	**traído** / brought
ver / to see	**visto** / seen
volver / to return	**vuelto** / returned

§58.18 **Uses of the past participle**

§58.19 **To form the compound tenses:**

As in English, the past participle is needed to form the compound tenses in Spanish, of which there are seven. For the complete conjugation showing the forms of the six persons in each of the following compound tenses and for an explanation of how they are formed, see the specific name of each tense in the General Index.

The Compound Tenses / Los Tiempos compuestos

Name of tense in Spanish / English	Example (1st pers., sing.)
Perfecto de Indicativo / Present Perfect Indicative	**he hablado**
Pluscuamperfecto de Indicativo / Pluperfect Indicative	**había hablado**
Pretérito Anterior / Preterit Perfect	**hube hablado**
Futuro Perfecto / Future Perfect	**habré hablado**
Potencial Compuesto / Conditional Perfect	**habría hablado**
Perfecto de Subjuntivo / Present Perfect Subjunctive	**haya hablado**
Pluscuamperfecto de Subjuntivo / Pluperfect Subjunctive	**hubiera hablado** *or* **hubiese hablado**

§58.20   To form the Perfect Infinitive: **haber hablado** / to have spoken

§58.21   To form the Perfect Participle: **habiendo hablado** / having spoken

§58.22   To serve as an adjective, which must agree in gender and number with the noun it modifies: **El señor Molina es muy respetado de todos los alumnos** / Mr. Molina is very respected by all the students; **La señora González es muy conocida** / Mrs. González is very well known.

§58.23   To express the result of an action with **estar** and sometimes with **quedar** or **quedarse**: **La puerta está abierta** / The door is open; **Las cartas están escritas** / The letters are written; **Los niños se quedaron asustados** / The children remained frightened.

§58.24   To express the passive voice with **ser**: **La ventana fue abierta por el ladrón** / The window was opened by the robber.

§59.   PASSIVE VOICE

§59.1   Passive voice means that the action of the verb falls on the subject; in other words, the subject receives the action: **La ventana fue abierta por el ladrón** / The window was opened by the robber. NOTE that **abierta** (really a form of the past part. **abrir** / **abierto**) is used as an adjective and it must agree in gender and number with the subject that it describes.

§59.2   Active voice means that the subject performs the action and the subject is always stated: **El ladrón abrió la ventana** / The robber opened the window.

§59.3   To form the true passive, use **ser** + the past participle of the verb you have in mind; the past part. then serves as an adjective and it must agree in gender and number with the subject that it describes, as in the example given in **§59.1.** In the true passive, the agent (the doer) is always expressed with the prep. **por** in front of it. The formula for the true passive construction is: subject + tense of **ser** + past participle + por + the agent (the doer): **Estas composiciones fueron escritas por Juan** / These compositions were written by John.

§59.4   The reflexive pronoun **se** may be used to substitute for the true passive voice construction. When you use the **se** construction, the subject is a thing (not a person) and the doer (agent) is not stated: **Aquí se habla español** / Spanish is spoken here; **Aquí se hablan español e inglés** / Spanish and English are spoken here; **Se venden libros en esta tienda** / Books are sold in this store.

§59.5   There are a few standard idiomatic expressions that are commonly used with the pronoun **se.** These expressions are not truly passive, the pronoun **se** is not truly a reflexive pronoun, and the verb form is in the 3rd pers. sing. only. In this construction, there is no subject expressed; the subject is contained in the use of **se** + the 3rd pers. sing. of the verb at all times and the common translations into English are: it is . . . , people . . . , they . . . , one . . . :

§59.6   **Se cree que . . .** / It is believed that . . . , people believe that . . . , they believe that . . . , one believes that . . .

Se cree que este criminal es culpable / It is believed that this criminal is guilty.

§59.7   **Se dice que . . .** / It is said that . . . , people say that . . . , they say that . . . , one says that . . . , you say . . . .

Se dice que va a nevar esta noche / They say that it's going to snow tonight; **¿Cómo se dice en español** ice cream**?** / How do you say ice cream in Spanish?

§59.8   **Se sabe que . . .** / It is known that . . . , people know that . . . , they know that . . . , one knows that . . .

Se sabe que María va a casarse con Juan / People know that Mary is going to marry John.

§59.9   The **se** reflexive pronoun construction (see **§59.4** above) is avoided if the subject is a person because there can be ambiguity in meaning. For example, how would you translate into English the following: **Se da un regalo.** Which of the following two meanings is intended? She (he) is being given a present, or She (he) is giving a present to himself (to herself). In correct Spanish you would have to say: **Le da (a María, a Juan,** etc.**) un regalo** / He (she) is giving a present to Mary (to John, etc.) Avoid using the **se** construction in the passive when the subject is a person; change your sentence around and state it in the active voice to make the meaning clear. Otherwise, the pronoun **se** seems to go with the verb, as if the verb itself is reflexive, which gives an entirely different meaning. Another example: **Se miró** would mean He (she) looked at himself (herself), not He (she) was looked at! If you mean to say He (she) looked at him (at her), say: **La miró** or, if in the plural, say: **La miraron** / They looked at her.

§60.   POR OR DE

§60.1   The preposition **por** is sometimes translated into English as by, although it has other meanings, such as through, for, etc. (See **§52.7–§52.18** and **§53.22**).

§60.2   The preposition **de** is sometimes translated into English as by and it has other meanings, too, such as of, from, in, etc. (See **§1.46, §5.24, §53.7,** and other references under the entry **de** in the Comprehensive Index.)

§60.3   When using a passive meaning that expresses an action performed by someone or something, **por** is generally used. (See also **§58.24** and **§59.–§59.9**)

§60.4   Use the prep. **de** to express by when using a passive meaning if some emotion or feeling is expressed instead of an action:

La señora Gómez es respetada de todos los alumnos / Mrs. Gómez is respected by all the students. (See also **§58.22** above)
Notice, of course, that the adjective **respetada** (which is really a past participial form (**respetar / respetado**) agrees in gender and number with the subject it modifies or describes.

§61.   ¿QUÉ . . . ? AND ¿CUÁL . . . ?

§61.1   These two interrogative words both mean what or which but there is a difference in their use:

§61.2   Use **¿Qué . . . ?** as a pronoun (when there is no noun right after it) if you are inquiring about something, if you want an explanation about something, if you want something defined or described, e.g.: **¿Qué es esto?** / What is this?

§61.3   Use **¿Qué . . . ?** as an adjective, when there is a noun right after it: **¿Qué día es hoy?** / What day is it today?

§61.4 Use **¿Cuál . . . ?** as a pronoun, when there is no noun right after it. If by *what* you mean *which* or, *which one*, it is better Spanish to use **¿Cuál . . . ?** For example: **¿Cuál de estos lápices es mejor?** / Which (Which one) of these pencils is better?

§61.5 The same is true in the plural: **¿Cuáles son buenos?** / Which ones are good?

§61.6 Do not use **cuál** if there is a noun right after it; in that case, you must use **qué,** as in **§61.3** above.

§61.7 Do not assume that just because you can use *what* or *which* interchangeably in English that you can do the same in Spanish. If by *what* or *which* you mean *which one*, you must use **cuál** because in that case there is no noun right after **cuál.** Note the following examples:

§61.8 **¿Qué libro tiene Ud.?** / What book do you have? *or* Which book do you have? You must use **qué** here because there is a noun right after it.

§61.9 **Cuál** and **cuáles** are pronouns and there cannot be a noun right after these words. In colloquial Spanish they are sometimes used as adjectives (when there is a noun right after them), but this does not mean that it is correct Spanish.

§61.10 Certain words need accent marks when they are used in interrogative sentences. For other interrogative words, see **§2.10, §9., §11.**

§62. **PREPOSITIONS** (*See also* verbs that take certain prepositions in **§67.16–§67.30**)

§62.1 A preposition is a word that connects words and, according to the thought expressed in the sentence, it serves to indicate the relationship between the words.

§62.2 **Common prepositions in Spanish are:**
a / at, to (plus other meanings, depending on idiomatic use; see **a** in idioms, **§53.1–§53.3**)
ante / before, in the presence of
bajo / under
con / with (plus other meanings, depending on idiomatic use; see **con** in idioms, **§53.4**)
contra / against
de / of, from (plus other meanings, depending on idiomatic use; see **de** in idioms, **§53.7**)
desde / after, from, since
durante / during
en / in, on (plus other meanings, depending on idiomatic use; see **en** in idioms, **§53.10**)
entre / among, between
hacia / toward
hasta / until, up to, as far as (plus other meanings, depending on idiomatic use; see **hasta** in idioms, **§53.14**)
menos / except
para / for, in order to (plus other meanings, depending on idiomatic use; see **para** in idioms, **§53.20;** see also **para** and **por** in **§52.–§52.18**)
por / by, for (plus other meanings, depending on idiomatic use; see **por** in idioms, **§53.22;** see also **por** and **para** in **§52.–§52.18**)
salvo / except, save
según / according to
sin / without (plus other meanings, depending on idiomatic use; see **sin** in idioms, **§53.26**); after **sin, nada** is used instead of **algo;** after **sin, nadie** is used instead of **alguien**
sobre / on, upon, over, above
tras / after, behind

§62.3 **Common prepositional phrases in Spanish are:**
acerca de / about (see **de** in idioms, **§53.7,** for other uses of the prep. **de**)

además de / in addition to, besides

alrededor de / around

antes de / before; (after **antes de,** use **nada** instead of **algo: antes de nada** / before anything; use **nadie** instead of **alguien: antes de nadie** / before anyone)

cerca de / near

con rumbo a / in the direction of (see **con** in idioms, **§53.4,** for other uses of the prep. **con**)

debajo de / underneath

delante de / in front of

dentro de / within, inside (of)

después de / after

detrás de / in back of, behind

en contra de / against (see **en** in idioms, **§53.10,** for other uses of the prep. **en**)

en cuanto a / as far as (see **a** in idioms, **§53.1–§53.3,** for other uses of the prep. **a**)

en lugar de / in place of, instead of

en medio de / in the middle of

en vez de / instead of

encima de / on top of, upon

enfrente de / opposite

frente a / in front of

fuera de / outside of

junto a / next to

lejos de / far from

por valor de / worth (see **por** in idioms, **§53.22,** for other uses of the prep. **por**)

§62.4 **Distinction between a preposition and an adverb**

Many prepositional phrases, such as the ones given above in **§62.3,** would not be prepositional if the prep. **de** were not included in the phrase; without the prep. **de,** most of them are adverbs, for example:

además / furthermore; **además de** / in addition to

alrededor / around; **alrededor de** / around

debajo / under; **debajo de** / underneath

lejos / far, far off; **lejos de** / far from

§62.5 The use of the prep. **de** with these adverbs, and others, changes the part of speech to a preposition, as in such prepositional phrases: **lejos de la escuela** / far from the school; **alrededor de la casa** / around the house. Generally speaking, prepositions require a noun or a pronoun right after them (sometimes an infinitive, as in **sin decir nada** / without saying anything), which become objects of prepositions. In the examples cited here, **la escuela** is object of **lejos de; la casa** is object of **alrededor de.**

§62.6 **Uses of prepositions**

§62.7 Generally speaking, prepositions are used in the following categories:

prep. + a noun: **con María** / with Mary; **con mi amigo** / with my friend

prep. + a pronoun: **para ella** / for her; **para usted** / for you

prep. + inf.: **sin hablar** / without talking

verb + prep.: **gozar de algo** / to enjoy something

§62.8 **Personal a**

§62.9 In Spanish, the prep. **a** is used in front of a noun direct object of a verb if the direct object is a person or something personified:

§62.10 **Conozco a su hermana Elena** / I know your sister Helen; **¿Conoce Ud. a Roberto?** / Do you know Robert? **Llamo al médico** / I am calling the doctor.

However, if the direct object is a person not definitely specified by name or noun whom you have in mind, the personal **a** is not generally used: **Llamo un médico** / I am calling a doctor. Here, no definite doctor is specified. This exception is not always observed by everyone and it is possible for you to read or hear: **Llamo a un médico.**

§62.11   The personal **a** is used in front of an indefinite pronoun when it is direct object of a verb and it refers to a person, for example: **nadie, ninguno (ninguna), alguien, alguno (alguna), quien: Mis padres están visitando a alguien en el hospital** / My parents are visiting someone in the hospital; **¿Ve Ud. a alguien?** / Do you see anybody? **No veo a nadie** / I don't see anybody.

§62.12   The personal **a** is used in front of a geographic name if it is used as direct object: **Este verano pensamos visitar a Colombia** / This summer we plan to visit Colombia.

But if the geographic place contains a definite article in front of it (which is part of its name), the personal **a** is not used: **¿Ha visitado Ud. la Argentina?** / Have you visited Argentina? **La familia Gómez en Guadalajara quiere visitar los Estados Unidos** / The Gómez family in Guadalajara wants to visit the United States. The trend these days is not to use the prep. **a** in front of a geographic name even if it does not contain a def. art.

§62.13   The personal **a** is used in front of a noun which is a domestic animal when personified and when it is direct object: **Quiero a mi gatito** / I love my kitten.

§62.14   The personal **a** is not generally used with the verb **tener** when it means *to have:* **Tengo dos hermanas y dos hermanos** / I have two sisters and two brothers.

But when **tener** means *to hold,* the personal **a** is generally used: **La enfermera tenía al niño en los brazos** / The nurse was holding the child in her arms.

§62.15   The prepositional expression **para con,** meaning *to* or *toward,* in the sense of *with respect to* or *as regards,* is used to denote a mental attitude or feeling about a person: **Nuestra profesora de español es muy amable para con nosotros** / Our Spanish teacher is very kind to us.

§62.16   For prepositions that are used with certain verbs, see the entry Verbs in the General Index.

§62.17   For the use of prepositions with infinitives, see the entry Infinitives in the General Index.

§62.18   For additional comments, explanations and examples regarding the use of prepositions, consult the General Index under a specific preposition, of which the most commonly used are: **a, con, de, en, para, por, sin.** See also **Verbs and prepositions, §67.16–§67.30.**

§63.   TELLING TIME

§63.1   **¿Qué hora es?** / What time is it?

§63.2   **Es la una** / It is one o'clock. Note that the 3rd pers. sing. of **ser** is used because the time is one (o'clock), which is singular.

§63.3   **Son las dos** / It is two o'clock. Note that the 3rd pers. pl. of **ser** is used because the time is two (o'clock), which is more than one.

§63.4   **Son las tres, son las cuatro,** *etc.* / It is three o'clock, it is four o'clock, *etc.*

§63.5   When the time is a certain number of minutes after the hour, the hour is stated first (**Es la una**) + **y** + the number of minutes:

Es la una y cinco / It is five minutes after one o'clock / It is 1:05.
Son las dos y diez / It is ten minutes after two o'clock / It is 2:10.

§63.6   When the hour is a quarter after, you can express it by using either **y cuarto** or **y quince (minutos):**

Son las dos y cuarto or **Son las dos y quince (minutos)** / It is 2:15.

§63.7 When it is half past the hour, you can express it by using either **y media** or **y treinta (minutos)**:

Son las dos y media or **Son las dos y treinta** / It is 2:30.

§63.8 When telling time, the verb **ser** is used in the 3rd pers. sing. if the time is one and in the 3rd pers. plural if the time is more than one.

§63.9 When the time is of (to, toward, before) the hour, state the hour that it will be + **menos** + the number of minutes or **menos cuarto** (a quarter of):

Son las cuatro menos cuarto / It is a quarter of (to) four *or* It is 3:45.

Son las cinco menos veinte / It is twenty minutes to five *or* It is 4:40.

§63.10 When you are not telling what time it is and you want only to say *at* a certain time, merely say: **a la una, a las dos, a las tres** / at one o'clock, at two o'clock, at three o'clock; **a la una y cuarto** / at 1:15; **a las cuatro y media** / at 4:30, *etc.*

§63.11 **¿A qué hora va Ud. a la clase de español?** / At what time do you go to Spanish class? **Voy a la clase a las dos y veinte** / I go to class at 2:20.

§63.12 **¿A qué hora toma Ud. el almuerzo?** / At what time do you have lunch? **Tomo el almuerzo a las doce en punto** / I have lunch at exactly twelve o'clock.

¿A qué hora toma Ud. el autobús para ir a la escuela? / At what time do you take the bus to go to school? **Tomo el autobús a las ocho en punto** / I take the bus at eight o'clock sharp.

§63.13 **¿Llega Ud. a la escuela a tiempo?** / Do you arrive at school on time? **Llego a la escuela a eso de las ocho y media** / I arrive at school at about 8:30.

§63.14 When you state what time it is or at what time you are going to do something, sometimes you have to make it clear whether it is in the morning (A.M.), in the afternoon (P.M.), or in the evening (P.M.):

Tomo el tren a las ocho de la noche / I am taking the train at 8:00 P.M. (at eight o'clock in the evening).

Tomo el tren a las ocho de la mañana / I am taking the train at 8:00 A.M. (at eight o'clock in the morning).

Tomo el tren a las cuatro de la tarde / I am taking the train at 4:00 P.M. (at four o'clock in the afternoon).

Tomo el tren a las tres de la madrugada / I am taking the train at 3:00 A.M. (at three o'clock in the morning). Note that in Spanish we say **de la madrugada** (before daylight hours) instead of **de la noche** if the time is between midnight and the break of dawn.

§63.15 **¿Qué hora es?** / What time is it? **Es mediodía** / It is noon.

§63.16 **¿Qué hora es?** / What time is it? **Es medianoche** / It is midnight.

§63.17 **¿A qué hora toma Ud. el almuerzo?** / At what time do you have lunch? **Tomo el almuerzo a mediodía** (or **al mediodía**).

§63.18 **¿A qué hora se acuesta Ud. por lo general?** / At what time do you generally get to bed? **Generalmente, me acuesto a medianoche** (or **a la medianoche**).

§63.19 When telling time in the past, use the imperfect indicative tense of the verb **ser**: It was two o'clock when I had lunch today / **Eran las dos cuando tomé el almuerzo hoy**; It was one o'clock when I saw them / **Era la una cuando los vi**; **¿Qué hora era cuando sus padres llegaron a casa?** / What time was it when your parents arrived home? **Eran las dos de la madrugada** / It was two in the morning.

§63.20 The future tense is used when telling time in the future or when you wonder what time it is at present or when you want to state what time it probably is:

En algunos minutos serán las tres / In a few minutes it will be three o'clock.
¿Qué hora será? / I wonder what time it is; **Serán las seis** / It is probably six o'clock.

§63.21 When wondering what time it was in the past or when stating what time it probably was in the past, use the conditional: **¿Qué hora sería?** / I wonder what time it was; **Serían las seis cuando llegaron** / It was probably six o'clock when they arrived.

§63.22 When no specific time is stated and you merely want to say *in the morning, in the afternoon, in the evening,* use the prep. **por** instead of **de: Los sábados estudio mis lecciones por la mañana, juego por la tarde, y salgo por la noche** / On Saturdays I study my lessons in the morning, I play in the afternoon, and I go out in the evening.

§63.23 To express *a little after the hour,* state the hour + **y pico: Cuando salí eran las seis y pico** / When I went out it was a little after six o'clock.

§63.24 To say *about* or *around* a particular time, say **a eso de** + the hour: **Te veré a eso de la una** / I will see you about one o'clock; **Te veré a eso de las tres** / I will see you around three o'clock.

§63.25 Instead of using **menos** (of, to, toward, before the hour)—see **§63.9** above—you may use the verb **faltar,** which means *to be lacking:* **Faltan cinco minutos para las tres** / It's five minutes to three (in other words, five minutes are lacking before it is three o'clock). In this construction, which is idiomatic, note the use of the prep. **para.**

§63.26 Finally, note another way to tell time, which is used on radio and TV, in railroad and bus stations, at airports, and at other places where many people gather:

§63.27 It is the 24 hour system around the clock.

§63.28 When using the 24 hours around the clock, the stated time is perfectly clear and there is no need to say **de la madrugada, de la mañana, de la tarde,** or **de la noche** (see **§63.14**).

§63.29 When using the 24 hour system around the clock, there is no need to use **cuarto, media, menos** or **y** (except when **y** is required in the cardinal number, *e.g.,* diez y seis).

§63.30 When you hear or see the stated time using this system, subtract 12 from the number that you hear or see. If the number is less than 12, it is A.M. time. Midnight is **veinticuatro horas.** This system uses the cardinal numbers (see **§57.1**). Examples:

trece horas / 1 P.M.   **quince horas treinta** or 15.30 / 3:30 P.M.
catorce horas / 2 P.M.   **veinte horas cuarenta y dos** or 20.42 / 8:42 P.M.
veinte horas / 8 P.M.   **nueve horas diez** or 09.10 / 9:10 A.M.

§64. WEATHER EXPRESSIONS

§64.1 with **hacer**

¿Qué tiempo hace? / What is the weather like?
Hace buen tiempo / The weather is good.
Hace calor / It is warm (hot).
Hace fresco hoy / It is cool today.
Hace frío / It is cold.
Hace mal tiempo / The weather is bad.
Hace sol / It is sunny.
Hace viento / It is windy.

¿Qué tiempo hacía cuando usted salió esta mañana? / What was the weather like when you went out this morning?

Hacía mucho frío ayer por la noche / It was very cold yesterday evening.

Hacía mucho viento / It was very windy.

¿Qué tiempo hará mañana? / What will the weather be like tomorrow?

Se dice que hará mucho calor / They say it will be very hot.

§64.2   with **haber**

Hay lodo / It is muddy; **Había lodo** / It was muddy.

Hay luna / The moon is shining *or* There is moonlight; **Había luna ayer por la noche** / There was moonlight yesterday evening.

Hay mucha nieve aquí en el invierno? / Is there much snow here in winter?

Hay neblina / It is foggy; **Había mucha neblina** / It was very foggy.

Hay polvo / It is dusty; **Había mucho polvo** / It was very dusty.

§64.3   **Other weather expressions**

Está lloviendo ahora / It is raining now.

Está nevando / It is snowing.

Esta mañana llovía cuando tomé el autobús / This morning it was raining when I took the bus.

Estaba lloviendo cuando tomé el autobús / It was raining when I took the bus.

Estaba nevando cuando me desperté / It was snowing when I woke up.

¿Nieva mucho aquí en el invierno? / Does it snow much here in winter?

Las estrellas brillan / The stars are shining.

¿Le gusta a usted la lluvia? / Do you like rain?

¿Le gusta a usted la nieve? / Do you like snow?

§65.   **SYNONYMS**

Another very good way to increase your Spanish vocabulary in preparation for a standardized test in Spanish is to think of a synonym (similar meaning) for every word in Spanish that you already know. Of course, there is no synonym for all words in the Spanish language—nor in English. If you hope to achieve a high score on standardized tests, you must try now to increase your vocabulary. Study the following synonyms. You can be sure that a good number of them will be on standardized tests. They are standard words of high frequency.

For suggestions as to how to study vocabulary, consult the entry **Vocabulary, how to study** in the Comprehensive Index. Also, that entry in the Index gives you references in this Grammar Part where you can find other vocabulary that you ought to know in preparation for a standardized test in Spanish, for example, adjectives, adverbs, antonyms, cognates, conjunctions, conjunctive locutions and correlative conjunctions, and other types of words.

acercarse (a), aproximarse (a) / to approach, to come near

acordarse (de), recordar / to remember

alabar, elogiar / to praise, to glorify, to eulogize

alimento, comida / food, nourishment

alumno (alumna), estudiante / pupil, student

andar, caminar / to walk

anillo, sortija / ring (finger)

antiguo (antigua), viejo (vieja) / ancient, old

así que, luego que, tan pronto como / as soon as

asustar, espantar / to frighten, to terrify, to scare

atreverse (a), osar / to dare, to venture

aún, todavía / still, yet, even

ayuda, socorro, auxilio / aid, succor, help, assistance

barco, buque, vapor / boat, ship

bastante, suficiente / enough, sufficient
batalla, combate, lucha / battle, combat, struggle, fight
bonito (bonita), lindo (linda) / pretty
breve, corto (corta) / brief, short
burlarse de, mofarse de / to make fun of, to mock
camarero, mozo / waiter
campesino, rústico, labrador / farmer, peasant
cara, rostro, semblante / face
cariño, amor / affection, love
cocinar, cocer, guisar / to cook
comenzar, empezar, principiar / to begin, to start, to commence
comprender, entender / to understand, to comprehend
conquistar, vencer / to conquer, to vanquish
contento (contenta), feliz, alegre / content, happy, glad
contestar, responder / to answer, to reply
continuar, seguir / to continue
cruzar, atravesar / to cross
cuarto, habitación / room
cura, sacerdote / priest
chiste, chanza, broma / jest, joke, fun
dar un paseo, pasearse / to take a walk, to go for a walk
dar voces, gritar / to shout, to cry out
de manera que, de modo que / so that
dejar de + inf., cesar de + inf. / to cease + pres. part., to stop + pres. part.
delgado, esbelto, flaco / thin, slender, slim, svelte
desafortunado, desgraciado / unfortunate
desaparecer, desvanecerse / to disappear, to vanish
desear, querer / to desire, to want, to wish
desprecio, desdén / scorn, disdain, contempt
diablo, demonio / devil, demon
diferente, distinto (distinta) / different, distinct
diligente, trabajador (trabajadora), aplicado (aplicada) / diligent, hard working, industrious
diversión, pasatiempo / diversion, pastime
dueño (dueña), propietario (propietaria), amo (ama) / owner, master, boss
echar, lanzar, tirar, arrojar / to throw, to lance, to hurl
elevar, levantar, alzar / to elevate, to raise, to lift
empleado (empleada), dependiente / employee, clerk
enojarse, enfadarse / to become angry, to become annoyed
enviar, mandar / to send
error, falta / error, mistake, fault
escoger, elegir / to choose, to select, to elect
esperar, aguardar / to wait for
esposa, mujer / wife, spouse
estrecho (estrecha), angosto (angosta) / narrow
famoso (famosa), célebre, ilustre / famous, celebrated, renowned, illustrious
fatigado (fatigada), cansado (cansada), rendido (rendida) / tired, exhausted, worn out
fiebre, calentura / fever
grave, serio (seria) / serious, grave
habilidad, destreza / ability, skill, dexterity
hablador (habladora), locuaz / talkative, loquacious
halagar, lisonjear, adular / to flatter
hallar, encontrar / to find
hermoso (hermosa), bello (bella) / beautiful, handsome

igual, semejante / equal, alike, similar
invitar, convidar / to invite
irse, marcharse / to leave, to go away
joya, alhaja / jewel, gem
lanzar, tirar, echar / to throw, to lance, to hurl
lengua, idioma / language, idiom
lentamente, despacio / slowly
luchar, combatir, pelear, pugnar / to fight, to battle, to combat, to struggle
lugar, sitio / place, site
llevar, conducir / to take, to lead
maestro (maestra), profesor (profesora) / teacher, professor
marido, esposo / husband, spouse
mendigo (mendiga), pordiosero (pordiosera), limosnero (limosnera) / beggar
miedo, temor / fear, dread
morir, fallecer, fenecer / to die, to expire
mostrar, enseñar / to show
nobleza, hidalguez, hidalguía / nobility
nunca, jamás / never
obtener, conseguir / to obtain, to get
ocurrir, suceder, acontecer, acaecer / to occur, to happen, to come about, to come to pass
odiar, aborrecer / to hate, to abhor
onda, ola / wave
país, nación / country, nation
pájaro, ave / bird
pararse, detenerse / to stop (oneself)
parecido, semejante / like, similar
pasar un buen rato, divertirse / to have a good time
pena, dolor / pain, grief
perezoso (perezosa), flojo (floja) / lazy
periódico, diario / newspaper
permiso, licencia / permission, leave
permitir, dejar / to permit, to allow, to let
poner, colocar / to put, to place
porfiado (porfiada), terco (terca), testarudo (testaruda) / obstinate, stubborn
posponer, diferir, aplazar / to postpone, to defer, to put off, to delay
premio, galardón / prize, reward
quedarse, permanecer / to remain, to stay
rapidez, prisa, velocidad / rapidity, haste, speed, velocity
regresar, volver / to return (to a place)
rezar, orar / to pray
rogar, suplicar / to beg, to implore, to entreat
romper, quebrar / to break
sin embargo, no obstante / nevertheless, however
solamente, sólo / only
sorprender, asombrar / to surprise, to astonish
suceso, acontecimiento / happening, event
sufrir, padecer / to suffer, to endure
susto, espanto / fright, scare, dread
tal vez, acaso, quizá, quizás / maybe, perhaps
terminar, acabar, concluir / to terminate, to finish, to end
tonto (tonta), necio (necia) / foolish, stupid, idiotic
trabajo, tarea, obra / work, task
tratar de, intentar / to try to, to attempt
ya que, puesto que / since, inasmuch as

§66. PRONOUNS

§66.1   **Definition:** A pronoun is a word that takes the place of a noun; for example, in English there are these common pronouns: I, you, he, she, it, we, they, me, him, her, us, them—just to mention a few.

§66.2   **Pronouns are divided into certain types:** personal, prepositional, relative, interrogative, demonstrative, possessive, indefinite and negative.

§66.3   A personal pronoun is used as the subject of a verb, direct or indirect object of a verb or verb form, as a reflexive pronoun object, and as object of a preposition.

Correct use of pronouns in Spanish is not easy—nor in English, for that matter. For example, in English, you can often hear people using pronouns incorrectly: "between you and *I*" ought to be stated as "between you and *me*"; "if you have any questions, see *myself*" ought to be stated as "if you have any questions, see *me*"; "*Who* did you see?" ought to be stated as "*Whom* did you see?" And there are many more incorrect uses of pronouns in English.

§66.4   **Personal pronouns**

Subject pronouns	Examples
Singular	
1. **yo** / I	**Yo** hablo.
2. **tú** / you *(familiar)*	**Tú** hablas.
3. **usted** / you *(polite)*	**Usted** habla.
él / he, it	**Él** habla.
ella / she, it	**Ella** habla.
Plural	
1. **nosotros (nosotras)** / we	**Nosotros** hablamos.
2. **vosotros (vosotras)** / you *(fam.)*	**Vosotros** habláis.
3. **ustedes** / you *(polite)*	**Ustedes** hablan.
ellos / they	**Ellos** hablan.
ellas / they	**Ellas** hablan.

As you can see in the examples given here, a subject pronoun is ordinarily placed in front of the main verb. For other positions, see **§66.34ff.**

§66.5   In Spanish, subject pronouns are not used at all times. The ending of the verb tells you if the subject is 1st, 2nd, or 3rd person in the singular or plural. Of course, in the 3rd person sing. and pl. there is more than one possible subject with the same ending on the verb form. In that case, if there is any doubt as to what the subject is, it is mentioned for the sake of clarity. At other times, subject pronouns in Spanish are used when you want to be emphatic, to make a contrast between this person and that person, or out of simple courtesy. To prepare yourself for a standardized test in Spanish, you must be certain to know the endings of the verb forms in all the tenses (see the entry **Verbs** in the Comprehensive Index) in the three persons of the singular and of the plural so that you can figure out the subject if it is not clearly stated. In addition to pronouns as subjects, nouns are also used as subjects. Any noun—whether common (el hombre, la mujer, el cielo, la silla, *etc.*) or proper (María, Juan y Elena, los Estados Unidos, *etc.*) are always 3rd person, either singular or plural.

§66.6   Generally speaking, in Latin American countries **ustedes** (3rd pers., pl.) is used in place of **vosotros** or **vosotras** (2nd pers., pl.).

§66.7

Direct object pronouns	Examples
Singular	
1. **me** / me	**María me ha visto** / Mary has seen me.
2. **te** / you *(fam.)*	**María te había visto** / Mary had seen you.

3. **le, la** / you   **María le (la) ve** / Mary sees you.
    le / him; **lo** / him, it   **María le (lo) ve** / Mary sees him (it).
    la / her, it   **María la ve** / Mary sees her (it).

Plural
1. **nos** / us   **María nos había visto** / Mary had seen us.
2. **os** / you (*fam.*)   **María os ha visto** / Mary has seen you.
3. **los, las** / you   **María los (las) ve** / Mary sees you.
    los / them   **María los ve** / Mary sees them.
    las / them   **María las ve** / Mary sees them.

§66.8   In Latin American countries, **lo** is generally used instead of **le** to mean *him*. You can tell from the context of what is written or said if **lo** means *him* or *it* (masc.). NOTE that the plural of **le** as direct object pronoun is **los**.

§66.9   NOTE that in the 3rd pers., plural, the direct objects **los** (masc.) and **las** (fem.) refer to people and things.

§66.10   ALSO NOTE that in the 3rd pers. singular, the direct object pronoun **le** is masc. and **la** is fem. and both mean *you*. You can tell from the context of what is written or said if **le** means *you* (masc. sing.) or if it means *him*.

§66.11   Here is a summing up of the various meanings of the direct object pronouns **le, lo, la, los, las:**

le: him, you (*masc.*)
lo: him, it (*masc.*)
la: her, you (*fem.*), it (*fem.*)
los: you (*masc. pl.*), them (*people or things, masc., pl.*)
las: you (*fem. pl.*), them (*people or things, fem., pl.*)

As you can see in the examples given in **§66.7,** a direct object pronoun ordinarily is placed in front of the main verb. For other positions, see **§66.34ff.**

§66.12   There is also the neuter **lo** direct object pronoun. It does not refer to any particular noun that is f. or m.; that is why it has no gender and is called *neuter*. It usually refers to an idea or a statement:

    ¿Está Ud. enfermo? / Are you sick?   **Sí, lo estoy** / Yes, I am.
    ¿Son amigos? / Are they friends?   **Sí, lo son** / Yes, they are.

Of course, your reply could be **Sí, estoy enfermo** and **Sí, son amigos.** But because your verb is a form of **estar** or **ser,** you do not have to repeat what was mentioned; neuter **lo** takes its place as a direct object pronoun. This neuter **lo** direct object pronoun is also used with other verbs, *e.g.,* **pedir, preguntar** and **parecer:**

    María parece contenta / Mary seems happy. **Sí, lo parece** / Yes, she does (Yes, she does seem *so*).

§66.13   To make the examples in Spanish given above in **§66.7** negative, place **no** in front of the direct object pronouns: **María no me ve,** *etc.* To make the examples negative in **§66.4,** place **no** in front of the verb.

§66.14   **Indirect object pronouns**   **Examples**

Singular
1. **me** / to me   **Pablo me ha hablado** / Paul has talked to me.
2. **te** / to you (*fam.*)   **Pablo te habla** / Paul talks to you.
3. **le** / to you, to him,   **Pablo le habla** / Paul talks to you (to him,
    to her, to it   to her, to it).

Plural
1. **nos** / to us   **Pablo nos ha hablado** / Paul has talked to us.

2. **os** / to you *(fam.)*   **Pablo os habla** / Paul talks to you.
3. **les** / to you, to them   **Pablo les habla** / Paul talks to you (to them).

§66.15   To make these sentences negative, place **no** in front of the indirect object pronouns: **Pablo no me habla** / Paul does not talk to me.

§66.16   NOTE that **me, te, nos, os** are direct object pronouns and indirect object pronouns. See **§66.7ff.**

§66.17   NOTE that **le** as an indirect object pronoun has more than one meaning. If there is any doubt as to the meaning, merely add after the verb any of the following accordingly to clarify the meaning: **a Ud., a él, a ella: Pablo le habla a usted** / Paul is talking to you.

§66.18   NOTE that **les** has more than one meaning. If there is any doubt as to the meaning, merely add after the verb any of the following, accordingly: **a Uds., a ellos, a ellas: Pablo no les habla a ellos** / Paul is not talking to them.

As you can see in the examples given in **§66.14,** an indirect object pronoun ordinarily is placed in front of the main verb. For other positions, see **§66.34ff.**

§66.19   An indirect object pronoun is needed when you use a verb that indicates a person is being deprived of something, *e.g.,* to steal something *from* someone, to take something *off* or *from* someone, to buy something from someone, and actions of this sort. The reason why an indirect object pronoun is needed is that you are dealing with the preposition **a + noun** or **pronoun** and it must be accounted for. Examples:

Los ladrones le robaron todo el dinero a él / The robbers stole all the money from him.
La madre le quitó al niño el sombrero / The mother took off the child's hat.
Les compré mi automóvil a ellos / I bought my car from them.

§66.20   The indirect object pronouns are used with the verb **gustar** (see **§25.**) and with the following verbs: **bastar, faltar** or **hacer falta, sobrar, quedarle (a uno), tocarle (a uno), placer, parecer.** Examples:

A Ricardo le gusta el helado / Richard likes ice cream (*i.e.,* Ice cream is pleasing to him, to Richard).
A Juan le bastan cien dólares / One hundred dollars are enough for John.
A los muchachos les faltan cinco dólares / The boys need five dollars (*i.e.,* Five dollars are lacking to them, to the boys). OR: **A la mujer le hacen falta cinco dólares** / The woman needs five dollars (*i.e.,* Five dollars are lacking to her, to the woman).

To put it simply, the indirect object pronoun is needed in the examples given in **§66.19** and **§66.20** above because some kind of action is being done *to* someone.

§66.21   **Reflexive pronouns**   **Examples**

Singular
1. **me** / myself   **Me lavo** / I wash myself.
2. **te** / yourself   **Te lavas** / You wash yourself.
3. **se** / yourself, himself,   **Ud. se lava** / You wash yourself; **Pablo se**
     herself, itself   **lava** / Paul washes himself, *etc.*

Plural
1. **nos** / ourselves   **Nosotros (-as) nos lavamos.**
2. **os** / yourselves   **Vosotros (-as) os laváis.**
3. **se** / yourselves, themselves   **Uds. se lavan** / You wash yourselves; **Ellos (Ellas) se lavan** / They wash themselves.

§66.22   A reflexive verb contains a reflexive pronoun, and the action of the verb falls on the subject and its reflexive pronoun either directly or indirectly. For that reason the reflexive pronoun must agree with the subject: **yo me . . . , tú te . . . , Ud. se . . . , él se . . . , ella se . . . , nosotros nos . . . , vosotros os . . . , Uds. se . . . , ellos se . . . , ellas se . . . .**

A reflexive pronoun is ordinarily placed in front of the verb form, as you can see in the examples given in §66.21. For other positions, see §66.34ff.

§66.23   To make these sentences negative, place **no** in front of the reflexive pronoun: **Yo no me lavo, Tú no te lavas, Ud. no se lava,** *etc.*

§66.24   NOTE that **me, te, nos, os** are not only reflexive pronouns but they are also direct object pronouns and indirect object pronouns. See §66.16.

§66.25   A reflexive verb in Spanish is not always reflexive in English, for example:

Spanish	English
levantarse	to get up
sentarse	to sit down

§66.26   There are some reflexive verbs in Spanish that are also reflexive in English, for example:

Spanish	English
bañarse	to bathe oneself
lavarse	to wash oneself

§66.27   The following reflexive pronouns are also used as reciprocal pronouns, meaning "each other" or "to each other": **se, nos, os.** Examples:

Ayer por la noche, María y yo nos vimos en el cine / Yesterday evening, Mary and I saw each other at the movies.

Roberto y Teresa se escriben todos los días / Robert and Teresa write to each other every day.

§66.28   If the meaning of these three reflexive pronouns (**se, nos, os**) is not clear when they are used in a reciprocal meaning, any of the following may be added accordingly to express the idea of "each other" or "to each other": **uno a otro, una a otra, unos a otros,** *etc.*

§66.29   For the position of reflexive pronouns with reflexive verbs in the imperative (command) and for other comments on reflexive verbs, see Imperative, with reflexive verbs in §68.62 and Verbs, reflexive in §1.64, §66.21—§66.29, §66.53, §68.62 (h), (k) and (l).

§66.30   **Prepositional pronouns**

§66.31   Pronouns that are used as objects of prepositions are called prepositional pronouns or disjunctive pronouns. They are as follows:

Singular
1. **para mí** / for me, for myself
2. **para tí** / for you, for yourself
3. **para usted (Ud.)** / for you
   para él / for him, for it
   para ella / for her, for it

Plural
1. **para nosotros (nosotras)** / for us, for ourselves
2. **para vosotros (vosotras)** / for you, for yourselves
3. **para ustedes (Uds.)** / for you
   para ellos / for them
   para ellas / for them

§66.32   Also note the following:

Singular
3. **para sí** / for yourself, for himself, for herself, for itself

Plural
3. **para sí** / for yourselves, for themselves

§66.33   NOTE the following exceptions with the prepositions **con, entre,** and **menos:**

conmigo / with me
contigo / with you *(fam.)*
consigo / with yourself, with yourselves, with himself, with herself, with themselves
entre tú y yo / between you and me
menos yo / except me

§66.34   **Position of object pronouns**

§66.35   In preparation for the next standardized test in Spanish, you surely must review pronouns and their positions beginning with **§66.** above. You can expect to find them in short sentences and in reading passages because they are used very commonly in the Spanish language. In the reading passages, you will have to recognize their meaning according to their position with regard to a verb form. In sentences, sometimes short or long, you will probably have to choose the correct pronoun to fit in the blank space. Many questions, by the way, on standardized tests are the multiple choice type and if you do not recognize the correct answer from among the choices it will mean that you did not review this section and other sections in this Grammar Part thoroughly enough.

In the sections above, I reviewed for you single object pronouns and their position, beginning in **§66.7.** In this section, there is a summary review of the position of a single object pronoun and a review of double object pronouns and their position with regard to a verb or verb form. By double object pronouns is meant one direct object pronoun and one indirect object pronoun. Which one comes first and where do you put them?

§66.36   **Position of a single object pronoun: a summary**

Review the normal position of a single object pronoun as given above in the examples beginning in **§66.7** when dealing with a simple tense or a compound tense.

§66.37   Attach the single object pronoun to an infinitive: **Juan quiere escribirlo** / John wants to write it.

OR

§66.38   If the main verb is **poder, querer, saber, ir a,** you may place the object pronoun in front of the main verb:

Juan lo quiere escribir / John wants to write it; **¿Puedo levantarme?** or **¿Me puedo levantar?** / May I get up?

§66.39   Attach the single object pronoun to a present participle: **Juan está escribiéndolo** / John is writing it.

NOTE that when you attach an object pronoun to a present participle, you must add an accent mark on the vowel that was stressed in the present participle before the object pronoun was attached. The accent mark is needed to keep the stress where it originally was.

OR

§66.40   If the main verb is a progressive form with **estar** or another auxiliary, you may place the object pronoun in front of the main verb:

Juan lo está escribiendo / John is writing it.

§66.41   When you are dealing with a verb form in the affirmative imperative (command), you must attach the single object pronoun to the verb form and add an accent mark on the vowel that was stressed in the verb form before the single object pronoun was added. The accent mark is needed to keep the stress where it originally was:

¡Hábleme Ud., por favor! / Talk to me, please!

§66.42   When you are dealing with a verb form in the negative imperative (command), you must place the object pronoun in front of the verb form, where it normally goes:

¡No me hable Ud., por favor! / Do not talk to me, please!

§66.43 **Position of double object pronouns: a summary**

§66.44 An indirect object pronoun is always placed in front of a direct object pronoun. They are never separated from each other.

§66.45 **With a verb in a simple tense or in a compound tense in the affirmative or negative:**

The indirect object pronoun is placed in front of the direct object pronoun and both are placed in front of the verb form:

Juan me lo da. / John is giving it to me.
Juan te la daba / John was giving it to you.
Juan nos los dio / John gave them to us.
Juan os las dará / John will give them to you.

María no me lo ha dado / Mary has not given it to me.
María no te la había dado / Mary had not given it to you.
María no nos los habrá dado / Mary will not have given them to us.
María no os las habría dado / Mary would not have given them to you.

§66.46 **With a verb in a simple tense or in a compound tense in the interrogative:**

The indirect object pronoun still remains in front of the direct object pronoun and both still remain in front of the verb form. The subject (whether a noun or pronoun) is placed after the verb form:

¿Nos la dio Juan? / Did John give it to us?
¿Te lo ha dado Juan? / Has John given it to you?

§66.47 **With a verb in the affirmative imperative (command):**

The object pronouns are still in the same order (indirect object + direct object) but they are attached to the verb form and an accent mark is added on the vowel that was stressed in the verb form before the two object pronouns were added. The accent mark is needed to keep the stress where it originally was:

¡Dígamelo Ud., por favor! / Tell it to me, please!

§66.48 **With a verb in the negative imperative (command):**

The position of **no** and the two object pronouns is still the same as usual, in front of the verb form:

¡No me lo diga Ud., por favor! / Don't tell it to me, please!

§66.49 **When dealing with an infinitive,** attach both object pronouns (indirect, direct) to the infinitive:

Juan quiere dármelo / John wants to give it to me.
Juan no quiere dármelo / John does not want to give it to me.

OR

If the main verb is **poder, querer, saber, ir a,** you may place the two object pronouns in front of the main verb:

Juan me lo quiere dar / John wants to give it to me.
Juan no me lo quiere dar / John does not want to give it to me.

§66.50 **When dealing with a present participle,** attach both object pronouns (indirect, direct) to the present participle:

Juan está escribiéndomelo / John is writing it to me.

Juan no está escribiéndomelo / John is not writing it to me.

OR

§66.51   If the main verb is a progressive form with **estar** or another auxiliary, you may place the two object pronouns (indirect, direct) in front of the main verb:

Juan me lo está escribiendo / John is writing it to me.
Juan no me lo está escribiendo / John is not writing it to me.

Juana me lo estaba escribiendo / Jane was writing it to me.

§66.52   When an indirect object pronoun and a direct object pronoun are both 3rd person, either singular or plural or both singular or both plural, the indirect object pronoun (**le** or **les**) changes to **se** because it cannot stand as **le** or **les** in front of a direct object pronoun beginning with the letter "**l**". Review the direct object pronouns, 3rd person sing. and plural in §66.7. Also, review the indirect object pronouns, 3rd person sing. and plural in §66.14.

Juan se lo da / John is giving it to you (to him, to her, to it, to you *plural*, to them).

¡Dígaselo Ud.! / Tell it to him!
¡No se lo diga Ud.! / Don't tell it to him!

Juan quiere dárselo.
Juan se lo quiere dar. } John wants to give it to her.

Juan está escribiéndoselo.
Juan se lo está escribiendo. } John is writing it to them.

Since the form **se** can have more than one meaning (to him, to her, to them, *etc.*), in addition to the fact that it looks exactly like the reflexive pronoun **se,** any doubt as to its meaning can be clarified merely by adding any of the following accordingly: **a Ud., a él, a ella, a Uds., a ellos, a ellas.**

§66.53   If you are dealing with a reflexive pronoun, it is normally placed in front of an object pronoun:

Yo me lo puse / I put it on (me, on myself).

§66.54   **Demonstrative pronouns**

§66.55   Demonstrative pronouns are formed from the demonstrative adjectives. To form a demonstrative pronoun write an accent mark on the stressed vowel of a demonstrative adjective. See §1.54 and §1.55.

§66.56   A demonstrative pronoun is used to take the place of a noun. It agrees in gender and number with the noun it replaces. The demonstrative pronouns are:

MASCULINE	FEMININE	NEUTER	ENGLISH MEANING
éste	**ésta**	**esto**	this one *(here)*
éstos	**éstas**		these *(here)*
ése	**ésa**	**eso**	that one *(there)*
ésos	**ésas**		those *(there)*
aquél	**aquélla**	**aquello**	that one { *(farther away or*
aquéllos	**aquéllas**		those { *out of sight)*

§66.57   EXAMPLES

Me gustan este cuadro y ése / I like this picture and that one.
Me gustan estos guantes y aquéllos / I like these gloves and those.
Esta falda y ésa son bonitas / This skirt and that one are pretty.
Estas camisas y aquéllas son hermosas / These shirts and those are beautiful.

§66.58   NOTE that the neuter forms do not have an accent mark. They are not used when you are referring to a particular noun. They are used when referring to an idea, a statement, a situation, a clause, a phrase. Never use the neuter pronouns to refer to a person. Examples:

> **Qué es esto?** / What is this?
> **Qué es eso?** / What is that?
> **Qué es aquello?** / What is that (way over there)?

> **Eso es fácil de hacer** / That is easy to do.
> **Es fácil hacer eso** / It is easy to do that.
> **Eso es** / That's right.

> **Juan no estudia y esto me inquieta** / John does not study and this worries me.

§66.59   NOTE also that the English term *the latter* is expressed in Spanish as **éste, ésta, éstos,** or **éstas;** and *the fomer* is expressed in Spanish as **aquél, aquélla, aquéllos, aquéllas**—depending on the gender and number of the noun referred to.

AND NOTE that in English the order is generally "the former . . . the latter"—in other words, "the one that was mentioned first . . . the one that was mentioned last". In Spanish, however, the stated order is the opposite: "the latter . . . the former"—in other words, "the one that was just mentioned last . . . the one that was mentioned first:

> **Roberto y Antonio son inteligentes; éste** (meaning Antonio) **es alto y aquél es pequeño** / Robert and Anthony are intelligent; the former (meaning Roberto) is short and the latter is tall.

§66.60   The pronouns **el de, la de, los de, las de; el que, la que, los que, las que**
These pronouns are used in place of nouns.

> EXAMPLES:
> **mi hermano y el** *(hermano)* **de mi amigo** / my brother and my friend's (the one of my friend *or* that of my friend)
> **mi hermana y la** *(hermana)* **de mi amigo** / my sister and my friend's (the one of my friend *or* that of my friend)
> **mis hermanos y los** *(hermanos)* **del muchacho** / my brothers and the boy's (the ones of the boy *or* those of the boy)
> **mis hermanas y las** *(hermanas)* **de la muchacha** / my sisters and the girl's (the ones of the girl *or* those of the girl)
> **El** *(muchacho)* **que baila con María es mi hermano** / The one who (The boy who) is dancing with Mary is my brother.
> **La** *(muchacha)* **que baila con Roberto es mi hermana** / The one who (The girl who) is dancing with Robert is my sister.
> **Los** *(muchachos)* **que bailan son mis amigos** / The ones who (The boys who) are dancing are my friends.
> **Las** *(muchachas)* **que bailan son mis amigas** / The ones who (The girls who) are dancing are my friends.

§66.61   **Possessive pronouns**

§66.62   Definition: A possessive pronoun is a word that takes the place of a noun to show possession, as in English: *mine, yours,* etc., instead of saying *my mother, your car,* etc.

§66.63   You form a possessive pronoun by using the appropriate definite article (**el, la, los, las**) + the long form of the possessive adj., all of which are given in **§1.60.** As you realize by now, a pronoun must agree in gender and number with the noun it takes the place of. Therefore, a possessive pronoun must agree in gender and number with the noun it replaces. It does not agree with the possessor.

§66.64   **The possessive pronouns are:**

ENGLISH MEANING	SINGULAR FORM (agreement in gender and number with the noun it replaces)	PLURAL FORM (agreement in gender and number with the noun it replaces)
1. mine	**el mío, la mía**	**los míos, las mías**
2. yours *(fam. sing.)*	**el tuyo, la tuya**	**los tuyos, las tuyas**
3. yours, his, hers, its	**el suyo, la suya**	**los suyos, las suyas**
1. ours	**el nuestro, la nuestra**	**los nuestros, las nuestras**
2. yours *(fam. pl.)*	**el vuestro, la vuestra**	**los vuestros, las vuestras**
3. yours, theirs	**el suyo, la suya**	**los suyos, las suyas**

EXAMPLES:

§66.65   **Mi hermano es más alto que el suyo** / My brother is taller than yours (his, hers, theirs).
Su hermana es más alta que la mía / Your sister is taller than mine.
Mi casa es más grande que la suya / My house is larger than yours (his, hers, theirs).

§66.66   In order to clarify the meanings of **el suyo, la suya, los suyos, las suyas** (since they can mean *yours, his, hers, its, theirs*), do the following: drop the **suyo** form, keep the appropriate definite article (**el, la, los, las**), and add, appropriately, any of the following: **de Ud., de él, de ella, de Uds., de ellos, de ellas:**

mi libro y el de Ud., mi casa y la de él, mis amigos y los de ella, mis amigas y las de Uds., mis libros y los de ellos, mis cuadernos y los de ellas / my book and yours, my house and his, my friends and hers, my friends and yours, *etc.* See also **§1.59.**

§66.67   **¿De quién es . . . ? ¿De quiénes es . . . ? ¿De quién son . . . ? ¿De quiénes son . . . ?**   Whose is . . . ? Whose are . . . ?

Whose, when asking a question (usually at the beginning of a sentence), is expressed by any of the above. If you believe that the possessor is singular, use **¿De quién es . . . ?** If you think that the possessor is plural, use **¿De quiénes es . . . ?** And if the noun you have in mind (**whose . . .**) is plural, use the third person plural form of **ser:**

¿De quién es esta casa? / Whose is this house?   **Es de mi tío** / It is my uncle's.
¿De quiénes es esta casa? / Whose is this house?   **Es de mis amigos** / It is my friends'.
¿De quién son estos guantes? / Whose are these gloves?   **Son de Juan** / They are John's.
¿De quiénes son estos niños? / Whose are these children?   **Son de los Señores Pardo** / They are Mr. and Mrs. Pardo's.

§66.68   NOTE that the verb **ser** is used in these expressions showing possession.

§66.69   ALSO NOTE that if a possessive pronoun is used with the verb **ser,** the definite article is dropped:

¿De quién es este lápiz? / Whose is this pencil?   **Es mío** / It is mine.
¿De quién son estas camisas? / Whose are these shirts?   **Son suyas** / They are theirs (yours, his, hers). OR, to clarify **suyas,** say: **Son de Ud., Son de él, Son de ella,** *etc.* / They are yours, They are his, They are hers, *etc.* See also **§66.66.**

§66.70   **Relative pronouns**

§66.71   **Definition:** A pronoun is a word that takes the place of a noun (see **§66.1**). A relative pronoun is a pronoun that refers (relates) to an **antecedent.** An antecedent is something that comes before something; it can be a word, a phrase, a clause which is replaced by a pronoun or some other substitute. Example: *Is it Mary who did that?* In this sentence, *who* is the relative pronoun and *Mary* is the antecedent. Another example, a longer one: *It seems to me that you are right, which is what I had thought right along.* The relative pronoun in this example is *which* and the antecedent of it is the clause, *that you are right.*

In Spanish, a relative pronoun can refer to an antecedent which is a person or a thing, or an idea. A relative pronoun can be subject or object of a verb, or object of a preposition.

§66.72 **Common relative pronouns**

§66.73   **que** / who, that, whom, which. This is the most common relative pronoun.

§66.74   **As subject referring to a person:** La muchacha **que** habla con Juan es mi hermana / The girl **who** is talking with John is my sister.

Here, the relative pronoun **que** is subject of the verb **habla** and it refers to **la muchacha,** which is the subject of the verb **es.**

§66.75   **As subject referring to a thing:** El libro **que** está en la mesa es mío / The book **which (that)** is on the table is mine.

Here, the relative pronoun **que** is subject of the verb **está** and it refers to **el libro,** which is the subject of **es.**

§66.76   **As direct object of a verb referring to a person:** El señor Molina es el profesor **que** admiro / Mr. Molina is the professor **whom** I admire.

Here, the relative pronoun **que** is object of the verb form **admiro.** It refers to **el profesor.**

§66.77   **As direct object of a verb referring to a thing:** La composición **que** Ud. lee es mía / The composition (**that, which**) you are reading is mine.

Here, the relative pronoun **que** is object of the verb form **lee.** It refers to **la composición,** which is the subject of **es.** The subject of **lee** is **Ud.**

§66.78   NOTE here, in the English translation of this example, that we do not always have to use a relative pronoun in English. In Spanish, it must be stated.

§66.79   **As object of a preposition referring only to a thing:** La cama **en que** duermo es grande / The bed **in which** I sleep is large.

Here, the relative pronoun **que** is object of the preposition **en.** It refers to **la cama.** Other prepositions used commonly with **que** are **a, con, de.**

As object of a preposition, **que** refers to a thing only—not to a person. Use **quien** or **quienes** as object of a preposition referring to persons. See §66.87.

§66.80   **quien** / who (after a preposition, whom)

§66.81   **As subject of a verb referring only to persons:** Yo sé **quien** lo hizo / I know **who** did it.

Here, **quien** is the subject of **hizo.** It does not refer to a specific antecedent. Here, **quien** includes its antecedent.

§66.82   When used as a subject, **quien** (or **quienes,** if plural) can also mean *he who, she who, the or* who, *the ones who, those who.* In place of **quien** or **quienes** in this sense, you can also use **el que, la que, los que, las que:**

§66.83   **Quien escucha** oye / Who listens hears; He who listens hears; She who listens hears; The one who listens hears.

    OR: **El que escucha** oye / He who listens hears; **La que escucha** oye / She who listens hears; The one who listens hears.

§66.84   **Quienes escuchan** oyen / Who listen hear; Those who listen hear; The ones who listen hear.

    OR: **Los que escuchan** oyen; **Las que escuchan** oyen / Those who listen hear; The ones who listen hear.

§66.85   **As subject of a verb,** the relative pronoun **quien** may be used instead of **que** referring only to persons (see also §66.74) when it is the subject of a non-restrictive dependent clause set off by commas: La señora Gómez, **quien** (or **que**) es profesora, conoce a mi madre / Mrs. Gómez, who is a teacher, knows my mother.

§66.86   **As direct object of a verb referring only to persons,** the relative pronoun **quien** or **quienes** may be used with the personal **a** (**a quien, a quienes**) instead of **que** (see also §66.76): La muchacha **que** (*or* **a quien**) Ud. vio al baile es mi hermana / The girl **whom** you saw at the dance is my sister.

§66.87   **As object of a preposition referring only to persons:** ¿Conoces a la chica **con quien** tomé el almuerzo? / Do you know the girl **with whom** I had lunch? ¿Conoces a los chicos **con quienes** María tomó el almuerzo? / Do you know the boys **with whom** Mary had lunch? ¿Conoce Ud. a los hombres **de quienes** hablo? / Do you know the men **of whom** (**about whom**) I am talking?

§66.88   **el cual, la cual, los cuales, las cuales** / who, that, whom, which, the one which, the ones which, the one who, the ones who.

These relative pronouns may be used in place of **que,** as given in §66.73ff. This can be especially needed when it is desired to clarify the gender and number of **que:** La madre de José, **la cual** es muy inteligente, es dentista / Joseph's mother, **who** is very intelligent, is a dentist.

§66.89   These substitute relative pronouns may also refer to things: El libro, **el cual** está sobre la mesa, es mío / The book, **which** (**the one which**) is on the table, is mine.

§66.90   These relative pronouns may also be used as substitutes for **el que, la que, los que, las que** (see §66.82) when used as the subject of a non-restrictive dependent clause set off by commas, as given in §66.85: La señora Gómez, **la cual** (or **la que,** or **quien,** or **que**) es profesora, conoce a mi madre / Mrs. Gómez, **who** is a teacher, knows my mother.

§66.91   These relative pronouns, as well as **el que, la que, los que, las que,** are used as objects of prepositions except with **a, con, de, en**—in which case the relative pronoun **que** is preferred with things (see §66.79). These relative pronouns (**el cual, la cual, los cuales, las cuales** and **el que, la que, los que, las que**) are commonly used with the following prepositions: **para, por, sin, delante de, cerca de,** and **sobre:** En este cuarto, hay una gran ventana **por la cual** se ve el sol por la mañana / In this room, there is a large window **through which** you (one, anyone) can see the sun in the morning.

§66.92   These compound relative pronouns (**el cual, el que,** *etc.*) refer to persons as well as things and can be used as subject of a verb or direct object of a verb when used in a non-restrictive dependent clause separated from its antecedent and set off with commas, as in §66.88. See also §66.89–§66.91.

§66.93   **lo cual** / which; **lo que** / what, that which
These are neuter compound relative pronouns. They do not refer to an antecedent of any gender or number. That is why they are called *neuter.*

§66.94   **Lo cual** or **lo que** are used to refer to a statement, a clause, an idea: Mi hijo Juan estudia sus lecciones todos los días, **lo cual** es bueno / My son John studies his lessons every day, **which** is good. Mi hija recibió buenas notas, **lo que** me gustó / My daughter received good marks, **which** pleased me.

§66.95   **Lo que** is also used to express *what* in the sense of *that which:* Comprendo **lo que** Ud. dice / I understand **what** (**that which**) you say. **Lo que** Ud. dice es verdad / **What** (**That which**) you say is true.

§66.96   **cuanto = todo lo que** / all that

As a relative pronoun, **cuanto** may be used in place of **todo lo que:** Todo lo que Ud. dice es verdad; OR: **Cuanto** Ud. dice es verdad / **All that** (**All that which**) you say is true. See also §66.95.

§66.97   **cuyo, cuya, cuyos, cuyas** / whose

This word (and its forms as given) refers to persons and things. Strictly speaking, **cuyo,** *etc.* is not regarded as a relative pronoun but rather as a relative possessive adjective. It agrees in gender and number with what is possessed (whose . . .), not with the possessor. Its position is directly in front of the noun it modifies. Examples:

§66.98   El señor García, **cuyos hijos** son inteligentes, es profesor / Mr. García, **whose children** are intelligent, is a professor.

§66.99   La muchacha, **cuyo padre** es profesor, es inteligente / The girl, **whose father** is a professor, is intelligent.

§66.100   El muchacho, **cuya madre** es profesora, es inteligente / The boy, **whose mother** is a professor, is intelligent.

§66.101   The forms of **cuyo** cannot be used as an interrogative when you ask: Whose is . . . ? You must use **de quién: ¿De quien es este libro?** See also **§66.67–§66.69.**

§66.102   When referring to parts of the body, use **a quien** instead of **cuyo:** La niña, **a quien** la madre lavó las manos, es bonita / The child, **whose** hands the mother washed, is pretty.

§66.103   **Interrogative pronouns.** See **§9.** and the entry **Interrogative words,** as well as specific interrogatives, *e.g.,* **qué, cuál,** *etc.,* in the General Index.

§66.104   **Indefinite pronouns.** See **§55.** and the entry **Indefinite and negative words,** as well as specific indefinite words, *e.g.,* **algo, alguien,** *etc.,* in the General Index.

§66.105   **Negative pronouns.** See **§55.** and the entry **Negative and indefinite words,** as well as specific negative words, *e.g.,* **nada, nadie,** *etc.,* in the General Index.

§67.   VERBS

§67.1   Introduction

A verb is where the action is! A verb is a word that expresses an action (like *go, eat, write*) or a state of being (like *think, believe, be*). Tense means time. Spanish and English verb tenses are divided into three main groups of time: past, present, and future. A verb tense shows if an action or state of being took place, is taking place, or will take place.

Spanish and English verbs are also used in four moods, or modes. (There is also the Infinitive Mood, but we are not concerned with that here.) Mood has to do with the *way* a person regards an action or a state that he expresses. For example, a person may merely make a statement or ask a question—this is the Indicative Mood, which we use most of the time in Spanish and English. A person may say that he *would do* something if something else were possible or that he *would have done* something if something else had been possible—this is the Conditional Mood. A person may use a verb *in such a way* that a wish, a fear, a regret, a joy, a request, a supposition, or something of this sort is indicated—this is the Subjunctive Mood. The Subjunctive Mood is used in Spanish much more than in English. Finally, a person may command someone to do something or demand that something be done—this is the Imperative Mood.

There are six verb tenses in English: Present, Past, Future, Present Perfect, Past Perfect, and Future Perfect. The first three are simple tenses. The other three tenses are compound and are based on the simple tenses. In Spanish, however, there are fourteen tenses, seven of which are simple and seven of which are compound. The seven compound tenses are based on the seven simple tenses. In Spanish and English a verb tense is simple if it consists of one verb form, *e.g.,* **estudio.** A verb tense is compound if it consists of two parts—the auxiliary (or helping) verb plus the past participle of the verb you have in mind, *e.g.,* **he estudiado.** See the list of **Verb Tenses and Moods in Spanish with English Equivalents** in **§68.**

In Spanish there is also another tense which is used to express an action in the present. It is called the *Progressive Present.* It is used only if an action is actually in progress at the present time;

for example, **Estoy leyendo,** *I am reading (right now).* It is formed by using the *Present Indicative* of **estar** plus the present participle of the verb you have in mind. There is still another tense in Spanish which is used to express an action that was taking place in the past. It is called the *Progressive Past.* It is used if an action was actually in progress at a certain moment in the past; for example, **Estaba leyendo cuando mi hermano entró,** *I was reading when my brother came in.* The *Progressive Past* is formed by using the *Imperfect Indicative* of **estar** plus the present participle of the verb you have in mind. See **§68.63** and **§68.64.**

In **§68.** and beginning with **§68.14,** the tenses and moods are given in Spanish and the equivalent name or names in English are given in parentheses. Although some of the names given in English are not considered to be tenses (for there are only six), they are given for the purpose of identification as they are related to the Spanish names. The comparison includes only the essential points you need to know about the meanings and uses of Spanish verb tenses and moods as related to English usage to help prepare you for standardized tests in Spanish. I shall use examples to illustrate their meanings and uses. This is not intended to be a treatise in detail. It is merely a summary. I hope you find it helpful so that you can understand Spanish verbs better.

But first, here are some essential points you need to know about Spanish verbs:

§67.2 Agreement of subject and verb

A subject and verb form must agree in person and number. By *person* is meant 1st, 2nd, or 3rd; by *number* is meant singular or plural. To get a picture of the three persons in the singular and in the plural, see Subject pronouns, **§66.4ff.** This may seem elementary and obvious to you, but too often students become careless on a standardized test in Spanish and they neglect to watch for the correct ending of a verb form to agree with the subject in person and number. You must be aware of this. For example, if you had to select the correct subject for the verb form **hablaron** on a standardized test in Spanish, and if you were offered the following choices, which would you select? **(A) Ud. (B) vosotros (C) María y Pablo (D) José y yo.** First, you have to look at the ending of the verb form that is given: **hablaron** is 3rd plural because the ending is **-aron,** which is preterit. Therefore, the correct choice for an answer is (C). You do not really have to memorize verb form endings in all the tenses (unless you want to!). All you have to do is open your eyes and observe the verb form by looking at the ending. After constant practice (haven't you been studying Spanish for about three years already?), you should be able *to recognize* the endings and know right away what the subject would have to be: 1st, 2nd or 3rd person, singular or plural.

§67.3 Agreement of subject and reflexive pronoun of a reflexive verb

A subject and reflexive pronoun must agree in person and number. Here, too, students often are careless on a standardized test and neglect to select the proper reflexive pronoun that matches the subject. To get a picture of the correct reflexive pronoun that goes with the subject, according to the person you need (1st, 2nd or 3rd, singular or plural), see Reflexive pronouns in **§66.21–§66.29.** You must be aware of this so that you can choose the correct answer for the easy questions that test this on standardized tests in Spanish.

§67.4 Formation of past participle

The past participle is regularly formed from the infinitive:

—**ar** ending verbs, drop the —**ar** and add **ado: hablar, hablado**
—**er** ending verbs, drop the —**er** and add **ido: beber, bebido**
—**ir** ending verbs, drop the —**ir** and **ido: recibir, recibido**

§67.5 Common irregular past participles

For a listing of all commonly used irregular past participles, see **§58.17.** You ought to know them so that you may be able to recognize them on standardized tests in Spanish.

§67.6 Auxiliary verb: haber (to have)

The auxiliary verb **haber** (also called *helping verb*) is used in any of the 7 simple tenses + the past participle of the main verb to form the 7 compound tenses. For a complete picture of **haber** in the 7 simple tenses, see **§68.11.**

§67.7 **Transitive verbs**

A transitive verb is a verb that takes a direct object. Such a verb is called *transitive* because the action passes over from the subject and directly affects someone or something in some way:

(a) **Veo a mi amigo** / I see my friend.

(b) **Abro la ventana** / I open the window.

(c) **Estudié mis lecciones esta mañana en la biblioteca** / I studied my lessons this morning in the library.

(d) **Antes de salir, la profesora cerró las ventanas de la sala de clase** / Before going out, the teacher closed the classroom windows.

NOTE that in the above examples, the direct object is a noun in every sentence. Let me diagram them for you so you can see that a transitive verb performs an action that passes over from the subject and affects someone or something:

(a)
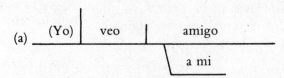

Here, **Yo** is the subject understood; it does not have to be mentioned because the verb ending is 1st person singular and we know it must be **yo.** The verb is **veo; amigo** is the direct object; **mi** is a possessive adjective that modifies **amigo; a** is the *personal a* used in front of the noun direct object because it is a person.

(b)
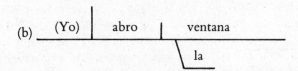

Here, **Yo** is the subject understood; **abro** is the verb; **ventana** is the direct object; **la** is the definite article fem. sing. used with the fem. sing. noun **ventana.**

(c)
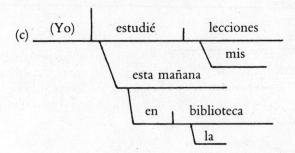

Here, **Yo** is the subject understood; **estudié** is the verb; **lecciones** is the direct object; **mis** is a possessive adjective that modifies **lecciones; esta mañana** has an adverbial value that tells you when the action of the verb took place; **en la biblioteca** is an adverbial prepositional phrase that tells you where the action of the verb took place; hence, they are placed under the words they are related to.

(d)
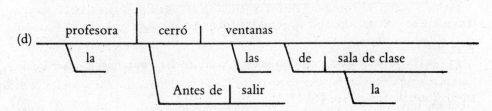

Here, **profesora** is the subject; **la** is the def. art. fem. sing. used with the fem. sing. noun **profesora; cerró** is the verb; **antes de salir** is an adverbial prepositional phrase that tells you when the action of the verb took place; **ventanas** is the direct object; **las** is the def. art. fem. plural used with the fem. plural noun **ventanas** so it is placed under it because it is related to it; **de la sala de clase** is an adjectival prepositional phrase that describes the noun **ventanas; la** is the def. art. sing. fem. used with the fem. sing. noun **sala** and it is placed under it because it is related to it.

§67.8   When the direct object of the verb is a pronoun, it is placed in front of the verb most of the time, generally speaking; at other times it is attached to an infinitive (see **§66.37**); if the main verb is **poder, querer, saber, ir a** + inf., the direct object pronoun may be placed in front of the main verb instead of attaching it to the infinitive (see **§66.38**); at other times, the direct object pronoun is attached to a present participle (see **§66.39**). For an in-depth analysis of the word order of elements in Spanish sentences, particularly pronouns, review **§66.4–§66.53.**

§67.9   Let me diagram the same sentences given above in **§67.7** using them with direct object pronouns instead of direct object nouns so that you may see their position, as in a picture:

(a) **(Yo) le veo** / I see him.

$$\text{(Yo)} \mid \text{le} \mid \text{veo}$$

The subject is **yo** understood; the verb is **veo;** the direct object pronoun is **le** and it is placed directly in front of the verb. Here, you can use **lo** instead of **le** as a dir. obj. pronoun, masc. sing.

(b) **(Yo) la abro** / I open it.

$$\text{(Yo)} \mid \text{la} \mid \text{abro}$$

The subject is **yo** understood; the verb is **abro;** the direct object pronoun is **la** (referring to **la ventana**) and it is placed directly in front of the verb.

(c) **(Yo) las estudié esta mañana en la biblioteca** / I studied them this morning in the library.

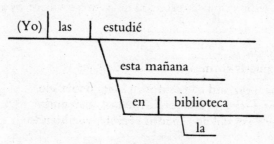

The direct object pronoun **las** (referring to **lecciones**) is placed directly in front of the verb. The other elements in this sentence are the same as in **§67.7(c).**

(d) **Antes de salir, la profesora las cerró** / Before going out, the professor closed them.

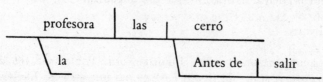

The direct object pronoun **las** (referring to **las ventanas**) is placed directly in front of the verb.

§67.10   For the position of pronouns in other types of sentences in Spanish, review **§66.4–§66.53.**

§67.11   Intransitive verbs

An intransitive verb is a verb that does not take a direct object. Such a verb is called *intransitive* because the action does not pass over from the subject and directly affect anyone or anything.

(a) **La profesora está hablando** / The teacher is talking.

(b) **La señora Gómez salió temprano** / Mrs. Gómez left early.

§67.12   An intransitive verb takes an indirect object:

(a) **La profesora está hablando a los alumnos** / The teacher is talking to the students.

Here, the indirect object noun is **alumnos** because it is preceded by **a los** (to the).

(b) **La profesora les está hablando** / The teacher is talking to them (meaning, of course, **a los alumnos** (to the students).

Here, the indirect object is the pronoun **les,** meaning *to them*.

For a review of direct object pronouns, see **§66.7–§66.13;** for a review of indirect object pronouns, see **§66.14–§66.20.**

§67.13   Of course, a transitive verb can take an indirect object, too:

(a) **La profesora da los libros a los alumnos** / The teacher is giving the books to the pupils.

The direct object is **los libros** and the indirect object is **a los alumnos.**

(b) **La profesora los da a los alumnos** / The teacher is giving them to the pupils.

The direct object pronoun is **los** (meaning **los libros**) and the indirect object noun is still **a los alumnos.**

(c) **La profesora les da los libros** / The teacher is giving the books to them.

The indirect object pronoun is **les** (meaning *to them, i.e.,* **a los alumnos**).

(d) **La profesora se los da** / The teacher is giving them to them.

The indirect object pronoun **les** changes to **se** because **les** is 3rd person and it is followed by **los,** a direct object pronoun, which is also 3rd person. For a review of this point in Spanish grammar, see Position of double object pronouns, beginning in **§66.43,** specifically **§66.52.**

You may clarify the indirect object pronoun **se** in this sentence by adding **a ellos** or **a los alumnos.**

§67.14   Formation of present participle

The present participle is regularly formed from the infinitive:

—**ar** ending verbs, drop the —**ar** and add **ando: hablar, hablando**
—**er** ending verbs, drop the —**er** and add **iendo: beber, bebiendo**
—**ir** ending verbs, drop the —**ir** and add **iendo: recibir, recibiendo**

§67.15   Common irregular present participles

For a listing of all commonly used irregular present participles, see **§58.2.** You ought to know them so that you may be able to recognize them on standardized tests in Spanish that you take.

For uses of the present participle in Spanish, see **§58.3–§58.15.**

§67.16   Verbs with prepositions

§67.17   A verb right after a preposition is in the infinitive form: Pablo salió **sin hablar** / Paul went out **without talking;** María acaba **de llegar** / Mary has just arrived; Elena va **a jugar** / Helen is going to play.

§67.18   On standardized tests in Spanish you may be asked to fill in a blank space by selecting the appropriate preposition that is required after a particular verb. Note the following.

§67.19 **Verbs of motion take the prep. a + inf.**

> **apresurarse a** / to hasten to, to hurry to
> **dirigirse a** / to go to, to go toward
> **ir a** / to go to
> **regresar a** / to return to
> **salir a** / to go out to
> **venir a** / to come to
> **volver a** / to return to

> EXAMPLES:
> **Me apresuré a tomar el tren** / I hurried to take the train.
> **El profesor se dirigió a abrir la puerta** / The teacher went to open the door.
> **María fue a comer** / Mary went to eat.

§67.20 **The following verbs take the prep. a + inf.**

> **acertar a** / to happen to
> **acostumbrarse a** / to become used to, to become accustomed to
> **aficionarse a hacer algo** / to become fond of doing something
> **alcanzar a** / to succeed in (doing something)
> **aprender a** / to learn to, to learn how to
> **aspirar a** / to aspire to
> **atreverse a** / to dare to
> **ayudar a (hacer algo)** / to help to
> **comenzar a** / to begin to
> **condenar a** / to condemn to
> **convidar a** / to invite to
> **decidirse a** / to decide to
> **dedicarse a** / to devote oneself to
> **detenerse a** / to pause to, to stop to
> **disponerse a** / to get ready to
> **echarse a** / to begin to, to start to
> **empezar a** / to begin to, to start to
> **enseñar a** / to teach to
> **exponerse a** / to run the risk of
> **invitar a** / to invite to
> **negarse a** / to refuse to
> **obligar a** / to oblige to, to obligate to
> **ponerse a** / to begin to, to start to
> **prepararse a** / to prepare (oneself) to
> **principiar a** / to begin to, to start to
> **resignarse a** / to resign oneself to
> **resolverse a** / to make up one's mind to
> **someter a** / to submit to, to subdue to
> **venir a** / to end up by
> **volver a** / to (do something) again

> EXAMPLES:
> **Me acostumbré a estudiar mis lecciones todas las noches** / I became used to studying my lessons every evening.
> **No me atreví a responder** / I did not dare to answer.
> **El hombre comenzó a llorar** / The man began to cry.
> **Me dispuse a salir** / I got ready to go out.
> **Me eché a llorar** / I began to cry.
> **El señor Gómez se negó a ir** / Mr. Gómez refused to go.

Juana se puso a correr / Jane began to run.
El muchacho volvió a jugar / The boy played again.

§67.21 **The following verbs take the prep. a + noun** (or pronoun if that is the required dependent element)

acercarse a / to approach
acostumbrarse a / to become accustomed to, to become used to
aficionarse a / to become fond of
asemejarse a / to resemble, to look like
asistir a / to attend, to be present at
asomarse a / to appear at
cuidar a alguien / to take care of someone
dar a / to face, to overlook, to look out upon, to look out over
dedicarse a / to devote oneself to
echar una carta al correo / to mail, to post a letter
echar la culpa a alguien / to blame someone, to put the blame on someone
jugar a / to play (a game, sport, cards)
llegar a ser / to become
llevar a cabo / to carry out, to accomplish
oler a / to smell of, to smell like
parecerse a / to resemble, to look like
querer a / to love
saber a / to taste of, to taste like, to have the flavor of
ser aficionado a / to be fond of, to be a fan of
sonar a / to sound like
subir a / to get on, to get into (a bus, a train, a vehicle)
tocarle a una persona / to be a person's turn

EXAMPLES:

Nos acercamos a la ciudad / We are approaching the city.
Una muchacha bonita se asomó a la puerta / A pretty girl appeared at the door.
Mi cuarto da al jardín / My room faces the garden.
Me dedico a mis estudios / I devote myself to my studies.
Me gusta jugar al tenis / I like to play tennis.
Enrique llegó a ser profesor de matemáticas / Henry became a mathematics teacher.
Jorge llevó a cabo sus responsabilidades / George carried out his responsibilities.
Mi hermano se parece a mi padre y yo me parezco a mi madre / My brother resembles my father and I resemble my mother.
Quiero a mi patria / I love my country.
Soy aficionado a los deportes / I am fond of sports.
Subí al tren / I got on the train.
Le toca a Juan / It is John's turn.

§67.22 **The following verbs take the prep. con + inf.**

amenazar con / to threaten to
contar con / to count on, to rely on
contentarse con / to be satisfied with
soñar con / to dream of, to dream about

EXAMPLES:

Cuento con tener éxito / I am counting on being successful.
Me contento con quedarme en casa / I am satisfied with staying at home.
Sueño con ir a Chile / I dream of going to Chile.

§67.23 **The following verbs take the prep. con + noun** (or pronoun if that is the required dependent element)

acabar con / to finish, to put an end to, to make an end of, to finish off
casarse con / to marry, to get married to
conformarse con / to put up with
contar con / to count on, to rely on
contentarse con / to be satisfied with
cumplir con / to fulfill
dar con / to meet, to find, to come upon
encontrarse con / to run into, to meet by chance
entenderse con / to come to an understanding with
meterse con / to pick a quarrel with
quedarse con / to keep, to hold on to
soñar con / to dream of, to dream about
tropezar con / to come upon, to run across unexpectedly, to run into

EXAMPLES:

José se casó con Ana / Joseph married Anna.
Me conformo con tus ideas / I put up with your ideas.
Contamos con nuestros padres / We count on our parents.
Me contento con poco dinero / I am satisfied with little money.
Siempre cumplo con mi promesa / I always fulfill my promise.
Anoche di con mis amigos en el cine / Last night I met my friends at the movies.
Ayer por la tarde me encontré con un amigo mío / Yesterday afternoon I ran into a friend of mine.
Me quedo con el dinero / I am keeping the money; I am holding on to the money.
Sueño con un verano agradable / I am dreaming of a pleasant summer.

§67.24 **The following verbs take the prep. de + inf.**

acabar de / to have just
acordarse de / to remember to
alegrarse de / to be glad to
arrepentirse de / to repent
cansarse de / to become tired of
cesar de / to cease, to stop
dejar de / to stop, to fail to
encargarse de / to take charge of
haber de / *see* §26.ff
ocuparse de / to be busy with, to attend to
olvidarse de / to forget to
tratar de / to try to
tratarse de / to be a question of

EXAMPLES:

Guillermo acaba de llegar / William has just arrived.
Felipe acababa de partir / Philip had just left.
Me alegro de hablarle / I am glad to talk to you.
Me canso de esperar el autobús / I'm getting tired of waiting for the bus.
Cesó de llover / It stopped raining.
Jaime dejó de escribir la composición / James failed to write the composition.
Mi padre se ocupa de preparar la comida / My father is busy preparing the meal.
Andrés se olvidó de estudiar / Andrew forgot to study.
Siempre trato de hacer un buen trabajo / I always try to do a good job.
Se trata de abstenerse / It is a question of abstaining.

§67.25 **The following verbs take the prep. de + noun** (or pronoun if that is the required dependent element)

abusar de / to abuse, to overindulge in
acordarse de / to remember
alejarse de / to go away from
apartarse de / to keep away from
apoderarse de / to take possession of
aprovecharse de / to take advantage of
bajar de / to get out of, to descend from, to get off
burlarse de / to make fun of
cambiar de / to change (trains, buses, clothes, *etc.*)
cansarse de / to become tired of
carecer de / to lack
compadecerse de / to feel sorry for, to pity, to sympathize with
constar de / to consist of
cuidar de algo / to take care of something
depender de / to depend on
despedirse de / to say good-bye to, to take leave of
despojar de / to take off (clothing)
disfrutar de / to enjoy
enamorarse de / to fall in love with
encogerse de hombros / to shrug one's shoulders
enterarse de / to find out about
fiarse de alguien / to trust someone
gozar de algo / to enjoy something
ocuparse de / to be busy with, to attend to
oír hablar de / to hear of, to hear about
olvidarse de / to forget
pensar de / to think of [**pensar de** is used when asking for an opinion]
perder de vista / to lose sight of
ponerse de acuerdo / to come to an agreement
preocuparse de / to worry about, to be concerned about
quejarse de / to complain about
reírse de / to laugh at
saber de memoria / to know by heart, to memorize
salir de / to go out of, to leave from
servir de / to serve as
servirse de / to make use of, to use
tratarse de / to be a question of, to deal with

EXAMPLES:

Me acuerdo de aquel hombre / I remember that man.
Vamos a aprovecharnos de esta oportunidad / Let's take advantage of this opportunity.
Después de bajar del tren, fui a comer / After getting off the train, I went to eat.
Todos los días cambio de ropa / Every day I change my clothes.
Me canso de este trabajo / I am getting tired of this work.
Esta composición carece de calidad / This composition lacks quality.
Me compadezco de ese pobre hombre / I pity that poor man.
Ahora tengo que despedirme de usted / Now I have to say good-bye.
Eduardo se enamoró de Carmen / Edward fell in love with Carmen.
Mi madre se ocupa de mi padre que está enfermo / My mother is busy with my father who is sick.
Oí hablar de la boda de Anita / I heard about Anita's wedding.

Carlos se olvidó del aniversario de sus padres / Charles forgot about his parents' anniversary.

¿Qué piensa Ud. de nuestro profesor de español? / What do you think of our Spanish teacher?

¡Mira! El mono se ríe de nosotros / Look! The monkey is laughing at us.

Siempre salgo de casa a las ocho de la mañana / I always leave (from, go out of) the house at eight in the morning.

En nuestro club, Cristóbal sirve de presidente / In our club, Christopher serves as president.

§67.26 **The following verbs generally take the prep. en + inf.**

complacerse en / to be pleased to, to delight in
consentir en / to consent to
convenir en / to agree to, to agree on
empeñarse en / to persist in, to insist on
esforzarse en / to strive for, to force oneself to, to try hard to
insistir en / to insist on
quedar en / to agree to, to agree on
tardar en / to be late (to delay) in

EXAMPLES:

La señora Pardo consintió en asistir a la conferencia / Mrs. Pardo consented to attending the meeting.

El muchacho se empeñó en salir / The boy insisted on going out.

Mis amigos insistieron en venir a verme / My friends insisted on coming to see me.

El avión tardó en llegar / The plane was late in arriving.

§67.27 **The following verbs generally take the prep. en + noun** (or pronoun if that is the required dependent element)

apoyarse en / to lean against, to lean on
confiar en / to rely on, to trust in
consistir en / to consist of
convertirse en / to become, to convert to
entrar en / to enter (into), to go into
fijarse en / to stare at, to notice, to take notice, to observe
meterse en / to get involved in, to plunge into
pensar en / to think of, to think about [**pensar en** is used when asking or when stating what or whom a person is thinking of]
ponerse en camino / to set out, to start out
reparar en / to notice, to observe
volver en sí / to regain consciousness, to be oneself again

EXAMPLES:

Me apoyé en la puerta / I leaned against the door.

Entré en el restaurante / I entered (I went in) the restaurant.

¿En qué piensa Ud.? / What are you thinking of?

Pienso en mi trabajo / I am thinking of my work.

¿En quién piensa Ud.? / Whom are you thinking of?

Pienso en mi madre / I am thinking of my mother.

¿En quiénes piensa Ud.? / Whom are you thinking of?

Pienso en mis padres / I am thinking of my parents.

§67.28 **The following verbs generally take the prep. por + inf., noun, pronoun, adj., if that is the required dependent element**

acabar por / to end up by
dar por / to consider, to regard as
darse por / to pretend (to be something), to think oneself (to be something)
estar por / to be in favor of
interesarse por / to take an interest in
pasar por / to be considered as
preguntar por / to ask for, to inquire about
tener por / to consider something, to have an opinion on something
tomar por / to take someone for

EXAMPLES:
Domingo acabó por casarse con Elena / Dominic finally ended up by marrying Helen.
¿Mi libro de español? Lo doy por perdido / My Spanish book? I consider it lost.
La señorita López se da por actriz / Miss López pretends to be an actress.
Estamos por quedarnos en casa esta noche / We are in favor of staying at home this evening.
El señor Pizarro pasa por experto / Mr. Pizarro is considered an expert.
Pregunto por el señor Pardo. ¿Está en casa? / I am asking for Mr. Pardo. Is he at home?

§67.29 **Verb + NO PREPOSITION + inf. The following verbs do not ordinarily take a preposition when followed by an infinitive**

deber + inf. / must, ought to
Debo hacer mis lecciones / I must (ought to) do my lessons.
Exception: *see* **deber de + inf.** in **§20.2.**

decidir + inf. / to decide

dejar + inf. / to allow to, to let
Mi madre me dejó salir / My mother allowed me to go out.
Dejé caer mi libro / I dropped my book (I let my book fall.)

desear + inf. / to desire to, to wish to
Deseo tomar un café / I wish to have a cup of coffee.

esperar + inf. / to expect to, to hope to
Espero ir a la América del Sur este invierno / I expect to go to South America this winter.

hacer + inf. / to do, to make, to have something made or done
Tú me haces llorar / You make me cry.
Mi padre hace construir una casita / My father is having a small house built [by someone].
NOTE that the use of **hacer + inf.** can be described as the "causative (causal)" use of **hacer** when there is an inf. directly after it. The construction **hacer + inf.** indicates that something is being made or being done by someone. Further examples: **hacer firmar** / to have (something) signed (by someone); **hacer confesar** / to have (someone) confess or to make (someone) confess. This causative use of **hacer** is used in a verb tense that is needed + inf. form of the verb which tells what action is being done or being made: **Mi padre hizo construir una casita** / My father had a little house made; **Le haré confesar** / I shall make him confess; **El señor López lo hizo firmar la carta** / Mr. López made him sign the letter.

necesitar + inf. / to need
Necesito pasar una hora en la biblioteca / I need to spend an hour in the library.

oír + inf. / to hear

Le oí entrar por la ventana / I heard him enter through the window.

He oído hablar de su buena fortuna / I have heard (talk) about your good fortune; **He oído decir que la señora Sierra está enferma** / I have heard (tell) that Mrs. Sierra is sick.

pensar + inf. / to intend to, to plan to
Pienso hacer un viaje a México / I plan to take a trip to Mexico.

poder + inf. / to be able to, can
Puedo venir a verle a la una / I can come to see you at one o'clock.

preferir + inf. / to prefer
Prefiero quedarme en casa esta noche / I prefer to stay at home this evening.

prometer + inf. / to promise
Prometo venir a verle a las ocho / I promise to come to see you at eight o'clock.

querer + inf. / to want to, to wish to
Quiero comer ahora / I want to eat now.
¿Qué quiere decir este muchacho? / What does this boy mean?
María quiere hacerse profesora / Mary wants to become a teacher.

saber + inf. / to know how to
¿Sabe Ud. nadar? / Do you know how to swim?
Sí, yo sé nadar / Yes, I know how to swim.

ver + inf. / to see
Veo venir el tren / I see the train coming.

§67.30 The following verbs do not ordinarily require a preposition, whereas in English a preposition is used

agradecer / to thank for, to be thankful (to someone) for (something)
Le agradecí su paciencia / I thanked him for his patience.

aprovechar / to take advantage of
¿No quiere Ud. aprovechar la oportunidad? / Don't you want to take advantage of the opportunity?

buscar / to look for, to search for
Busco mi libro / I am looking for my book.

escuchar / to listen to
Escucho la música / I am listening to the music.

esperar / to wait for
Espero el autobús / I am waiting for the bus.

guardar cama / to stay in bed
La semana pasada guardé cama / Last week I stayed in bed.

lograr / to succeed in
El alumno logró hacerlo / The pupil succeeded in doing it.

mirar / to look at
Miro el cielo / I am looking at the sky.

pagar / to pay for
Pagué los billetes / I paid for the tickets.

pedir / to ask for
Pido un libro / I am asking for a book.

soler + inf. / to be accustomed to, to be in the habit of
(Yo) suelo acompañar a mis amigos en el autobús / I am in the habit of accompanying my friends on the bus.

§67.31 Principal parts of some important verbs

Infinitive	Present Participle	Past Participle	Present Indicative	Preterit
abrir	abriendo	abierto	abro	abrí
andar	andando	andado	ando	anduve
caber	cabiendo	cabido	quepo	cupe
caer	cayendo	caído	caigo	caí
conseguir	consiguiendo	conseguido	consigo	conseguí
construir	construyendo	construido	construyo	construí
corregir	corrigiendo	corregido	corrijo	corregí
creer	creyendo	creído	creo	creí
cubrir	cubriendo	cubierto	cubro	cubrí
dar	dando	dado	doy	di
decir	diciendo	dicho	digo	dije
descubrir	descubriendo	descubierto	descubro	descubrí
deshacer	deshaciendo	deshecho	deshago	deshice
despedirse	despidiéndose	despedido	me despido	me despedí
destruir	destruyendo	destruido	destruyo	destruí
devolver	devolviendo	devuelto	devuelvo	devolví
divertirse	divirtiéndose	divertido	me divierto	me divertí
dormir	durmiendo	dormido	duermo	dormí
escribir	escribiendo	escrito	escribo	escribí
estar	estando	estado	estoy	estuve
haber	habiendo	habido	he	hube
hacer	haciendo	hecho	hago	hice
huir	huyendo	huido	huyo	huí
ir	yendo	ido	voy	fui
irse	yéndose	ido	me voy	me fui
leer	leyendo	leído	leo	leí
mentir	mintiendo	mentido	miento	mentí
morir	muriendo	muerto	muero	morí
oír	oyendo	oído	oigo	oí
oler	oliendo	olido	huelo	olí
pedir	pidiendo	pedido	pido	pedí
poder	pudiendo	podido	puedo	pude
poner	poniendo	puesto	pongo	puse
querer	queriendo	querido	quiero	quise
reír	riendo	reído	río	reí
repetir	repitiendo	repetido	repito	repetí
resolver	resolviendo	resuelto	resuelvo	resolví
romper	rompiendo	roto	rompo	rompí
saber	sabiendo	sabido	sé	supe
salir	saliendo	salido	salgo	salí
seguir	siguiendo	seguido	sigo	seguí
sentir	sintiendo	sentido	siento	sentí
ser	siendo	sido	soy	fui
servir	sirviendo	servido	sirvo	serví
tener	teniendo	tenido	tengo	tuve
traer	trayendo	traído	traigo	traje
venir	viniendo	venido	vengo	vine
ver	viendo	visto	veo	vi
vestir	vistiendo	vestido	visto	vestí
volver	volviendo	vuelto	vuelvo	volví

§67.32 **Orthographical (spelling) changes in verb forms and stem-changing (radical-changing) verb forms.** See Present Indicative, **§68.19**; Preterit, **§68.30**; Present Subjunctive, **§68.42–§68.49**; Imperfect Subjunctive, **§68.51–§68.54**.

§67.33 **Subjunctive**

The subjunctive is not a tense; it is a mood or mode. Usually, when we speak in Spanish or English, we use the indicative mood. We use the subjunctive mood in Spanish for certain reasons. The following are the principal reasons.

§67.34 **After certain conjunctions**

When the following conjunctions introduce a new clause, the verb in that new clause is in the subjunctive mood:

a fin de que / so that, in order that
a menos que / unless
a no ser que / unless
antes que *or* **antes de que** / before
como si / as if
con tal que *or* **con tal de que** / provided that
en caso que *or* **en caso de que** / in case, in case that, supposing that
para que / in order that, so that
sin que / without

EXAMPLES:

§67.35 **Se lo explico a ustedes a fin de que puedan comprenderlo** / I am explaining it to you so that (in order that) you may be able to understand it.

§67.36 **Saldré a las tres y media a menos que esté lloviendo** / I will go out at three thirty unless it is raining.

§67.37 When the following conjunctions introduce a new clause, the verb in that new clause is sometimes in the indicative mood, sometimes in the subjunctive mood. Use the subjunctive mood if what is being expressed indicates some sort of anxious anticipation, doubt, indefiniteness, vagueness, or uncertainty. If these are not implied and if the action was completed in the past, use the indicative mood:

a pesar de que / in spite of the fact that
así que / as soon as, after
aunque / although, even if, even though
cuando / when
de manera que / so that, so as
de modo que / so that, in such a way that
después que *or* **después de que** / after
en cuanto / as soon as
hasta que / until
luego que / as soon as, after
mientras / while, as long as
siempre que / whenever, provided that
tan pronto como / as soon as

EXAMPLES:

§67.38 **Le daré el dinero a Roberto cuando me lo pida** / I shall give the money to Robert when he asks me for it. (**pida** is in the subjunctive mood because some doubt or uncertainty is suggested and Robert may not ask for it)

§67.39 **BUT: Se lo di a Roberto cuando me lo pidió** / I gave it to Robert when he asked me for it. (No subjunctive of **pedir** here because he actually did ask me for it.)

§67.40 **Esperaré hasta que llegue el autobús** / I shall wait until the bus arrives. **(llegue is in the subjunctive mood here because some doubt or uncertainty is suggested and the bus may never arrive)**

§67.41 BUT: **Esperé hasta que llegó el autobús** / I waited until the bus arrived. **(No subjunctive of llegar here because the bus actually did arrive)**

§67.42 **Trabajaré hasta que Ud. venga** / I shall work until you come. **(venga is used here because some doubt or uncertainty is suggested and Ud. may never come)**

§67.43 BUT: **Trabajé hasta que Ud. vino** / I worked until you came. (No subjunctive of **venir** here because **Ud.** actually did come)

§67.44 **After certain adverbs**

acaso
quizá *or* **quizás** ⎫ perhaps, maybe
tal vez ⎭

§67.45 **Tal vez hayan perdido** / Perhaps they have lost. (Subjunctive is used here because some degree of uncertainty or pessimism is implied.)

§67.46 **Tal vez han ganado** / Perhaps they have won. (No subjunctive is used here because some degree of certainty or optimism is implied.)

§67.47 **Por + adj.** or **adv. + que** / however, no matter how

§67.48 **Por (más) interesante que sea, no quiero ver esa película** / No matter how interesting it may be, I do not want to see that film.

§67.49 **Por bien que juegue Roberto, no quiero jugar con él** / However well (No matter how well) Robert plays, I do not want to play with him.

§67.50 **After certain indefinite expressions**

cualquier, cualquiera, cualesquier, cualesquiera / whatever, whichever, any (the final **a** drops in **cualquiera** and **cualesquiera** when the word is in front of a noun)
cuandoquiera / whenever
dondequiera / wherever; **adondequiera** / to wherever
quienquiera, quienesquiera / whoever

EXAMPLES:

§67.51 **No abriré la puerta, quienquiera que sea** / I will not open the door, whoever it may be.

§67.52 **Dondequiera que Ud. esté, escríbame** / Wherever you may be, write to me.

§67.53 **Adondequiera que Ud. vaya, dígamelo** / Wherever you may go, tell me.

§67.54 **After an indefinite or negative antecedent**
See **§66.71** for a brief definition of an antecedent with examples. Remember to use the General Index for references to explanations and examples located in different parts of this book.

§67.55 The reason why the subjunctive is needed after an indefinite or negative antecedent is that the person or thing desired may possibly not exist; or, if it does exist, you may never find it.

EXAMPLES:

§67.56 **Busco un libro que sea interesante** / I am looking for a book which is interesting.

§67.57 BUT: **Tengo un libro que es interesante** / I have a book which is interesting.

§67.58 ¿Conoce Ud. a alguien que tenga paciencia? / Do you know someone who has patience?

§67.59 BUT: Conozco a alguien que tiene paciencia / I know someone who has patience.

§67.60 No encontré a nadie que supiera la respuesta / I did not find anyone who knew the answer.

§67.61 No encuentro a nadie que sepa la respuesta / I do not find anyone who knows the answer.

§67.62 BUT: Encontré a alguien que sabe la respuesta / I found someone who knows the answer.

§67.63 No puedo encontrar a nadie que pueda prestarme dinero / I can't meet (find) anyone who can lend me money.

§67.64 BUT: Conozco a alguien que puede prestarme dinero / I know somebody who can lend me money.

§67.65 AND: Encontré a alguien que puede prestarme dinero / I met (found) someone who can lend me money.

§67.66 **After ¡Que . . . !**

In order to express indirectly a wish, an order, a command in the 3rd person singular or plural, you may use the exclamatory ¡Que . . . ! alone to introduce the subjunctive clause. The words generally understood to be omitted are: Quiero que . . . or Deje que . . . , which mean I want . . . or Let . . . Examples:

¡Que lo haga Jorge! / Let George do it! (In other words, the complete statement would be: ¡Deje que lo haga Jorge! or ¡Quiero que lo haga Jorge! / I want George to do it!

¡Que entre! / Let him enter! or I want him to enter! (¡Quiero que entre!)

§67.67 **After ¡Ojalá que . . . !**

§67.68 The exclamatory expression **Ojalá** is of Arabic origin meaning "Oh, God!" (Oh, Allah!). Examples:

§67.69 ¡Ojalá que vengan! / If only they would come! (Would that they come! Oh, God, let them come!)

§67.70 ¡Ojalá que lleguen! / If only they would arrive! (Would that they arrive! Oh, God, let them arrive!)

§67.71 **After certain impersonal expressions**

Generally speaking, the following impersonal expressions require the subjunctive form of the verb in the clause that follows.

§67.72 Basta que . . . / It is enough that . . . ; It is sufficient that . . .
Conviene que . . . / It is fitting that . . . ; It is proper that . . .
Importa que . . . / It is important that . . .
Más vale que . . . / It is better that . . .
Es aconsejable que . . . / It is advisable that . . .
Es bueno que . . . / It is good that . . .
Es importante que . . . / It is important that . . .
Es imposible que . . . / It is impossible that . . .
Es lástima que . . . / It is a pity that . . .
Es malo que . . . / It is bad that . . .
Es mejor que . . . / It is better that . . .
Es menester que . . . / It is necessary that . . .
Es necesario que . . . / It is necessary that . . .
Es posible que . . . / It is possible that . . .
Es preciso que . . . / It is necessary that . . .

Es probable que . . . / It is probable that . . .
Es raro que . . . / It is rare that . . .
Es urgente que . . . / It is urgent that . . .

    EXAMPLES:

§67.73   **Basta que sepan la verdad** / It is sufficient that they know the truth.

§67.74   **Conviene que venga ahora mismo** / It is proper that she come right now.

§67.75   **Es aconsejable que salga inmediatamente** / It is advisable that she leave immediately.

§67.76   **Es probable que María regrese a las tres** / It is probable that Mary will return at three o'clock.

§67.77   **Es necesario que Ud. escriba la composición** / It is necessary that you write the composition *or* It is necessary for you to write the composition.

§67.78   **After verbs or expressions that indicate denial, doubt or lack of belief, and uncertainty**

dudar que . . . / to doubt that . . .
negar que . . . / to deny that . . .
no creer que . . . / not to believe that . . .
Es dudoso que . . . / It is doubtful that . . .
Es incierto que . . . / It is uncertain that . . .
Hay duda que . . . / There is doubt that . . .
No es cierto que . . . / It is not certain that . . .
No estar seguro que . . . / Not to be sure that . . .
No suponer que . . . / Not to suppose that . . .

    EXAMPLES:

§67.79   **Dudo que mis amigos vengan a verme** / I doubt that my friends are coming (will come) to see me.

§67.80   **No creo que sea urgente** / I do not believe that it is urgent.

§67.81   **Es dudoso que Pablo lo haga** / It is doubtful that Paul will do it.

§67.82   **After verbs or expressions that indicate an emotion of joy, gladness, happiness, sorrow, regret, fear, surprise**

§67.83   estar contento que . . . / to be happy that . . . , to be pleased that . . .
estar feliz que . . . / to be happy that . . .
estar triste que . . . / to be sad that . . .
alegrarse (de) que . . . / to be glad that . . .
sentir que . . . / to regret that . . . , to feel sorry that . . .
sorprenderse (de) que . . . / to be surprised that . . .
temer que . . . / to fear that . . .
tener miedo (de) que . . . / to be afraid that . . .

    EXAMPLES:

§67.84   **Estoy muy contento que mis amigos vengan a verme** / I am very pleased that my friends are coming (will come) to see me.

§67.85   **Me alegro de que ellos hayan venido** / I am glad that they have come.

§67.86   **Siento mucho que su madre esté enferma** / I am very sorry that your mother is ill.

§67.87   **After certain verbs that imply a wish or desire that something be done, including a command, order, preference, advice, permission, request, plea, insistence, suggestion**

aconsejar / to advise
consentir / to consent
decir / to tell (someone to do something)
dejar / to allow, to let
desear / to want, to wish
esperar / to hope
exigir / to demand, to require
hacer / to make (someone do something or that something be done)
insistir (en) / to insist (on, upon)
mandar / to order, to command
pedir / to ask, to request
permitir / to allow, to permit
preferir / to prefer
prohibir / to forbid, to prohibit
querer / to want, to wish (someone to do something or that something be done)
recomendar / to recommend
rogar / to beg, to request
sugerir / to suggest
suplicar / to beg, to plead, to make a plea

EXAMPLES:

§67.88 **Les aconsejo a ellos que hagan el trabajo** / I advise them to do the work.

§67.89 **Les digo a ellos que escriban los ejercicios** / I am telling them to write the exercises.

§67.90 **Mi madre quiere que yo vaya a la escuela ahora** / My mother wants me to go to school now.

§67.91 BUT: **Yo quiero ir a la escuela ahora** / I want to go to school now.

§67.92 NOTE: In this example, there is no change in subject; therefore, the infinitive **ir** is used. But in the example in §67.90, there is a new subject (**yo**) in the dependent clause and **ir** is in the subjunctive because the verb **querer** is used in the main clause.

§67.93 **El capitán me manda que yo entre** / The captain orders me to come in.

§67.94 OR: **El capitán me manda entrar** / The captain orders me to come in.
(NOTE that **mandar** can take a new clause in the subjunctive or it can take an infinitive)

§67.95 **El coronel me permite que yo salga** / The colonel permits me to leave.

§67.96 OR: **El coronel me permite salir** / The colonel permits me to leave.
(NOTE that **permitir** can take a new clause in the subjunctive or it can take an infinitive. You can do the same with the verbs **dejar, hacer, mandar** and **prohibir**.)

§67.97 **Mi profesor exige que yo escriba los ejercicios** / My professor demands that I write the exercises.

§67.98 **Espero que mi perrito vuelva pronto** / I hope that my little dog returns soon.

§67.99 **Le ruego a usted que me devuelva mi libro** / I beg you to return my book to me.

§67.100 IN SUM, NOTE THAT:

(a) Beginning with §67.33, the subjunctive form of the verb in the dependent clause is used because what precedes is either a certain conjunction, a certain adverb, the expression **por + adj.** or **adv. + que,** a certain indefinite expression, an indefinite or negative antecedent, a superlative, an indirect wish or command or order introduced by **¡Que**

. . . ! (which is short for **"Quiero que . . .** or **"Deje que . . ."**), **¡Ojalá que . . . !** or a certain impersonal expression, or a certain verb (**§67.78–§67.99**).

(b) When you are dealing with two different subjects, you need two clauses: the main clause (also known as independent clause) and the dependent clause which contains the new subject. See, for example, **§67.90**. When there is no change in subject, there is no need for a second clause, as in **§67.91**.

(c) Generally speaking, only the verbs **dejar, hacer, mandar, permitir, prohibir** (as in **§67.93–§67.96**) can be followed by just the infinitive or a new clause with its verb in the subjunctive.

(d) In English, it is possible not to use a second clause even when the subject changes and to use an infinitive, but this is not so in Spanish—except for what is noted in **§67.93–§67.96**. Example: I want you to leave / **Quiero que Ud. salga.**

§67.101   **Sequence of tenses when the subjunctive is required: a summary**

When the verb in the main clause is in the:	The verb in the following clause (the dependent clause) most likely will be in the:
1. Present Indicative or Future or Present Perfect Indicative or Imperative (Command)	1. Present Subjunctive or Present Perfect Subjunctive
2. Conditional or a past tense (Imperfect Indicative or Preterit or Pluperfect Indicative)	2. Imperfect Subjunctive or Pluperfect Subjunctive

EXAMPLES:

§67.102   **Deseo que Ana cante** / I want Anna to sing.

§67.103   **Le diré a Ana que baile** / I will tell Anna to dance.

§67.104   **Le he dicho a Ana que cante y baile** / I have said to Anna to sing and dance.

§67.105   **Dígale a Ana que cante y baile** / Tell Anna to sing and dance.

§67.106   **Dudo que mi madre tome el tren** / I doubt that my mother is taking (*or* will take) the train.

§67.107   **Dudo que mi madre haya tomado el tren** / I doubt that my mother has taken the train.

§67.108   **Le gustaría al profesor que los alumnos hicieran los ejercicios** / The professor would like the pupils to do the exercises.

§67.109   **Sentía que su madre estuviera enferma** / I felt sorry that your mother was ill.

§67.110   **Dudé que mi madre hubiera tomado el tren** / I doubted that my mother had taken the train.

§67.111   Si clause: a summary of contrary-to-fact conditions

When the verb in the **Si** clause is:	The verb in the main or result clause is:
1. Present Indicative	1. Future

Example: **Si tengo bastante tiempo, vendré a verle** / If I have enough time, I will come to see you.

Note that the present subjunctive form of a verb is never used in a clause beginning with the conjunction *si*.

2. Imperfect Subjunctive (**-se** form or **-ra** form)	2. Conditional or Imperfect Subjunctive (**-ra** form)

Example: **Si yo tuviese** (*or* **tuviera**) **bastante tiempo, vendría a verle** / If I had enough time, I would come to see you.

    OR: **Si yo tuviese** (*or* **tuviera**) **bastante tiempo, viniera a verle** / If I had enough time, I would come to see you.

3. Pluperfect Subjunctive (**-se** form or **-ra** form)	3. Conditional Perfect or Pluperfect Subjunctive (**-ra** form)

Example: **Si yo hubiese tenido** (*or* **hubiera tenido**) **bastante tiempo, habría venido a verle** / If I had had enough time, I would have come to see you.

    OR: **Si yo hubiese tenido** (*or* **hubiera tenido**) **bastante tiempo, hubiera venido a verle** / If I had had enough time, I would have come to see you.

§68. THE NAMES OF TENSES AND MOODS IN SPANISH WITH ENGLISH EQUIVALENTS ARE AS FOLLOWS:

Spanish

Los tiempos simples

1. **Presente de indicativo**
2. **Imperfecto de indicativo**
3. **Pretérito**
4. **Futuro**
5. **Potencial simple**
6. **Presente de subjuntivo**
7. **Imperfecto de subjuntivo**

Los tiempos compuestos

8. **Perfecto de indicativo**
9. **Pluscuamperfecto de indicativo**
10. **Pretérito anterior**
11. **Futuro perfecto**
12. **Potencial compuesto**
13. **Perfecto de subjuntivo**
14. **Pluscuamperfecto de subjuntivo**

English

The simple tenses

1. Present indicative
2. Imperfect indicative
3. Preterit
4. Future
5. Conditional
6. Present subjunctive
7. Imperfect subjunctive

The compound tenses

8. Present perfect indicative
9. Pluperfect *or* Past perfect indicative
10. Past anterior *or* Preterit perfect
11. Future perfect *or* Future anterior
12. Conditional perfect
13. Present perfect *or* Past subjunctive
14. Pluperfect *or* Past perfect subjunctive

Imperative *or* Command **(Imperativo)**

§68.1   OBSERVATIONS:

§68.2   In Spanish, there are 7 simple tenses and 7 compound tenses. A simple tense means that the verb form consists of one word. A compound tense means that the verb form consists of two words (the auxiliary verb and the past participle). The auxiliary verb is also called a helping verb and in Spanish, as you know, it is any of the 7 simple tenses of **haber** *(to have)*.

§68.3   Each compound tense is based on each simple tense. The 14 tenses given above are arranged in the following logical order:

§68.4   Tense number 8 is based on Tense number 1; in other words, you form the **Perfecto de indicativo** by using the auxiliary **haber** in the **Presente de indicativo** plus the past participle of the verb you are dealing with.

§68.5   Tense number 9 is based on Tense number 2; in other words, you form the **Pluscuamperfecto de indicativo** by using the auxiliary **haber** in the **Imperfecto de indicativo** plus the past participle of the verb you are dealing with.

§68.6   Tense number 10 is based on Tense number 3; in other words, you form the **Pretérito anterior** by using the auxiliary **haber** in the **Pretérito** plus the past participle of the verb you are dealing with.

§68.7   Tense number 11 is based on Tense number 4; in other words, you form the **Futuro perfecto** by using the auxiliary **haber** in the **Futuro** plus the past participle of the verb you are dealing with.

§68.8   Tense number 12 is based on Tense number 5; in other words, you form the **Potencial compuesto** by using the auxiliary **haber** in the **Potencial simple** plus the past participle of the verb you are dealing with.

§68.9   Tense number 13 is based on Tense number 6; in other words, you form the **Perfecto de subjuntivo** by using the auxiliary **haber** in the **Presente de subjuntivo** plus the past participle of the verb you are dealing with.

§68.10   Tense number 14 is based on Tense number 7; in other words, you form the **Pluscuamperfecto de subjuntivo** by using the auxiliary **haber** in the **Imperfecto de subjuntivo** plus the past participle of the verb you are dealing with.

§68.11   What does all the above mean? This: If you ever expect to know or even recognize the meaning of any of the 7 compound tenses, you certainly have to know **haber** in the 7 simple tenses. If you do not, you cannot form the 7 compound tenses. This is one perfect example to illustrate that learning Spanish verb forms is a cumulative experience. In order to know the 7 compound tenses, you must first know the forms of **haber** in the 7 simple tenses, which are as follows. Study them or memorize them!

HABER (helping verb) in the 7 simple tenses

Present participle: **habiendo**   Past participle: **habido**   Infinitive: **haber**

1. **Presente indicativo**	**he, has, ha;** **hemos, habéis, han**
Present indicative	I have, you have, you *or* he *or* she *or* it has; we have, you have, you *or* they have
2. **Imperfecto indicativo**	**había, habías, había;** **habíamos, habíais, habían**
Imperfect indicative	I had, you had, you *or* he *or* she *or* it had; we had, you had, you *or* they had
3. **Pretérito**	**hube, hubiste, hubo;** **hubimos, hubisteis, hubieron**
Preterit	I had, you had, you *or* he *or* she *or* it had; we had, you had, you *or* they had

4. Futuro

habré, habrás, habrá;
habremos, habréis, habrán

Future

I shall have, you will have, you *or* he *or* she *or* it will have; we shall have, you will have, you *or* they will have

5. Potencial simple

habría, habrías, habría;
habríamos, habríais, habrían

Conditional

I would have, you would have, you *or* he *or* she *or* it would have; we would have, you would have, you *or* they would have

6. Presente subjuntivo

haya, hayas, haya;
hayamos, hayáis, hayan

Present subjunctive

that I may have, that you may have, that you *or* he *or* she *or* it may have; that we may have, that you may have, that you *or* they may have

7. Imperfecto subjuntivo

(the **-ra** form): **hubiera, hubieras, hubiera;**
hubiéramos, hubierais, hubieran

OR

(the **-se** form): **hubiese, hubieses, hubiese;**
hubiésemos, hubieseis, hubiesen

Imperfect subjunctive

that I might have, that you might have, that you *or* he *or* she *or* it might have; that we might have, that you might have, that you *or* they might have

NOTE: The subject pronouns in Spanish have been omitted above in order to emphasize the verb forms of the auxiliary verb **haber** in the 7 simple tenses, which you must know so that you can form the 7 compound tenses from these. As you know, the subject pronouns are as follows:

Singular: **yo, tú, Ud.** *or* **él** *or* **ella;**
Plural: **nosotros (nosotras), vosotros (vosotras), Uds.** *or* **ellos** *or* **ellas**

§68.12 COMPARISON OF MEANINGS AND USES OF SPANISH VERB TENSES AND MOODS AS RELATED TO ENGLISH VERB TENSES AND MOODS

§68.13   The following verb tenses and moods are presented in the same numbered order as given in §68.–§68.11. Compare them with these that follow here.

§68.14   **Tense No. 1: Presente de indicativo** (Present indicative)
This tense is used most of the time in Spanish and English. It indicates:

(a) An action or a state of being at the present time.
EXAMPLES:
1. **Hablo** español / *I speak* Spanish, or *I am speaking* Spanish, or *I do speak* Spanish.
2. **Creo en** Dios / *I believe* in God.

(b) Habitual action.
EXAMPLE:
Voy a la biblioteca todos los días / *I go* to the library every day, or *I do go* to the library every day.

(c) A general truth, something which is permanently true.
EXAMPLES:
1. Seis menos dos **son** cuatro / Six minus two *are* four.
2. El ejercicio **hace** maestro al novicio / Practice *makes* perfect.

(d) Vividness when talking or writing about past events.
EXAMPLE:
El asesino **se pone** pálido. **Tiene** miedo. **Sale** de la casa y **corre** a lo largo del río / The murderer *turns* pale. *He is* afraid. *He goes out* of the house and *runs* along the river.

(e) A near future.

EXAMPLES:

Mi hermano **llega** mañana / My brother *arrives* tomorrow.

¿Escuchamos un disco ahora? / Shall we listen to a record now?

(f) An action or state of being that occurred in the past and *continues up to the present.* In Spanish this is an idiomatic use of the *Present tense* of a verb with **hace,** which is also in the *Present.*

EXAMPLE:

Hace tres horas que **miro** la televisión / *I have been watching* television for three hours. See also §28.–§31.

(g) The meaning of *almost* or *nearly* when used with **por poco.**

EXAMPLE:

Por poco me **matan** / They almost *killed* me.

§68.15　**This tense is regularly formed as follows:**

§68.16　Drop the —**ar** ending of an infinitive, like **hablar,** and add the following endings: **o, as, a; amos, áis, an**

You then get: **hablo, hablas, habla;**
hablamos, habláis, hablan

§68.17　Drop the —**er** ending of an infinitive, like **beber,** and add the following endings: **o, es, e; emos, éis, en**

You then get: **bebo, bebes, bebe;**
bebemos, bebéis, beben

§68.18　Drop the —**ir** ending of an infinitive, like **recibir,** and add the following endings: **o, es, e; imos, ís, en**

You then get: **recibo, recibes, recibe;**
recibimos, recibís, reciben

§68.19　**Verbs irregular in the present indicative, including stem-changing verbs and orthographical changing verbs**

NOTE that the first three forms up to the semicolon are the 1st, 2nd, and 3rd persons of the singular; the three verb forms under those are the 1st, 2nd, and 3rd persons of the plural. The subject pronouns are not given in order to emphasize the verb forms. See my note at the end of **§68.11** where **haber** is given in all its forms in the seven simple tenses. See also **§66.4.**

acertar / to hit the mark, to hit upon, to do (something) right
acierto, aciertas, acierta;
acertamos, acertáis, aciertan

This is a stem-changing verb. The **e** in the stem changes to **ie** when stressed.

acordar / to agree (upon)
acuerdo, acuerdas, acuerda;
acordamos, acordáis, acuerdan

This is a stem-changing verb. The **o** in the stem changes to **ue** when stressed.

acordarse / to remember
me acuerdo, te acuerdas, se acuerda;
nos acordamos, os acordáis, se acuerdan

This is a stem-changing verb. The **o** in the stem changes to **ue** when stressed.

acostarse / to go to bed, to lie down
me acuesto, te acuestas, se acuesta;
nos acostamos, os acostáis, se acuestan

This is a stem-changing verb. The **o** in the stem changes to **ue** when stressed.

actuar / to act, to actuate
actúo, actúas, actúa;
actuamos, actuáis, actúan

This —**uar** verb is a stem-changing verb. The **u** in the stem changes to **ú** when stressed.

adquirir / to acquire, to get, to obtain
adquiero, adquieres, adquiere;
adquirimos, adquirís, adquieren

This is a stem-changing verb. The **i** in the stem changes to **ie** when stressed.

advertir / to notify, to warn, to give notice, to give warning
adv**ie**rto, adv**ie**rtes, adv**ie**rte;
advertimos, advertís, adv**ie**rten

This is a stem-changing verb. The **e** in the stem changes to **ie** when stressed. Present participle is **advirtiendo**.

afligir / to afflict, to grieve
afli**j**o, afli**g**es, afli**g**e;
afli**g**imos, afli**g**ís, afli**g**en

This is an orthographical changing verb, which means that it changes in spelling. The **g** changes to **j** in front of **o** or **a** in order to keep its original sound of *h*, as in the English word *hello*.

almorzar / to lunch, to have lunch
alm**ue**rzo, alm**ue**rzas, alm**ue**rza;
almorzamos, almorzáis, alm**ue**rzan

This is a stem-changing verb. The **o** in the stem changes to **ue** when stressed.

aparecer / to appear, to show up
apare**zc**o, apareces, aparece;
aparecemos, aparecéis, aparecen

This —**cer** verb changes only in the 1st person singular where the **c** changes to **zc**.

apretar / to squeeze, to tighten, to clench
apr**ie**to, apr**ie**tas, apr**ie**ta;
apretamos, apretáis, apr**ie**tan

This is a stem-changing verb. The **e** in the stem changes to **ie** when stressed.

ascender / to ascend
asc**ie**ndo, asc**ie**ndes, asc**ie**nde;
ascendemos, ascendéis, asc**ie**nden

This is a stem-changing verb. The **e** in the stem changes to **ie** when stressed.

asir / to grasp, to seize
as**g**o, ases, ase;
asimos, asís, asen

This verb is irregular only in the 1st person singular of this tense because the letter **g** is added.

atravesar / to cross, to go through, to run through
atrav**ie**so, atrav**ie**sas, atrav**ie**sa;
atravesamos, atravesáis, atrav**ie**san

This is a stem-changing verb. The **e** in the stem changes to **ie** when stressed.

atribuir / to attribute
atribu**y**o, atribu**y**es, atribu**y**e;
atribuimos, atribuís, atribu**y**en

This —**uir** verb requires the insertion of the letter **y** in front of the regular present tense endings **o, es, e,** and **en.** Pres. part. is **atribuyendo.**

bendecir / to bless
bendigo, bendices, bendice;
bendecimos, bendecís, **bendicen**

In addition to the four irregular forms noted here, the past participle is ordinarily **bendecido** but it changes to **bendito** when used as an adjective with **estar** and requires an agreement in gender and number. Also, the pres. part. is **bendiciendo.**

caber / to fit, to be contained
quepo, cabes, cabe;
cabemos, cabéis, caben

Irregular in the 1st pers. sing. only in this tense.

caer / to fall
caigo, caes, cae;
caemos, caéis, caen

Irregular in the 1st pers. sing. only in this tense. Pres. part. is **cayendo.**

calentar / to warm (up), to heat
cal**ie**nto, cal**ie**ntas, cal**ie**nta;
calentamos, calentáis, cal**ie**ntan

A stem-changing verb. The **e** in the stem changes to **ie** when stressed.

cerrar / to close
c**ie**rro, c**ie**rras, c**ie**rra;
cerramos, cerráis, c**ie**rran

A stem-changing verb. The **e** in the stem changes to **ie** when stressed.

cocer / to cook
c**ue**zo, c**ue**ces, c**ue**ce;
cocemos, cocéis, c**ue**cen

A stem-changing and orthographical changing verb. The **o** in the stem changes to **ue** when stressed. Also, this —**cer** verb changes **c** to **z** in front of **o** or **a.**

coger / to seize, to grasp, to grab, to catch
co**j**o, co**g**es, co**g**e;
co**g**emos, co**g**éis, co**g**en

An orthographical changing verb. This —**ger** verb changes **g** to **j** in front of **o** or **a.**

colegir / to collect
coli**j**o, coli**g**es, coli**g**e;
colegimos, colegís, coligen

An orthographical and stem-changing verb. This —**gir** verb changes **g** to **j** in front of **o** or **a.** Also, **e** in stem changes to **i** when stressed. Pres. part. is **coligiendo.**

colgar / to hang
cuelgo, cuelgas, cuelga;
colgamos, colgáis, cuelgan

A stem-changing verb. The **o** in the stem changes to **ue** when stressed.

comenzar / to begin, to start, to commence
comienzo, comienzas, comienza;
comenzamos, comenzáis, comienzan

A stem-changing verb. The **e** in the stem changes to **ie** when stressed.

concluir / to conclude, to end
concluyo, concluyes, concluye;
concluimos, concluís, concluyen

This —**uir** verb requires the insertion of **y** in front of the regular present tense endings **o, es, e,** and **en**. Pres. part. is **concluyendo.**

conducir / to conduct, to lead, to drive
conduzco, conduces, conduce;
conducimos, conducís, conducen

This —**cir** verb changes only in the 1st pers. sing. of this tense where the **c** changes to **zc.**

confesar / to confess
confieso, confiesas, confiesa;
confesamos, confesáis, confiesan

A stem-changing verb. The **e** in the stem changes to **ie** when stressed.

confiar (en) / to rely (on), to confide (in)
confío, confías, confía;
confiamos, confiáis, confían

This —**iar** verb changes **i** to **í** in the stem when stressed in order to split the dipthongs **io, ia.**

conocer / to know, to be acquainted with
conozco, conoces, conoce;
conocemos, conocéis, conocen

An orthographical changing verb. This —**cer** verb changes **c** to **zc** only in the 1st pers. sing. of this tense.

conseguir / to get, to obtain, to attain, to succeed in
consigo, consigues, consigue;
conseguimos, conseguís, consiguen

A stem-changing and orthographical changing verb. The **e** in the stem changes to **i** when stressed and the **u** in the stem drops only in the 1st pers. sing. in this tense. Pres. part. is **consiguiendo.**

consentir / to consent
consiento, consientes, consiente;
consentimos, consentís, consienten

A stem-changing verb. The **e** in the stem changes to **ie** when stressed. Pres. part. is **consintiendo.**

constituir / to constitute
constituyo, constituyes, constituye;
constituimos, constituís, constituyen

This —**uir** verb requires the insertion of **y** in front of the regular present tense endings **o, es, e,** and **en**. Pres. part. is **constituyendo.**

construir / to construct, to build
construyo, construyes, construye;
construimos, construís, construyen

This —**uir** verb requires the insertion of **y** in front of the regular present tense endings **o, es, e,** and **en**. Pres. part. is **construyendo.**

contar / to count, to relate
cuento, cuentas, cuenta;
contamos, contáis, cuentan

A stem-changing verb. The **o** in the stem changes to **ue** when stressed.

contener / to contain, to hold
contengo, contienes, contiene;
contenemos, contenéis, contienen

A stem-changing verb and an irregular form in the 1st pers. sing. of this tense. The **e** in the stem changes to **ie** when stressed.

continuar / to continue
continúo, continúas, continúa;
continuamos, continuáis, continúan

This —**uar** verb is a stem-changing verb. The **u** in the stem changes to **ú** when stressed.

contribuir / to contribute
contribuyo, contribuyes, contribuye;
contribuimos, contribuís, contribuyen

This —**uir** verb requires the insertion of **y** in front of the regular present tense endings **o, es, e,** and **en**. Pres. part. is **contribuyendo.**

convencer / to convince
convenzo, convences, convence;
convencemos, convencéis, convencen

An orthographical changing verb. This —**cer** verb changes **c** and **z** in front of **o** or **a.**

convertir / to convert
convierto, conviertes, convierte;
convertimos, convertís, convierten

A stem-changing verb. The **e** in the stem changes to **ie** when stressed. Pres. part. is **convirtiendo.**

corregir / to correct
corrijo, corriges, corrige;
corregimos, corregís, corrigen

An orthographical and stem-changing verb. The **g** changes to **j** in front of **o** or **a** in order to keep its original sound of *h*, as in the English word *hello*. Also, **e** in stem changes to **i** when stressed. Pres. part. is **corrigiendo**.

costar / to cost
cuesta;
cuestan

An impersonal verb used in the 3rd pers. sing. and plural. A stem-changing verb. The **o** in the stem changes to **ue** because of stress.

crecer / to grow
crezco, creces, crece;
crecemos, crecéis, crecen

An orthographical changing verb. This —**cer** verb changes **c** to **zc** only in the 1st pers. sing. of this tense.

dar / to give
doy, das, da;
damos, **dais**, dan

An irregular form in the 1st pers. sing. and no accent mark is needed in the 2nd pers. plural.

decir / to say, to tell
digo, dices, dice;
decimos, decís, **dicen**

An irregular form in the 1st pers. sing. Also, the **e** in the stem changes to **i** when stressed. Pres. part. is **diciendo**.

defender / to defend
defiendo, defiendes, defiende;
defendemos, defendéis, defienden

A stem-changing verb. The **e** in the stem changes to **ie** when stressed.

delinquir / to be guilty, to offend, to commit an offense
delinco, delinques, delinque;
delinquimos, delinquís, delinquen

An orthographical changing verb. This —**quir** verb changes **qu** to **c** in front of **o** or **a**.

desaparecer / to disappear
desaparezco, desapareces, desaparece;
desaparecemos, desaparecéis, desaparecen

This —**cer** verb changes only in the 1st pers. sing. where **c** changes to **zc**.

descender / to descend
desciendo, desciendes, desciende;
descendemos, descendéis, descienden

A stem-changing verb. The **e** in the stem changes to **ie** when stressed.

despedir / to dismiss
despido, despides, despide;
despedimos, despedís, despiden

A stem-changing verb. The **e** in the stem changes to **i** when stressed. Pres. part. is **despidiendo**.

despedirse (de) / to say good-bye (to), to take leave (of)
me despido, te despides, se despide;
nos despedimos, os despedís, se despiden

A stem-changing verb. The **e** in the stem changes to **i** when stressed. Pres. part. is **despidiéndose**.

despertarse / to awaken, to wake up (oneself)
me despierto, te despiertas, se despierta;
nos despertamos, os despertáis, se despiertan

A stem-changing verb. The **e** in the stem changes to **ie** when stressed.

destruir / to destroy
destruyo, destruyes, destruye;
destruimos, destruís, destruyen

This —**uir** verb requires the insertion of **y** in front of the regular present tense endings **o, es, e,** and **en**. Pres. part. is **destruyendo**.

detener / to detain, to stop (someone or something)
detengo, detienes, detiene;
detenemos, detenéis, detienen

An irregular form in the 1st pers. sing. Also, the **e** in the stem changes to **ie** when stressed in the forms noted.

devolver / to return (something), to give back (something)
devuelvo, devuelves, devuelve;
devolvemos, devolvéis, devuelven

A stem-changing verb. The **o** in the stem changes to **ue** when stressed.

dirigir / to direct
dirijo, diriges, dirige;
dirigimos, dirigís, dirigen

An orthographical changing verb. The **g** changes to **j** in front of **o** or **a** in order to keep its original sound of *h*, as in the English word *hello*.

disminuir / to diminish
disminuyo, disminuyes, disminuye;
disminuimos, disminuís, disminuyen

This —**uir** verb requires the insertion of **y** in front of the regular present tense endings **o, es, e,** and **en**. Pres. part. is **disminuyendo**.

disponer / to dispose
dispon**go**, dispones, dispone;
disponemos, dispon**é**is, disponen

Irregular only in the 1st pers. sing. of this tense.

distinguir / to distinguish
distin**go**, distingues, distingue;
distinguimos, distingu**í**s, distinguen

An orthographical changing verb. This **—guir** verb changes **gu** to **g** in front of **o** or **a**.

distribuir / to distribute
distribu**yo**, distribu**ye**s, distribu**ye**;
distribuimos, distribu**í**s, distribu**ye**n

This **—uir** verb requires the insertion of **y** in front of the regular present tense endings **o, es, e,** and **en**. Pres. part. is **distribuyendo**.

divertirse / to have a good time, to enjoy oneself
me div**ie**rto, te div**ie**rtes, se div**ie**rte;
nos divertimos, os divert**í**s, se div**ie**rten

A stem-changing verb. The **e** in the stem changes to **ie** when stressed. Pres. part. is **divirtiéndose**.

doler / to ache, to pain, to hurt, to cause grief, to cause regret
d**ue**lo, d**ue**les, d**ue**le;
dolemos, dol**é**is, d**ue**len

A stem-changing verb. The **o** in the stem changes to **ue** when stressed.

dormir / to sleep
d**ue**rmo, d**ue**rmes, d**ue**rme;
dormimos, dorm**í**s, d**ue**rmen

A stem-changing verb. The **o** in the stem changes to **ue** when stressed. Pres. part. is **durmiendo**.

dormirse / to fall asleep
me d**ue**rmo, te d**ue**rmes, se d**ue**rme;
nos dormimos, os dorm**í**s, se d**ue**rmen

A stem-changing verb. The **o** in the stem changes to **ue** when stressed. Pres. part. is **durmiéndose**.

ejercer / to exert, to exercise
ejer**zo**, ejerces, ejerce;
ejercemos, ejerc**é**is, ejercen

An orthographical changing verb. This **—cer** verb changes **c** to **z** in front of **o** or **a**.

elegir / to elect
eli**jo**, eliges, elige;
elegimos, eleg**í**s, eligen

An orthographical and stem-changing verb. The **g** changes to **j** in front of **o** or **a** in order to keep its original sound of *h*, as in the English

word *hello*. Also, the second **e** in the stem changes to **i** when stressed. Pres. part. is **eligiendo**.

empezar / to begin, to start
emp**ie**zo, emp**ie**zas, emp**ie**za;
empezamos, empez**á**is, emp**ie**zan

A stem-changing verb. The second **e** in the stem changes to **ie** when stressed.

encender / to light, to incite, to inflame, to kindle
enc**ie**ndo, enc**ie**ndes, enc**ie**nde;
encendemos, encend**é**is, enc**ie**nden

A stem-changing verb. The second **e** in the stem changes to **ie** when stressed.

encontrar / to meet, to encounter, to find
enc**ue**ntro, enc**ue**ntras, enc**ue**ntra;
encontramos, encontr**á**is, enc**ue**ntran

An orthographical changing verb. The **o** in the stem changes to **ue** when stressed.

entender / to understand
ent**ie**ndo, ent**ie**ndes, ent**ie**nde;
entendemos, entend**é**is, ent**ie**nden

A stem-changing verb. The second **e** in the stem changes to **ie** when stressed.

enviar / to send
env**í**o, env**í**as, env**í**a;
enviamos, envi**á**is, env**í**an

This **—iar** verb changes **i** to **í** in the stem when stressed.

envolver / to wrap
env**ue**lvo, env**ue**lves, env**ue**lve;
envolvemos, envolv**é**is, env**ue**lven

A stem-changing verb. The **o** in the stem changes to **ue** when stressed.

erguir / to erect, to set up straight
irgo, irgues, irgue; OR: yergo, yergues, yergue;
erguimos, ergu**í**s, irguen OR: yerguen

An orthographical and stem-changing verb, as noted here. Pres. part. is **irguiendo**.

errar / to err, to wander, to roam, to miss
yerro, yerras, yerra;
erramos, err**á**is, yerran

An orthographical changing verb, as noted here. Pres. part. is regular: **errando**.

escoger / to choose, to select
esco**jo**, escoges, escoge;
escogemos, escog**é**is, escogen

An orthographical changing verb. This **—ger** verb changes **g** to **j** in front of **o** or **a**.

espiar / to spy
espío, espías, espía;
espiamos, espiáis, espían

This —**iar** verb changes **i** to **í** in the stem when stressed.

estar / to be
estoy, estás, está;
estamos, estáis, están

exigir / to demand, to urge, to require
exijo, exiges, exige;
exigimos, exigís, exigen

An orthographical changing verb. The **g** in the stem changes to **j** in front of **o** or **a** in order to keep its original sound of *h*, as in the English word *hello*.

exponer / to expose
expon**go**, expones, expone;
exponemos, exponéis, exponen

Irregular only in the 1st pers. sing. of this tense.

extinguir / to extinguish
extin**go**, extingues, extingue;
extinguimos, extinguís, extinguen

An orthographical changing verb. This —**guir** verb changes **gu** to **g** in front of **o** or **a**.

fiarse (de) / to trust
me fío, te fías, se fía;
nos fiamos, os fiáis, se fían

This —**iar** verb changes **i** to **í** in the stem when stressed.

fingir / to pretend, to feign
finjo, finges, finge;
fingimos, fingís, fingen

An orthographical changing verb. The **g** changes to **j** in front of **o** or **a**.

freír / to fry
frío, fríes, fríe;
freímos, freís, fríen

Pres. part. is **friendo.**

gemir / to groan, to moan
gimo, gimes, gime;
gemimos, gemís, gimen

A stem-changing verb. The **e** in the stem changes to **i** when stressed. Pres. part. is **gimiendo.**

graduarse / to be graduated, to graduate
me grad**ú**o, te grad**ú**as, se grad**ú**a;
nos graduamos, os graduáis, se grad**ú**an

This —**uar** verb changes **u** in the stem to **ú** when stressed.

guiar / to guide, to drive, to lead
guío, guías, guía;
guiamos, guiáis, guían

This —**iar** verb changes **i** in the stem to **í** when stressed.

haber / to have (as an auxiliary or helping verb)
he, has, ha;
hemos, habéis, han

hacer / to do, to make
ha**go**, haces, hace;
hacemos, hacéis, hacen

Irregular form only in the 1st pers. sing. in this tense, as noted.

helar / to freeze
hiela OR está helando (in the present progressive form)

This impersonal verb, referring to the weather, is used in the 3rd pers. The **e** in the stem changes to **ie** because it is stressed. The present progressive form may be used also when referring to weather conditions in the present, as noted here.

herir / to harm, to hurt, to wound
hiero, hieres, hiere;
herimos, herís, hieren

A stem-changing verb because the **e** in the stem changes to **ie** when stressed. Pres. part is **hiriendo.**

hervir / to boil
hiervo, hierves, hierve;
hervimos, hervís, hierven

A stem-changing verb because the **e** in the stem changes to **ie** when stressed. Pres. part. is **hirviendo.**

huir / to flee, to escape, to run away, to slip away
huyo, huyes, huye;
huimos, huís, huyen

This —**uir** verb requires the insertion of **y** in front of the regular present tense endings **o, es, e,** and **en.** Pres. part. is **huyendo.**

impedir / to prevent, to impede, to hinder
impido, impides, impide;
impedimos, impedís, impiden

A stem-changing verb because the **e** in the stem changes to **i** when stressed. Pres. part. is **impidiendo.**

imponer / to impose
impon**go**, impones, impone;
imponemos, imponéis, imponen

Irregular only in the 1st pers. sing. of this tense.

incluir / to include
incluyo, incluyes, incluye;
incluimos, incluís, incluyen

This —uir verb requires the insertion of **y** in front of the regular present tense endings **o, es, e,** and **en.** Pres. part. is **incluyendo.**

influir / to influence
influyo, influyes, influye;
influimos, influís, influyen

This —uir verb requires the insertion of **y** in front of the regular present tense endings **o, es, e,** and **en.** Pres. part. is **influyendo.**

ir / to go
voy, vas, va;
vamos, vais, van

Pres. part. is **yendo.**

irse / to go away
me voy, te vas, se va;
nos vamos, os vais, se van

Pres. part. is **yéndose.**

jugar / to play
juego, juegas, juega;
jugamos, jugáis, juegan

A stem-changing verb because **u** in the stem changes to **ue** when stressed.

llover / to rain
llueve OR está lloviendo (in the present progressive form)

This impersonal verb, referring to the weather, is used in the 3rd pers. The **o** in the stem changes to **ue** because it is stressed. The present progressive form may be used also when referring to weather conditions in the present, as noted here.

medir / to measure
mido, mides, mide;
medimos, medís, miden

A stem-changing verb because **e** in the stem changes to **i** when stressed. Pres. part. is **midiendo.**

mentir / to lie, to tell a lie
miento, mientes, miente;
mentimos, mentís, mienten

A stem-changing verb because **e** in the stem changes to **ie** when stressed. Pres. part. is **mintiendo.**

morir / to die
muero, mueres, muere;
morimos, morís, mueren

A stem-changing verb because **o** in the stem changes to **ue** when stressed. Pres. part. is **muriendo.**

mostrar / to show, to point out
muestro, muestras, muestra;
mostramos, mostráis, muestran

A stem-changing verb because **o** in the stem changes to **ue** when stressed.

mover / to move, to persuade, to induce
muevo, mueves, mueve;
movemos, movéis, mueven

A stem-changing verb because **o** in the stem changes to **ue** when stressed.

nacer / to be born
nazco, naces, nace;
nacemos, nacéis, nacen

This —cer verb changes only in the 1st pers. sing. where **c** changes to **zc.**

negar / to deny
niego, niegas, niega;
negamos, negáis, niegan

A stem-changing verb because **e** in the stem changes to **ie** when stressed.

nevar / to snow
nieva OR está nevando (in the present progressive form)

This impersonal verb, referring to the weather, is used in the 3rd pers. The **e** in the stem changes to **ie** because it is stressed. The present progressive form may be used also when referring to weather conditions in the present, as noted here.

obedecer / to obey
obedezco, obedeces, obedece;
obedecemos, obedecéis, obedecen

An orthographical changing verb. This —cer verb changes **c** to **zc** only in the 1st pers. sing. of this tense.

obtener / to obtain, to get
obtengo, obtienes, obtiene;
obtenemos, obtenéis, obtienen

The 1st pers. sing. form is irregular. As a stem-changing verb, the **e** in the stem changes to **ie** when stressed.

ofrecer / to offer
ofrezco, ofreces, ofrece;
ofrecemos, ofrecéis, ofrecen

An orthographical changing verb. This —cer verb changes **c** to **zc** only in the 1st pers. sing. of this tense.

oír / to hear

oigo, oyes, oye;
oímos, oís, oyen

An irregular verb. Pres. part. is **oyendo.**

oler / to smell
huelo, hueles, huele;
olemos, oléis, **huelen**

An orthographical and stem-changing verb because **o** in the stem changes to **ue** when stressed and *h* is added as noted. Pres. part. is regular: **oliendo.**

pedir / to ask for, to request
pido, pides, pide;
pedimos, pedís, piden

A stem-changing verb because **e** in the stem changes to **i** when stressed. Pres. part. is **pidiendo.**

pensar / to think
pienso, piensas, piensa;
pensamos, pensáis, piensan

A stem-changing verb because **e** in the stem changes to **ie** when stressed.

perder / to lose
pierdo, pierdes, pierde;
perdemos, perdéis, pierden

A stem-changing verb because **e** in the stem changes to **ie** when stressed.

perseguir / to pursue, to follow after
persigo, persigues, persigue;
perseguimos, perseguís, persiguen

An orthographical and stem-changing verb because **u** in the stem drops only in the 1st pers. sing. since it is not needed. Also, the second **e** in the stem changes to **i** when stressed. Pres. part. is **persiguiendo.**

poder / to be able, can
puedo, puedes, puede;
podemos, podéis, pueden

A stem-changing verb because **o** in the stem changes to **ue** when stressed. Pres. part. is **pudiendo.**

poner / to put, to place
pongo, pones, pone;
ponemos, ponéis, ponen

Irregular in the 1st pers. sing. only of this tense.

preferir / to prefer
prefiero, prefieres, prefiere;
preferimos, preferís, prefieren

A stem-changing verb because the second **e** in the stem changes to **ie** when stressed. Pres. part. is **prefiriendo.**

probar / to prove, to test, to try
pruebo, pruebas, prueba;
probamos, probáis, prueban

A stem-changing verb because **o** in the stem changes to **ue** when stressed.

producir / to produce
produzco, produces, produce;
producimos, producís, producen

This —**cir** verb changes **c** to **zc** only in the 1st pers. sing. of this tense.

proseguir / to continue, to proceed
prosigo, prosigues, prosigue;
proseguimos, proseguís, prosiguen

An orthographical changing verb because **u** in the stem drops only in the 1st pers. sing. Also, a stem-changing verb because **e** in the stem changes to **i** when stressed. Pres. part. is **prosiguiendo.**

proteger / to protect
protejo, proteges, protege;
protegemos, protegéis, protegen

An orthographical changing verb because this —**ger** verb changes **g** to **j** in front of **o** or **a.**

quebrar / to break
quiebro, quiebras, quiebra;
quebramos, quebráis, quiebran

A stem-changing verb because **e** in the stem changes to **ie** when stressed.

querer / to want, to wish
quiero, quieres, quiere;
queremos, queréis, quieren

A stem-changing verb because **e** in the stem changes to **ie** when stressed.

recoger / to pick, to pick up, to gather
recojo, recoges, recoge;
recogemos, recogéis, recogen

An orthographical changing verb because this —**ger** verb changes **g** to **j** in front of **o** or **a.**

recomendar / to recommend, to advise, to commend
recomiendo, recomiendas, recomienda;
recomendamos, recomendáis, recomiendan

A stem-changing verb because **e** in the stem changes to **ie** when stressed.

recordar / to remember
recuerdo, recuerdas, recuerda;
recordamos, recordáis, recuerdan

A stem-changing verb because **o** in the stem changes to **ue** when stressed.

referir / to refer
refiero, refieres, refiere;
referimos, referís, refieren

A stem-changing verb because the second **e** in the stem changes to **ie** when stressed. Pres. part. is **refiriendo**.

reír / to laugh
río, ríes, ríe;
reímos, reís, ríen

The pres. part. is also irregular: **riendo**.

reñir / to scold, to quarrel, to argue
riño, riñes, riñe;
reñimos, reñís, riñen

A stem-changing verb because **e** in the stem changes to **i** when stressed. Past part. is also irregular: **riñendo**.

renovar / to renew, to remodel
renuevo, renuevas, renueva;
renovamos, renováis, renuevan

A stem-changing verb because **o** in the stem changes to **ue** when stressed.

repetir / to repeat
repito, repites, repite;
repetimos, repetís, repiten

A stem-changing verb because the second **e** in the stem changes to **i** when stressed. Pres. part. is also irregular: **repitiendo**.

resfriarse / to catch cold
me resfrío, te resfrías, se resfría;
nos resfriamos, os resfriáis, se resfrían

This —iar verb changes **i** to **í** when stressed.

resolver / to resolve, to solve (a problem)
resuelvo, resuelves, resuelve;
resolvemos, resolvéis, resuelven

A stem-changing verb because **o** in the stem changes to **ue** when stressed.

reunir / to gather, to join, to unite
reúno, reúnes, reúne;
reunimos, reunís, reúnen

The **u** in the stem changes to **ú** when stressed.

rogar / to beg, to request
ruego, ruegas, ruega;
rogamos, rogáis, ruegan

A stem-changing verb because **o** in the stem changes to **ue** when stressed.

saber / to know, to know how
sé, sabes, sabe;
sabemos, sabéis, saben

Irregular only in the 1st pers. sing. of this tense.

salir / to go out
salgo, sales, sale;
salimos, salís, salen

Irregular only in the 1st pers. sing. of this tense.

seguir / to follow, to pursue, to continue
sigo, sigues, sigue;
seguimos, seguís, siguen

An orthographical changing verb because **u** in the stem drops only in the 1st pers. sing. of this tense. Also, a stem-changing verb because **e** in the stem changes to **i** when stressed. Pres. part. is also irregular: **siguiendo**.

sentarse / to sit down
me siento, te sientas, se sienta;
nos sentamos, os sentáis, se sientan

A stem-changing verb because **e** in the stem changes to **ie** when stressed.

sentir / to feel sorry, to regret, to feel, to experience, to sense
siento, sientes, siente;
sentimos, sentís, sienten

A stem-changing verb because **e** in the stem changes to **ie** when stressed. Pres. part. is also irregular: **sintiendo**.

sentirse / to feel (well, sick)
me siento, te sientes, se siente;
nos sentimos, os sentís, se sienten

A stem-changing verb because **e** in the stem changes to **ie** when stressed. Pres. part. is also irregular: **sintiéndose**.

ser / to be
soy, eres, es;
somos, sois, son

Pres. part. is **siendo**.

servir / to serve
sirvo, sirves, sirve;
servimos, servís, sirven

A stem-changing verb because **e** in the stem changes to **i** when stressed. Pres. part. is also irregular: **sirviendo**.

soler / to be in the habit of, to be accustomed to, to have the custom of
suelo, sueles, suele;
solemos, soléis, suelen

A stem-changing verb because **o** in the stem changes to **ue** when stressed. This verb is generally used in this tense, in the imperfect indicative, and in the present subjunctive. It is followed by an inf.: **Suelo lavarme las manos antes de comer** / I am in the habit of washing my hands before eating.

sonar / to ring, to sound
sueno, suenas, suena;
sonamos, sonáis, suenan

A stem-changing verb because **o** in the stem changes to **ue** when stressed.

soñar / to dream
sueño, sueñas, sueña;
soñamos, soñáis, sueñan

A stem-changing verb because **o** in the stem changes to **ue** when stressed.

sonreír / to smile
sonrío, sonríes, sonríe;
sonreímos, sonreís, sonríen

The pres. part. is also irregular: **sonriendo.**

sugerir / to suggest, to hint
sugiero, sugieres, sugiere;
sugerimos, sugerís, sugieren

A stem-changing verb because **e** in the stem changes to **ie** when stressed. Pres. part. is also irregular: **sugiriendo.**

suponer / to suppose, to assume
supongo, supones, supone;
suponemos, suponéis, suponen

Irregular in the 1st pers. sing. only of this tense.

sustituir / to substitute
sustituyo, sustituyes, sustituye;
sustituimos, sustituís, sustituyen

This —**uir** verb requires the insertion of **y** in front of the regular present tense endings **o, es, e,** and **en.** Pres. part. is also irregular: **sustituyendo.**

tener / to have, to hold
tengo, tienes, tiene;
tenemos, tenéis, tienen

An irregular form in the 1st pers. sing. of this tense. Also, **e** in the stem changes to **ie** when stressed.

torcer / to twist
tuerzo, tuerces; tuerce;
torcemos, torcéis, tuercen

A stem-changing verb because **o** in the stem changes to **ue** when stressed. Also an orthographical changing verb because **c** changes to **z** in front of **o** or **a.**

traducir / to translate
traduzco, traduces, traduce;
traducimos, traducís, traducen

An orthographical changing verb because this —**cer** verb changes **c** to **zc** only in the 1st pers. sing. of this tense.

traer / to bring
traigo, traes, trae;
traemos, traéis, traen

Irregular in the 1st pers. sing. only of this tense. Also, the pres. part. is irregular: **trayendo.**

tronar / to thunder
truena OR está tronando (in the present progressive form)

This impersonal verb, referring to the weather, is used in the 3rd pers. The **o** in the stem changes to **ue** because it is stressed. The present progressive form may be used also when referring to weather conditions in the present, as noted here.

valer / to be worth, to be worthy
valgo, vales, vale;
valemos, valéis, valen

Irregular only in the 1st pers. sing. of this tense.

vencer / to conquer, to overcome
venzo, vences, vence;
vencemos, vencéis, vencen

An orthographical changing verb because **c** changes to **z** in front of **o** or **a.**

venir / to come
vengo, vienes, viene;
venimos, venís, vienen

The pres. part. is also irregular: **viniendo.**

ver / to see
veo, ves, ve;
vemos, veis, ven

vestir / to clothe, to dress
visto, vistes, viste;
vestimos, vestís, visten

A stem-changing verb because **e** in the stem changes to **i** when stressed. Pres. part. is also irregular: **vistiendo.**

vestirse / to dress oneself, to get dressed
me visto, te vistes, se viste;
nos vestimos, os vestís, se visten

A stem-changing verb because **e** in the stem changes to **i** when stressed. Pres. part. is also irregular: **vistiéndose.**

volar / to fly
vuelo, vuelas, vuela;
volamos, voláis, vuelan

A stem-changing verb because **o** in the stem changes to **ue** when stressed.

volver / to return
vuelvo, vuelves, vuelve;
volvemos, volvéis, **vuelven**

A stem-changing verb because **o** in the stem
changes to **ue** when stressed.

NOTE: If I have inadvertently omitted any verb you have in mind, which is irregular in the present indicative in some way, consult my book *501 Spanish verbs fully conjugated in all the tenses in a new easy to learn format,* Second Edition, also published by Barron's.

§68.20   Tense No. 2: Imperfecto de indicativo (Imperfect indicative)

This is a past tense. Imperfect suggests incomplete. The *Imperfect tense* expresses **an action or a state of being that was continuous in the past and its completion is not indicated. This tense** is used, therefore, to express:

(a) An action that was going on in the past at the same time as another action.
EXAMPLE:
Mi hermano **leía** y mi padre **hablaba** / My brother *was reading* and my father *was talking*.

(b) An action that was going on in the past when another action occurred.
EXAMPLE:
Mi hermana **cantaba** cuando yo entré / My sister *was singing* when I came in.

(c) An action that a person did habitually in the past.
EXAMPLES:
1. Cuando **estábamos** en Nueva York, **íbamos** al cine todos los sábados / When *we were* in New York, *we went* to the movies every Saturday; When *we were* in New York, *we used to go* to the movies every Saturday.
2. Cuando **vivíamos** en California, **íbamos** a la playa todos los días / When *we used to live* in California, *we would go* to the beach every day.

NOTE: In this last example, *we would go* looks like the Conditional, but it is not. It is the *Imperfect tense* in this sentence because habitual action in the past is expressed.

(d) A description of a mental, emotional, or physical condition in the past.
EXAMPLES:
1. (mental condition)   **Quería** ir al cine / *I wanted* to go to the movies.
   Common verbs in this use are **creer, desear, pensar, poder, preferir, querer, saber, sentir.**
2. (emotional condition)   **Estaba** contento de verlo / *I was* happy to see him.
3. (physical condition)   Mi madre **era** hermosa cuando **era** pequeña / My mother *was* beautiful when she *was* young.

(e) The time of day in the past.
EXAMPLES:
1. ¿Qué hora **era**? / What time *was* it?
2. **Eran** las tres / *It was* three o'clock.

(f) An action or state of being that occurred in the past and *lasted for a certain length of time* prior to another past action. In English it is usually translated as a Pluperfect tense and is formed with *had been* plus the present participle of the verb you are using. It is like the special use of the **Presente de indicativo** explained in the above section in paragraph (f), **§68.14,** except that the action or state of being no longer exists at present. This is an idiomatic use of the *Imperfect tense* of a verb with **hacía,** which is also in the *Imperfect*.
EXAMPLE:
Hacía tres horas que **miraba** la televisión cuando mi hermano entró / *I had been watching* television for three hours when my brother came in.
See also **§32.–§35.**

(g) An indirect quotation in the past.

EXAMPLE:
Present: Dice que **quiere** venir a mi casa / He says *he wants* to come to my house.
Past: Dijo que **quería** venir a mi casa / He said *he wanted* to come to my house.

§68.21   This tense is regularly formed as follows:

§68.22   Drop the **—ar** ending of an infinitive, like **hablar,** and add the following endings: **aba, abas, aba; ábamos, abais, aban**

You then get: **hablaba, hablabas, hablaba;**
                hablábamos, hablabais, hablaban

The usual equivalent in English is: I was talking OR I used to talk OR I talked; you were talking OR you used to talk OR you talked, *etc.*

§68.23   Drop the **—er** ending of an infinitive, like **beber,** or the **—ir** ending of an infinitive, like **recibir,** and add the following endings: **ía, ías, ía; íamos, íais, ían**
You then get: **bebía, bebías, bebía;**
                bebíamos, bebíais, bebían

                recibía, recibías, recibía;
                recibíamos, recibíais, recibían

The usual equivalent in English is: I was drinking OR I used to drink OR I drank; you were drinking OR you used to drink OR you drank, *etc.*; I was receiving OR I used to receive OR I received; you were receiving OR you used to receive OR you received, *etc.*

§68.24   Verbs irregular in the imperfect indicative

ir / to go   **iba, ibas, iba;** (I was going, I used to go, *etc.*)
                    íbamos, ibais, iban
ser / to be   **era, eras, era;** (I was, I used to be, *etc.*)
                    éramos, erais, eran
ver / to see   **veía, veías, veía;** (I was seeing, I used to see, *etc.*)
                    veíamos, veíais, veían

NOTE: If I have inadvertently omitted any verb you have in mind, which is irregular in the imperfect indicative in some way, consult my book *501 Spanish verbs fully conjugated in all the tenses in a new easy to learn format*, Second Edition, also published by Barron's.

§68.25   Tense No. 3: Pretérito (Preterit)
This tense expresses an action that was completed at some time in the past.

EXAMPLES:
1. Mi padre **llegó** ayer / My father *arrived* yesterday; My father *did arrive* yesterday.
2. María **fue** a la iglesia esta mañana / Mary *went* to church this morning; Mary *did go* to church this morning.
3. ¿Qué **pasó**?   What *happened?* What *did happen?*
4. **Tomé** el desayuno a las siete / I *had* breakfast at seven o'clock. I *did have* breakfast at seven o'clock.
5. **Salí** de casa, **tomé** el autobús y **llegué** a la escuela a las ocho / I *left* the house, I *took* the bus and I *arrived* at school at eight o'clock.

§68.26   In Spanish, some verbs that express a mental state have a different meaning when used in the Preterit.

EXAMPLES:
1. La **conocí** la semana pasada en el baile / I *met* her last week at the dance. (**Conocer,** which means *to know* or *be acquainted with*, means *met*, that is, introduced to for the first time, in the Preterit.)

2. **Pude** hacerlo / *I succeeded* in doing it. (**Poder,** which means *to be able*, means *succeeded* in the Preterit.)

3. **No pude** hacerlo / *I failed* to do it. (**Poder,** when used in the negative in the Preterit, means *failed* or *did not succeed*.)

4. **Quise** llamarlo / *I tried* to call you. (**Querer,** which means *to wish* or *want*, means tried in the Preterit.)

5. **No quise** hacerlo / *I refused* to do it. (**Querer,** when used in the negative in the Preterit, means *refused*.)

6. **Supe** la verdad / *I found out* the truth. (**Saber,** which means *to know*, means *found out* in the Preterit.)

7. **Tuve** una carta de mi amigo Roberto / *I received* a letter from my friend Robert. (**Tener,** which means *to have*, means *received* in the Preterit.)

§68.27 This tense is regularly formed as follows:

§68.28 Drop the —**ar** ending of an infinitive, like **hablar,** and add the following endings: **é, aste, ó; amos, asteis, aron**

You then get: **hablé, hablaste, habló;**
                      hablamos, hablasteis, hablaron

The usual equivalent in English is: I talked OR I did talk; you talked OR you did talk, *etc.* OR I spoke OR I did speak; you spoke OR you did speak, *etc.*

§68.29 Drop the —**er** ending of an infinitive, like **beber,** or the —**ir** ending of an infinitive, like **recibir,** and add the following endings: **í, iste, ió; imos, isteis, ieron**

You then get: **bebí, bebiste, bebió;**
                      bebimos, bebisteis, bebieron
                      recibí, recibiste, recibió;
                      recibimos, recibisteis, recibieron

The usual equivalent in English is: I drank OR I did drink; you drank OR you did drink, *etc.*; I received OR I did receive, *etc.*

§68.30 **Verbs irregular in the preterit, including stem-changing verbs and orthographical changing verbs**

NOTE that the first three forms up to the semicolon are the 1st, 2nd, and 3rd persons of the singular; the three verb forms under those are the 1st, 2nd, and 3rd persons of the plural. The subject pronouns are not given in order to emphasize the verb forms. See my note at the end of **§68.11** where **haber** is given in all its forms in the seven simple tenses. See also **§66.4.**

abrazar / to embrace, to hug
abracé, abrazaste, abrazó;
abrazamos, abrazasteis, abrazaron

An orthographical changing verb because **z** change to **c** in front of **é** in the 1st pers. sing. of this tense.

acercarse / to approach, to draw near
me acerqué, te acercaste, se acercó;
nos acercamos, os acercasteis, se acercaron

An orthographical changing verb because **c** changes to **qu** in front of **é** in the 1st pers. sing. of this tense.

advertir / to notify, to warn, to give notice, to give warning
advertí, advertiste, advirtió;
advertimos, advertisteis, advirtieron

A stem-changing verb because **e** in the stem changes to **i** in the 3rd pers. sing. and plural of this tense.

agregar / to add, to collect, to gather
agregué, agregaste, agregó;
agregamos, agregasteis, agregaron

An orthographical changing verb because **g** changes to **gu** in front of **é** in the 1st pers. sing. of this tense.

alcanzar / to reach, to overtake
alcancé, alcanzaste, alcanzó;
alcanzamos, alcanzasteis, alcanzaron

An orthographical changing verb because **z** changes to **c** in front of **é** in the 1st pers. sing. of this tense.

almorzar / to have lunch, to eat lunch
almorcé, almorzaste, almorzó;
almorzamos, almorzasteis, almorzaron

An orthographical changing verb because **z** changes to **c** in front of **é** in the 1st pers. sing. of this tense.

alzar / to heave, to lift, to pick up, to raise (prices)
alcé, alzaste, alzó;
alzamos, alzasteis, alzaron

An orthographical changing verb because **z** changes to **c** in front of **é** in the 1st pers. sing. of this tense.

amenazar / to threaten
amenacé, amenazaste, amenazó;
amenazamos, amenazasteis, amenazaron

An orthographical changing verb because **z** changes to **c** in front of **é** in the 1st pers. sing. of this tense.

andar / to walk
anduve, anduviste, anduvo;
anduvimos, anduvisteis, anduvieron

apagar / to extinguish
apagué, apagaste, apagó;
apagamos, apagasteis, apagaron

An orthographical changing verb because **g** changes to **gu** in front of **é** in the 1st pers. sing. of this tense.

aplicar / to apply
apliqué, aplicaste, aplicó;
aplicamos, aplicasteis, aplicaron

An orthographical changing verb because **c** changes to **qu** in front of **é** in the 1st pers. sing. of this tense.

arrancar / to pull out, to uproot
arranqué, arrancaste, arrancó;
arrancamos, arrancasteis, arrancaron

An orthographical changing verb because **c** changes to **qu** in front of **é** in the 1st pers. sing. of this tense.

atacar / to attack
ataqué, atacaste, atacó;
atacamos, atacasteis, atacaron

An orthographical changing verb because **c** changes to **qu** in front of **é** in the 1st pers. sing. of this tense.

atraer / to attract, to allure, to charm
atraje, atrajiste, atrajo;
atrajimos, atrajisteis, atrajeron

avanzar / to advance
avancé, avanzcaste, avanzó;
avanzamos, avanzasteis, avanzaron

An orthographical changing verb because **z** changes to **c** in front of **é** in the 1st pers. sing. of this tense.

averiguar / to find out, to inquire, to investigate
averigüé, averiguaste, averiguó;
averiguamos, averiguasteis, averiguaron

An orthographical changing verb because **u** changes to **ü** in front of **é** in the 1st pers. sing. of this tense. The two dots over the **ü** are called dieresis or diaeresis; in Spanish, they are called *diéresis*. They indicate that each of the two vowels (**üé**) has a separate and distinct pronunciation. The dieresis mark is used in **averigüé** to tell you that **güe** should be pronounced as *gway*, not *gay*. Why? In order to preserve the *gw* sound in the infinitive.

bautizar / to baptize, to christen
bauticé, bautizaste, bautizó;
bautizamos, bautizasteis, bautizaron

An orthographical changing verb because **z** changes to **c** in front of **é** in the 1st pers. sing. of this tense.

bendecir / to bless
bendije, bendijiste, bendijo;
bendijimos, bendijisteis, bendijeron

bostezar / to gape, to yawn
bostecé, bostezaste, bostezó;
bostezamos, bostezasteis, bostezaron

An orthographical changing verb because **z** changes to **c** in front of **é** in the 1st pers. sing. of this tense.

buscar / to look for, to search, to seek
busqué, buscaste, buscó;
buscamos, buscasteis, buscaron

An orthographical changing verb because **c** changes to **qu** in front of **é** in the 1st pers. sing. of this tense.

caber / to fit, to be contained
cupe, cupiste, cupo;
cupimos, cupisteis, cupieron

caer / to fall
caí, caíste, cayó;
caímos, caísteis, cayeron

An orthographical changing verb because **i** in **ió** of the 3rd pers. sing. ending changes to **y** and **i** in **ieron** of the 3rd pers. plural ending changes to **y**. The reason for this spelling change is the strong vowel **a** right in front of those two endings.

ALSO NOTE that **i** in **iste** changes to **í** in the 2nd pers. sing. and **i** in **isteis** changes to **í** in the 2nd pers. plural because of the strong vowel **a** in front of those two endings. The same thing happens in **caímos**.

caracterizar / to characterize
caractericé, caracterizaste, caracterizó;
caracterizamos, caracterizasteis, caracterizaron

An orthographical changing verb because **z** changes to **c** in front of **é** in the 1st pers. sing. of this tense.

cargar / to load, to burden
cargué, cargaste, cargó;
cargamos, cargasteis, cargaron

An orthographical changing verb because **g** changes to **gu** in front of **é** in the 1st pers. sing. of this tense.

castigar / to punish
castigué, castigaste, castigó;
castigamos, castigasteis, castigaron

An orthographical changing verb because **g** changes to **gu** in front of **é** in the 1st pers. sing. of this tense.

certificar / to certify, to register (a letter), to attest
certifiqué, certificaste, certificó;
certificamos, certificasteis, certificaron

An orthographical changing verb because **c** changes to **qu** in front of **é** in the 1st pers. sing. of this tense.

colgar / to hang
colgué, colgaste, colgó;
colgamos, colgasteis, colgaron

An orthographical changing verb because **g** changes to **gu** in front of **é** in the 1st pers. sing. of this tense.

colocar / to place, to put
coloqué, colocaste, colocó;
colocamos, colocasteis, colocaron

An orthographical changing verb because **c** changes to **qu** in front of **é** in the 1st pers. sing. of this tense.

comenzar / to begin, to commence, to start
comencé, comenzaste, comenzó;
comenzamos, comenzasteis, comenzaron

An orthographical changing verb because **z** changes to **c** in front of **é** in the 1st pers. sing. of this tense.

componer / to compose
compuse, compusiste, compuso;
compusimos, compusisteis, compusieron

comunicar / to communicate
comuniqué, comunicaste, comunicó;
comunicamos, comunicasteis, comunicaron

An orthographical changing verb because **c** changes to **que** in front of **é** in the 1st pers. sing. of this tense.

conducir / to conduct, to lead, to drive
conduje, condujiste, condujo;
condujimos, condujisteis, condujeron

conseguir / to get, to obtain, to attain, to succeed in
conseguí, conseguiste, consiguió;
conseguimos, conseguisteis, consiguieron

A stem-changing verb because **e** in the stem changes to **i** in the 3rd pers. sing. and pl. of this tense. Pres. part. is **consiguiendo**.

constituir / to constitute
constituí, constituiste, constituyó;
constituimos, constituisteis, constituyeron

This —**uir** verb changes **i** to **y** in the 3rd pers. sing. and pl. of this tense.

construir / to construct, to build
construí, construiste, construyó;
construimos, construisteis, construyeron

This —**uir** verb changes **i** to **y** in the 3rd pers. sing. and pl. of this tense.

contener / to contain, to hold
contuve, contuviste, contuvo;
contuvimos, contuvisteis, contuvieron

contradecir / to contradict
contradije, contradijiste, contradijo;
contradijimos, contradijisteis, contradijeron

contribuir / to contribute
contribuí, contribuiste, contribuyó;
contribuimos, contribuisteis, contribuyeron

This —**uir** verb changes **i** to **y** in the 3rd pers. sing. and pl. of this tense.

convenir / to agree
convine, conviniste, convino;
convinimos, convinisteis, convinieron

Pres. part. is also irregular: **conviniendo**.

convertir / to convert
convertí, convertiste, convirtió;
convertimos, convertisteis, convirtieron

A stem-changing verb because **e** in the stem

changes to **i** in the 3rd pers. sing. and pl. of this tense. Pres. part. is also irregular: **convirtiendo.**

convocar / to call together, to convene
convoqué, convocaste, convocó;
convocamos, convocasteis, convocaron

An orthographical changing verb because **c** changes to **qu** in front of **é** in the 1st pers. sing. of this tense.

corregir / to correct
corregí, corregiste, corrigió;
corregimos, corregisteis, corrigieron

A stem-changing verb because **e** in the stem changes to **i** in the 3rd pers. sing. and pl. of this tense. Pres. part. is also irregular: **corrigiendo.**

creer / to believe
creí, creíste, creyó;
creímos, creísteis, creyeron

An orthographical changing verb because **i** in **ió** of the 3rd pers. sing. ending changes to **y** and **i** in **ieron** of the 3rd pers. plural ending changes to **y**. Also note that **i** in **iste** changes to **í** in the 2nd pers. sing. and **i** in **isteis** changes to **í** in the 2nd pers. pl. because of the strong vowel **e** in front of those two endings. The same thing happens in **creímos.**

cruzar / to cross
crucé, cruzaste, cruzó;
cruzamos, cruzasteis, cruzaron

An orthographical changing verb because **z** changes to **c** in front of **é** in the 1st pers. sing. of this tense.

dar / to give
di, diste, dio;
dimos, disteis, dieron

decir / to say, to tell
dije, dijiste, dijo;
dijimos, dijisteis, dijeron

dedicar / to dedicate, to devote
dediqué, dedicaste, dedicó;
dedicamos, dedicasteis, dedicaron

An orthographical changing verb because **c** changes to **qu** in front of **é** in the 1st pers. sing. of this tense.

deslizarse / to slip away, to let slip, to let slide
me deslicé, te deslizaste, se deslizó;
nos deslizamos, os deslizasteis, se deslizaron

An orthographical changing verb because **z** changes to **c** in front of **é** in the 1st pers. sing. of this tense.

despedir / to dismiss
despedí, despediste, despidió;
despedimos, despedisteis, despidieron

A stem-changing verb because **e** in the stem changes to **i** in the 3rd pers. sing. and pl. of this tense. Pres. part. is **despidiendo.**

despedirse (de) / to say good-bye (to), to take leave (of)
me despedí, te despediste, se despidió;
nos despedimos, os despedisteis, se despidieron

A stem-changing verb because **e** in the stem changes to **i** in the 3rd pers. sing. and pl. of this tense. Pres. part. is **despidiéndose.**

desperezarse / to stretch (oneself)
me desperecé, te desperezaste, se desperezó;
nos desperezamos, os desperezasteis, se desperezaron

An orthographical changing verb because **z** changes to **c** in front of **é** in the 1st pers. sing. of this tense.

destruir / to destroy
destruí, destruiste, destruyó;
destruimos, destruisteis, destruyeron

This —**uir** verb changes **i** to **y** in the 3rd pers. sing. and pl. of this tense.

desvestirse / to undress, to get undressed
me desvestí, te desvestiste, se desvistió;
nos desvestimos, os desvestisteis, se desvistieron

A stem-changing verb because **e** in the stem changes to **i** in the 3rd pers. sing. and pl. of this tense. Pres. part. is **desvistiéndose.**

detener / to detain, to stop (someone or something)
detuve, detuviste, detuvo;
detuvimos, detuvisteis, detuvieron

detenerse / to stop (oneself or itself)
me detuve, te detuviste, se detuvo;
nos detuvimos, os detuvisteis, se detuvieron

divertirse / to have a good time, to enjoy oneself
me divertí, te divertiste, se divirtió;
nos divertimos, os divertisteis, se divirtieron

A stem-changing verb because **e** in the stem changes to **i** in the 3rd pers. sing. and pl. of this tense. Pres. part. is **divirtiéndose.**

dormir / to sleep
dormí, dormiste, durmió;
dormimos, dormisteis, durmieron

A stem-changing verb because **o** in the stem

changes to **u** in the 3rd pers. sing. and pl. of this tense. Pres. part. is **durmiendo**.

dormirse / to fall asleep
me dormí, te dormiste, se durmió;
nos dormimos, os dormisteis, se durmieron

A stem-changing verb because **o** in the stem changes to **u** in the 3rd pers. sing. and pl. of this tense. Pres. part. is **durmiéndose**.

educar / to educate
eduqué, educaste, educó;
educamos, educasteis, educaron

An orthographical changing verb because **c** changes to **qu** in front of **é** in the 1st pers. sing. of this tense.

elegir / to elect
elegí, elegiste, eligió;
elegimos, elegisteis, eligieron

A stem-changing verb because **e** in the stem changes to **i** in the 3rd pers. sing. and pl. of this tense. Pres. part. is **eligiendo**.

embarcarse / to embark
me embarqué, te embarcaste, se embarcó;
nos embarcamos, os embarcasteis, se embarcaron

An orthographical changing verb because **c** changes to **qu** in front of **é** in the 1st pers. sing. of this tense.

empezar / to begin, to start
empecé, empezaste, empezó;
empezamos, empezasteis, empezaron

An orthographical changing verb because **z** changes to **c** in front of **é** in the 1st pers. sing. of this tense.

encargar / to entrust, to put in charge
encargué, encargaste, encargó;
encargamos, encargasteis, encargaron

An orthographical changing verb because **g** changes to **gu** in front of **é** in the 1st pers. sing. of this tense.

entregar / to surrender, to give up, to hand over, to deliver
entregué, entregaste, entregó;
entregamos, entregasteis, entregaron

An orthographical changing verb because **g** changes to **gu** in front of **é** in the 1st pers. sing. of this tense.

equivocarse / to be mistaken
me equivoqué, te equivocaste, se equivocó;
nos equivocamos, os equivocasteis, se equivocaron

An orthographical changing verb because **c** changes to **qu** in front of **é** in the 1st pers. sing. of this tense.

erguir / to erect, to set up straight
erguí, erguiste, irguió;
erguimos, erguisteis, irguieron

A stem-changing verb because **e** in the stem changes to **i** in the 3rd pers. sing. and pl. of this tense. Pres. part. is **irguiendo**.

estar / to be
estuve, estuviste, estuvo;
estuvimos, estuvisteis, estuvieron

explicar / to explain
expliqué, explicaste, explicó;
explicamos, explicasteis, explicaron

An orthographical changing verb because **c** changes to **qu** in front of **é** in the 1st pers. sing. of this tense.

fabricar / to manufacture, to fabricate
fabriqué, fabricaste, fabricó;
fabricamos, fabricasteis, fabricaron

An orthographical changing verb because **c** changes to **qu** in front of **é** in the 1st pers. sing. of this tense.

gemir / to groan, to moan
gemí, gemiste, gimió;
gemimos, gemisteis, gimieron

A stem-changing verb because **e** in the stem changes to **i** in the 3rd pers. sing. and pl. of this tense. Pres. part. is **gimiendo**.

gozar / to enjoy
gocé, gozaste, gozó;
gozamos, gozasteis, gozaron

An orthographical changing verb because **z** changes to **c** in front of **é** in the 1st pers. sing. of this tense.

gruñir / to grumble, to grunt, to growl, to creak (as doors, hinges, *etc.*)
gruñí, gruñiste, gruñó;
gruñimos, gruñisteis, gruñeron

This —**ñir** verb drops **i** in the ending **ió** in the 3rd pers. sing. and drops **i** in the ending **ieron** in the 3rd pers. pl. because **ñ** is in front of those two endings. The sound of **ieron** is still the same without **i** because of the sound of **ñ**. Pres. part. is **gruñendo**.

haber / to have (as an auxiliary or helping verb)
hube, hubiste, hubo;
hubimos, hubisteis, hubieron

hacer / to do, to make
hice, hiciste, hizo;
hicimos, hicisteis, hicieron

herir / to harm, to hurt, to wound
herí, heriste, hirió;
herimos, heristeis, hirieron

A stem-changing verb because **e** changes to **i** in the stem in the 3rd pers. sing. and pl. of this tense. Pres. part. is **hiriendo.**

huir / to flee, to escape, to run away, to slip away
huí, huiste, huyó;
huimos, huisteis, huyeron

This —**uir** verb changes **i** to **y** in the 3rd pers. sing. and pl. of this tense. Pres. part. is **huyendo.**

impedir / to prevent, to impede, to hinder
impedí, impediste, impidió;
impedimos, impedisteis, impidieron

A stem-changing verb because **e** in the stem changes to **i** in the 3rd pers. sing. and pl. of this tense. Pres. part. is **impidiendo.**

imponer / to impose
impuse, impusiste, impuso;
impusimos, impusisteis, impusieron

incluir / to enclose, to include
incluí, incluiste, incluyó;
incluimos, incluisteis, incluyeron

This —**uir** verb changes **i** to **y** in the 3rd pers. sing. and pl. of this tense. Pres. part. is **incluyendo.**

indicar / to indicate
indiqué, indicaste, indicó;
indicamos, indicasteis, indicaron

An orthographical changing verb because **c** changes to **qu** in front of **é** in the 1st pers. sing. of this tense.

inducir / to induce, to influence, to persuade
induje, indujiste, indujo;
indujimos, indujisteis, indujeron

influir / to influence
influí, influiste, influyó;
influimos, influisteis, influyeron

This —**uir** verb changes **i** to **y** in the 3rd pers. sing. and pl. of this tense. Pres. part. is **influyendo.**

introducir / to introduce
introduje, introdujiste, introdujo;
introdujimos, introdujisteis, introdujeron

ir / to go

fui, fuiste, fue;
fuimos, fuisteis, fueron

NOTE that these forms are the same for **ser** in the preterit.

irse / to go away
me fui, te fuiste, se fue;
nos fuimos, os fuisteis, se fueron

jugar / to play (game or sport)
jugué, jugaste, jugó;
jugamos, jugasteis, jugaron

An orthographical changing verb because **g** changes to **gu** in front of **é** in the 1st pers. sing. of this tense.

lanzar / to throw, to hurl, to fling, to launch
lancé, lanzaste, lanzó;
lanzamos, lanzasteis, lanzaron

An orthographical changing verb because **z** changes to **c** in front of **é** in the 1st pers. sing. of this tense.

leer / to read
leí, leíste, leyó;
leímos, leísteis, leyeron

An orthographical changing verb because **i** in **ió** of the 3rd pers. sing. ending changes to **y** and **i** in **ieron** of the 3rd pers. plural ending changes to **y.** Also note that **i** in **iste** changes to **í** in the 2nd pers. sing. and **i** in **isteis** changes to **í** in the 2nd pers. pl. because of the strong vowel **e** in front of those two endings. The same thing happens in **leímos.** Remember that the regular endings in the preterit of an —**er** and —**ir** verb are: **í, iste, ió; imos, isteis, ieron.**

llegar / to arrive
llegué, llegaste, llegó;
llegamos, llegasteis, llegaron

An orthographical changing verb because **g** changes to **gu** in front of **é** in the 1st pers. sing. of this tense.

marcar / to mark
marqué, marcaste, marcó;
marcamos, marcasteis, marcaron

An orthographical changing verb because **c** changes to **qu** in front of **é** in the 1st pers. sing. of this tense.

mascar / to mask
masqué, mascaste, mascó;
mascamos, mascasteis, mascaron

An orthographical changing verb because **c** changes to **qu** in front of **é** in the 1st pers. sing. of this tense.

medir / to measure
medí, mediste, midió;
medimos, medisteis, midieron

A stem-changing verb because **e** in the stem
changes to **i** in the 3rd pers. sing. and pl. of this
tense. Pres. part. is **midiendo.**

mentir / to lie, to tell a lie
mentí, mentiste, mintió;
mentimos, mentisteis, mintieron

A stem-changing verb because **e** in the stem
changes to **i** in the 3rd pers. sing. and pl. of this
tense. Pres. part. is **mintiendo.**

morir / to die
morí, moriste, murió;
morimos, moristeis, murieron

A stem-changing verb because **o** in the stem
changes to **u** in the 3rd pers. sing. and pl. of
this tense. Pres. part. is **muriendo.**

negar / to deny
negué, negaste, negó;
negamos, negasteis, negaron

An orthographical changing verb because **g**
changes to **gu** in front of **é** in the 1st pers. sing.
of this tense.

obligar / to obligate, to compel
obligué, obligaste, obligó;
obligamos, obligasteis, obligaron

An orthographical changing verb because **g**
changes to **gu** in front of **é** in the 1st pers. sing.
of this tense.

obtener / to obtain, to get
obtuve, obtuviste, obtuvo;
obtuvimos, obtuvisteis, obtuvieron

oír / to hear (sometimes can mean *to understand*)
oí, oíste, oyó;
oímos, oísteis, oyeron

An orthographical changing verb because **i** in
ió of the 3rd pers. sing. ending and **i** in **ieron**
of the 3rd pers. plural ending both change to
y.

ALSO NOTE that **iste** changes to **íste, imos** to
ímos, and **isteis** to **ísteis** because of the strong
vowel **o** in front of those endings. Remember
that the regular endings in the preterit of an
—er and **—ir** verb are: **í, iste, ió, imos, isteis,**
ieron.

oponer / to oppose
opuse, opusiste, opuso;
opusimos, opusisteis, opusieron

pagar / to pay

pagué, pagaste, pagó;
pagamos, pagasteis, pagaron

An orthographical changing verb because **g**
changes to **gu** in front of **é** in the 1st pers. sing.
of this tense.

pedir / to ask for, to request
pedí, pediste, pidió;
pedimos, pedisteis, pidieron

A stem-changing verb because **e** in the stem
changes to **i** in the 3rd pers. sing. and pl. of this
tense. Pres. part. is **pidiendo.**

pegar / to beat, to hit, to slap
pegué, pegaste, pegó;
pegamos, pegasteis, pegaron

An orthographical changing verb because **g**
changes to **gu** in front of **é** in the 1st pers. sing.
of this tense.

pescar / to fish
pesqué, pescaste, pescó;
pescamos, pescasteis, pescaron

An orthographical changing verb because **c**
changes to **qu** in front of **é** in the 1st pers. sing.
of this tense.

poder / to be able, can
pude, pudiste, pudo;
pudimos, pudisteis, pudieron

See also §68.26.

poner / to put, to place
puse, pusiste, puso;
pusimos, pusisteis, pusieron

ponerse / to put on, to become (pale, angry, *etc.*),
to set (of the sun)
me puse, te pusiste, se puso;
nos pusimos, os pusisteis, se pusieron

poseer / to possess, to own
poseí, poseíste, poseyó;
poseímos, poseísteis, poseyeron

An orthographical changing verb because **i** in
ió of the 3rd pers. sing. ending and **i** in **ieron**
of the 3rd pers. plural ending both change to
y.

ALSO NOTE that **iste** changes to **íste, imos** to
ímos, and **isteis** to **ísteis** because of the strong
vowel **e** in front of those endings. Remember
that the regular endings in the preterit of an
—er and **—ir** verb are: **í, iste, ió; imos, isteis,**
ieron.

predecir / to predict, to forecast, to foretell
predije, predijiste, predijo;
predijimos, predijisteis, predijeron

predicar / to preach
prediqué, predicaste, predicó;
predicamos, predicasteis, predicaron

preferir / to prefer
preferí, preferiste, prefirió;
preferimos, preferisteis, prefirieron

A stem-changing verb because **e** in the stem changes to **i** in the 3rd pers. sing. and pl. of this tense. Pres. part. is **prefiriendo.**

producir / to produce
produje, produjiste, produjo;
produjimos, produjisteis, produjeron

proponer / to propose
propuse, propusiste, propuso;
propusimos, propusisteis, propusieron

publicar / to publish
publiqué, publicaste, publicó;
publicamos, publicasteis, publicaron

An orthographical changing verb because **c** change to **qu** in front of **é** in the 1st pers. sing. of this tense.

querer / to want, to wish
quise, quisiste, quiso;
quisimos, quisisteis, quisieron

See also §68.26.

raer / to erase, to wipe out, to scrape, to rub off
raí, raíste, rayó;
raímos, raísteis, rayeron

An orthographical changing verb because **i** in **ió** of the 3rd pers. sing. ending and **i** in **ieron** of the 3rd pers. plural ending both change to **y**.

ALSO NOTE that **iste** changes to **íste, imos** to **ímos,** and **isteis** to **ísteis** because of the strong vowel **a** in front of those endings. Remember that the regular endings in the preterit of an —er and —ir verb are: **í, iste, ió; imos, isteis, ieron.** Pres. part. is **rayendo.**

realizar / to realize, to carry out, to fulfill
realicé, realizaste, realizó;
realizamos, realizasteis, realizaron

An orthographical changing verb because **z** changes to **c** in front of **é** in the 1st pers. sing. of this tense.

referir / to refer
referí, referiste, refirió;
referimos, referisteis, refirieron

A stem-changing verb because **e** in the stem changes to **i** in the 3rd pers. sing. and pl. of this tense. Pres. part. is **refiriendo.**

reír / to laugh
reí, reíste, rió;
reímos, reísteis, rieron

Pres. part. is **riendo.**

reñir / to scold, to quarrel, to argue
reñí, reñiste, riñó;
reñimos, reñisteis, riñeron

Pres. part. is **riñendo.** Compare these forms of **reñir** with those of **gruñir** given above.

repetir / to repeat
repetí, repetiste, repitió;
repetimos, repetisteis, repitieron

A stem-changing verb because **e** in the stem changes to **i** in the 3rd pers. sing. and pl. of this tense. Pres. part. is **repitiendo.**

replicar / to reply
repliqué, replicaste, replicó;
replicamos, replicasteis, replicaron

An orthographical changing verb because **c** changes to **qu** in front of **é** in the 1st pers. sing. of this tense.

rezar / to pray
recé, rezaste, rezó;
rezamos, rezasteis, rezaron

An orthographical changing verb because **z** changes to **c** in front of **é** in the 1st pers. sing. of this tense.

rogar / to beg, to request
rogué, rogaste, rogó;
rogamos, rogasteis, rogaron

An orthographical changing verb because **g** changes to **gu** in front of **é** in the 1st pers. sing. of this tense.

saber / to know, to know how
supe, supiste, supo;
supimos, supisteis, supieron

See also §68.26.

sacar / to take out
saqué, sacaste, sacó;
sacamos, sacasteis, sacaron

An orthographical changing verb because **c** changes to **qu** in front of **é** in the 1st pers. sing. of this tense.

sacrificar / to sacrifice
sacrifiqué, sacrificaste, sacrificó;
sacrificamos, sacrificasteis, sacrificaron

An orthographical changing verb because **c** changes to **qu** in front of **é** in the 1st pers. sing. of this tense.

satisfacer / to satisfy
satisfice, satisficiste, satisfizo;
satisficimos, satisficisteis, satisficieron

Compare these forms of **satisfacer** with those of **hacer** given above.

secar / to dry, to wipe dry
sequé, secaste, secó;
secamos, secasteis, secaron

An orthographical changing verb because **c** changes to **qu** in front of **é** in the 1st pers. sing. of this tense.

seguir / to follow, to pursue, to continue
seguí, seguiste, siguió;
seguimos, seguisteis, siguieron

A stem-changing verb because **e** in the stem changes to **i** in the 3rd pers. sing. and pl. of this tense. Pres. part. is **siguiendo.**

ser / to be
fui, fuiste, fue;
fuimos, fuisteis, fueron

NOTE that these forms are the same for **ir** in the preterit.

sentir / to feel sorry, to regret, to feel, to experience, to sense
sentí, sentiste, sintió;
sentimos, sentisteis, sintieron

A stem-changing verb because **e** in the stem changes to **i** in the 3rd pers. sing. and pl. of this tense. Pres. part. is **sintiendo.**

servir / to serve
serví, serviste, sirvió;
servimos, servisteis, sirvieron

A stem-changing verb because **e** in the stem changes to **i** in the 3rd pers. sing. and pl. of this tense. Pres. part. is **sirviendo.**

significar / to mean, to signify
signifiqué, significaste, significó;
significamos, significasteis, significaron

An orthographical changing verb because **c** changes to **qu** in front of **é** in the 1st pers. sing. of this tense.

sollozar / to sob
sollocé, sollozaste, sollozó;
sollozamos, sollozasteis, sollozaron

An orthographical changing verb because **z** changes to **c** in front of **é** in the 1st pers. sing. of this tense.

sonreír / to smile
sonreí, sonreíste, sonrió;
sonreímos, sonreísteis, sonrieron

Pres. part. is **sonriendo.**

sugerir / to suggest, to hint
sugerí, sugeriste, sugirió;
sugerimos, sugeristeis, sugirieron

A stem-changing verb because **e** in the stem changes to **i** in the 3rd pers. sing. and pl. of this tense. Pres. part. is **sugiriendo.**

suplicar / to supplicate, to beseech, to entreat, to beg
supliqué, suplicaste, suplicó;
suplicamos, suplicasteis, suplicaron

An orthographical changing verb because **c** changes to **qu** in front of **é** in the 1st pers. sing. of this tense.

suponer / to suppose
supuse, supusiste, supuso;
supusimos, supusisteis, supusieron

tener / to have, to hold
tuve, tuviste, tuvo;
tuvimos, tuvisteis, tuvieron

See also §68.26.

tocar / to touch, to play (music or a musical instrument)
toqué, tocaste, tocó;
tocamos, tocasteis, tocaron

An orthographical changing verb because **c** changes to **qu** in front of **é** in the 1st pers. sing. of this tense.

traducir / to translate
traduje, tradujiste, tradujo;
tradujimos, tradujisteis, tradujeron

traer / to bring
traje, trajiste, trajo;
trajimos, trajisteis, trajeron

Pres. part. is **trayendo.**

tropezar / to stumble
tropecé, tropezaste, tropezó;
tropezamos, tropezasteis, tropezaron

An orthographical changing verb because **z** changes to **c** in front of **é** in the 1st pers. sing. of this tense.

utilizar / to utilize
utilicé, utilizaste, utilizó;
utilizamos, utilizasteis, utilizaron

An orthographical changing verb because **z** changes to **c** in front of **é** in the 1st pers. sing. of this tense.

venir / to come
vine, viniste, vino;

vinimos, vinisteis, vinieron

ver / to see
vi, viste, vio;
vimos, visteis, vieron

vestir / to dress, to clothe (someone)
vestí, vestiste, vistió;
vestimos, vestisteis, vistieron

A stem-changing verb because **e** in the stem

changes to **i** in the 3rd pers. sing. and pl. of this tense. Pres. part. is **vistiendo**.

vestirse / to dress, to clothe (oneself)
me vestí, te vestiste, se vistió;
nos vestimos, os vestisteis, se vistieron

A stem-changing verb because **e** in the stem changes to **i** in the 3rd pers. sing. and pl. of this tense. Pres. part. is **vistiéndose**.

NOTE: If I have inadvertently omitted any verb you have in mind, which is irregular in the preterit in some way, consult my book *501 Spanish verbs fully conjugated in all the tenses in a new easy to learn format,* Second Edition, also published by Barron's.

§68.31 **Tense No. 4: Futuro** (Future)

In Spanish and English, the future tense is used to express an action or a state of being that will take place at some time in the future.

EXAMPLES:
1. Lo **haré** / *I shall do* it; *I will do* it.
2. **Iremos** al campo la semana que viene / *We shall go* to the country next week; *We will go* to the country next week.

Also, in Spanish the future tense is used to indicate:

(a) Conjecture regarding the present.
EXAMPLES:
1. ¿Qué hora **será**? / *I wonder* what time *it is.*
2. ¿Quién **será**? / Who *can that be? I wonder who that is.*

(b) Probability regarding the present.
EXAMPLES:
1. **Serán** las cinco / *It is probably* five o'clock; *It must be* five o'clock.
2. **Tendrá** muchos amigos / *He probably has* many friends; *He must have* many friends.
3. María **estará** enferma / Mary *is probably* sick; Mary *must be* sick.

(c) An indirect quotation.
EXAMPLE: María dice que **vendrá** mañana / Mary says that she *will come* tomorrow.

Finally, remember that the future is never used in Spanish after *si* when *si* means *if.*

§68.32 **This tense is regularly formed as follows:**
Add the following endings to the whole infinitive: **é, ás, á; emos, éis, án**

NOTE that these future endings happen to be related to the endings of **haber** in the present indicative: **he, has, ha; hemos, habéis, han.** ALSO NOTE the accent marks on the future endings, except for **emos.**

§68.33 You then get: **hablaré, hablarás, hablará;**
hablaremos, hablaréis, hablarán

beberé, beberás, beberá;
beberemos, beberéis, beberán

recibiré, recibirás, recibirá;
recibiremos, recibiréis, recibirán

§68.34 The usual equivalent in English is: I shall talk OR I will talk, you will talk, *etc.*; I shall drink OR I will drink, you will drink, *etc.*; I shall receive OR I will receive, you will receive, *etc.*

§68.35 **Verbs irregular in the future**

caber / to fit, to be contained
cabré, cabrás, cabrá;
cabremos, cabréis, cabrán

The **e** of the inf. ending drops.

decir / to say, to tell
diré, dirás, dirá;
diremos, diréis, dirán

The **e** and **c** of the inf. drop.

haber / to have (as an auxiliary or helping verb)
habré, habrás, habrá;
habremos, habréis, habrán

The **e** of the inf. ending drops.

hacer / to do, to make
haré, harás, hará;
haremos, haréis, harán

The **c** and **e** of the inf. drop.

poder / to be able, can
podré, podrás, podrá;
podremos, podréis, podrán

The **e** of the inf. ending drops.

poner / to put, to place
pondré, pondrás, pondrá;
pondremos, pondréis, pondrán

The **e** of the inf. ending drops and **d** is added.

querer / to want, to wish
querré, querrás, querrá;
querremos, querréis, querrán

The **e** of the inf. ending drops and you are left with two **r**'s.

saber / to know, to know how
sabré, sabrás, sabrá;
sabremos, sabréis, sabrán

The **e** of the inf. ending drops.

salir / to go out
saldré, saldrás, saldrá;
saldremos, saldréis, saldrán

The **i** of the inf. ending drops and **d** is added.

tener / to have, to hold
tendré, tendrás, tendrá;
tendremos, tendréis, tendrán

The **e** of the inf. ending drops and **d** is added.

valer / to be worth, to be worthy
valdré, valdrás, valdrá;
valdremos, valdréis, valdrán

The **e** of the inf. ending drops and **d** is added.

venir / to come
vendré, vendrás, vendrá;
vendremos, vendréis, vendrán

The **i** of the inf. ending drops and **d** is added.

NOTE: If I have inadvertently omitted any verb you have in mind, which is irregular in the future in some way, consult my book *501 Spanish verbs fully conjugated in all the tenses in a new easy to learn format,* Second Edition, also published by Barron's.

§68.36 **Tense No. 5: Potencial simple** (Conditional)

The Conditional is used in Spanish and in English to express:

(a) An action that you *would do* if something else were possible.

EXAMPLE:

Iría a España si tuviera dinero / *I would go* to Spain if I had money. (For an explanation of **tuviera,** imperfect subjunctive, see **§67.111(2)** and **§68.50.**)

(b) A conditional desire. This is a conditional of courtesy.

EXAMPLE:

Me **gustaría** tomar una limonada / *I would like (I should like)* to have a lemonade . . . (if you are willing to let me have it).

(c) An indirect quotation.

EXAMPLES:

María *dijo* que **vendría** mañana / Mary *said* that she *would come* tomorrow.
María *decía* que **vendría** mañana / Mary *was saying* that she *would come tomorrow.*
María *había dicho* que **vendría** mañana / Mary *had said* that she *would come* tomorrow.

(d) Conjecture regarding the past.

EXAMPLE:

¿Quién **sería**? / *I wonder who that was.*

(e) Probability regarding the past.
EXAMPLE:
Serían las cinco cuando salieron / *It was probably* five o'clock when they went out.

See also the use of **deber de + inf.** in §20.2.

§68.37 **This tense is regularly formed as follows:**
Add the following endings to the whole infinitive: **ía, ías, ía; íamos, íais, ían**

NOTE that these conditional endings are the same endings of the imperfect indicative for **—er** and **—ir** verbs. See §68.23.

§68.38 You then get: **hablaría, hablarías, hablaría;
hablaríamos, hablaríais, hablarían**

**bebería, beberías, bebería;
beberíamos, beberíais, beberían**

**recibiría, recibirías, recibiría;
recibiríamos, recibiríais, recibirían**

§68.39 The usual translation in English is: I would talk, you would talk, *etc.*; I would drink, you would drink, *etc.*; I would receive, you would receive, *etc.*

§68.40 **Verbs irregular in the conditional**

caber / to fit, to be contained
**cabría, cabrías, cabría;
cabríamos, cabríais, cabrían**
The **e** of the inf. ending drops.

decir / to say, to tell
**diría, dirías, diría;
diríamos, diríais, dirían**
The **e** and **c** of the inf. drop.

haber / to have (as an auxiliary or helping verb)
**habría, habrías, habría;
habríamos, habríais, habrían**
The **e** of the inf. ending drops.

hacer / to do, to make
**haría, harías, haría;
haríamos, haríais, harían**
The **c** and **e** of the inf. drop.

poder / to be able, can
**podría, podrías, podría;
podríamos, podríais, podrían**
The **e** of the inf. ending drops.

poner / to put, to place
**pondría, pondrías, pondría;
pondríamos, pondríais, pondrían**
The **e** of the inf. ending drops and **d** is added.

querer / to want, to wish
**querría, querrías, querría;
querríamos, querríais, querrían**
The **e** of the inf. ending drops and you are left with two **r**'s.

saber / to know, to know how
**sabría, sabrías, sabría;
sabríamos, sabríais, sabrían**
The **e** of the inf. ending drops.

salir / to go out
**saldría, saldrías, saldría;
saldríamos, saldríais, saldrían**
The **i** of the inf. ending drops and **d** is added.

tener / to have, to hold
**tendría, tendrías, tendría;
tendríamos, tendríais, tendrían**
The **e** of the inf. ending drops and **d** is added.

valer / to be worth, to be worthy
**valdría, valdrías, valdría;
valdríamos, valdríais, valdrían**
The **e** of the inf. ending drops and **d** is added.

venir / to come
**vendría, vendrías, vendría;
vendríamos, vendríais, vendrían**
The **i** of the inf. ending drops and **d** is added.

NOTE: If I have inadvertently omitted any verb you have in mind, which is irregular in the conditional in some way, consult my book *501 Spanish verbs fully conjugated in all the tenses in a new easy to learn format,* Second Edition, also published by Barron's.

§68.41   **Tense No. 6: Presente de subjuntivo** (Present subjunctive) (See also **§67.33**)

The subjunctive mood is used in Spanish much more than in English. In Spanish the present subjunctive is used:

(a) To express a command in the **usted** or **ustedes** form, either in the affirmative or negative.

EXAMPLES:

    1. **Siéntese** Vd. / *Sit down.*

    2. **No se siente** Vd. / *Don't sit down.*

    3. **Cierren** Vds. la puerta / *Close* the door.

    4. **No cierren** Vds. la puerta / *Don't close* the door.

    5. **Dígame** Vd. la verdad / *Tell me* the truth.

(b) To express a negative command in the familiar form (**tú**).

EXAMPLES:

    1. **No te sientes** / *Don't sit down.*

    2. **No entres** / *Don't come in.*

    3. **No duermas** / *Don't sleep.*

    4. **No lo hagas** / *Don't do it.*

(c) To express a negative command in the second person plural (**vosotros**).

EXAMPLES:

    1. **No os sentéis** / *Don't sit down.*

    2. **No entréis** / *Don't come in.*

    3. **No durmáis** / *Don't sleep.*

    4. **No lo hagáis** / *Don't do it.*

(d) To express a command in the first person plural, either in the affirmative or negative (**nosotros**).

EXAMPLES:

    1. **Sentémonos** / *Let's sit down.*

    2. **No entremos** / *Let's not go in.*

See also **Imperativo** (Imperative) in **§68.62.**

(e) After a verb that expresses some kind of wish, insistence, preference, suggestion, or request. For those verbs, see **§67.87–§67.100.**

EXAMPLES:

    1. *Quiero* que María lo **haga** / I want Mary to do it.

NOTE: In this example, English uses the infinitive form, *to do.* In Spanish, however, a new clause is needed introduced by *que* because there is a new subject, María. The present subjunctive of *hacer* is used (**haga**) because the main verb is *Quiero*, which indicates a wish. If there were no change in subject, Spanish would use the infinitive form, as we do in English, for example, **Quiero hacerlo** / *I want to do it.*

    2. *Insisto* en que María lo **haga** / I insist that Mary *do* it.

    3. *Prefiero* que María lo **haga** / I prefer that Mary *do* it.

    4. *Pido* que María lo **haga** / I ask that Mary *do* it.

NOTE: In examples 2, 3, and 4 here, English also uses the subjunctive form *do.* Not so in example no. 1, however.

(f) After a verb that expresses doubt, fear, joy, hope, sorrow, or some other emotion. Notice in the following examples, however, that the subjunctive is not used in English. For those verbs, see **§67.78–§67.86.**

EXAMPLES:

    1. *Dudo* que María lo **haga** / I doubt that Mary *is doing* it; I doubt that Mary *will do* it.

    2. *No creo* que María **venga** / I don't believe (I doubt) that Mary *is coming;* I don't believe (I doubt) that Mary *will come.*

    3. *Temo* que María **esté** enferma / I fear that Mary *is* ill.

4. *Me alegro* de que **venga** María / I'm glad that Mary *is coming;* I'm glad that Mary *will come.*

5. *Espero* que María no **esté** enferma / I hope that Mary *is* not ill.

(g) After certain impersonal expressions that show necessity, doubt, regret, importance, urgency, or possibility. Notice, however, that the subjunctive is not used in English in all of the following examples. For those impersonal expressions, see §67.71–§67.77.

EXAMPLES:

1. *Es necesario que* María lo **haga** / It is necessary for Mary to do it; It is necessary that Mary *do* it.

2. *No es cierto que* María **venga** / It is doubtful (not certain) that Mary *is coming;* It is doubtful (not certain) that Mary *will come.*

3. *Es lástima que* María **no venga** / It's too bad (a pity) that Mary *isn't coming.*

4. *Es importante que* María **venga** / It is important for Mary to come; It is important that Mary *come.*

5. *Es preciso que* María **venga** / It is necessary for Mary to come; It is necessary that Mary *come.*

6. *Es urgente que* María **venga** / It is urgent for Mary to come; It is urgent that Mary *come.*

(h) After certain conjunctions of time, such as **antes (de) que, cuando, en cuanto, después (de) que, hasta que, mientras,** and the like. The subjunctive form of the verb is used when introduced by any of these time conjunctions if the time referred to is either indefinite or is expected to take place in the future. However, if the action was completed in the past, the indicative mood is used. See §67.34–§67.43.

EXAMPLES:

1. Le hablaré a María cuando **venga** / I shall talk to Mary when she *comes.*

2. Vámonos antes (de) que **llueva** / Let's go before *it rains.*

3. En cuanto la **vea** yo, le hablaré / As soon as *I see* her, I shall talk to her.

4. Me quedo aquí hasta que **vuelva** / I'm staying here until *he returns.*

NOTE: In the above examples, the subjunctive is not used in English.

(i) After certain conjunctions that express a condition, negation, purpose, such as, **a menos que, con tal que, para que, a fin de que, sin que, en caso (de) que,** and the like. Notice, however, that the subjunctive is not used in English in the following examples. For these conjunctions, and others, see §67.34–§67.43.

EXAMPLES:

1. Démelo con tal que **sea** bueno / Give it to me provided that *it is* good.

2. Me voy a menos que **venga** / I'm leaving unless *he comes.*

(j) After certain adverbs, such as, **acaso, quizá,** and **tal vez.** See also §67.44–§67.46.

EXAMPLE:

Acaso **venga** mañana / Perhaps *he will come* tomorrow; Perhaps *he is coming* tomorrow.

(k) After **aunque** if the action has not yet occurred.

EXAMPLE:

Aunque María **venga** esta noche, no me quedo / Although Mary *may come* tonight, I'm not staying; Although Mary *is coming* tonight, I'm not staying.

(l) In an adjectival clause if the antecedent is something or someone that is indefinite, negative, vague, or nonexistent. See also §67.54–§67.62.

EXAMPLES:

1. Busco un libro que **sea** interesante / I'm looking for a book that *is* interesting.

NOTE: In this example, *que* (which is the relative pronoun) refers to *un libro* (which is the antecedent). Since *un libro* is indefinite, the verb in the following clause must be in the subjunctive (**sea**). Notice, however, that the subjunctive is not used in English.

2. ¿Hay alguien aquí que **hable** francés? / Is there anyone here who *speaks* French?

NOTE: In this example, *que* (which is the relative pronoun) refers to *alguien* (which is the antecedent). Since *alguien* is indefinite and somewhat vague—we do not know who this anyone might be—the verb in the following clause must be in the subjunctive (**hable**). Notice, however, that the subjunctive is not used in English.

3. No hay nadie que **pueda** hacerlo / There is no one who *can* do it.

NOTE: In this example, *que* (which is the relative pronoun) refers to *nadie* (which is the antecedent). Since *nadie* is nonexistent, the verb in the following clause must be in the subjunctive (**pueda**). Notice, however, that the subjunctive is not used in English.

(m) After **por más que** or **por mucho que**. See also §67.47ff.

EXAMPLES:

1. **Por más que hable usted,** no quiero escuchar / *No matter how much you talk,* I don't want to listen.

2. **Por mucho que se alegre,** no me importa / *No matter how glad he is,* I don't care.

(n) After the expression **ojalá (que),** which expresses a great desire. This interjection means *would to God!* or *may God grant!* . . . It is derived from the Arabic, **ya Allah!** / (Oh, God!) See also §67.67ff.

EXAMPLE:

¡**Ojalá que vengan** mañana! / *Would to God that they come* tomorrow! *May God grant that they come* tomorrow! *How I wish that they would come* tomorrow! *If only they would come* tomorrow!

Finally, remember that the present subjunctive is never used in Spanish after *si* when *si* means *if*. See also §67.50–§67.53, §67.63–§67.66, and §67.101–§67.111.

§68.42
The present subjunctive of regular verbs and many irregular verbs is normally formed as follows:

Go to the present indicative, 1st pers. sing., of the verb you have in mind, drop the ending **o**, and

for an —**ar** ending type, add: **e, es, e; emos, éis, en**

for an —**er** or —**ir** ending type, add: **a, as, a; amos, áis, an**

As you can see, the characteristic vowel in the present subjunctive endings for an —**ar** type verb is **e** in the six persons.

As you can see, the characteristic vowel in the present subjunctive endings for an —**er** or —**ir** type verb is **a** in the six persons.

§68.43
You then get, for example: **hable, hables, hable;
hablemos, habléis, hablen
beba, bebas, beba;
bebamos, bebáis, beban
reciba, recibas, reciba;
recibamos, recibáis, reciban**

§68.44
The usual equivalent in English is: (that I) talk OR (that I) may talk, (that you) talk OR (that you) may talk, (that he/she) talk OR (that he/she) may talk, *etc.*; (that I) drink OR (that I) may drink, (that you) drink OR (that you) may drink, (that he/she) drink OR (that he/she) may drink, *etc.*; (that I) receive OR (that I) may receive, (that you) receive OR (that you) may receive, (that he/she) receive OR (that he/she) may receive, *etc.*

§68.45 Verbs irregular in the present subjunctive commonly used
The following verbs are irregular because if you go to the present indicative, 1st pers. sing. of these verbs, you will find a form which you cannot work with according to the process of forming the present subjunctive normally, as explained in **§68.42** above. Also, see the irregular verbs in the present indicative where they are arranged alphabetically in **§68.19**.

dar / to give
dé, des, dé;
demos, deis, den

estar / to be
esté, estés, esté;
estemos, estéis, estén

haber / to have (as an auxiliary or helping verb)
haya, hayas, haya;
hayamos, hayáis, hayan

ir / to go
vaya, vayas, vaya;
vayamos, vayáis, vayan

saber / to know, to know how
sepa, sepas, sepa;
sepamos, sepáis, sepan

ser / to be
sea, seas, sea;
seamos, seáis, sean

§68.46 **Other verbs irregular in the present subjunctive**

§68.47 Stem-changing verbs in the present indicative have the same stem changes in the present subjunctive, generally speaking. If you go to the present indicative, 1st pers. sing. of those verbs, you will find the stem change there. Drop the ending **o** and add the appropriate endings of the present subjunctive, as explained in §68.42 above. For example, to form the present subjunctive of **pensar,** go to the 1st pers. sing. of the present indicative and there you will find **pienso.** Drop the ending **o** and add: **e, es, e; emos, éis, en.** The verbs irregular in the present indicative, including stem-changing and orthographical changing verbs, are given to you alphabetically in §68.19.

§68.48 Orthographical changing verbs (those that change in spelling), which end in **car, gar,** and **zar** in the infinitive form, have the same spelling changes in the present subjunctive as they do in the 1st pers. sing. of the preterit. Just drop the accent mark on **é** and you have the form of the present subjunctive, generally speaking. Those verbs are given to you in §68.30 where they are listed alphabetically under **Verbs irregular in the preterit, including stem-changing verbs and orthographical changing verbs.**

FOR EXAMPLE:

Preterit, 1st pers. sing.	Present subjunctive
abracé (abra**zar**)	**abrace, abraces, abrace;** **abracemos, abracéis, abracen**
busqué (bus**car**)	**busque, busques, busque;** **busquemos, busquéis, busquen**
pagué (pa**gar**)	**pague, pagues, pague;** **paguemos, paguéis, paguen**

§68.49 However, there are some verbs of the type that end in **car, gar,** and **zar** which are stem-changing when stressed and the process described in §68.48 above will not work for them. For example:

Take **almorzar.** If you go to the preterit, 1st pers. sing., you will find **almorcé.** If you drop the accent mark on **é,** you are left with **almorce,** which is not the correct form in the present subjunctive. The **o** in the stem is stressed and it changes to **ue;** the forms in the present subjunctive for this verb contain the stem change, which is found in the present indicative. The forms of **almorzar** in the present subjunctive, therefore, are: **almuerce, almuerces, almuerce; almor-**

cemos, almorcéis, almuercen.

See the verb **almorzar** in sections §68.19 and §68.30.

Finally, remember that there is really no easy perfect system of arriving at verb forms no matter what process is used because there is usually some exception—even if only one exception. The best thing for you to do, since you are preparing to take standardized tests in Spanish, is to be sure you know the regular forms in all the tenses and the irregular forms that are commonly used just so that you can recognize them. All those that you need to know and to recognize are given to you in these sections on Spanish verbs.

If I have inadvertently omitted any verb you have in mind, which is irregular in the present subjunctive in some way, consult my book *501 Spanish verbs fully conjugated in all the tenses in a new easy to learn format*, Second Edition, also published by Barron's.

§68.50 **Tense No. 7: Imperfecto de subjuntivo** (!mperfect subjunctive) (See also §67.33)

This past tense is used for the same reasons as the **presente de subjuntivo**—that is, after certain verbs, conjunctions, impersonal expressions, etc., which were explained and illustrated above in §68.37–§68.45. The main difference between these two tenses is the time of the action.

If the verb in the main clause is in the present indicative or future or present perfect indicative or imperative, the *present subjunctive* or the *present perfect subjunctive* (see §67.101, no. 1) is used in the dependent clause—provided, of course, that there is some element which requires the use of the subjunctive.

However, if the verb in the main clause is in the imperfect indicative, preterit, conditional, or pluperfect indicative, the *imperfect subjunctive* (this tense) or *pluperfect subjunctive* is ordinarily used in the dependent clause—provided, of course, that there is some element which requires the use of the subjunctive. See also §67.101, no. 2.

EXAMPLES:
1. *Insistí* en que María lo **hiciera** / I insisted that Mary *do* it.
2. Se lo *explicaba* a María **para que lo comprendiera** / I was explaining it to Mary *so that she might understand it.*

NOTE that the *imperfect subjunctive* is used after **como si** to express a condition contrary to fact. See also §67.34.

EXAMPLE:
Me habla como si **fuera** un niño / He speaks to me as if *I were* a child.

NOTE: In this last example, the subjunctive is used in English also for the same reason.

Finally, note that **quisiera** (the imperfect subjunctive or **querer**) can be used to express in a very polite way, *I should like:* **Quisiera hablar ahora** / I should like to speak now.

§68.51 **The imperfect subjunctive is regularly formed as follows:**

For all verbs, drop the **ron** ending of the 3rd pers. pl. of the preterit and add the following endings:

ra, ras, ra;	OR	**se, ses, se;**
ramos, rais, ran		**semos, seis, sen**

§68.52 The only accent mark on the forms of the imperfect subjunctive is on the 1st pers. pl. form (**nosotros**) and it is placed on the vowel which is right in front of the ending **ramos** or **semos**.

§68.53 EXAMPLES:

Preterit, 3rd pers. plural	Imperfect subjunctive
bebieron (beber)	**bebiera, bebieras, bebiera;**
	bebiéramos, bebierais, bebieran
	OR
	bebiese, bebieses, bebiese;
	bebiésemos, bebieseis, bebiesen

creyeron (creer)	**creyera, creyeras, creyera;** **creyéramos, creyerais, creyeran**
	OR
	creyese, creyeses, creyese; **creyésemos, creyeseis, creyesen**
dieron (dar)	**diera, dieras, diera;** **diéramos, dierais, dieran**
	OR
	diese, dieses, diese; **diésemos, dieseis, diesen**
dijeron (decir)	**dijera, dijeras, dijera;** **dijéramos, dijerais, dijeran**
	OR
	dijese, dijeses, dijese; **dijésemos, dijeseis, dijesen**
durmieron (dormir)	**durmiera, durmieras, durmiera;** **durmiéramos, durmierais, durmieran**
	OR
	durmiese, durmieses, durmiese; **durmiésemos, durmieseis, durmiesen**
hubieron (haber)	**hubiera, hubieras, hubiera;** **hubiéramos, hubieras, hubieran**
	OR
	hubiese, hubieses, hubiese; **hubiésemos, hubieseis, hubiesen**
hablaron (hablar)	**hablara, hablaras, hablara;** **habláramos, hablarais, hablaran**
	OR
	hablase, hablases, hablase; **hablásemos, hablaseis, hablasen**
hicieron (hacer)	**hiciera, hicieras, hiciera;** **hiciéramos, hicierais, hicieran**
	OR
	hiciese, hicieses, hiciese; **hiciésemos, hicieseis, hiciesen**
fueron (ir)	**fuera, fueras, fuera;** **fuéramos, fuerais, fueran**
	OR
	fuese, fueses, fuese; **fuésemos, fueseis, fuesen**

leyeron (leer)	**leyera, leyeras, leyera;**
	leyéramos, leyerais, leyeran
	OR
	leyese, leyeses, leyese;
	leyésemos, leyeseis, leyesen
recibieron (recibir)	**recibiera, recibieras, recibiera;**
	recibiéramos, recibierais, recibieran
	OR
	recibiese, recibieses, recibiese;
	recibiésemos, recibieseis, recibiesen
fueron (ser)	**fuera, fueras, fuera;**
	fuéramos, fuerais, fueran
	OR
	fuese, fueses, fuese;
	fuésemos, fueseis, fuesen
tuvieron (tener)	**tuviera, tuvieras, tuviera;**
	tuviéramos, tuvierais, tuvieran
	OR
	tuviese, tuvieses, tuviese;
	tuviésemos, tuvieseis, tuviesen

§68.54 Using the first three examples given above in **§68.53** (**beber, creer, dar**), the usual English equivalents are as follows:

(that I) might drink, (that you) might drink, (that he/she) might drink, *etc.*
(that I) might believe, (that you) might believe, (that he/she) might believe, *etc.*
(that I) might give, (that you) might give, (that he/she) might give, *etc.*

§68.55 Tense No. 8: Perfecto de indicativo (Present perfect indicative)

This is the first of the seven compound tenses that follow here. This tense expresses an action that took place at no definite time in the past. It is also called Past Indefinite. It is a compound tense because it is formed with the present indicative of **haber** (the auxiliary or helping verb) plus the past participle of the verb you have in mind. Note the translation into English in the examples that follow. Then compare this tense with the Perfecto de Subjuntivo and the examples given in **§68.60.** For the seven simple tenses of **haber** (which you need to know to form these seven compound tenses), see **§68.11.** See also **§68.4.**

1. (Yo) **he hablado** / *I have spoken.*
2. (Tú) no **has venido** a verme / *You have not come* to see me.
3. Elena **ha ganado** el premio / Helen *has won* the prize.

§68.56 Tense No. 9: Pluscuamperfecto de indicativo (Pluperfect *or* Past perfect indicative)

This is the second of the compound tenses. In Spanish and English, this past tense is used to express an action which happened in the past *before* another past action. Since it is used in relation to another past action, the other past action is ordinarily expressed in the preterit. However, it is not always necessary to have the other past action expressed, as in example no. 2 below.

In English, this tense is formed with the past tense of *to have* (had) plus the past participle of the verb you have in mind. In Spanish, this tense is formed with the imperfect indicative of **haber** plus the past participle of the verb you have in mind. Note the translation into English in the examples that follow. Then compare this tense with the **pluscuamperfecto de subjuntivo** and the examples given in **§68.61.** For the seven simple tenses of **haber** (which you need to know to form these seven compound tenses), see §68.11. See also §68.5.

1. Cuando **llegué** a casa, mi hermano **había salido** / When I *arrived* home, my brother *had gone out*.

   NOTE: *First,* my brother went out; *then,* I arrived home. Both actions happened in the past. The action that occurred in the past *before* the other past action is in the pluperfect, and in this example it is *my brother had gone out* (**mi hermano había salido**).

   NOTE ALSO that **llegué** (*I arrived*) is in the preterit because it is an action that happened in the past and it was completed.

2. Juan lo **había perdido** en la calle / John *had lost* it in the street.

   NOTE: In this example, the pluperfect indicative is used even though no other past action is expressed. It is assumed that John *had lost* something **before** some other past action.

§68.57   Tense No. 10: Pretérito anterior (Past anterior or Preterit perfect)

This is the third of the compound tenses. This past tense is compound because it is formed with the preterit of **haber** plus the past participle of the verb you are using. It is translated into English like the pluperfect indicative explained in §68.56 above. This tense is not used much in spoken Spanish. Ordinarily, the pluperfect indicative is used in spoken Spanish (and sometimes even the simple preterit) in place of the past anterior.

This tense is ordinarily used in formal writing, such as history and literature. It is normally used after certain conjunctions of time, *e.g.,* **después que, cuando, apenas, luego que, en cuanto.**

For your purposes, since you are preparing to take standardized tests in Spanish, you must become familiar with this tense because you will have to recognize its meaning in reading comprehension selections. Remember that it is translated into English the same as the pluperfect indicative in §68.56 above. It is used in literature and formal writings, rarely in informal conversation. See §68.6 and §68.11.

   EXAMPLE:
   Después que **hubo hablado,** salió / After *he had spoken,* he left.

§68.58   Tense No. 11: Futuro perfecto (Future perfect or Future anterior)

This is the fourth of the compound tenses. This compound tense is formed with the future of **haber** plus the past participle of the verb you have in mind. In Spanish and in English, this tense is used to express an action that will happen in the future *before* another future action. In English, this tense is formed by using *shall have* or *will have* plus the past participle of the verb you have in mind.

   NOTE the translation into English in the examples that follow. See §68.7 and §68.11.

   EXAMPLE:
   María llegará mañana y **habré terminado** mi trabajo / Mary will arrive tomorrow and *I shall have finished* my work.

   NOTE: *First,* I shall finish my work; *then,* Mary will arrive. The action that will occur in the future *before* the other future action is in the **Futuro perfecto,** and in this example it is (yo) **habré terminado mi trabajo.**

Also, in Spanish the future perfect is used to indicate conjecture or probability regarding recent past time.

   EXAMPLES:
   1. María **se habrá acostado** / Mary *has probably gone to bed;* Mary *must have gone to bed.*
   2. José **habrá llegado** / Joseph *has probably arrived;* Joseph *must have arrived.*

§68.59   Tense No. 12: Potencial compuesto (Conditional perfect)

This is the fifth of the compound tenses. It is formed with the conditional of **haber** (see §68.8 and §68.11) plus the past participle of the verb you have in mind. It is used in Spanish and English to express an action that you *would have done* if something else had been possible; that is, you would have done something *on condition* that something else had been possible.

In English it is formed by using *would have* plus the past participle of the verb you have in mind. Observe the difference between the following example and the one given for the use of the **Potencial simple** which was explained and illustrated in **§68.36(a)**.

> EXAMPLE:
>
> (a) **Habría ido** a España si hubiera tenido dinero / *I would have gone* to Spain if I had had money. (For an explanation of **hubiera tenido**, see **§67.111(3)** and **§68.61.**

Also, in Spanish the Conditional perfect is used to indicate probability or conjecture in the past.

> EXAMPLE:
>
> (b) **Habrían sido** las cinco cuando salieron / *It must have been* five o'clock when they went out. [Compare this with the example given for the simple conditional in **§68.36(e)**].
>
> (c) ¿Quién **habría sido**? / Who *could that have been* (or I wonder *who that could have been*). [Compare this with the example given for the simple conditional in **§68.36(d)**.]

§68.60   **Tense No. 13: Perfecto de subjuntivo** (Present perfect *or* Past subjunctive) (See also **§67.33ff**)

This is the sixth of the compound tenses. It is formed by using the present subjunctive of **haber** as the helping verb (see **§68.9** and **§68.11**) plus the past participle of the verb you have in mind.

If the verb in the main clause is in the present indicative, future, or present perfect tense, the present subjunctive (see **§68.41**) is used *or* this tense is used in the dependent clause—provided, of course, that there is some element which requires the use of the subjunctive.

The Present subjunctive is used if the action is not past. However, if the action is past, this tense (present perfect subjunctive) is used, as in the examples given below.

Review the present subjunctive in **§68.41** and the imperfect subjunctive in **§68.50**.

NOTE the following examples in which this tense is used. Then compare them with the examples given in **§68.55** where the **Perfecto de indicativo** is explained and illustrated:

1. María duda que yo le **haya hablado** al profesor / Mary doubts that *I have spoken* to the professor.
2. Siento que tú no **hayas venido** a verme / I am sorry that you *have not come* to see me.
3. Me alegro de que Elena **haya ganado** el premio / I am glad that Helen *has won* the prize.

In these three examples, the auxiliary verb **haber** is used in the present subjunctive because the main verb in the clause that precedes is one that requires the subjunctive mood of the verb in the dependent clause. See the special verbs that require the subjunctive form of a verb in a dependent clause in **§67.78–§67.99**.

§68.61   **Tense No. 14: Pluscuamperfecto de subjuntivo** (Pluperfect *or* Past perfect subjunctive) (See also **§67.33ff**)

This is the seventh of the compound tenses. It is formed by using the imperfect subjunctive of **haber** as the helping verb (see **§68.10** and **§68.11**) plus the past participle of the verb you have in mind.

The translation of this tense into English is often like the pluperfect indicative (see **§68.56**).

If the verb in the main clause is in a past tense, this tense is used in the dependent clause—provided, of course, that there is some element which requires the use of the subjunctive. Review **§67.101(2)**.

> EXAMPLES:
>
> 1. Sentí mucho que **no hubiera venido** María / I was very sorry that Mary *had not come.*
> 2. Me alegraba de que **hubiera venido** María / I was glad that Mary *had come.*
> 3. No creía que María **hubiera llegado** / I did not believe that Mary *had arrived.*

So much for the seven simple tenses and the seven compound tenses. Now, let's look at the Imperative Mood.

§68.62   **Imperativo** (Imperative *or* Command)

The Imperative mood is used in Spanish and in English to express a command. We saw earlier in §68.41 that the subjunctive mood is used to express commands in the **Ud.** and **Uds.** forms, in addition to other uses of the subjunctive mood. Review §68.41(a) to (d) and (n).

Here are other points you ought to know about the Imperative.

(a) An indirect command or deep desire expressed in the third pers. sing. or pl. is in the subjunctive. Notice the use of *Let* or *May* in the English translations. **Que** introduces this kind of command. Examples:

1. ¡Que lo **haga** Jorge!
   Let George do it!
2. ¡Que Dios se lo **pague**!
   May God reward you!
3. ¡Que **vengan** pronto!
   Let them come quickly!
4. ¡Que **entre** Roberto!
   Let Robert enter!
5. ¡Que **salgan**!
   Let them leave!
6. ¡Que **entren** las muchachas!
   Let the girls come in!

(b) In some indirect commands, **que** is omitted. Here, too, the subjunctive is used. Example: ¡**Viva** el presidente! / Long live the president!

(c) The verb form of the affirmative sing. familiar (**tú**) is the same as the 3rd pers. sing. of the present indicative when expressing a command. Examples:

1. ¡**Entra** pronto! / *Come in* quickly!
2. ¡**Sigue** leyendo! / *Keep on* reading! or *Continue* reading!

(d) There are some exceptions, however, to (c) above. The following verb forms are irregular in the affirmative sing. imperative (**tú** form only).

di (decir)   **sal** (salir)   **val** (valer)
haz (hacer)   **sé** (ser)   **ve** (ir)
he (haber)   **ten** (tener)   **ven** (venir)
pon (poner)

(e) In the affirmative command, 1st pers. pl., instead of using the present subjunctive hortatory command, **vamos a** (*Let's* or *Let us*) **+ inf.** may be used. Examples:

1. **Vamos a** comer / Let's eat.
   or: **Comamos** (1st pers. pl., present subj., hortatory command)
2. **Vamos a** cantar / Let's sing.
   or: **Cantemos** (1st pers. pl., present subj., hortatory command)

(f) In the affirmative command, 1st pers. pl., **vamos** may be used to mean *Let's go:* **Vamos** al cine / Let's go to the movies.

(g) However, if in the negative (*Let's not go*), the present subjunctive of **ir** must be used: **No vayamos** al cine / Let's not go to the movies.

(h) Note that **vámonos** (1st pers. pl. of **irse,** imperative) means *Let's go,* or *Let's go away,* or *Let's leave.* See (m) below.

(i) Also note that **no nos vayamos** (1st pers. pl. of **irse,** present subjunctive) means *Let's not go,* or *Let's not go away,* or *Let's not leave.*

(j) The imperative in the affirmative familiar plural (**vosotros, vosotras**) is formed by dropping the final **r** of the inf. and adding **d**. Examples:

1. ¡**Hablad**! / Speak!
2. ¡**Comed**! / Eat!
3. ¡**Id**! / Go!
4. ¡**Venid**! / Come!

(k) When forming the affirmative familiar plural (**vosotros, vosotras**) imperative of a reflexive verb, the final **d** on the inf. must be dropped before the reflexive pronoun **os** is added, and both elements are joined to make one word. Examples:

1. ¡**Levantaos**! / Get up!
2. ¡**Sentaos**! / Sit down!

(l) Referring to (k) above, when the final **d** is dropped in a reflexive verb ending in **—ir,** an accent mark must be written on the **i.** Examples:

1. **¡Vestíos!** / Get dressed!   2. **¡Divertíos!** / Have a good time!

(m) When forming the 1st pers. pl. affirmative imperative of a reflexive verb, the final **s** must drop before the reflexive pronoun **os** is added, and both elements are joined to make one word. This requires an accent mark on the vowel of the syllable that was stressed before **os** was added. Example:

Vamos + nos changes to: **Vámonos!** / *Let's go!* or *Let's go away!* or *Let's leave!* See (h) above.

(n) All negative imperatives in the familiar 2nd pers. sing. (**tú**) and plural (**vosotros, vosotras**) are expressed in the present subjunctive. Review §68.41(b) and (c). Examples:

1. **¡No corras (tú)!** / Don't run!
2. **¡No corráis (vosotros or vosotras)!** / Don't run!
3. **¡No vengas (tú)!** / Don't come!
4. **¡No vengáis (vosotros or vosotras)!** / Don't come!

(o) Object pronouns (direct, indirect, or reflexive) with an imperative verb form in the **affirmative** are attached to the verb form. See also **Position of object pronouns** in §66.34–§66.53 and the entry **accent mark** in the Comprehensive Index in the back pages of this book for section references in this Grammar Part. Examples:

1. **¡Hágalo (Ud.)!** / Do it!
2. **¡Díganoslo (Ud.)!** / Tell it to us!
3. **¡Dímelo (tú)!** / Tell it to me!
4. **¡Levántate (tú)!** / Get up!
5. **¡Siéntese (Ud.)!** / Sit down!
6. **¡Hacedlo (vosotros, vosotras)!** / Do it!
7. **¡Démelo (Ud.)!** / Give it to me!

(p) Object pronouns (direct, indirect, or reflexive) with an imperative verb form in the **negative** are placed in front of the verb form. See also **Position of object pronouns** in §66.34–§66.53 and the entry **accent mark** in the Comprehensive Index in the back pages of this book for section references in this Grammar Part. Compare the following examples with those given in (o) above:

1. **¡No lo haga (Ud.)!** / Don't do it!
2. **¡No nos lo diga (Ud.)!** / Don't tell it to us!
3. **¡No me lo digas (tú)!** / Don't tell it to me!
4. **¡No te levantes (tú)!** / Don't get up!
5. **¡No se siente (Ud.)!** / Don't sit down!
6. **¡No lo hagáis (vosotros, vosotras)!** / Don't do it!
7. **¡No me lo dé (Ud.)!** / Don't give it to me!

(q) Note that in some countries in Latin America the 2nd pers. pl. familiar (**vosotros, vosotras**) forms are avoided. In place of them, the 3rd pers. pl. **Uds.** forms are customarily used.

§68.63   The Progressive forms of tenses: a note

(1) In Spanish, there are also progressive forms of tenses. They are the Progressive Present and the Progressive Past.

(2) The Progressive Present is formed by using **estar** in the present tense plus the present participle of your main verb; *e.g.,* **Estoy hablando** (*I am talking*), *i.e., I am* (in the act of) *talking* (right now).

(3) The Progressive Past is formed by using **estar** in the imperfect indicative plus the present participle of your main verb; *e.g.,* **Estaba hablando** (*I was talking*), *i.e., I was* (in the act of) *talking* (right then).

(4) The progressive forms are used when you want to emphasize or intensify an action; if you don't want to do that, then just use the simple present or simple imperfect; *e.g.,* say **Hablo,** *not* **Estoy hablando;** or **Hablaba,** *not* **Estaba hablando.**

(5) Sometimes **ir** is used instead of **estar** to form the progressive tenses; *e.g.,* **Va hablando** (*he/she keeps right on talking*), **Iba hablando** (*he/she kept right on talking*). Note that they do not have the exact same meaning as **Está hablando** and **Estaba hablando.** See (2) and (3) above.

(6) See also the General Index in the back pages of this book for other references about these forms under the entry **Progressive forms.**

§68.64　The Future Subjunctive and the Future Perfect Subjunctive: a note

The Future Subjunctive and the Future Perfect Subjunctive exist in Spanish, but they are rarely used. Nowadays, instead of using the Future Subjunctive, one uses the Present Subjunctive or the Present Indicative. Instead of using the Future Perfect Subjunctive, one uses the Future Perfect Indicative or the Present Perfect Subjunctive. However, if you are curious to know how to form the Future Subjunctive and the Future Perfect Subjunctive in Spanish, the following is offered:

(1) To form the Future Subjunctive, take the third person plural of the Pretèrit of any Spanish verb and change the ending **—ron** to **re, res, re; remos, reis, ren.** An accent mark is needed as shown below on the first person plural form to preserve the stress.

EXAMPLES:

amar	**amare, amares, amare;** **amáremos, amareis, amaren**
comer	**comiere, comieres, comiere;** **comiéremos, comiereis, comieren**
dar	**diere, dieres, diere;** **diéremos, diereis, dieren**
haber	**hubiere, hubieres, hubiere;** **hubiéremos, hubiereis, hubieren**
hablar	**hablare, hablares, hablare;** **habláremos, hablareis, hablaren**
ir *or* **ser**	**fuere, fueres, fuere;** **fuéremos, fuereis, fueren**

(2) Let's look at the forms of **amar** above to see what the English translation is of this tense:

(que) yo amare, (that) I love . . .
(que) tú amares, (that) you love . . .
(que) Vd. (él, ella) amare, (that) you (he, she) love . . .
(que) nosotros (—tras) amáremos, (that) we love . . .
(que) vosotros (—tras) amareis, (that) you love . . .
(que) Vds. (ellos, ellas) amaren, (that) you (they) love . . .

(3) To form the Future Perfect Subjunctive, use the Future Subjunctive form of **haber** (shown above) as your auxiliary plus the past participle of the verb you have in mind.

EXAMPLES:
(que) hubiere amado, hubieres amado, hubiere amado;
(que) hubiéremos amado, hubiereis amado, hubieren amado

English translation:
(that) I have *or* I shall have loved, (that) you have *or* will have loved, *etc.*

§68.65 Common irregular Spanish verb forms and uncommon Spanish verb forms identified by infinitive

A

abierto **abrir**
acierto, *etc.* **acertar**
acuerdo, *etc.* **acordar**
acuesto, *etc.* **acostarse**
alce, *etc.* **alzar**
ase, *etc.* **asir**
asgo, *etc.* **asir**
ate, *etc.* **atar**

C

caí, *etc.* **caer**
caía, *etc.* **caer**
caigo, *etc.* **caer**
cayera, *etc.* **caer**
cierro, *etc.* **cerrar**
cojo, *etc.* **coger**
cuece, *etc.* **cocer**
cuelgo, *etc.* **colgar**
cuento, *etc.* **contar**
cuesta, *etc.* **costar**
cuezo, *etc.* **cocer**
cupiera, *etc.* **caber**

D

da, *etc.* **dar**
dad **dar**
dé **dar**
demos **dar**
den **dar**
des **dar**
di, *etc.* **dar, decir**
dice, *etc.* **decir**
diciendo **decir**
dicho **decir**
diera, *etc.* **dar**
diese, *etc.* **dar**
digo, *etc.* **decir**
dije, *etc.* **decir**
dimos, *etc.* **dar**
dio **dar**
diré, *etc.* **decir**
diría, *etc.* **decir**
doy **dar**
duelo, *etc.* **doler**
duermo, *etc.* **dormir**
durmamos **dormir**
durmiendo **dormir**

E

eliges, *etc.* **elegir**
eligiendo **elegir**
eligiera, *etc.* **elegir**
elijo, *etc.* **elegir**
era, *etc.* **ser**

eres **ser**
es **ser**

F

fíe, *etc.* **fiar**
fío, *etc.* **fiar**
friendo **freír**
friera, *etc.* **freír**
frío, *etc.* **freír**
frito **freír**
fue, *etc.* **ir, ser**
fuera, *etc.* **ir, ser**
fuese, *etc.* **ir, ser**
fui, *etc.* **ir, ser**

G

gima, *etc.* **gemir**
gimiendo **gemir**
gimiera, *etc.* **gemir**
gimiese, *etc.* **gemir**
gimo, *etc.* **gemir**
goce, *etc.* **gozar**
gocé **gozar**

H

ha **haber**
habré, *etc.* **haber**
haga, *etc.* **hacer**
hago, *etc.* **hacer**
han **haber**
haría, *etc.* **hacer**
has **haber**
haya, *etc.* **haber**
haz **hacer**
he **haber**
hecho **hacer**
hemos **haber**
hice, *etc.* **hacer**
hiciera, *etc.* **hacer**
hiciese, *etc.* **hacer**
hiela **helar**
hiele **helar**
hiera, *etc.* **herir**
hiero, *etc.* **herir**
hiramos **herir**
hiriendo **herir**
hiriera, *etc.* **herir**
hiriese, *etc.* **herir**
hizo **hacer**
hube, *etc.* **haber**
hubiera, *etc.* **haber**
hubiese, *etc.* **haber**
huela, *etc.* **oler**
huelo, *etc.* **oler**
huya, *etc.* **huir**

huyendo **huir**
huyera, *etc.* **huir**
huyese, *etc.* **huir**
huyo, *etc.* **huir**

I

iba, *etc.* **ir**
id **ir**
ido **ir**
idos **irse**
irgo, *etc.* **erguir**
irguiendo **erguir**
irguiera, *etc.* **erguir**
irguiese, *etc.* **erguir**

J

juego, *etc.* **jugar**
juegue, *etc.* **jugar**

L

lea, *etc.* **leer**
leído **leer**
leo, *etc.* **leer**
leyendo **leer**
leyera, *etc.* **leer**
leyese, *etc.* **leer**

LL

llueva **llover**
llueve **llover**

M

mida, *etc.* **medir**
midiendo **medir**
midiera, *etc.* **medir**
midiese, *etc.* **medir**
mido, *etc.* **medir**
mienta, *etc.* **mentir**
miento, *etc.* **mentir**
mintiendo **mentir**
mintiera, *etc.* **mentir**
mintiese, *etc.* **mentir**
muerda, *etc.* **morder**
muerdo, *etc.* **morder**
muero, *etc.* **morir**
muerto **morir**
muestre, *etc.* **mostrar**
muestro, *etc.* **mostrar**
mueva, *etc.* **mover**
muevo, *etc.* **mover**
muramos **morir**
muriendo **morir**
muriera, *etc.* **morir**
muriese, *etc.* **morir**

N

nazca, *etc.* **nacer**
nazco **nacer**
niego, *etc.* **negar**
niegue, *etc.* **negar**
nieva **nevar**
nieve **nevar**

O

oíd **oír**
oiga, *etc.* **oír**
oigo, *etc.* **oír**
oliendo **oler**
oliera, *etc.* **oler**
oliese, *etc.* **oler**
oye, *etc.* **oír**
oyendo **oír**
oyera, *etc.* **oír**
oyese, *etc.* **oír**

P

pida, *etc.* **pedir**
pidamos **pedir**
pidiendo **pedir**
pidiera, *etc.* **pedir**
pidiese, *etc.* **pedir**
pido, *etc.* **pedir**
pienso, *etc.* **pensar**
pierda, *etc.* **perder**
pierdo, *etc.* **perder**
plegue **placer**
plugo **placer**
pluguiera **placer**
pluguieron **placer**
pluguiese **placer**
ponga, *etc.* **poner**
pongámonos **ponerse**
ponte **ponerse**
pruebe, *etc.* **probar**
pruebo, *etc.* **probar**
pude, *etc.* **poder**
pudiendo **poder**
pudiera, *etc.* **poder**
pudiese, *etc.* **poder**
puedo, *etc.* **poder**
puesto **poner**
puse, *etc.* **poner**
pusiera, *etc.* **poner**
pusiese, *etc.* **poner**

Q

quepo, *etc.* **caber**
quiebro **quebrar**
quiero, *etc.* **querer**
quise, *etc.* **querer**
quisiera, *etc.* **querer**
quisiese, *etc.* **querer**

R

raí, *etc.* **raer**
raía, *etc.* **raer**
raiga, *etc.* **raer**
raigo, *etc.* **raer**
rayendo **raer**
rayera, *etc.* **raer**
rayese, *etc.* **raer**
ría, *etc.* **reír**
riamos **reír**
riendo **reír**
riera, *etc.* **reír**
riese, *etc.* **reír**
riña, *etc.* **reñir**
riñendo **reñir**
riñera, *etc.* **reñir**
riñese, *etc.* **reñir**
riño, *etc.* **reñir**
río, *etc.* **reír**
roto **romper**
ruego, *etc.* **rogar**
ruegue, *etc.* **rogar**

S

saque, *etc.* **sacar**
sé **saber, ser**
sea, *etc.* **ser**
sed **ser**
sepa, *etc.* **saber**
seque, *etc.* **secar**
sido **ser**
siendo **ser**
siento, *etc.* **sentar, sentir**
sigo, *etc.* **seguir**
siguiendo **seguir**
siguiera, *etc.* **seguir**
siguiese, *etc.* **seguir**
sintiendo **sentir**
sintiera, *etc.* **sentir**
sintiese, *etc.* **sentir**
sintió **sentir**
sirviendo **servir**
sirvo, *etc.* **servir**
sois **ser**
somos **ser**
son **ser**
soy **ser**
suela, *etc.* **soler**
suelo, *etc.* **soler**
suelto, *etc.* **soltar**
sueno, *etc.* **sonar**
sueño, *etc.* **soñar**
supe, *etc.* **saber**
supiera, *etc.* **saber**
supiese, *etc.* **saber**

T

tiemblo, *etc.* **temblar**
tiendo, *etc.* **tender**
tienes, *etc.* **tener**

tiento, *etc.* **tentar**
toque, *etc.* **tocar**
tuesto, *etc.* **tostar**
tuve, *etc.* **tener**

U

uno, *etc.* **unir**

V

va **ir**
vais **ir**
vámonos **irse**
vamos **ir**
van **ir**
vas **ir**
vaya, *etc.* **ir**
ve **ir, ver**
vea, *etc.* **ver**
ved **ver**
vendré, *etc.* **venir**
venga, vengo **venir**
veo, *etc.* **ver**
ves **ver**
vete **irse**
vi **ver**
viendo **ver**
viene **venir**
viera, *etc.* **ver**
viese, *etc.* **ver**
vimos, *etc.* **ver**
vine, vino, *etc.* **venir**
vio **ver**
viste **ver, vestir**
vistiendo **vestir**
vistiéndose **vestirse**
vistiese, *etc.* **vestir(se)**
visto **ver, vestir**
voy **ir**
vuelo, *etc.* **volar**
vuelto **volver**
vuelvo, *etc.* **volver**

Y

yaz **yacer**
yazco, *etc.* **yacer**
yendo **ir**
yergo, *etc.* **erguir**
yerro, *etc.* **errar**

§68.66 **Irregular Spanish verbs commonly used (conjugation of)**

Here are fifty commonly used irregular verbs conjugated for you fully in all the tenses and moods. If there are any that are not given here, but are of interest to you, consult my *501 Spanish Verbs fully conjugated in all the tenses in a new easy to learn format*, Second Edition, also published by Barron's Educational Series, Inc., Woodbury, New York.

In the format of the verbs that follow, the subject pronouns have been omitted in order to emphasize the verb forms. The subject pronouns are, as you know, as follows:

singular	*plural*
yo	**nosotros (nosotras)**
tú	**vosotros (vosotras)**
Ud. (él, ella)	**Uds. (ellos, ellas)**

A Note About the Spanish Alphabet

The Spanish alphabet contains the letters **ch, ll, ñ,** and **rr,** which are considered separately. A Spanish word that contains **ch** is alphabetized *after* the letter **c; ll** is alphabetized *after* the letter **l;** and **ñ** is alphabetized *after* the letter **n.** This rule does not apply to the double consonant **rr.**

Note Further

The numbered sequence of the verb tenses on the pages that follow is that used in **§68.–§68.11** and **§68.14–§68.62.**

acostarse
Gerundio **acostándose** Part. pas. **acostado**

to go to bed, to lie down

The Seven Simple Tenses		The Seven Compound Tenses	
Singular	Plural	Singular	Plural

1 presente de indicativo

me acuesto	nos acostamos
te acuestas	os acostáis
se acuesta	se acuestan

8 perfecto de indicativo

me he acostado	nos hemos acostado
te has acostado	os habéis acostado
se ha acostado	se han acostado

2 imperfecto de indicativo

me acostaba	nos acostábamos
te acostabas	os acostabais
se acostaba	se acostaban

9 pluscuamperfecto de indicativo

me había acostado	nos habíamos acostado
te habías acostado	os habíais acostado
se había acostado	se habían acostado

3 pretérito

me acosté	nos acostamos
te acostaste	os acostasteis
se acostó	se acostaron

10 pretérito anterior

me hube acostado	nos hubimos acostado
te hubiste acostado	os hubisteis acostado
se hubo acostado	se hubieron acostado

4 futuro

me acostaré	nos acostaremos
te acostarás	os acostaréis
se acostará	se acostarán

11 futuro perfecto

me habré acostado	nos habremos acostado
te habrás acostado	os habréis acostado
se habrá acostado	se habrán acostado

5 potencial simple

me acostaría	nos acostaríamos
te acostarías	os acostaríais
se acostaría	se acostarían

12 potencial compuesto

me habría acostado	nos habríamos acostado
te habrías acostado	os habríais acostado
se habría acostado	se habrían acostado

6 presente de subjuntivo

me acueste	nos acostemos
te acuestes	os acostéis
se acueste	se acuesten

13 perfecto de subjuntivo

me haya acostado	nos hayamos acostado
te hayas acostado	os hayáis acostado
se haya acostado	se hayan acostado

7 imperfecto de subjuntivo

me acostara	nos acostáramos
te acostaras	os acostarais
se acostara	se acostaran
OR	
me acostase	nos acostásemos
te acostases	os acostaseis
se acostase	se acostasen

14 pluscuamperfecto de subjuntivo

me hubiera acostado	nos hubiéramos acostado
te hubieras acostado	os hubierais acostado
se hubiera acostado	se hubieran acostado
OR	
me hubiese acostado	nos hubiésemos acostado
te hubieses acostado	os hubieseis acostado
se hubiese acostado	se hubiesen acostado

imperativo

—	acostémonos
acuéstate; no te acuestes	acostaos; no os acostéis
acuéstese	acuéstense

Sentences using this verb and words and expressions related to it

Todas las noches me acuesto a las diez, mi hermanito se acuesta a las ocho, y mis padres se acuestan a las once.

el acostamiento lying down, stretching
acostado, acostada in bed, lying down

acostar to put to bed
acostarse con las gallinas to go to bed
  very early

Gerundio **almorzando**   Part. pas. **almorzado**   **almorzar**

to lunch, to have lunch

The Seven Simple Tenses		The Seven Compound Tenses	
Singular	Plural	Singular	Plural

1   presente de indicativo

		8 perfecto de indicativo	
almuerzo	almorzamos	he almorzado	hemos almorzado
almuerzas	almorzáis	has almorzado	habéis almorzado
almuerza	almuerzan	ha almorzado	han almorzado

2   imperfecto de indicativo

		9 pluscuamperfecto de indicativo	
almorzaba	almorzábamos	había almorzado	habíamos almorzado
almorzabas	almorzabais	habías almorzado	habíais almorzado
almorzaba	almorzaban	había almorzado	habían almorzado

3   pretérito

		10 pretérito anterior	
almorcé	almorzamos	hube almorzado	hubimos almorzado
almorzaste	almorzasteis	hubiste almorzado	hubisteis almorzado
almorzó	almorzaron	hubo almorzado	hubieron almorzado

4   futuro

		11 futuro perfecto	
almorzaré	almorzaremos	habré almorzado	habremos almorzado
almorzarás	almorzaréis	habrás almorzado	habréis almorzado
almorzará	almorzarán	habrá almorzado	habrán almorzado

5   potencial simple

		12 potencial compuesto	
almorzaría	almorzaríamos	habría almorzado	habríamos almorzado
almorzarías	almorzaríais	habrías almorzado	habríais almorzado
almorzaría	almorzarían	habría almorzado	habrían almorzado

6   presente de subjuntivo

		13 perfecto de subjuntivo	
almuerce	almorcemos	haya almorzado	hayamos almorzado
almuerces	almorcéis	hayas almorzado	hayáis almorzado
almuerce	almuercen	haya almorzado	hayan almorzado

7   imperfecto de subjuntivo

		14 pluscuamperfecto de subjuntivo	
almorzara	almorzáramos	hubiera almorzado	hubiéramos almorzado
almorzaras	almorzarais	hubieras almorzado	hubierais almorzado
almorzara	almorzaran	hubiera almorzado	hubieran almorzado
OR		OR	
almorzase	almorzásemos	hubiese almorzado	hubiésemos almorzado
almorzases	almorzaseis	hubieses almorzado	hubieseis almorzado
almorzase	almorzasen	hubiese almorzado	hubiesen almorzado

imperativo

—	almorcemos
almuerza; no almuerces	almorzad; no almorcéis
almuerce	almuercen

Sentences using this verb and words related to it

Todos los días tomo el desayuno en casa, tomo el almuerzo en la escuela con mis amigos, y ceno con mi familia a las ocho.

el desayuno breakfast
el almuerzo lunch

la cena dinner, supper
cenar to have dinner, supper

The subject pronouns are found in §68.66.

andar

Gerundio **andando**   Part. pas. **andado**

to walk

The Seven Simple Tenses		The Seven Compound Tenses	
Singular	Plural	Singular	Plural

1   presente de indicativo

		8 perfecto de indicativo	
ando	andamos	he andado	hemos andado
andas	andáis	has andado	habéis andado
anda	andan	ha andado	han andado

2   imperfecto de indicativo

		9 pluscuamperfecto de indicativo	
andaba	andábamos	había andado	habíamos andado
andabas	andabais	habías andado	habíais andado
andaba	andaban	había andado	habían andado

3   pretérito

		10 pretérito anterior	
anduve	anduvimos	hube andado	hubimos andado
anduviste	anduvisteis	hubiste andado	hubisteis andado
anduvo	anduvieron	hubo andado	hubieron andado

4   futuro

		11 futuro perfecto	
andaré	andaremos	habré andado	habremos andado
andarás	andaréis	habrás andado	habréis andado
andará	andarán	habrá andado	habrán andado

5   potencial simple

		12 potencial compuesto	
andaría	andaríamos	habría andado	habríamos andado
andarías	andaríais	habrías andado	habríais andado
andaría	andarían	habría andado	habrían andado

6   presente de subjuntivo

		13 perfecto de subjuntivo	
ande	andemos	haya andado	hayamos andado
andes	andéis	hayas andado	hayáis andado
ande	anden	haya andado	hayan andado

7   imperfecto de subjuntivo

		14 pluscuamperfecto de subjuntivo	
anduviera	anduviéramos	hubiera andado	hubiéramos andado
anduvieras	anduvierais	hubieras andado	hubierais andado
anduviera	anduvieran	hubiera andado	hubieran andado
OR		OR	
anduviese	anduviésemos	hubiese andado	hubiésemos andado
anduvieses	anduvieseis	hubieses andado	hubieseis andado
anduviese	anduviesen	hubiese andado	hubiesen andado

imperativo

—	andemos
anda; no andes	andad; no andéis
ande	anden

Words and expressions related to this verb

las andanzas   running about
buena andanza   good fortune
mala andanza   bad fortune

a todo andar   at full speed
a largo andar   in the long run
desandar   to retrace

Anda despacio que tengo prisa.   Make haste slowly.
Díme con quien andas y te diré quien eres.   Tell me who your friends are and I will tell you who you are.

Gerundio **buscando**   Part. pas. **buscado**   **buscar**

to look for, to seek

The Seven Simple Tenses		The Seven Compound Tenses	
Singular	Plural	Singular	Plural
1 presente de indicativo		**8 perfecto de indicativo**	
busco	buscamos	he buscado	hemos buscado
buscas	buscáis	has buscado	habéis buscado
busca	buscan	ha buscado	han buscado
2 imperfecto de indicativo		**9 pluscuamperfecto de indicativo**	
buscaba	buscábamos	había buscado	habíamos buscado
buscabas	buscabais	habías buscado	habíais buscado
buscaba	buscaban	había buscado	habían buscado
3 pretérito		**10 pretérito anterior**	
busqué	buscamos	hube buscado	hubimos buscado
buscaste	buscasteis	hubiste buscado	hubisteis buscado
buscó	buscaron	hubo buscado	hubieron buscado
4 futuro		**11 futuro perfecto**	
buscaré	buscaremos	habré buscado	habremos buscado
buscarás	buscaréis	habrás buscado	habréis buscado
buscará	buscarán	habrá buscado	habrán buscado
5 potencial simple		**12 potencial compuesto**	
buscaría	buscaríamos	habría buscado	habríamos buscado
buscarías	buscaríais	habrías buscado	habríais buscado
buscaría	buscarían	habría buscado	habrían buscado
6 presente de subjuntivo		**13 perfecto de subjuntivo**	
busque	busquemos	haya buscado	hayamos buscado
busques	busquéis	hayas buscado	hayáis buscado
busque	busquen	haya buscado	hayan buscado
7 imperfecto de subjuntivo		**14 pluscuamperfecto de subjuntivo**	
buscara	buscáramos	hubiera buscado	hubiéramos buscado
buscaras	buscarais	hubieras buscado	hubierais buscado
buscara	buscaran	hubiera buscado	hubieran buscado
OR		OR	
buscase	buscásemos	hubiese buscado	hubiésemos buscado
buscases	buscaseis	hubieses buscado	hubieseis buscado
buscase	buscasen	hubiese buscado	hubiesen buscado

imperativo

—	busquemos
busca; no busques	buscad; no busquéis
busque	busquen

Sentences using this verb and words related to it

¿Qué busca Ud.?   What are you looking for?
Busco mis libros.   I'm looking for my books.

la busca, la buscada   research, search
la búsqueda   search

rebuscar   to search into
el rebuscamiento   searching

Consult §67.16–§67.30 for verbs with prepositions.

The subject pronouns are found in §68.66.

caber

Gerundio **cabiendo**   Part. pas. **cabido**

to be contained, to fit into

The Seven Simple Tenses		The Seven Compound Tenses	
Singular	Plural	Singular	Plural
1 presente de indicativo		**8 perfecto de indicativo**	
quepo	cabemos	he cabido	hemos cabido
cabes	cabéis	has cabido	habéis cabido
cabe	caben	ha cabido	han cabido
2 imperfecto de indicativo		**9 pluscuamperfecto de indicativo**	
cabía	cabíamos	había cabido	habíamos cabido
cabías	cabíais	habías cabido	habíais cabido
cabía	cabían	había cabido	habían cabido
3 pretérito		**10 pretérito anterior**	
cupe	cupimos	hube cabido	hubimos cabido
cupiste	cupisteis	hubiste cabido	hubisteis cabido
cupo	cupieron	hubo cabido	hubieron cabido
4 futuro		**11 futuro perfecto**	
cabré	cabremos	habré cabido	habremos cabido
cabrás	cabréis	habrás cabido	habréis cabido
cabrá	cabrán	habrá cabido	habrán cabido
5 potencial simple		**12 potencial compuesto**	
cabría	cabríamos	habría cabido	habríamos cabido
cabrías	cabríais	habrías cabido	habríais cabido
cabría	cabrían	habría cabido	habrían cabido
6 presente de subjuntivo		**13 perfecto de subjuntivo**	
quepa	quepamos	haya cabido	hayamos cabido
quepas	quepáis	hayas cabido	hayáis cabido
quepa	quepan	haya cabido	hayan cabido
7 imperfecto de subjuntivo		**14 pluscuamperfecto de subjuntivo**	
cupiera	cupiéramos	hubiera cabido	hubiéramos cabido
cupieras	cupierais	hubieras cabido	hubierais cabido
cupiera	cupieran	hubiera cabido	hubieran cabido
OR		OR	
cupiese	cupiésemos	hubiese cabido	huviésemos cabido
cupieses	cupieseis	hubieses cabido	hubieseis cabido
cupiese	cupiesen	hubiese cabido	hubiesen cabido

imperativo

—	quepamos
cabe; no quepas	cabed; no quepáis
quepa	quepan

Common idiomatic expressions using this verb

Pablo no cabe en sí.   Paul has a swelled head.
No quepo aquí.   I don't have enough room here.
No cabe duda de que . . .   There is no doubt that . . .

Gerundio **cayendo**   Part. pas. **caído**   **caer**

to fall

The Seven Simple Tenses		The Seven Compound Tenses	
Singular	Plural	Singular	Plural
1 presente de indicativo		**8 perfecto de indicativo**	
caigo	caemos	he caído	hemos caído
caes	caéis	has caído	habéis caído
cae	caen	ha caído	han caído
2 imperfecto de indicativo		**9 pluscuamperfecto de indicativo**	
caía	caíamos	había caído	habíamos caído
caías	caíais	habías caído	habíais caído
caía	caían	había caído	habían caído
3 pretérito		**10 pretérito anterior**	
caí	caímos	hube caído	hubimos caído
caíste	caísteis	hubiste caído	hubisteis caído
cayó	cayeron	hubo caído	hubieron caído
4 futuro		**11 futuro perfecto**	
caeré	caeremos	habré caído	habremos caído
caerás	caeréis	habrás caído	habréis caído
caerá	caerán	habrá caído	habrán caído
5 potencial simple		**12 potencial compuesto**	
caería	caeríamos	habría caído	habríamos caído
caerías	caeríais	habrías caído	habríais caído
caería	caerían	habría caído	habrían caído
6 presente de subjuntivo		**13 perfecto de subjuntivo**	
caiga	caigamos	haya caído	hayamos caído
caigas	caigáis	hayas caído	hayáis caído
caiga	caigan	haya caído	hayan caído
7 imperfecto de subjuntivo		**14 pluscuamperfecto de subjuntivo**	
cayera	cayéramos	hubiera caído	hubiéramos caído
cayeras	cayerais	hubieras caído	hubierais caído
cayera	cayeran	hubiera caído	hubieran caído
OR		OR	
cayese	cayésemos	hubiese caído	hubiésemos caído
cayeses	cayeseis	hubieses caído	hubieseis caído
cayese	cayesen	hubiese caído	hubiesen caído

imperativo

—	caigamos
cae; no caigas	caed; no caigáis
caiga	caigan

Words and expressions related to this verb

la caída   the fall
a la caída del sol   at sunset
a la caída de la tarde   at the end of the afternoon
caer enfermo (enferma)   to fall sick
dejar caer   to drop

caer de espaldas   to fall backwards
decaer   to decay, decline
recaer   to relapse, fall back
caer con   to come down with

The subject pronouns are found in §68.66.

comenzar

Gerundio **comenzando**   Part. pas. **comenzado**

to begin, to start, to commence

The Seven Simple Tenses		The Seven Compound Tenses	
Singular	Plural	Singular	Plural
1 presente de indicativo		**8 perfecto de indicativo**	
comienzo	comenzamos	he comenzado	hemos comenzado
comienzas	comenzáis	has comenzado	habéis comenzado
comienza	comienzan	ha comenzado	han comenzado
2 imperfecto de indicativo		**9 pluscuamperfecto de indicativo**	
comenzaba	comenzábamos	había comenzado	habíamos comenzado
comenzabas	comenzabais	habías comenzado	habíais comenzado
comenzaba	comenzaban	había comenzado	habían comenzado
3 pretérito		**10 pretérito anterior**	
comencé	comenzamos	hube comenzado	hubimos comenzado
comenzaste	comenzasteis	hubiste comenzado	hubisteis comenzado
comenzó	comenzaron	hubo comenzado	hubieron comenzado
4 futuro		**11 futuro perfecto**	
comenzaré	comenzaremos	habré comenzado	habremos comenzado
comenzarás	comenzaréis	habrás comenzado	habréis comenzado
comenzará	comenzarán	habrá comenzado	habrán comenzado
5 potencial simple		**12 potencial compuesto**	
comenzaría	comenzaríamos	habría comenzado	habríamos comenzado
comenzarías	comenzaríais	habrías comenzado	habríais comenzado
comenzaría	comenzarían	habría comenzado	habrían comenzado
6 presente de subjuntivo		**13 perfecto de subjuntivo**	
comience	comencemos	haya comenzado	hayamos comenzado
comiences	comencéis	hayas comenzado	hayáis comenzado
comience	comiencen	haya comenzado	hayan comenzado
7 imperfecto de subjuntivo		**14 pluscuamperfecto de subjuntivo**	
comenzara	comenzáramos	hubiera comenzado	hubiéramos comenzado
comenzaras	comenzarais	hubieras comenzado	hubierais comenzado
comenzara	comenzaran	hubiera comenzado	hubieran comenzado
OR		OR	
comenzase	comenzásemos	hubiese comenzado	hubiésemos comenzado
comenzases	comenzaseis	hubieses comenzado	hubieseis comenzado
comenzase	comenzasen	hubiese comenzado	hubiesen comenzado

	imperativo	
—	comencemos
comienza; no comiences	comenzad; no comencéis
comience	comiencen

Words and expressions related to this verb

—¿Qué tiempo hace?

—Comienza a llover.

el comienzo beginning

comenzante beginner

El comenzante comenzó al comienzo.

The beginner began at the beginning.

comenzar a + inf. to begin + inf.

comenzar por + inf. to begin by + pres. part.

Gerundio **conociendo**   Part. pas. **conocido**   **conocer**

to know, to be acquainted with

The Seven Simple Tenses		The Seven Compound Tenses	
Singular	Plural	Singular	Plural
1 presente de indicativo		**8 perfecto de indicativo**	
conozco	conocemos	he conocido	hemos conocido
conoces	conocéis	has conocido	habéis conocido
conoce	conocen	ha conocido	han conocido
2 imperfecto de indicativo		**9 pluscuamperfecto de indicativo**	
conocía	conocíamos	había conocido	habíamos conocido
conocías	conocíais	habías conocido	habíais conocido
conocía	conocían	había conocido	habían conocido
3 pretérito		**10 pretérito anterior**	
conocí	conocimos	hube conocido	hubimos conocido
conociste	conocisteis	hubiste conocido	hubisteis conocido
conoció	conocieron	hubo conocido	hubieron conocido
4 futuro		**11 futuro perfecto**	
conoceré	conoceremos	habré conocido	habremos conocido
conocerás	conoceréis	habrás conocido	habréis conocido
conocerá	conocerán	habrá conocido	habrán conocido
5 potencial simple		**12 potencial compuesto**	
conocería	conoceríamos	habría conocido	habríamos conocido
conocerías	conoceríais	habrías conocido	habríais conocido
conocería	conocerían	habría conocido	habrían conocido
6 presente de subjuntivo		**13 perfecto de subjuntivo**	
conozca	conozcamos	haya conocido	hayamos conocido
conozcas	conozcáis	hayas conocido	hayáis conocido
conozca	conozcan	haya conocido	hayan conocido
7 imperfecto de subjuntivo		**14 pluscuamperfecto de subjuntivo**	
conociera	conociéramos	hubiera conocido	hubiéramos conocido
conocieras	conocierais	hubieras conocido	hubierais conocido
conociera	conocieran	hubiera conocido	hubieran conocido
OR		OR	
conociese	conociésemos	hubiese conocido	hubiésemos conocido
conocieses	conocieseis	hubieses conocido	hubieseis conocido
conociese	conociesen	hubiese conocido	hubiesen conocido

imperativo

—	conozcamos
conoce; no conozcas	conoced; no conozcáis
conozca	conozcan

Sentences using this verb and words related to it

—¿**Conoce Ud. a esa mujer?**
—**Sí, la conozco.**

un conocido, una conocida an acquaintance
el conocimiento knowledge
poner en conocimiento de to inform (about)

reconocer to recognize, to admit
desconocer to be ignorant of

Consult the Appendix for the section on verbs used in idiomatic expressions and §53.–§53.31.

The subject pronouns are found in §68.66.

creer

Gerundio **creyendo**   Part. pas. **creído**

to believe

The Seven Simple Tenses		The Seven Compound Tenses	
Singular	Plural	Singular	Plural
1 presente de indicativo		**8 perfecto de indicativo**	
creo	creemos	he creído	hemos creído
crees	creéis	has creído	habéis creído
cree	creen	ha creído	han creído
2 imperfecto de indicativo		**9 pluscuamperfecto de indicativo**	
creía	creíamos	había creído	habíamos creído
creías	creíais	habías creído	habíais creído
creía	creían	había creído	habían creído
3 pretérito		**10 pretérito anterior**	
creí	creímos	hube creído	hubimos creído
creíste	creísteis	hubiste creído	hubisteis creído
creyó	creyeron	hubo creído	hubieron creído
4 futuro		**11 futuro perfecto**	
creeré	creeremos	habré creído	habremos creído
creerás	creeréis	habrás creído	habréis creído
creerá	creerán	habrá creído	habrán creído
5 potencial simple		**12 potencial compuesto**	
creería	creeríamos	habría creído	habríamos creído
creerías	creeríais	habrías creído	habríais creído
creería	creerían	habría creído	habrían creído
6 presente de subjuntivo		**13 perfecto de subjuntivo**	
crea	creamos	haya creído	hayamos creído
creas	creáis	hayas creído	hayáis creído
crea	crean	haya creído	hayan creído
7 imperfecto de subjuntivo		**14 pluscuamperfecto de subjuntivo**	
creyera	creyéramos	hubiera creído	hubiéramos creído
creyeras	creyerais	hubieras creído	hubierais creído
creyera	creyeran	hubiera creído	hubieran creído
OR		OR	
creyese	creyésemos	hubiese creído	hubiésemos creído
creyeses	creyeseis	hubieses creído	hubieseis creído
creyese	creyesen	hubiese creído	hubiesen creído

imperativo	
—	creamos
cree; no creas	creed; no creáis
crea	crean

Words and expressions related to this verb

Ver y creer Seeing is believing.
¡Ya lo creo! Of course!
crédulo, crédula credulous
descreer to disbelieve

la credulidad credulity
el credo creed
dar crédito to believe

Gerundio **dando**   Part. pas. **dado**   **dar**

to give

The Seven Simple Tenses		The Seven Compound Tenses	
Singular	Plural	Singular	Plural
1 presente de indicativo		**8 perfecto de indicativo**	
doy	damos	he dado	hemos dado
das	dais	has dado	habéis dado
da	dan	ha dado	han dado
2 imperfecto de indicativo		**9 pluscuamperfecto de indicativo**	
daba	dábamos	había dado	habíamos dado
dabas	dabais	habías dado	habíais dado
daba	daban	había dado	habían dado
3 pretérito		**10 pretérito anterior**	
di	dimos	hube dado	hubimos dado
diste	disteis	hubiste dado	hubisteis dado
dio	dieron	hubo dado	hubieron dado
4 futuro		**11 futuro perfecto**	
daré	daremos	habré dado	habremos dado
darás	daréis	habrás dado	habréis dado
dará	darán	habrá dado	habrán dado
5 potencial simple		**12 potencial compuesto**	
daría	daríamos	habría dado	habríamos dado
darías	daríais	habrías dado	habríais dado
daría	darían	habría dado	habrían dado
6 presente de subjuntivo		**13 perfecto de subjuntivo**	
dé	demos	haya dado	hayamos dado
des	deis	hayas dado	hayáis dado
dé	den	haya dado	hayan dado
7 imperfecto de subjuntivo		**14 pluscuamperfecto de subjuntivo**	
diera	diéramos	hubiera dado	hubiéramos dado
dieras	dierais	hubieras dado	hubierais dado
diera	dieran	hubiera dado	hubieran dado
OR		OR	
diese	diésemos	hubiese dado	hubiésemos dado
dieses	dieseis	hubieses dado	hubieseis dado
diese	diesen	hubiese dado	hubiesen dado

imperativo

—	demos
da; no des	dad; no deis
dé	den

Common idiomatic expressions using this verb

A Dios rogando y con el mazo dando.   Put your faith in God and keep your powder dry.
El tiempo da buen consejo.   Time will tell.
dar la mano (las manos) a alguien   to shake hands with someone
dar de comer   to feed
darse   to give oneself up, to give in

Consult the Appendix for the section on verbs used in idiomatic expressions and §53.–§53.31.

The subject pronouns are found in §68.66.

decir

Gerundio **diciendo**   Part. pas. **dicho**

to say, to tell

The Seven Simple Tenses		The Seven Compound Tenses	
Singular	Plural	Singular	Plural

1 presente de indicativo		8 perfecto de indicativo	
digo	decimos	he dicho	hemos dicho
dices	decís	has dicho	habéis dicho
dice	dicen	ha dicho	han dicho

2 imperfecto de indicativo		9 pluscuamperfecto de indicativo	
decía	decíamos	había dicho	habíamos dicho
decías	decíais	habías dicho	habíais dicho
decía	decían	había dicho	habían dicho

3 pretérito		10 pretérito anterior	
dije	dijimos	hube dicho	hubimos dicho
dijiste	dijisteis	hubiste dicho	hubisteis dicho
dijo	dijeron	hubo dicho	hubieron dicho

4 futuro		11 futuro perfecto	
diré	diremos	habré dicho	habremos dicho
dirás	diréis	habrás dicho	habréis dicho
dirá	dirán	habrá dicho	habrán dicho

5 potencial simple		12 potencial compuesto	
diría	diríamos	habría dicho	habríamos dicho
dirías	diríais	habrías dicho	habríais dicho
diría	dirían	habría dicho	habrían dicho

6 presente de subjuntivo		13 perfecto de subjuntivo	
diga	digamos	haya dicho	hayamos dicho
digas	digáis	hayas dicho	hayáis dicho
diga	digan	haya dicho	hayan dicho

7 imperfecto de subjuntivo		14 pluscuamperfecto de subjuntivo	
dijera	dijéramos	hubiera dicho	hubiéramos dicho
dijeras	dijerais	hubieras dicho	hubierais dicho
dijera	dijeran	hubiera dicho	hubieran dicho
OR		OR	
dijese	dijésemos	hubiese dicho	hubiésemos dicho
dijeses	dijeseis	hubieses dicho	hubieseis dicho
dijese	dijesen	hubiese dicho	hubiesen dicho

	imperativo	
—	digamos
di; no digas	decid; no digáis
diga	digan

Sentences using this verb and words related to it

Dicho y hecho.   No sooner said than done.
Díme con quien andas y te diré quien eres.   Tell me who your friends are and I will tell you who you are.

querer decir   to mean
un decir   a familiar saying

See the Appendix for verbs used in idiomatic expressions and §53.–§53.31.

Gerundio **despertándose**   Part. pas. **despertado**   **despertarse**

to wake up oneself

The Seven Simple Tenses		The Seven Compound Tenses	
Singular	Plural	Singular	Plural

1   presente de indicativo

me despierto	nos despertamos
te despiertas	os despertáis
se despierta	se despiertan

8   perfecto de indicativo

me he despertado	nos hemos despertado
te has despertado	os habéis despertado
se ha despertado	se han despertado

2   imperfecto de indicativo

me despertaba	nos despertábamos
te despertabas	os despertabais
se despertaba	se despertaban

9   pluscuamperfecto de indicativo

me había despertado	nos habíamos despertado
te habías despertado	os habíais despertado
se había despertado	se habían despertado

3   pretérito

me desperté	nos despertamos
te despertaste	os despertasteis
se despertó	se despertaron

10   pretérito anterior

me hube despertado	nos hubimos despertado
te hubiste despertado	os hubisteis despertado
se hubo despertado	se hubieron despertado

4   futuro

me despertaré	nos despertaremos
te despertarás	os despertaréis
se despertará	se despertarán

11   futuro perfecto

me habré despertado	nos habremos despertado
te habrás despertado	os habréis despertado
se habrá despertado	se habrán despertado

5   potencial simple

me despertaría	nos despertaríamos
te despertarías	os despertaríais
se despertaría	se despertarían

12   potencial compuesto

me habría despertado	nos habríamos despertado
te habrías despertado	os habríais despertado
se habría despertado	se habrían despertado

6   presente de subjuntivo

me despierte	nos despertemos
te despiertes	os despertéis
se despierte	se despierten

13   perfecto de subjuntivo

me haya despertado	nos hayamos despertado
te hayas despertado	os hayáis despertado
se haya despertado	se hayan despertado

7   imperfecto de subjuntivo

me despertara	nos despertáramos
te despertaras	os despertarais
se despertara	se despertaran

OR

me despertase	nos despertásemos
te despertases	os despertaseis
se despertase	se despertasen

14   pluscuamperfecto de subjuntivo

me hubiera despertado	nos hubiéramos despertado
te hubieras despertado	os hubierais despertado
se hubiera despertado	se hubieran despertado

OR

me hubiese despertado	nos hubiésemos despertado
te hubieses despertado	os hubieseis despertado
se hubiese despertado	se hubiesen despertado

imperativo

—	despertémonos
despiértate; no te despiertes	despertaos; no os despertéis
despiértese	despiértense

Words related to this verb

despertar   to awaken (someone), to enliven
un despertador   alarm clock
el despertamiento   awakening

The subject pronouns are found in §68.66.

desvestirse
Gerundio **desvistiéndose**   Part. pas. **desvestido**

to undress oneself, to get undressed

The Seven Simple Tenses		The Seven Compound Tenses	
Singular	Plural	Singular	Plural
1 presente de indicativo		**8 perfecto de indicativo**	
me desvisto	nos desvestimos	me he desvestido	nos hemos desvestido
te desvistes	os desvestís	te has desvestido	os habéis desvestido
se desviste	se desvisten	se ha desvestido	se han desvestido
2 imperfecto de indicativo		**9 pluscuamperfecto de indicativo**	
me desvestía	nos desvestíamos	me había desvestido	nos habíamos desvestido
te desvestías	os desvestíais	te habías desvestido	os habíais desvestido
se desvestía	se desvestían	se había desvestido	se habían desvestido
3 pretérito		**10 pretérito anterior**	
me desvestí	nos desvestimos	me hube desvestido	nos hubimos desvestido
te desvestiste	os desvestisteis	te hubiste desvestido	os hubisteis desvestido
se desvistió	se desvistieron	se hubo desvestido	se hubieron desvestido
4 futuro		**11 futuro perfecto**	
me desvestiré	nos desvestiremos	me habré desvestido	nos habremos desvestido
te desvestirás	os desvestiréis	te habrás desvestido	os habréis desvestido
se desvestirá	se desvestirán	se habrá desvestido	se habrán desvestido
5 potencial simple		**12 potencial compuesto**	
me desvestiría	nos desvestiríamos	me habría desvestido	nos habríamos desvestido
te desvestirías	os desvestiríais	te habrías desvestido	os habríais desvestido
se desvestiría	se desvestirían	se habría desvestido	se habrían desvestido
6 presente de subjuntivo		**13 perfecto de subjuntivo**	
me desvista	nos desvistamos	me haya desvestido	nos hayamos desvestido
te desvistas	os desvistáis	te hayas desvestido	os hayáis desvestido
se desvista	se desvistan	se haya desvestido	se hayan desvestido
7 imperfecto de subjuntivo		**14 pluscuamperfecto de subjuntivo**	
me desvistiera	nos desvistiéramos	me hubiera desvestido	nos hubiéramos desvestido
te desvistieras	os desvistierais	te hubieras desvestido	os hubierais desvestido
se desvistiera	se desvistieran	se hubiera desvestido	se hubieran desvestido
OR		OR	
me desvistiese	nos desvistiésemos	me hubiese desvestido	nos hubiésemos desvestido
te desvistieses	os desvistieseis	te hubieses desvestido	os hubieseis desvestido
se desvistiese	se desvistiesen	se hubiese desvestido	se hubiesen desvestido

imperativo

—	desvistámonos
desvístete; no te desvistas	desvestíos; no os desvistáis
desvístase	desvístanse

Words related to this verb

vestir   to clothe, to dress
vestirse   to clothe oneself, to dress oneself
el vestido   clothing, clothes, dress
vestidos usados   secondhand clothing

Gerundio **divirtiéndose**   Part. pas. **divertido**   **divertirse**

to have a good time, to enjoy oneself

The Seven Simple Tenses		The Seven Compound Tenses	
Singular	Plural	Singular	Plural

1   presente de indicativo

me divierto	nos divertimos		
te diviertes	os divertís		
se divierte	se divierten		

8   perfecto de indicativo

me he divertido	nos hemos divertido
te has divertido	os habéis divertido
se ha divertido	se han divertido

2   imperfecto de indicativo

me divertía	nos divertíamos
te divertías	os divertíais
se divertía	se divertían

9   pluscuamperfecto de indicativo

me había divertido	nos habíamos divertido
te habías divertido	os habíais divertido
se había divertido	se habían divertido

3   pretérito

me divertí	nos divertimos
te divertiste	os divertisteis
se divirtió	se divirtieron

10   pretérito anterior

me hube divertido	nos hubimos divertido
te hubiste divertido	os hubisteis divertido
se hubo divertido	se hubieron divertido

4   futuro

me divertiré	nos divertiremos
te divertirás	os divertiréis
se divertirá	se divertirán

11   futuro perfecto

me habré divertido	nos habremos divertido
te habrás divertido	os habréis divertido
se habrá divertido	se habrán divertido

5   potencial simple

me divertiría	nos divertiríamos
te divertirías	os divertiríais
se divertiría	se divertirían

12   potencial compuesto

me habría divertido	nos habríamos divertido
te habrías divertido	os habríais divertido
se habría divertido	se habrían divertido

6   presente de subjuntivo

me divierta	nos divirtamos
te diviertas	os divirtáis
se divierta	se diviertan

13   perfecto de subjuntivo

me haya divertido	nos hayamos divertido
te hayas divertido	os hayáis divertido
se haya divertido	se hayan divertido

7   imperfecto de subjuntivo

me divirtiera	nos divirtiéramos
te divirtieras	os divirtierais
se divirtiera	se divirtieran
OR	
me divirtiese	nos divirtiésemos
te divirtieses	os divirtieseis
se divirtiese	se divirtiesen

14   pluscuamperfecto de subjuntivo

me hubiera divertido	nos hubiéramos divertido
te hubieras divertido	os hubierais divertido
se hubiera divertido	se hubieran divertido
OR	
me hubiese divertido	nos hubiésemos divertido
te hubieses divertido	os hubieseis divertido
se hubiese divertido	se hubiesen divertido

imperativo

—	divirtámonos
diviértete; no te diviertas	divertíos; no os divirtáis
diviértase	diviértanse

Words related to this verb

el divertimiento   amusement, diversion
diverso, diversa   diverse, different
la diversión   entertainment
divertir   to entertain

The subject pronouns are found in §68.66.

dormir

Gerundio **durmiendo**   Part. pas. **dormido**

to sleep

The Seven Simple Tenses		The Seven Compound Tenses	
Singular	Plural	Singular	Plural

1 presente de indicativo		8 perfecto de indicativo	
duermo	dormimos	he dormido	hemos dormido
duermes	dormís	has dormido	habéis dormido
duerme	duermen	ha dormido	han dormido

2 imperfecto de indicativo		9 pluscuamperfecto de indicativo	
dormía	dormíamos	había dormido	habíamos dormido
dormías	dormíais	habías dormido	habíais dormido
dormía	dormían	había dormido	habían dormido

3 pretérito		10 pretérito anterior	
dormí	dormimos	hube dormido	hubimos dormido
dormiste	dormisteis	hubiste dormido	hubisteis dormido
durmió	durmieron	hubo dormido	hubieron dormido

4 futuro		11 futuro perfecto	
dormiré	dormiremos	habré dormido	habremos dormido
dormirás	dormiréis	habrás dormido	habréis dormido
dormirá	dormirán	habrá dormido	habrán dormido

5 potencial simple		12 potencial compuesto	
dormiría	dormiríamos	habría dormido	habríamos dormido
dormirías	dormiríais	habrías dormido	habríais dormido
dormiría	dormirían	habría dormido	habrían dormido

6 presente de subjuntivo		13 perfecto de subjuntivo	
duerma	durmamos	haya dormido	hayamos dormido
duermas	durmáis	hayas dormido	hayáis dormido
duerma	duerman	haya dormido	hayan dormido

7 imperfecto de subjuntivo		14 pluscuamperfecto de subjuntivo	
durmiera	durmiéramos	hubiera dormido	hubiéramos dormido
durmieras	durmierais	hubieras dormido	hubierais dormido
durmiera	durmieran	hubiera dormido	hubieran dormido
OR		OR	
durmiese	durmiésemos	hubiese dormido	hubiésemos dormido
durmieses	durmieseis	hubieses dormido	hubieseis dormido
durmiese	durmiesen	hubiese dormido	hubiesen dormido

imperativo

—	durmamos
duerme; no duermas	dormid; no durmáis
duerma	duerman

Words and expressions related to this verb

dormirse   to fall asleep; (pres. part.: **durmiéndose**)
dormir a pierna suelta   to sleep soundly
dormitar   to doze
el dormitorio   bedroom, dormitory

Gerundio **empezando**   Part. pas. **empezado**   **empezar**

to begin, to start

The Seven Simple Tenses		The Seven Compound Tenses	
Singular	Plural	Singular	Plural
1 presente de indicativo		**8 perfecto de indicativo**	
empiezo	empezamos	he empezado	hemos empezado
empiezas	empezáis	has empezado	habéis empezado
empieza	empiezan	ha empezado	han empezado
2 imperfecto de indicativo		**9 pluscuamperfecto de indicativo**	
empezaba	empezábamos	había empezado	habíamos empezado
empezabas	empezabais	habías empezado	habíais empezado
empezaba	empezaban	había empezado	habían empezado
3 pretérito		**10 pretérito anterior**	
empecé	empezamos	hube empezado	hubimos empezado
empezaste	empezasteis	hubiste empezado	hubisteis empezado
empezó	empezaron	hubo empezado	hubieron empezado
4 futuro		**11 futuro perfecto**	
empezaré	empezaremos	habré empezado	habremos empezado
empezarás	empezaréis	habrás empezado	habréis empezado
empezará	empezarán	habrá empezado	habrán empezado
5 potencial simple		**12 potencial compuesto**	
empezaría	empezaríamos	habría empezado	habríamos empezado
empezarías	empezaríais	habrías empezado	habríais empezado
empezaría	empezarían	habría empezado	habrían empezado
6 presente de subjuntivo		**13 perfecto de subjuntivo**	
empiece	empecemos	haya empezado	hayamos empezado
empieces	empecéis	hayas empezado	hayáis empezado
empiece	empiecen	haya empezado	hayan empezado
7 imperfecto de subjuntivo		**14 pluscuamperfecto de subjuntivo**	
empezara	empezáramos	hubiera empezado	hubiéramos empezado
empezaras	empezarais	hubieras empezado	hubierais empezado
empezara	empezaran	hubiera empezado	hubieran empezado
OR		OR	
empezase	empezásemos	hubiese empezado	hubiésemos empezado
empezases	empezaseis	hubieses empezado	hubieseis empezado
empezase	empezasen	hubiese empezado	hubiesen empezado

imperativo

–	empecemos
empieza; no empieces	empezad; no empecéis
empiece	empiecen

Common idiomatic expressions using this verb

empezar por + inf.   to begin by + pres. part.
empezar a + inf.   to begin + inf.; **Ricardo empieza a escribir en inglés.**
para empezar   to begin with

Consult §67.16–§67.30 for the section on verbs used with prepositions.

The subject pronouns are found in §68.66.

encontrar

Gerundio **encontrando**   Part. pas. **encontrado**

to meet, to encounter, to find

The Seven Simple Tenses		The Seven Compound Tenses	
Singular	Plural	Singular	Plural
1 presente de indicativo		**8 perfecto de indicativo**	
encuentro	encontramos	he encontrado	hemos encontrado
encuentras	encontráis	has encontrado	habéis encontrado
encuentra	encuentran	ha encontrado	han encontrado
2 imperfecto de indicativo		**9 pluscuamperfecto de indicativo**	
encontraba	encontrábamos	había encontrado	habíamos encontrado
encontrabas	encontrabais	habías encontrado	habíais encontrado
encontraba	encontraban	había encontrado	habían encontrado
3 pretérito		**10 pretérito anterior**	
encontré	encontramos	hube encontrado	hubimos encontrado
encontraste	encontrasteis	hubiste encontrado	hubisteis encontrado
encontró	encontraron	hubo encontrado	hubieron encontrado
4 futuro		**11 futuro perfecto**	
encontraré	encontraremos	habré encontrado	habremos encontrado
encontrarás	encontraréis	habrás encontrado	habréis encontrado
encontrará	encontrarán	habrá encontrado	habrán encontrado
5 potencial simple		**12 potencial compuesto**	
encontraría	encontraríamos	habría encontrado	habríamos encontrado
encontrarías	encontraríais	habrías encontrado	habríais encontrado
encontraría	encontrarían	habría encontrado	habrían encontrado
6 presente de subjuntivo		**13 perfecto de subjuntivo**	
encuentre	encontremos	haya encontrado	hayamos encontrado
encuentres	encontréis	hayas encontrado	hayáis encontrado
encuentre	encuentren	haya encontrado	hayan encontrado
7 imperfecto de subjuntivo		**14 pluscuamperfecto de subjuntivo**	
encontrara	encontráramos	hubiera encontrado	hubiéramos encontrado
encontraras	encontrarais	hubieras encontrado	hubierais encontrado
encontrara	encontraran	hubiera encontrado	hubieran encontrado
OR		OR	
encontrase	encontrásemos	hubiese encontrado	hubiésemos encontrado
encontrases	encontraseis	hubieses encontrado	hubieseis encontrado
encontrase	encontrasen	hubiese encontrado	hubiesen encontrado

imperativo	
—	encontremos
encuentra; no encuentres	encontrad; no encontréis
encuentre	encuentren

Words and expressions related to this verb

un encuentro   encounter, meeting
salir al encuentro de   to go to meet
encontrarse con alguien   to meet someone, to run across someone
(pres. part.: encontrándose)

Gerundio **entendiendo**   Part. pas. **entendido**   **entender**

to understand

The Seven Simple Tenses		The Seven Compound Tenses	
Singular	Plural	Singular	Plural
1 presente de indicativo		**8 perfecto de indicativo**	
entiendo	entendemos	he entendido	hemos entendido
entiendes	entendéis	has entendido	habéis entendido
entiende	entienden	ha entendido	han entendido
2 imperfecto de indicativo		**9 pluscuamperfecto de indicativo**	
entendía	entendíamos	había entendido	habíamos entendido
entendías	entendíais	habías entendido	habíais entendido
entendía	entendían	había entendido	habían entendido
3 pretérito		**10 pretérito anterior**	
entendí	entendimos	hube entendido	hubimos entendido
entendiste	entendisteis	hubiste entendido	hubisteis entendido
entendió	entendieron	hubo entendido	hubieron entendido
4 futuro		**11 futuro perfecto**	
entenderé	entenderemos	habré entendido	habremos entendido
entenderás	entenderéis	habrás entendido	habréis entendido
entenderá	entenderán	habrá entendido	habrán entendido
5 potencial simple		**12 potencial compuesto**	
entendería	entenderíamos	habría entendido	habríamos entendido
entenderías	entenderíais	habrías entendido	habríais entendido
entendería	entenderían	habría entendido	habrían entendido
6 presente de subjuntivo		**13 perfecto de subjuntivo**	
entienda	entendamos	haya entendido	hayamos entendido
entiendas	entendáis	hayas entendido	hayáis entendido
entienda	entiendan	haya entendido	hayan entendido
7 imperfecto de subjuntivo		**14 pluscuamperfecto de subjuntivo**	
entendiera	entendiéramos	hubiera entendido	hubiéramos entendido
entendieras	entendierais	hubieras entendido	hubierais entendido
entendiera	entendieran	hubiera entendido	hubieran entendido
OR		OR	
entendiese	entendiésemos	hubiese entendido	hubiésemos entendido
entendieses	entendieseis	hubieses entendido	hubieseis entendido
entendiese	entendiesen	hubiese entendido	hubiesen entendido

imperativo

—	entendamos
entiende; no entiendas	entended; no entendáis
entienda	entiendan

Words and expressions related to this verb

dar a entender to insinuate, to hint
el entender understanding
según mi entender according to my understanding
el entendimiento comprehension, understanding

entenderse to understand
 each other
desentenderse de to pay no
 attention to

The subject pronouns are found in §68.66.

estar

Gerundio **estando**   Part. pas. **estado**

to be

The Seven Simple Tenses		The Seven Compound Tenses	
Singular	Plural	Singular	Plural

1   presente de indicativo

		8 perfecto de indicativo	
estoy	estamos	he estado	hemos estado
estás	estáis	has estado	habéis estado
está	están	ha estado	han estado

2   imperfecto de indicativo

		9 pluscuamperfecto de indicativo	
estaba	estábamos	había estado	habíamos estado
estabas	estabais	habías estado	habíais estado
estaba	estaban	había estado	habían estado

3   pretérito

		10 pretérito anterior	
estuve	estuvimos	hube estado	hubimos estado
estuviste	estuvisteis	hubiste estado	hubisteis estado
estuvo	estuvieron	hubo estado	hubieron estado

4   futuro

		11 futuro perfecto	
estaré	estaremos	habré estado	habremos estado
estarás	estaréis	habrás estado	habréis estado
estará	estarán	habrá estado	habrán estado

5   potencial simple

		12 potencial compuesto	
estaría	estaríamos	habría estado	habríamos estado
estarías	estaríais	habrías estado	habríais estado
estaría	estarían	habría estado	habrían estado

6   presente de subjuntivo

		13 perfecto de subjuntivo	
esté	estemos	haya estado	hayamos estado
estés	estéis	hayas estado	hayáis estado
esté	estén	haya estado	hayan estado

7   imperfecto de subjuntivo

		14 pluscuamperfecto de subjuntivo	
estuviera	estuviéramos	hubiera estado	hubiéramos estado
estuvieras	estuvierais	hubieras estado	hubierais estado
estuviera	estuvieran	hubiera estado	hubieran estado
OR		OR	
estuviese	estuviésemos	hubiese estado	hubiésemos estado
estuvieses	estuvieseis	hubieses estado	hubieseis estado
estuviese	estuviesen	hubiese estado	hubiesen estado

imperativo

—	estemos
está; no estés	estad; no estéis
esté	estén

Common idiomatic expressions using this verb

—¿Cómo está Ud.?
—Estoy muy bien, gracias. ¿Y usted?
—Estoy enfermo hoy.

estar para + inf.   to be about + inf.
  Estoy para salir.   I am about to go out.   Consult the Appendix for verbs used in
estar por   to be in favor of   idiomatic expressions and §53.–§53.31.

Gerundio **habiendo**   Part. pas. **habido**   **haber**

to have (as an auxiliary, helping verb to form the compound tenses)

The Seven Simple Tenses		The Seven Compound Tenses	
Singular	Plural	Singular	Plural

1 presente de indicativo

he	hemos
has	habéis
ha	han

8 perfecto de indicativo

he habido	hemos habido
has habido	habéis habido
ha habido	han habido

2 imperfecto de indicativo

había	habíamos
habías	habíais
había	habían

9 pluscuamperfecto de indicativo

había habido	habíamos habido
habías habido	habíais habido
había habido	habían habido

3 pretérito

hube	hubimos
hubiste	hubisteis
hubo	hubieron

10 pretérito anterior

hube habido	hubimos habido
hubiste habido	hubisteis habido
hubo habido	hubieron habido

4 futuro

habré	habremos
habrás	habréis
habrá	habrán

11 futuro perfecto

habré habido	habremos habido
habrás habido	habréis habido
habrá habido	habrán habido

5 potencial simple

habría	habríamos
habrías	habríais
habría	habrían

12 potencial compuesto

habría habido	habríamos habido
habrías habido	habríais habido
habría habido	habrían habido

6 presente de subjuntivo

haya	hayamos
hayas	hayáis
haya	hayan

13 perfecto de subjuntivo

haya habido	hayamos habido
hayas habido	hayáis habido
haya habido	hayan habido

7 imperfecto de subjuntivo

hubiera	hubiéramos
hubieras	hubierais
hubiera	hubieran
OR	
hubiese	hubiésemos
hubieses	hubieseis
hubiese	hubiesen

14 pluscuamperfecto de subjuntivo

hubiera habido	hubiéramos habido
hubieras habido	hubierais habido
hubiera habido	hubieran habido
OR	
hubiese habido	hubiésemos habido
hubieses habido	hubieseis habido
hubiese habido	hubiesen habido

imperativo

—	hayamos
he; no hayas	habed; no hayáis
haya	hayan

Words and expressions related to this verb

el haber   credit (in bookkeeping)
los haberes   assets, possessions, property
habérselas con alguien   to have a showdown with someone

Consult the Appendix and §53.–§53.31 for more idiomatic expressions using this verb.

The subject pronouns are found in §68.66.

hacer

Gerundio **haciendo**   Part. pas. **hecho**

to do, to make

The Seven Simple Tenses		The Seven Compound Tenses	
Singular	Plural	Singular	Plural
1 presente de indicativo		**8 perfecto de indicativo**	
hago	hacemos	he hecho	hemos hecho
haces	hacéis	has hecho	habéis hecho
hace	hacen	ha hecho	han hecho
2 imperfecto de indicativo		**9 pluscuamperfecto de indicativo**	
hacía	hacíamos	había hecho	habíamos hecho
hacías	hacíais	habías hecho	habíais hecho
hacía	hacían	había hecho	habían hecho
3 pretérito		**10 pretérito anterior**	
hice	hicimos	hube hecho	hubimos hecho
hiciste	hicisteis	hubiste hecho	hubisteis hecho
hizo	hicieron	hubo hecho	hubieron hecho
4 futuro		**11 futuro perfecto**	
haré	haremos	habré hecho	habremos hecho
harás	haréis	habrás hecho	habréis hecho
hará	harán	habrá hecho	habrán hecho
5 potencial simple		**12 potencial compuesto**	
haría	haríamos	habría hecho	habríamos hecho
harías	haríais	habrías hecho	habríais hecho
haría	harían	habría hecho	habrían hecho
6 presente de subjuntivo		**13 perfecto de subjuntivo**	
haga	hagamos	haya hecho	hayamos hecho
hagas	hagáis	hayas hecho	hayáis hecho
haga	hagan	haya hecho	hayan hecho
7 imperfecto de subjuntivo		**14 pluscuamperfecto de subjuntivo**	
hiciera	hiciéramos	hubiera hecho	hubiéramos hecho
hicieras	hicierais	hubieras hecho	hubierais hecho
hiciera	hicieran	hubiera hecho	hubieran hecho
OR		OR	
hiciese	hiciésemos	hubiese hecho	hubiésemos hecho
hicieses	hicieseis	hubieses hecho	hubieseis hecho
hiciese	hiciesen	hubiese hecho	hubiesen hecho

imperativo

—	**hagamos**
haz; no hagas	**haced; no hagáis**
haga	**hagan**

Common idiomatic expressions using this verb

Dicho y hecho.   No sooner said than done.
El ejercicio hace maestro al novicio.   Practice makes perfect.
Si a Roma fueres, haz como vieres.   When in Rome do as the Romans do. [Note that it is
   not uncommon to use the future subjunctive in proverbs, as in *fueres* (ir or ser) and
   vieres (ver); see §68.64.

Consult the Appendix for verbs used in idiomatic expressions and §53.–§53.31.

Gerundio **yendo**   Part. pas. **ido**   **ir**

to go

The Seven Simple Tenses		The Seven Compound Tenses	
Singular	Plural	Singular	Plural
1 presente de indicativo		**8 perfecto de indicativo**	
voy	vamos	he ido	hemos ido
vas	vais	has ido	habéis ido
va	van	ha ido	han ido
2 imperfecto de indicativo		**9 pluscuamperfecto de indicativo**	
iba	íbamos	había ido	habíamos ido
ibas	ibais	habías ido	habíais ido
iba	iban	había ido	habían ido
3 pretérito		**10 pretérito anterior**	
fui	fuimos	hube ido	hubimos ido
fuiste	fuisteis	hubiste ido	hubisteis ido
fue	fueron	hubo ido	hubieron ido
4 futuro		**11 futuro perfecto**	
iré	iremos	habré ido	habremos ido
irás	iréis	habrás ido	habréis ido
irá	irán	habrá ido	habrán ido
5 potencial simple		**12 potencial compuesto**	
iría	iríamos	habría ido	habríamos ido
irías	iríais	habrías ido	habríais ido
iría	irían	habría ido	habrían ido
6 presente de subjuntivo		**13 perfecto de subjuntivo**	
vaya	vayamos	haya ido	hayamos ido
vayas	vayáis	hayas ido	hayáis ido
vaya	vayan	haya ido	hayan ido
7 imperfecto de subjuntivo		**14 pluscuamperfecto de subjuntivo**	
fuera	fuéramos	hubiera ido	hubiéramos ido
fueras	fuerais	hubieras ido	hubierais ido
fuera	fueran	hubiera ido	hubieran ido
OR		OR	
fuese	fuésemos	hubiese ido	hubiésemos ido
fueses	fueseis	hubieses ido	hubieseis ido
fuese	fuesen	hubiese ido	hubiesen ido

imperativo

—	vamos (no vayamos)
ve; no vayas	id; no vayáis
vaya	vayan

Common idiomatic expressions using this verb

ir de compras   to go shopping   **ir a caballo**   to ride horseback
ir de brazo   to walk arm in arm   **un billete de ida y vuelta**   return ticket
¿Cómo le va?   How goes it? How are you?   **¡Qué va!**   Nonsense!
Cuando el gato va a sus devociones, bailan los ratones.   When the cat is away, the mice will play.

Consult the Appendix for verbs used in idiomatic expressions and §53.–§53.31.

The subject pronouns are found in §68.66.

irse

Gerundio **yéndose**   Part. pas. **ido**

to go away

The Seven Simple Tenses		The Seven Compound Tenses	
Singular	Plural	Singular	Plural
1 presente de indicativo		**8 perfecto de indicativo**	
me voy	nos vamos	me he ido	nos hemos ido
te vas	os vais	te has ido	os habéis ido
se va	se van	se ha ido	se han ido
2 imperfecto de indicativo		**9 pluscuamperfecto de indicativo**	
me iba	nos íbamos	me había ido	nos habíamos ido
te ibas	os ibais	te habías ido	os habíais ido
se iba	se iban	se había ido	se habían ido
3 pretérito		**10 pretérito anterior**	
me fui	nos fuimos	me hube ido	nos hubimos ido
te fuiste	os fuisteis	te hubiste ido	os hubisteis ido
se fue	se fueron	se hubo ido	se hubieron ido
4 futuro		**11 futuro perfecto**	
me iré	nos iremos	me habré ido	nos habremos ido
te irás	os iréis	te habrás ido	os habréis ido
se irá	se irán	se habrá ido	se habrán ido
5 potencial simple		**12 potencial compuesto**	
me iría	nos iríamos	me habría ido	nos habríamos ido
te irías	os iríais	te habrías ido	os habríais ido
se iría	se irían	se habría ido	se habrían ido
6 presente de subjuntivo		**13 perfecto de subjuntivo**	
me vaya	nos vayamos	me haya ido	nos hayamos ido
te vayas	os vayáis	te hayas ido	os hayáis ido
se vaya	se vayan	se haya ido	se hayan ido
7 imperfecto de subjuntivo		**14 pluscuamperfecto de subjuntivo**	
me fuera	nos fuéramos	me hubiera ido	nos hubiéramos ido
te fueras	os fuerais	te hubieras ido	os hubierais ido
se fuera	se fueran	se hubiera ido	se hubieran ido
OR		OR	
me fuese	nos fuésemos	me hubiese ido	nos hubiésemos ido
te fueses	os fueseis	te hubieses ido	os hubieseis ido
se fuese	se fuesen	se hubiese ido	se hubiesen ido

imperativo	
—	vámonos
vete; no te vayas	idos; no os vayáis
váyase	váyanse

Common idiomatic expressions using this verb

Vámonos!   Let's go! Let's leave! **¡Vete!**   Go away! **¡Váyase!**   Go away!
Si a Roma fueres, haz como vieres.   When in Rome do as the Romans do. [Note that it is not uncommon to use the future subjunctive in proverbs, as in *fueres* (**ir** or **ser**) and *vieres* (**ver**); see §68.64.

For additional common idiomatic expressions, see **ir**, which is related to **irse**.
See also the Appendix for verbs used in idiomatic expressions and §53.–§53.31.

Gerundio **jugando**   Part. pas. **jugado**   **jugar**

to play (a game, sport)

The Seven Simple Tenses		The Seven Compound Tenses	
Singular	Plural	Singular	Plural

1   presente de indicativo

		8 perfecto de indicativo	
juego	jugamos	he jugado	hemos jugado
juegas	jugáis	has jugado	habéis jugado
juega	juegan	ha jugado	han jugado

2   imperfecto de indicativo

		9 pluscuamperfecto de indicativo	
jugaba	jugábamos	había jugado	habíamos jugado
jugabas	jugabais	habías jugado	habíais jugado
jugaba	jugaban	había jugado	habían jugado

3   pretérito

		10 pretérito anterior	
jugué	jugamos	hube jugado	hubimos jugado
jugaste	jugasteis	hubiste jugado	hubisteis jugado
jugó	jugaron	hubo jugado	hubieron jugado

4   futuro

		11 futuro perfecto	
jugaré	jugaremos	habré jugado	habremos jugado
jugarás	jugaréis	habrás jugado	habréis jugado
jugará	jugarán	habrá jugado	habrán jugado

5   potencial simple

		12 potencial compuesto	
jugaría	jugaríamos	habría jugado	habríamos jugado
jugarías	jugaríais	habrías jugado	habríais jugado
jugaría	jugarían	habría jugado	habrían jugado

6   presente de subjuntivo

		13 perfecto de subjuntivo	
juegue	juguemos	haya jugado	hayamos jugado
juegues	juguéis	hayas jugado	hayáis jugado
juegue	jueguen	haya jugado	hayan jugado

7   imperfecto de subjuntivo

		14 pluscuamperfecto de subjuntivo	
jugara	jugáramos	hubiera jugado	hubiéramos jugado
jugaras	jugarais	hubieras jugado	hubierais jugado
jugara	jugaran	hubiera jugado	hubieran jugado
OR		OR	
jugase	jugásemos	hubiese jugado	hubiésemos jugado
jugases	jugaseis	hubieses jugado	hubieseis jugado
jugase	jugasen	hubiese jugado	hubiesen jugado

imperativo

—	juguemos
juega; no juegues	jugad; no juguéis
juegue	jueguen

Words and expressions related to this verb

un juguete   toy, plaything
jugador, jugadora   player
un juego   game

jugar a los naipes   to play cards
jugar al tenis   to play tennis
jugar al béisbol   to play baseball

Consult the Appendix for verbs used in idiomatic expressions and §53.–§53.31.

The subject pronouns are found in §68.66.

leer

Gerundio **leyendo**   Part. pas. **leído**

to read

The Seven Simple Tenses		The Seven Compound Tenses	
Singular	Plural	Singular	Plural
1 presente de indicativo		**8 perfecto de indicativo**	
leo	leemos	he leído	hemos leído
lees	leéis	has leído	habéis leído
lee	leen	ha leído	han leído
2 imperfecto de indicativo		**9 pluscuamperfecto de indicativo**	
leía	leíamos	había leído	habíamos leído
leías	leíais	habías leído	habíais leído
leía	leían	había leído	habían leído
3 pretérito		**10 pretérito anterior**	
leí	leímos	hube leído	hubimos leído
leíste	leísteis	hubiste leído	hubisteis leído
leyó	leyeron	hubo leído	hubieron leído
4 futuro		**11 futuro perfecto**	
leeré	leeremos	habré leído	habremos leído
leerás	leeréis	habrás leído	habréis leído
leerá	leerán	habrá leído	habrán leído
5 potencial simple		**12 potencial compuesto**	
leería	leeríamos	habría leído	habríamos leído
leerías	leeríais	habrías leído	habríais leído
leería	leerían	habría leído	habrían leído
6 presente de subjuntivo		**13 perfecto de subjuntivo**	
lea	leamos	haya leído	hayamos leído
leas	leáis	hayas leído	hayáis leído
lea	lean	haya leído	hayan leído
7 imperfecto de subjuntivo		**14 pluscuamperfecto de subjuntivo**	
leyera	leyéramos	hubiera leído	hubiéramos leído
leyeras	leyerais	hubieras leído	hubierais leído
leyera	leyeran	hubiera leído	hubieran leído
OR		OR	
leyese	leyésemos	hubiese leído	hubiésemos leído
leyeses	leyeseis	hubieses leído	hubieseis leído
leyese	leyesen	hubiese leído	hubiesen leído

imperativo	
—	leamos
lee; no leas	leed; no leáis
lea	lean

Words and expressions related to this verb

la lectura reading
  Me gusta la lectura. I like reading.
le lección lesson
lector, lectora reader
leer mal to misread

releer to read again, to reread
leer entre líneas to read between the lines
un, una leccionista private tutor
leer para sí to read to oneself

Gerundio **llegando**   Part. pas. **llegado**   **llegar**

to arrive

The Seven Simple Tenses		The Seven Compound Tenses	
Singular	Plural	Singular	Plural

1 presente de indicativo

llego	llegamos
llegas	llegáis
llega	llegan

8 perfecto de indicativo

he llegado	hemos llegado
has llegado	habéis llegado
ha llegado	han llegado

2 imperfecto de indicativo

llegaba	llegábamos
llegabas	llegabais
llegaba	llegaban

9 pluscuamperfecto de indicativo

había llegado	habíamos llegado
habías llegado	habíais llegado
había llegado	habían llegado

3 pretérito

llegué	llegamos
llegaste	llegasteis
llegó	llegaron

10 pretérito anterior

hube llegado	hubimos llegado
hubiste llegado	hubisteis llegado
hubo llegado	hubieron llegado

4 futuro

llegaré	llegaremos
llegarás	llegaréis
llegará	llegarán

11 futuro perfecto

habré llegado	habremos llegado
habrás llegado	habréis llegado
habrá llegado	habrán llegado

5 potencial simple

llegaría	llegaríamos
llegarías	llegaríais
llegaría	llegarían

12 potencial compuesto

habría llegado	habríamos llegado
habrías llegado	habríais llegado
habría llegado	habrían llegado

6 presente de subjuntivo

llegue	lleguemos
llegues	lleguéis
llegue	lleguen

13 perfecto de subjuntivo

haya llegado	hayamos llegado
hayas llegado	hayáis llegado
haya llegado	hayan llegado

7 imperfecto de subjuntivo

llegara	llegáramos
llegaras	llegarais
llegara	llegaran
OR	
llegase	llegásemos
llegases	llegaseis
llegase	llegasen

14 pluscuamperfecto de subjuntivo

hubiera llegado	hubiéramos llegado
hubieras llegado	hubierais llegado
hubiera llegado	hubieran llegado
OR	
hubiese llegado	hubiésemos llegado
hubieses llegado	hubieseis llegado
hubiese llegado	hubiesen llegado

imperativo

—	lleguemos
llega; no llegues	llegad; no lleguéis
llegue	lleguen

Words and expressions related to this verb

llegar a ser to become
   Luis y Luisa quieren llegar a ser médicos. Louis and Louise want to become doctors.
llegar a saber to find out   **llegar a** to reach
la llegada arrival   **al llegar** on arrival, upon arriving
llegar tarde to arrive late

Consult the Appendix for verbs used in idiomatic expressions and §53.–§53.31.

The subject pronouns are found in §68.66.

morir

to die

Gerundio **muriendo**   Part. pas. **muerto**

The Seven Simple Tenses		The Seven Compound Tenses	
Singular	Plural	Singular	Plural
1 presente de indicativo		**8 perfecto de indicativo**	
muero	morimos	he muerto	hemos muerto
mueres	morís	has muerto	habéis muerto
muere	mueren	ha muerto	han muerto
2 imperfecto de indicativo		**9 pluscuamperfecto de indicativo**	
moría	moríamos	había muerto	habíamos muerto
morías	moríais	habías muerto	habíais muerto
moría	morían	había muerto	habían muerto
3 pretérito		**10 pretérito anterior**	
morí	morimos	hube muerto	hubimos muerto
moriste	moristeis	hubiste muerto	hubisteis muerto
murió	murieron	hubo muerto	hubieron muerto
4 futuro		**11 futuro perfecto**	
moriré	moriremos	habré muerto	habremos muerto
morirás	moriréis	habrás muerto	habréis muerto
morirá	morirán	habrá muerto	habrán muerto
5 potencial simple		**12 potencial compuesto**	
moriría	moriríamos	habría muerto	habríamos muerto
morirías	moriríais	habrías muerto	habríais muerto
moriría	morirían	habría muerto	habrían muerto
6 presente de subjuntivo		**13 perfecto de subjuntivo**	
muera	muramos	haya muerto	hayamos muerto
mueras	muráis	hayas muerto	hayáis muerto
muera	mueran	haya muerto	hayan muerto
7 imperfecto de subjuntivo		**14 pluscuamperfecto de subjuntivo**	
muriera	muriéramos	hubiera muerto	hubiéramos muerto
murieras	murierais	hubieras muerto	hubierais muerto
muriera	murieran	hubiera muerto	hubieran muerto
OR		OR	
muriese	muriésemos	hubiese muerto	hubiésemos muerto
murieses	murieseis	hubieses muerto	hubieseis muerto
muriese	muriesen	hubiese muerto	hubiesen muerto

	imperativo
—	muramos
muere; no mueras	morid; no muráis
muera	mueran

Words and expressions related to this verb

la muerte death	**entremorir** to burn out, to flicker
mortal fatal, mortal	**morir de repente** to drop dead
la mortalidad mortality	**hasta morir** until death
morir de risa to die laughing	**morirse de miedo** to be scared to death

Gerundio **naciendo**   Part. pas. **nacido**   **nacer**

                                                                                   to be born

The Seven Simple Tenses		The Seven Compound Tenses	
Singular	Plural	Singular	Plural
1 presente de indicativo		**8 perfecto de indicativo**	
nazco	nacemos	he nacido	hemos nacido
naces	nacéis	has nacido	habéis nacido
nace	nacen	ha nacido	han nacido
2 imperfecto de indicativo		**9 pluscuamperfecto de indicativo**	
nacía	nacíamos	había nacido	habíamos nacido
nacías	nacíais	habías nacido	habíais nacido
nacía	nacían	había nacido	habían nacido
3 pretérito		**10 pretérito anterior**	
nací	nacimos	hube nacido	hubimos nacido
naciste	nacisteis	hubiste nacido	hubisteis nacido
nació	nacieron	hubo nacido	hubieron nacido
4 futuro		**11 futuro perfecto**	
naceré	naceremos	habré nacido	habremos nacido
nacerás	naceréis	habrás nacido	habréis nacido
nacerá	nacerán	habrá nacido	habrán nacido
5 potencial simple		**12 potencial compuesto**	
nacería	naceríamos	habría nacido	habríamos nacido
nacerías	naceríais	habrías nacido	habríais nacido
nacería	nacerían	habría nacido	habrían nacido
6 presente de subjuntivo		**13 perfecto de subjuntivo**	
nazca	nazcamos	haya nacido	hayamos nacido
nazcas	nazcáis	hayas nacido	hayáis nacido
nazca	nazcan	haya nacido	hayan nacido
7 imperfecto de subjuntivo		**14 pluscuamperfecto de subjuntivo**	
naciera	naciéramos	hubiera nacido	hubiéramos nacido
nacieras	nacierais	hubieras nacido	hubierais nacido
naciera	nacieran	hubiera nacido	hubieran nacido
OR		OR	
naciese	naciésemos	hubiese nacido	hubiésemos nacido
nacieses	nacieseis	hubieses nacido	hubieseis nacido
naciese	naciesen	hubiese nacido	hubiesen nacido

imperativo

—	nazcamos
nace; no nazcas	naced; no nazcáis
nazca	nazcan

Words and expressions related to this verb

bien nacido (nacida)   well bred; **mal nacido (nacida)**   ill bred
el nacimiento   birth
renacer   to be born again, to be reborn
nacer tarde   to be born yesterday (not much intelligence)
nacer de pies   to be born with a silver spoon in one's mouth

The subject pronouns are found in §68.66.

oír

Gerundio **oyendo**   Part. pas. **oído**

to hear

The Seven Simple Tenses		The Seven Compound Tenses	
Singular	Plural	Singular	Plural

1   presente de indicativo

		8 perfecto de indicativo	
oigo	oímos	he oído	hemos oído
oyes	oís	has oído	habéis oído
oye	oyen	ha oído	han oído

2   imperfecto de indicativo

		9 pluscuamperfecto de indicativo	
oía	oíamos	había oído	habíamos oído
oías	oíais	habías oído	habíais oído
oía	oían	había oído	habían oído

3   pretérito

		10 pretérito anterior	
oí	oímos	hube oído	hubimos oído
oíste	oísteis	hubiste oído	hubisteis oído
oyó	oyeron	hubo oído	hubieron oído

4   futuro

		11 futuro perfecto	
oiré	oiremos	habré oído	habremos oído
oirás	oiréis	habrás oído	habréis oído
oirá	oirán	habrá oído	habrán oído

5   potencial simple

		12 potencial compuesto	
oiría	oiríamos	habría oído	habríamos oído
oirías	oiríais	habrías oído	habríais oído
oiría	oirían	habría oído	habrían oído

6   presente de subjuntivo

		13 perfecto de subjuntivo	
oiga	oigamos	haya oído	hayamos oído
oigas	oigáis	hayas oído	hayáis oído
oiga	oigan	haya oído	hayan oído

7   imperfecto de subjuntivo

		14 pluscuamperfecto de subjuntivo	
oyera	oyéramos	hubiera oído	hubiéramos oído
oyeras	oyerais	hubieras oído	hubierais oído
oyera	oyeran	hubiera oído	hubieran oído
OR		OR	
oyese	oyésemos	hubiese oído	hubiésemos oído
oyeses	oyeseis	hubieses oído	hubieseis oído
oyese	oyesen	hubiese oído	hubiesen oído

imperativo

—	oigamos
oye; no oigas	oíd; no oigáis
oiga	oigan

Words and expressions related to this verb

la oída   hearing; **de oídas**   by hearsay
dar oídos   to lend an ear
oír decir   to hear tell, to hear say
oír hablar de   to hear of, to hear talk of

por oídos, de oídos   by hearing
al oído   confidentially
el oído   hearing (sense)
desoír   to ignore, to be deaf to

Gerundio **pagando**   Part. pas. **pagado**   **pagar**

to pay

The Seven Simple Tenses		The Seven Compound Tenses	
Singular	Plural	Singular	Plural
1 presente de indicativo		**8 perfecto de indicativo**	
pago	pagamos	he pagado	hemos pagado
pagas	pagáis	has pagado	habéis pagado
paga	pagan	ha pagado	han pagado
2 imperfecto de indicativo		**9 pluscuamperfecto de indicativo**	
pagaba	pagábamos	había pagado	habíamos pagado
pagabas	pagabais	habías pagado	habíais pagado
pagaba	pagaban	había pagado	habían pagado
3 pretérito		**10 pretérito anterior**	
pagué	pagamos	hube pagado	hubimos pagado
pagaste	pagasteis	hubiste pagado	hubisteis pagado
pagó	pagaron	hubo pagado	hubieron pagado
4 futuro		**11 futuro perfecto**	
pagaré	pagaremos	habré pagado	habremos pagado
pagarás	pagaréis	habrás pagado	habréis pagado
pagará	pagarán	habrá pagado	habrán pagado
5 potencial simple		**12 potencial compuesto**	
pagaría	pagaríamos	habría pagado	habríamos pagado
pagarías	pagaríais	habrías pagado	habríais pagado
pagaría	pagarían	habría pagado	habrían pagado
6 presente de subjuntivo		**13 perfecto de subjuntivo**	
pague	paguemos	haya pagado	hayamos pagado
pagues	paguéis	hayas pagado	hayáis pagado
pague	paguen	haya pagado	hayan pagado
7 imperfecto de subjuntivo		**14 pluscuamperfecto de subjuntivo**	
pagara	pagáramos	hubiera pagado	hubiéramos pagado
pagaras	pagarais	hubieras pagado	hubierais pagado
pagara	pagaran	hubiera pagado	hubieran pagado
OR		OR	
pagase	pagásemos	hubiese pagado	hubiésemos pagado
pagases	pagaseis	hubieses pagado	hubieseis pagado
pagase	pagasen	hubiese pagado	hubiesen pagado

imperativo

—	paguemos
paga; no pagues	pagad; no paguéis
pague	paguen

Words and expressions related to this verb

la paga   payment
pagable   payable
pagador, pagadora   payer
el pagaré   promissory note, I.O.U.

pagar al contado   to pay in cash
pagar contra entrega   C.O.D. (Collect on delivery)
pagar la cuenta   to pay the bill
pagar un ojo de la cara   to pay an arm and a leg; to pay through your nose

The subject pronouns are found in §68.66.

pedir

Gerundio **pidiendo**   Part. pas. **pedido**

to ask for, to request

The Seven Simple Tenses		The Seven Compound Tenses	
Singular	Plural	Singular	Plural

1   presente de indicativo

pido	pedimos	
pides	pedís	
pide	piden	

8   perfecto de indicativo

he pedido	hemos pedido
has pedido	habéis pedido
ha pedido	han pedido

2   imperfecto de indicativo

pedía	pedíamos
pedías	pedíais
pedía	pedían

9   pluscuamperfecto de indicativo

había pedido	habíamos pedido
habías pedido	habíais pedido
había pedido	habían pedido

3   pretérito

pedí	pedimos
pediste	pedisteis
pidió	pidieron

10   pretérito anterior

hube pedido	hubimos pedido
hubiste pedido	hubisteis pedido
hubo pedido	hubieron pedido

4   futuro

pediré	pediremos
pedirás	pediréis
pedirá	pedirán

11   futuro perfecto

habré pedido	habremos pedido
habrás pedido	habréis pedido
habrá pedido	habrán pedido

5   potencial simple

pediría	pediríamos
pedirías	pediríais
pediría	pedirían

12   potencial compuesto

habría pedido	habríamos pedido
habrías pedido	habríais pedido
habría pedido	habrían pedido

6   presente de subjuntivo

pida	pidamos
pidas	pidáis
pida	pidan

13   perfecto de subjuntivo

haya pedido	hayamos pedido
hayas pedido	hayáis pedido
haya pedido	hayan pedido

7   imperfecto de subjuntivo

pidiera	pidiéramos
pidieras	pidierais
pidiera	pidieran
OR	
pidiese	pidiésemos
pidieses	pidieseis
pidiese	pidiesen

14   pluscuamperfecto de subjuntivo

hubiera pedido	hubiéramos pedido
hubieras pedido	hubierais pedido
hubiera pedido	hubieran pedido
OR	
hubiese pedido	hubiésemos pedido
hubieses pedido	hubieseis pedido
hubiese pedido	hubiesen pedido

imperativo	
—	pidamos
pide; no pidas	pedid; no pidáis
pida	pidan

Words and expressions related to this verb

un pedimento   petition
hacer un pedido   to place an order

un pedido   request, order
colocar un pedido   to place an order
pedir prestado   to borrow

Consult the Appendix for the section on verbs used in idiomatic expressions and §53.–§53.31.

Gerundio **pensando**   Part. pas. **pensado**   **pensar**

to think

The Seven Simple Tenses		The Seven Compound Tenses	
Singular	Plural	Singular	Plural
1 presente de indicativo		**8 perfecto de indicativo**	
pienso	pensamos	he pensado	hemos pensado
piensas	pensáis	has pensado	habéis pensado
piensa	piensan	ha pensado	han pensado
2 imperfecto de indicativo		**9 pluscuamperfecto de indicativo**	
pensaba	pensábamos	había pensado	habíamos pensado
pensabas	pensabais	habías pensado	habíais pensado
pensaba	pensaban	había pensado	habían pensado
3 pretérito		**10 pretérito anterior**	
pensé	pensamos	hube pensado	hubimos pensado
pensaste	pensasteis	hubiste pensado	hubisteis pensado
pensó	pensaron	hubo pensado	hubieron pensado
4 futuro		**11 futuro perfecto**	
pensaré	pensaremos	habré pensado	habremos pensado
pensarás	pensaréis	habrás pensado	habréis pensado
pensará	pensarán	habrá pensado	habrán pensado
5 potencial simple		**12 potencial compuesto**	
pensaría	pensaríamos	habría pensado	habríamos pensado
pensarías	pensaríais	habrías pensado	habríais pensado
pensaría	pensarían	habría pensado	habrían pensado
6 presente de subjuntivo		**13 perfecto de subjuntivo**	
piense	pensemos	haya pensado	hayamos pensado
pienses	penséis	hayas pensado	hayáis pensado
piense	piensen	haya pensado	hayan pensado
7 imperfecto de subjuntivo		**14 pluscuamperfecto de subjuntivo**	
pensara	pensáramos	hubiera pensado	hubiéramos pensado
pensaras	pensarais	hubieras pensado	hubierais pensado
pensara	pensaran	hubiera pensado	hubieran pensado
OR		OR	
pensase	pensásemos	hubiese pensado	hubiésemos pensado
pensases	pensaseis	hubieses pensado	hubieseis pensado
pensase	pensasen	hubiese pensado	hubiesen pensado

imperativo

—	pensemos
piensa; no pienses	pensad; no penséis
piense	piensen

Words and expressions related to this verb

¿Qué piensa Ud. de eso? What do you think of that?
¿En qué piensa Ud.? What are you thinking of?
pensativo, pensativa thoughtful, pensive
un pensador, una pensadora thinker

pensar + inf. to intend + inf.
pensar en to think of, about
sin pensar thoughtlessly
repensar to think over (again)

Consult the Appendix for the section on verbs used in idiomatic expressions and §53.–§53.31.

The subject pronouns are found in §68.66.

poder

Gerundio **pudiendo**   Part. pas. **podido**

to be able, can

The Seven Simple Tenses		The Seven Compound Tenses	
Singular	Plural	Singular	Plural
1 presente de indicativo		**8 perfecto de indicativo**	
puedo	podemos	he podido	hemos podido
puedes	podéis	has podido	habéis podido
puede	pueden	ha podido	han podido
2 imperfecto de indicativo		**9 pluscuamperfecto de indicativo**	
podía	podíamos	había podido	habíamos podido
podías	podíais	habías podido	habíais podido
podía	podían	había podido	habían podido
3 pretérito		**10 pretérito anterior**	
pude	pudimos	hube podido	hubimos podido
pudiste	pudisteis	hubiste podido	hubisteis podido
pudo	pudieron	hubo podido	hubieron podido
4 futuro		**11 futuro perfecto**	
podré	podremos	habré podido	habremos podido
podrás	podréis	habrás podido	habréis podido
podrá	podrán	habrá podido	habrán podido
5 potencial simple		**12 potencial compuesto**	
podría	podríamos	habría podido	habríamos podido
podrías	podríais	habrías podido	habríais podido
podría	podrían	habría podido	habrían podido
6 presente de subjuntivo		**13 perfecto de subjuntivo**	
pueda	podamos	haya podido	hayamos podido
puedas	podáis	hayas podido	hayáis podido
pueda	puedan	haya podido	hayan podido
7 imperfecto de subjuntivo		**14 pluscuamperfecto de subjuntivo**	
pudiera	pudiéramos	hubiera podido	hubiéramos podido
pudieras	pudierais	hubieras podido	hubierais podido
pudiera	pudieran	hubiera podido	hubieran podido
OR		OR	
pudiese	pudiésemos	hubiese podido	hubiésemos podido
pudieses	pudieseis	hubieses podido	hubieseis podido
pudiese	pudiesen	hubiese podido	hubiesen podido

imperativo

—	podamos
puede; no puedas	poded; no podáis
pueda	puedan

Words and expressions related to this verb

el poder   power
apoderar   to empower
apoderarse de   to take possession, to take over
poderoso, poderosa   powerful
No se puede.   It can't be done.

a poder de   by dint of (by the power or force of)
estar en el poder   to be in power
Querer es poder   Where there's a will there's a way.

Consult the Appendix for verbs used in idiomatic expressions and §53.–§53.31.

Gerundio **poniendo**   Part. pas. **puesto**   **poner**

to put, to place

The Seven Simple Tenses		The Seven Compound Tenses	
Singular	Plural	Singular	Plural
1 presente de indicativo		**8 perfecto de indicativo**	
pongo	ponemos	he puesto	hemos puesto
pones	ponéis	has puesto	habéis puesto
pone	ponen	ha puesto	han puesto
2 imperfecto de indicativo		**9 pluscuamperfecto de indicativo**	
ponía	poníamos	había puesto	habíamos puesto
ponías	poníais	habías puesto	habíais puesto
ponía	ponían	había puesto	habían puesto
3 pretérito		**10 pretérito anterior**	
puse	pusimos	hube puesto	hubimos puesto
pusiste	pusisteis	hubiste puesto	hubisteis puesto
puso	pusieron	hubo puesto	hubieron puesto
4 futuro		**11 futuro perfecto**	
pondré	pondremos	habré puesto	habremos puesto
pondrás	pondréis	habrás puesto	habréis puesto
pondrá	pondrán	habrá puesto	habrán puesto
5 potencial simple		**12 potencial compuesto**	
pondría	pondríamos	habría puesto	habríamos puesto
pondrías	pondríais	habrías puesto	habríais puesto
pondría	pondrían	habría puesto	habrían puesto
6 presente de subjuntivo		**13 perfecto de subjuntivo**	
ponga	pongamos	haya puesto	hayamos puesto
pongas	pongáis	hayas puesto	hayáis puesto
ponga	pongan	haya puesto	hayan puesto
7 imperfecto de subjuntivo		**14 pluscuamperfecto de subjuntivo**	
pusiera	pusiéramos	hubiera puesto	hubiéramos puesto
pusieras	pusierais	hubieras puesto	hubierais puesto
pusiera	pusieran	hubiera puesto	hubieran puesto
OR		OR	
pusiese	pusiésemos	hubiese puesto	hubiésemos puesto
pusieses	pusieseis	hubieses puesto	hubieseis puesto
pusiese	pusiesen	hubiese puesto	hubiesen puesto

imperativo

—	pongamos
pon; no pongas	poned; no pongáis
ponga	pongan

Common idiomatic expressions using this verb

poner fin a   to put a stop to
poner la mesa   to set the table
poner de acuerdo   to reach an agreement
posponer   to postpone

la puesta de sol   sunset
buen puesto, buen puesta   well dressed
reponer   to replace, to put back

For additional words and expressions related to this verb, see **ponerse.**
See also the Appendix for verbs used in idiomatic expressions and §53.–§53.31.

The subject pronouns are found in §68.66.

ponerse

Gerundio **poniéndose** Part. pas. **puesto**

to put on (clothing), to become, to set (of sun)

The Seven Simple Tenses		The Seven Compound Tenses	
Singular	Plural	Singular	Plural
1 presente de indicativo		**8 perfecto de indicativo**	
me pongo	nos ponemos	me he puesto	nos hemos puesto
te pones	os ponéis	te has puesto	os habéis puesto
se pone	se ponen	se ha puesto	se han puesto
2 imperfecto de indicativo		**9 pluscuamperfecto de indicativo**	
me ponía	nos poníamos	me había puesto	nos habíamos puesto
te ponías	os poníais	te habías puesto	os habíais puesto
se ponía	se ponían	se había puesto	se habían puesto
3 pretérito		**10 pretérito anterior**	
me puse	nos pusimos	me hube puesto	nos hubimos puesto
te pusiste	os pusisteis	te hubiste puesto	os hubisteis puesto
se puso	se pusieron	se hubo puesto	se hubieron puesto
4 futuro		**11 futuro perfecto**	
me pondré	nos pondremos	me habré puesto	nos habremos puesto
te pondrás	os pondréis	te habrás puesto	os habréis puesto
se pondrá	se pondrán	se habrá puesto	se habrán puesto
5 potencial simple		**12 potencial compuesto**	
me pondría	nos pondríamos	me habría puesto	nos habríamos puesto
te pondrías	os pondríais	te habrías puesto	os habríais puesto
se pondría	se pondrían	se habría puesto	se habrían puesto
6 presente de subjuntivo		**13 perfecto de subjuntivo**	
me ponga	nos pongamos	me haya puesto	nos hayamos puesto
te pongas	os pongáis	te hayas puesto	os hayáis puesto
se ponga	se pongan	se haya puesto	se hayan puesto
7 imperfecto de subjuntivo		**14 pluscuamperfecto de subjuntivo**	
me pusiera	nos pusiéramos	me hubiera puesto	nos hubiéramos puesto
te pusieras	os pusierais	te hubieras puesto	os hubierais puesto
se pusiera	se pusieran	se hubiera puesto	se hubieran puesto
OR		OR	
me pusiese	nos pusiésemos	me hubiese puesto	nos hubiésemos puesto
te pusieses	os pusieseis	te hubieses puesto	os hubieseis puesto
se pusiese	se pusiesen	se hubiese puesto	se hubiesen puesto

imperativo	
—	pongámonos
ponte; no te pongas	poneos; no os pongáis
póngase	pónganse

Common idiomatic expressions using this verb

ponerse el abrigo to put on one's overcoat
ponerse a + inf. to begin, to start + inf.
María se puso pálida. Mary become pale.

reponerse to calm down, to recover (one's health)
indisponerse to become ill

For additional words and expressions related to this verb, see **poner.**
See also the Appendix for verbs used in idiomatic expressions and §53.–§53.31.

Gerundio **queriendo**   Part. pas. **querido**   **querer**

to want, to wish

The Seven Simple Tenses		The Seven Compound Tenses	
Singular	Plural	Singular	Plural
presente de indicativo		8 **perfecto de indicativo**	
quiero	queremos	he querido	hemos querido
quieres	queréis	has querido	habéis querido
quiere	quieren	ha querido	han querido
2 **imperfecto de indicativo**		9 **pluscuamperfecto de indicativo**	
quería	queríamos	había querido	habíamos querido
querías	queríais	habías querido	habíais querido
quería	querían	había querido	habían querido
3 **pretérito**		10 **pretérito anterior**	
quise	quisimos	hube querido	hubimos querido
quisiste	quisisteis	hubiste querido	hubisteis querido
quiso	quisieron	hubo querido	hubieron querido
4 **futuro**		11 **futuro perfecto**	
querré	querremos	habré querido	habremos querido
querrás	querréis	habrás querido	habréis querido
querrá	querrán	habrá querido	habrán querido
5 **potencial simple**		12 **potencial compuesto**	
querría	querríamos	habría querido	habríamos querido
querrías	querríais	habrías querido	habríais querido
querría	querrían	habría querido	habrían querido
6 **presente de subjuntivo**		13 **perfecto de subjuntivo**	
quiera	queramos	haya querido	hayamos querido
quieras	queráis	hayas querido	hayáis querido
quiera	quieran	haya querido	hayan querido
7 **imperfecto de subjuntivo**		14 **pluscuamperfecto de subjuntivo**	
quisiera	quisiéramos	hubiera querido	hubiéramos querido
quisieras	quisierais	hubieras querido	hubierais querido
quisiera	quisieran	hubiera querido	hubieran querido
OR		OR	
quisiese	quisiésemos	hubiese querido	hubiésemos querido
quisieses	quisieseis	hubieses querido	hubieseis querido
quisiese	quisiesen	hubiese querido	hubiesen querido

imperativo

—	queramos
quiere; no quieras	quered; no queráis
quiera	quieran

Words and expressions related to this verb

querer decir   to mean;   **¿Qué quiere Ud. decir?**   What do you mean?
  ¿Qué quiere decir esto?   What does this mean?
querido, querida   dear;   **querido amigo, querida amiga**   dear friend
querido mío, querida mía   my dear
querer bien a   to love
Querer es poder   Where there's a will there's a way.

The subject pronouns are found in §68.66.

recordar

Gerundio **recordando**   Part. pas. **recordado**

to remember, to recall, to remind

The Seven Simple Tenses		The Seven Compound Tenses	
Singular	Plural	Singular	Plural
1 presente de indicativo		**8 perfecto de indicativo**	
recuerdo	recordamos	he recordado	hemos recordado
recuerdas	recordáis	has recordado	habéis recordado
recuerda	recuerdan	ha recordado	han recordado
2 imperfecto de indicativo		**9 pluscuamperfecto de indicativo**	
recordaba	recordábamos	había recordado	habíamos recordado
recordabas	recordabais	habías recordado	habíais recordado
recordaba	recordaban	había recordado	habían recordado
3 pretérito		**10 pretérito anterior**	
recordé	recordamos	hube recordado	hubimos recordado
recordaste	recordasteis	hubiste recordado	hubisteis recordado
recordó	recordaron	hubo recordado	hubieron recordado
4 futuro		**11 futuro perfecto**	
recordaré	recordaremos	habré recordado	habremos recordado
recordarás	recordaréis	habrás recordado	habréis recordado
recordará	recordarán	habrá recordado	habrán recordado
5 potencial simple		**12 potencial compuesto**	
recordaría	recordaríamos	habría recordado	habríamos recordado
recordarías	recordaríais	habrías recordado	habríais recordado
recordaría	recordarían	habría recordado	habrían recordado
6 presente de subjuntivo		**13 perfecto de subjuntivo**	
recuerde	recordemos	haya recordado	hayamos recordado
recuerdes	recordéis	hayas recordado	hayáis recordado
recuerde	recuerden	haya recordado	hayan recordado
7 imperfecto de subjuntivo		**14 pluscuamperfecto de subjuntivo**	
recordara	recordáramos	hubiera recordado	hubiéramos recordado
recordaras	recordarais	hubieras recordado	hubierais recordado
recordara	recordaran	hubiera recordado	hubieran recordado
OR		OR	
recordase	recordásemos	hubiese recordado	hubiésemos recordado
recordases	recordaseis	hubieses recordado	hubieseis recordado
recordase	recordasen	hubiese recordado	hubiesen recordado

imperativo

—	recordemos
recuerda; no recuerdes	recordad; no recordéis
recuerde	recuerden

Words and expressions related to this verb

el recuerdo   memory, recollection
los recuerdos   regards, compliments
recordable   memorable

recordar algo a uno   to remind someone of something
un recordatorio   memento, reminder

Gerundio **riendo**   Part. pas. **reído**   **reír**

to laugh

The Seven Simple Tenses		The Seven Compound Tenses	
Singular	Plural	Singular	Plural
1 presente de indicativo		**8 perfecto de indicativo**	
río	reímos	he reído	hemos reído
ríes	reís	has reído	habéis reído
ríe	ríen	ha reído	han reído
2 imperfecto de indicativo		**9 pluscuamperfecto de indicativo**	
reía	reíamos	había reído	habíamos reído
reías	reíais	habías reído	habíais reído
reía	reían	había reído	habían reído
3 pretérito		**10 pretérito anterior**	
reí	reímos	hube reído	hubimos reído
reíste	reísteis	hubiste reído	hubisteis reído
rió	rieron	hubo reído	hubieron reído
4 futuro		**11 futuro perfecto**	
reiré	reiremos	habré reído	habremos reído
reirás	reiréis	habrás reído	habréis reído
reirá	reirán	habrá reído	habrán reído
5 potencial simple		**12 potencial compuesto**	
reiría	reiríamos	habría reído	habríamos reído
reirías	reiríais	habrías reído	habríais reído
reiría	reirían	habría reído	habrían reído
6 presente de subjuntivo		**13 perfecto de subjuntivo**	
ría	riamos	haya reído	hayamos reído
rías	riáis	hayas reído	hayáis reído
ría	rían	haya reído	hayan reído
7 imperfecto de subjuntivo		**14 pluscuamperfecto de subjuntivo**	
riera	riéramos	hubiera reído	hubiéramos reído
rieras	rierais	hubieras reído	hubierais reído
riera	rieran	hubiera reído	hubieran reído
OR		OR	
riese	riésemos	hubiese reído	hubiésemos reído
rieses	rieseis	hubieses reído	hubieseis reído
riese	riesen	hubiese reído	hubiesen reído

imperativo

—	riamos
ríe; no rías	reíd; no riáis
ría	rían

Common idiomatic expressions using this verb

reír a carcajadas to laugh loudly   **risible** laughable
reír de to laugh at, to make fun of   **risueño, risueña** smiling
la risa laugh, laughter

The subject pronouns are found in §68.66.

saber

Gerundio **sabiendo**   Part. pas. **sabido**

to know, to know how

The Seven Simple Tenses		The Seven Compound Tenses	
Singular	Plural	Singular	Plural
1 presente de indicativo		**8 perfecto de indicativo**	
sé	sabemos	he sabido	hemos sabido
sabes	sabéis	has sabido	habéis sabido
sabe	saben	ha sabido	han sabido
2 imperfecto de indicativo		**9 pluscuamperfecto de indicativo**	
sabía	sabíamos	había sabido	habíamos sabido
sabías	sabíais	habías sabido	habíais sabido
sabía	sabían	había sabido	habían sabido
3 pretérito		**10 pretérito anterior**	
supe	supimos	hube sabido	hubimos sabido
supiste	supisteis	hubiste sabido	hubisteis sabido
supo	supieron	hubo sabido	hubieron sabido
4 futuro		**11 futuro perfecto**	
sabré	sabremos	habré sabido	habremos sabido
sabrás	sabréis	habrás sabido	habréis sabido
sabrá	sabrán	habrá sabido	habrán sabido
5 potencial simple		**12 potencial compuesto**	
sabría	sabríamos	habría sabido	habríamos sabido
sabrías	sabríais	habrías sabido	habríais sabido
sabría	sabrían	habría sabido	habrían sabido
6 presente de subjuntivo		**13 perfecto de subjuntivo**	
sepa	sepamos	haya sabido	hayamos sabido
sepas	sepáis	hayas sabido	hayáis sabido
sepa	sepan	haya sabido	hayan sabido
7 imperfecto de subjuntivo		**14 pluscuamperfecto de subjuntivo**	
supiera	supiéramos	hubiera sabido	hubiéramos sabido
supieras	supierais	hubieras sabido	hubierais sabido
supiera	supieran	hubiera sabido	hubieran sabido
OR		OR	
supiese	supiésemos	hubiese sabido	hubiésemos sabido
supieses	supieseis	hubieses sabido	hubieseis sabido
supiese	supiesen	hubiese sabido	hubiesen sabido

imperativo

—	sepamos
sabe; no sepas	sabed; no sepáis
sepa	sepan

Words and expressions related to this verb

sabio, sabia wise, learned
un sabidillo, una sabidilla a know-it-all individual
la sabiduría knowledge, learning, wisdom
¿Sabe Ud. nadar? Do you know how to swim?
Sí, yo sé nadar. Yes, I know how to swim.

Que yo sepa. . . As far as I know. . .
¡Quién sabe! Who knows! Perhaps! Maybe!

Consult the Appendix for verbs used in idiomatic expressions and §53.–§53.31.

Gerundio **saliendo**   Part. pas. **salido**   **salir**

to go out, to leave

The Seven Simple Tenses		The Seven Compound Tenses	
Singular	Plural	Singular	Plural

1   presente de indicativo

		8 perfecto de indicativo	
salgo	salimos	he salido	hemos salido
sales	salís	has salido	habéis salido
sale	salen	ha salido	han salido

2   imperfecto de indicativo

		9 pluscuamperfecto de indicativo	
salía	salíamos	había salido	habíamos salido
salías	salíais	habías salido	habíais salido
salía	salían	había salido	habían salido

3   pretérito

		10 pretérito anterior	
salí	salimos	hube salido	hubimos salido
saliste	salisteis	hubiste salido	hubisteis salido
salió	salieron	hubo salido	hubieron salido

4   futuro

		11 futuro perfecto	
saldré	saldremos	habré salido	habremos salido
saldrás	saldréis	habrás salido	habréis salido
saldrá	saldrán	habrá salido	habrán salido

5   potencial simple

		12 potencial compuesto	
saldría	saldríamos	habría salido	habríamos salido
saldrías	saldríais	habrías salido	habríais salido
saldría	saldrían	habría salido	habrían salido

6   presente de subjuntivo

		13 perfecto de subjuntivo	
salga	salgamos	haya salido	hayamos salido
salgas	salgáis	hayas salido	hayáis salido
salga	salgan	haya salido	hayan salido

7   imperfecto de subjuntivo

		14 pluscuamperfecto de subjuntivo	
saliera	saliéramos	hubiera salido	hubiéramos salido
salieras	salierais	hubieras salido	hubierais salido
saliera	salieran	hubiera salido	hubieran salido
OR		OR	
saliese	saliésemos	hubiese salido	hubiésemos salido
salieses	salieseis	hubieses salido	hubieseis salido
saliese	saliesen	hubiese salido	hubiesen salido

imperativo

—	salgamos
sal; no salgas	salid; no salgáis
salga	salgan

Words and expressions related to this verb

la salida   exit
sin salida   no exit, dead-end street
salir de compras   to go out shopping
salir mal   to go wrong, to do badly

salir a   to resemble, to look like
salir al encuentro de   to go to meet
salir de   to leave from, to get out of

Consult the Appendix for verbs used in idiomatic expressions and §53.–§53.31.

The subject pronouns are found in §68.66.

sentarse
Gerundio **sentándose**   Part. pas. **sentado**

to sit down

The Seven Simple Tenses		The Seven Compound Tenses	
Singular	Plural	Singular	Plural
1 presente de indicativo		**8 perfecto de indicativo**	
me siento	nos sentamos	me he sentado	nos hemos sentado
te sientas	os sentáis	te has sentado	os habéis sentado
se sienta	se sientan	se ha sentado	se han sentado
2 imperfecto de indicativo		**9 pluscuamperfecto de indicativo**	
me sentaba	nos sentábamos	me había sentado	nos habíamos sentado
te sentabas	os sentabais	te habías sentado	os habíais sentado
se sentaba	se sentaban	se había sentado	se habían sentado
3 pretérito		**10 pretérito anterior**	
me senté	nos sentamos	me hube sentado	nos hubimos sentado
te sentaste	os sentasteis	te hubiste sentado	os hubisteis sentado
se sentó	se sentaron	se hubo sentado	se hubieron sentado
4 futuro		**11 futuro perfecto**	
me sentaré	nos sentaremos	me habré sentado	nos habremos sentado
te sentarás	os sentaréis	te habrás sentado	os habréis sentado
se sentará	se sentarán	se habrá sentado	se habrán sentado
5 potencial simple		**12 potencial compuesto**	
me sentaría	nos sentaríamos	me habría sentado	nos habríamos sentado
te sentarías	os sentaríais	te habrías sentado	os habríais sentado
se sentaría	se sentarían	se habría sentado	se habrían sentado
6 presente de subjuntivo		**13 perfecto de subjuntivo**	
me siente	nos sentemos	me haya sentado	nos hayamos sentado
te sientes	os sentéis	te hayas sentado	os hayáis sentado
se siente	se sienten	se haya sentado	se hayan sentado
7 imperfecto de subjuntivo		**14 pluscuamperfecto de subjuntivo**	
me sentara	nos sentáramos	me hubiera sentado	nos hubiéramos sentado
te sentaras	os sentarais	te hubieras sentado	os hubierais sentado
se sentara	se sentaran	se hubiera sentado	se hubieran sentado
OR		OR	
me sentase	nos sentásemos	me hubiese sentado	nos hubiésemos sentado
te sentases	os sentaseis	te hubieses sentado	os hubieseis sentado
se sentase	se sentasen	se hubiese sentado	se hubiesen sentado

imperativo	
—	sentémonos
siéntate; no te sientes	sentaos; no os sentéis
siéntese	siéntense

Words and expressions related to this verb

un asiento   a seat   sentar, asentar   to seat
sentado, sentada   seated   una sentada   a sitting; de una sentada   in one sitting
¡Siéntese Ud.!   Sit down!
¡Vamos a sentarnos!   Let's sit down!

Gerundio **sintiéndose**   Part. pas. **sentido**

sentirse

to feel (well, ill)

The Seven Simple Tenses		The Seven Compound Tenses	
Singular	Plural	Singular	Plural

1 presente de indicativo

		8 perfecto de indicativo	
me siento	nos sentimos	me he sentido	nos hemos sentido
te sientes	os sentís	te has sentido	os habéis sentido
se siente	se sienten	se ha sentido	se han sentido

2 imperfecto de indicativo

		9 pluscuamperfecto de indicativo	
me sentía	nos sentíamos	me había sentido	nos habíamos sentido
te sentías	os sentíais	te habías sentido	os habíais sentido
se sentía	se sentían	se había sentido	se habían sentido

3 pretérito

		10 pretérito anterior	
me sentí	nos sentimos	me hube sentido	nos hubimos sentido
te sentiste	os sentisteis	te hubiste sentido	os hubisteis sentido
se sintió	se sintieron	se hubo sentido	se hubieron sentido

4 futuro

		11 futuro perfecto	
me sentiré	nos sentiremos	me habré sentido	nos habremos sentido
te sentirás	os sentiréis	te habrás sentido	os habréis sentido
se sentirá	se sentirán	se habrá sentido	se habrán sentido

5 potencial simple

		12 potencial compuesto	
me sentiría	nos sentiríamos	me habría sentido	nos habríamos sentido
te sentirías	os sentiríais	te habrías sentido	os habríais sentido
se sentiría	se sentirían	se habría sentido	se habrían sentido

6 presente de subjuntivo

		13 perfecto de subjuntivo	
me sienta	nos sintamos	me haya sentido	nos hayamos sentido
te sientas	os sintáis	te hayas sentido	os hayáis sentido
se sienta	se sientan	se haya sentido	se hayan sentido

7 imperfecto de subjuntivo

		14 pluscuamperfecto de subjuntivo	
me sintiera	nos sintiéramos	me hubiera sentido	nos hubiéramos sentido
te sintieras	os sintierais	te hubieras sentido	os hubierais sentido
se sintiera	se sintieran	se hubiera sentido	se hubieran sentido
OR		OR	
me sintiese	nos sintiésemos	me hubiese sentido	nos hubiésemos sentido
te sintieses	os sintieseis	te hubieses sentido	os hubieseis sentido
se sintiese	se sintiesen	se hubiese sentido	se hubiesen sentido

imperativo

—	sintámonos
siéntete; no te sientas	sentíos; no os sintáis
siéntase	siéntanse

Words and expressions related to this verb

¿Cómo se siente Ud.?   How do you feel?   **Me siento mal.**   I feel sick.
el sentido   sense;   **los sentidos**   the senses

The subject pronouns are found in §68.66.

ser

Gerundio **siendo**   Part. pas. **sido**

to be

The Seven Simple Tenses		The Seven Compound Tenses	
Singular	Plural	Singular	Plural
1 presente de indicativo		**8 perfecto de indicativo**	
soy	somos	he sido	hemos sido
eres	sois	has sido	habéis sido
es	son	ha sido	han sido
2 imperfecto de indicativo		**9 pluscuamperfecto de indicativo**	
era	éramos	había sido	habíamos sido
eras	erais	habías sido	habíais sido
era	eran	había sido	habían sido
3 pretérito		**10 pretérito anterior**	
fui	fuimos	hube sido	hubimos sido
fuiste	fuisteis	hubiste sido	hubisteis sido
fue	fueron	hubo sido	hubieron sido
4 futuro		**11 futuro perfecto**	
seré	seremos	habré sido	habremos sido
serás	seréis	habrás sido	habréis sido
será	serán	habrá sido	habrán sido
5 potencial simple		**12 potencial compuesto**	
sería	seríamos	habría sido	habríamos sido
serías	seríais	habrías sido	habríais sido
sería	serían	habría sido	habrían sido
6 presente de subjuntivo		**13 perfecto de subjuntivo**	
sea	seamos	haya sido	hayamos sido
seas	seáis	hayas sido	hayáis sido
sea	sean	haya sido	hayan sido
7 imperfecto de subjuntivo		**14 pluscuamperfecto de subjuntivo**	
fuera	fuéramos	hubiera sido	hubiéramos sido
fueras	fuerais	hubieras sido	hubierais sido
fuera	fueran	hubiera sido	hubieran sido
OR		OR	
fuese	fuésemos	hubiese sido	hubiésemos sido
fueses	fueseis	hubieses sido	hubieseis sido
fuese	fuesen	hubiese sido	hubiesen sido

imperativo

—	seamos
sé; no seas	sed; no seáis
sea	sean

Common idiomatic expressions using this verb

Díme con quien andas y te diré quien eres.   Tell me who your friends are and I will tell
you who you are.
es decir   that is, that is to say; **Si yo fuera usted. . .**   If I were you. . .
¿Qué hora es?   What time is it?   **Es la una.**   It is one o'clock.   **Son las dos.**
It is two o'clock.
See the Appendix for verbs used in idiomatic expressions and §53.–§53.31.

Gerundio **teniendo** Part. pas. **tenido** **tener**

to have, to hold

The Seven Simple Tenses		The Seven Compound Tenses	
Singular	Plural	Singular	Plural
1 presente de indicativo		**8 perfecto de indicativo**	
tengo	tenemos	he tenido	hemos tenido
tienes	tenéis	has tenido	habéis tenido
tiene	tienen	ha tenido	han tenido
2 imperfecto de indicativo		**9 pluscuamperfecto de indicativo**	
tenía	teníamos	había tenido	habíamos tenido
tenías	teníais	habías tenido	habíais tenido
tenía	tenían	había tenido	habían tenido
3 pretérito		**10 pretérito anterior**	
tuve	tuvimos	hube tenido	hubimos tenido
tuviste	tuvisteis	hubiste tenido	hubisteis tenido
tuvo	tuvieron	hubo tenido	hubieron tenido
4 futuro		**11 futuro perfecto**	
tendré	tendremos	habré tenido	habremos tenido
tendrás	tendréis	habrás tenido	habréis tenido
tendrá	tendrán	habrá tenido	habrán tenido
5 potencial simple		**12 potencial compuesto**	
tendría	tendríamos	habría tenido	habríamos tenido
tendrías	tendríais	habrías tenido	habríais tenido
tendría	tendrían	habría tenido	habrían tenido
6 presente de subjuntivo		**13 perfecto de subjuntivo**	
tenga	tengamos	haya tenido	hayamos tenido
tengas	tengáis	hayas tenido	hayáis tenido
tenga	tengan	haya tenido	hayan tenido
7 imperfecto de subjuntivo		**14 pluscuamperfecto de subjuntivo**	
tuviera	tuviéramos	hubiera tenido	hubiéramos tenido
tuvieras	tuvierais	hubieras tenido	hubierais tenido
tuviera	tuvieran	hubiera tenido	hubieran tenido
OR		OR	
tuviese	tuviésemos	hubiese tenido	hubiésemos tenido
tuvieses	tuvieseis	hubieses tenido	hubieseis tenido
tuviese	tuviesen	hubiese tenido	hubiesen tenido

	imperativo
—	**tengamos**
ten; no tengas	**tened; no tengáis**
tenga	**tengan**

Common idiomatic expressions using this verb

Anda despacio que tengo prisa. Make haste slowly.
tener prisa to be in a hurry   **tener frío** to be (feel) cold (persons)
tener hambre to be hungry   **tener calor** to be (feel) warm (persons)
tener sed to be thirsty   **retener** to retain

Consult the Appendix for verbs used in idiomatic expressions and §53.–§53.31.

The subject pronouns are found in §68.66.

tocar
Gerundio **tocando**   Part. pas. **tocado**

to play (music or a musical instrument), to touch

The Seven Simple Tenses		The Seven Compound Tenses	
Singular	Plural	Singular	Plural
1 presente de indicativo		**8 perfecto de indicativo**	
toco	tocamos	he tocado	hemos tocado
tocas	tocáis	has tocado	habéis tocado
toca	tocan	ha tocado	han tocado
2 imperfecto de indicativo		**9 pluscuamperfecto de indicativo**	
tocaba	tocábamos	había tocado	habíamos tocado
tocabas	tocabais	habías tocado	habíais tocado
tocaba	tocaban	había tocado	habían tocado
3 pretérito		**10 pretérito anterior**	
toqué	tocamos	hube tocado	hubimos tocado
tocaste	tocasteis	hubiste tocado	hubisteis tocado
tocó	tocaron	hubo tocado	hubieron tocado
4 futuro		**11 futuro perfecto**	
tocaré	tocaremos	habré tocado	habremos tocado
tocarás	tocaréis	habrás tocado	habréis tocado
tocará	tocarán	habrá tocado	habrán tocado
5 potencial simple		**12 potencial compuesto**	
tocaría	tocaríamos	habría tocado	habríamos tocado
tocarías	tocaríais	habrías tocado	habríais tocado
tocaría	tocarían	habría tocado	habrían tocado
6 presente de subjuntivo		**13 perfecto de subjuntivo**	
toque	toquemos	haya tocado	hayamos tocado
toques	toquéis	hayas tocado	hayáis tocado
toque	toquen	haya tocado	hayan tocado
7 imperfecto de subjuntivo		**14 pluscuamperfecto de subjuntivo**	
tocara	tocáramos	hubiera tocado	hubiéramos tocado
tocaras	tocarais	hubieras tocado	hubierais tocado
tocara	tocaran	hubiera tocado	hubieran tocado
OR		OR	
tocase	tocásemos	hubiese tocado	hubiésemos tocado
tocases	tocaseis	hubieses tocado	hubieseis tocado
tocase	tocasen	hubiese tocado	hubiesen tocado

imperativo	
—	toquemos
toca; no toques	tocad; no toquéis
toque	toquen

Common idiomatic expressions using this verb

¿Sabe Ud. tocar el piano?   Do you know how to play the piano?
Sí, yo sé tocar el piano   Yes, I know how to play the piano.
tocar a la puerta   to knock on the door
el tocadiscos   record player
tocar a uno   to be someone's turn; **Le toca a Juan**   It's John's turn.

Consult the Appendix for verbs used in idiomatic expressions and §53.–§53.31.

Gerundio **trayendo**   Part. pas. **traído**   **traer**

to bring

The Seven Simple Tenses		The Seven Compound Tenses	
Singular	Plural	Singular	Plural
1 presente de indicativo		**8 perfecto de indicativo**	
traigo	traemos	he traído	hemos traído
traes	traéis	has traído	habéis traído
trae	traen	ha traído	han traído
2 imperfecto de indicativo		**9 pluscuamperfecto de indicativo**	
traía	traíamos	había traído	habíamos traído
traías	traíais	habías traído	habíais traído
traía	traían	había traído	habían traído
3 pretérito		**10 pretérito anterior**	
traje	trajimos	hube traído	hubimos traído
trajiste	trajisteis	hubiste traído	hubisteis traído
trajo	trajeron	hubo traído	hubieron traído
4 futuro		**11 futuro perfecto**	
traeré	traeremos	habré traído	habremos traído
traerás	traeréis	habrás traído	habréis traído
traerá	traerán	habrá traído	habrán traído
5 potencial simple		**12 potencial compuesto**	
traería	traeríamos	habría traído	habríamos traído
traerías	traeríais	habrías traído	habríais traído
traería	traerían	habría traído	habrían traído
6 presente de subjuntivo		**13 perfecto de subjuntivo**	
traiga	traigamos	haya traído	hayamos traído
traigas	traigáis	hayas traído	hayáis traído
traiga	traigan	haya traído	hayan traído
7 imperfecto de subjuntivo		**14 pluscuamperfecto de subjuntivo**	
trajera	trajéramos	hubiera traído	hubiéramos traído
trajeras	trajerais	hubieras traído	hubierais traído
trajera	trajeran	hubiera traído	hubieran traído
OR		OR	
trajese	trajésemos	hubiese traído	hubiésemos traído
trajeses	trajeseis	hubieses traído	hubieseis traído
trajese	trajesen	hubiese traído	hubiesen traído

imperativo

—	traigamos
trae; no traigas	traed; no traigáis
traiga	traigan

Words and expressions related to this verb

el traje costume, dress, suit
el traje de baño bathing suit
el traje hecho ready-made suit

traer daño to cause damage
traer entre ojos to hate
contraer to contract

The subject pronouns are found in §68.66.

venir

Gerundio **viniendo**   Part. pas. **venido**

to come

The Seven Simple Tenses		The Seven Compound Tenses	
Singular	Plural	Singular	Plural
1 presente de indicativo		**8 perfecto de indicativo**	
vengo	venimos	he venido	hemos venido
vienes	venís	has venido	habéis venido
viene	vienen	ha venido	han venido
2 imperfecto de indicativo		**9 pluscuamperfecto de indicativo**	
venía	veníamos	había venido	habíamos venido
venías	veníais	habías venido	habíais venido
venía	venían	había venido	habían venido
3 pretérito		**10 pretérito anterior**	
vine	vinimos	hube venido	hubimos venido
viniste	vinisteis	hubiste venido	hubisteis venido
vino	vinieron	hubo venido	hubieron venido
4 futuro		**11 futuro perfecto**	
vendré	vendremos	habré venido	habremos venido
vendrás	vendréis	habrás venido	habréis venido
vendrá	vendrán	habrá venido	habrán venido
5 potencial simple		**12 potencial compuesto**	
vendría	vendríamos	habría venido	habríamos venido
vendrías	vendríais	habrías venido	habríais venido
vendría	vendrían	habría venido	habrían venido
6 presente de subjuntivo		**13 perfecto de subjuntivo**	
venga	vengamos	haya venido	hayamos venido
vengas	vengáis	hayas venido	hayáis venido
venga	vengan	haya venido	hayan venido
7 imperfecto de subjuntivo		**14 pluscuamperfecto de subjuntivo**	
viniera	viniéramos	hubiera venido	hubiéramos venido
vinieras	vinierais	hubieras venido	hubierais venido
viniera	vinieran	hubiera venido	hubieran venido
OR		OR	
viniese	viniésemos	hubiese venido	hubiésemos venido
vinieses	vinieseis	hubieses venido	hubieseis venido
viniese	viniesen	hubiese venido	hubiesen venido

imperativo

—	vengamos
ven; no vengas	venid; no vengáis
venga	vengan

Common idiomatic expressions using this verb

la semana que viene next week
el mes que viene next month
el porvenir the future
Venga lo que viniere Come what may.

venir a las manos to come to blows
venir a buscar to come for, to get
en lo por venir hereafter

Gerundio viendo Part. pas. **visto** **ver**

to see

The Seven Simple Tenses		The Seven Compound Tenses	
Singular	Plural	Singular	Plural
1 presente de indicativo		**8 perfecto de indicativo**	
veo	vemos	he visto	hemos visto
ves	veis	has visto	habéis visto
ve	ven	ha visto	han visto
2 imperfecto de indicativo		**9 pluscuamperfecto de indicativo**	
veía	veíamos	había visto	habíamos visto
veías	veíais	habías visto	habíais visto
veía	veían	había visto	habían visto
3 pretérito		**10 pretérito anterior**	
vi	vimos	hube visto	hubimos visto
viste	visteis	hubiste visto	hubisteis visto
vio	vieron	hubo visto	hubieron visto
4 futuro		**11 futuro perfecto**	
veré	veremos	habré visto	habremos visto
verás	veréis	habrás visto	habréis visto
verá	verán	habrá visto	habrán visto
5 potencial simple		**12 potencial compuesto**	
vería	veríamos	habría visto	habríamos visto
verías	veríais	habrías visto	habríais visto
vería	verían	habría visto	habrían visto
6 presente de subjuntivo		**13 perfecto de subjuntivo**	
vea	veamos	haya visto	hayamos visto
veas	veáis	hayas visto	hayáis visto
vea	vean	haya visto	hayan visto
7 imperfecto de subjuntivo		**14 pluscuamperfecto de subjuntivo**	
viera	viéramos	hubiera visto	hubiéramos visto
vieras	vierais	hubieras visto	hubierais visto
viera	vieran	hubiera visto	hubieran visto
OR		OR	
viese	viésemos	hubiese visto	hubiésemos visto
vieses	vieseis	hubieses visto	hubieseis visto
viese	viesen	hubiese visto	hubiesen visto

imperativo

—	veamos
ve; no veas	ved; no veáis
vea	vean

Words and expressions related to this verb

¡Vamos a ver! Let's see
¡A ver! Let's see!
Ver es creer. Seeing is believing.
la vista sight, seeing, view, vision
vivir para ver to live and learn

Está por ver It remains to be seen.
Es de ver It is worth seeing.
ver claro to see clearly
¡Ya se ve! Of course! Certainly!

The subject pronouns are found in §68.66.

vestirse

Gerundio **vistiéndose**   Part. pas. **vestido**

to dress oneself, to get dressed

The Seven Simple Tenses		The Seven Compound Tenses	
Singular	Plural	Singular	Plural
1 presente de indicativo		**8 perfecto de indicativo**	
me visto	nos vestimos	me he vestido	nos hemos vestido
te vistes	os vestís	te has vestido	os habéis vestido
se viste	se visten	se ha vestido	se han vestido
2 imperfecto de indicativo		**9 pluscuamperfecto de indicativo**	
me vestía	nos vestíamos	me había vestido	nos habíamos vestido
te vestías	os vestíais	te habías vestido	os habíais vestido
se vestía	se vestían	se había vestido	se habían vestido
3 pretérito		**10 pretérito anterior**	
me vestí	nos vestimos	me hube vestido	nos hubimos vestido
te vestiste	os vestisteis	te hubiste vestido	os hubisteis vestido
se vistió	se vistieron	se hubo vestido	se hubieron vestido
4 futuro		**11 futuro perfecto**	
me vestiré	nos vestiremos	me habré vestido	nos habremos vestido
te vestirás	os vestiréis	te habrás vestido	os habréis vestido
se vestirá	se vestirán	se habrá vestido	se habrán vestido
5 potencial simple		**12 potencial compuesto**	
me vestiría	nos vestiríamos	me habría vestido	nos habríamos vestido
te vestirías	os vestiríais	te habrías vestido	os habríais vestido
se vestiría	se vestirían	se habría vestido	se habrían vestido
6 presente de subjuntivo		**13 perfecto de subjuntivo**	
me vista	nos vistamos	me haya vestido	nos hayamos vestido
te vistas	os vistáis	te hayas vestido	os hayáis vestido
se vista	se vistan	se haya vestido	se hayan vestido
7 imperfecto de subjuntivo		**14 pluscuamperfecto de subjuntivo**	
me vistiera	nos vistiéramos	me hubiera vestido	nos hubiéramos vestido
te vistieras	os vistierais	te hubieras vestido	os hubierais vestido
se vistiera	se vistieran	se hubiera vestido	se hubieran vestido
OR		OR	
me vistiese	nos vistiésemos	me hubiese vestido	nos hubiésemos vestido
te vistieses	os vistieseis	te hubieses vestido	os hubieseis vestido
se vistiese	se vistiesen	se hubiese vestido	se hubiesen vestido

imperativo	
—	vistámonos
vístete; no te vistas	vestíos; no os vistáis
vístase	vístanse

Words and expressions related to this verb

vestir   to clothe, to dress
desvestirse   to undress oneself, to get undressed
el vestido   clothing, clothes, dress
vestidos usados   secondhand clothing

bien vestido   well dressed
vestir de uniforme   to dress in uniform
vestir de blanco   to dress in white

Gerundio **volviendo**   Part. pas. **vuelto**   **volver**

to return, to go back

The Seven Simple Tenses		The Seven Compound Tenses	
Singular	Plural	Singular	Plural

1 presente de indicativo

		8 perfecto de indicativo	
vuelvo	**volvemos**	**he vuelto**	**hemos vuelto**
vuelves	**volvéis**	**has vuelto**	**habéis vuelto**
vuelve	**vuelven**	**ha vuelto**	**han vuelto**

2 imperfecto de indicativo

		9 pluscuamperfecto de indicativo	
volvía	**volvíamos**	**había vuelto**	**habíamos vuelto**
volvías	**volvíais**	**habías vuelto**	**habíais vuelto**
volvía	**volvían**	**había vuelto**	**habían vuelto**

3 pretérito

		10 pretérito anterior	
volví	**volvimos**	**hube vuelto**	**hubimos vuelto**
volviste	**volvisteis**	**hubiste vuelto**	**hubisteis vuelto**
volvió	**volvieron**	**hubo vuelto**	**hubieron vuelto**

4 futuro

		11 futuro perfecto	
volveré	**volveremos**	**habré vuelto**	**habremos vuelto**
volverás	**volveréis**	**habrás vuelto**	**habréis vuelto**
volverá	**volverán**	**habrá vuelto**	**habrán vuelto**

5 potencial simple

		12 potencial compuesto	
volvería	**volveríamos**	**habría vuelto**	**habríamos vuelto**
volverías	**volveríais**	**habrías vuelto**	**habríais vuelto**
volvería	**volverían**	**habría vuelto**	**habrían vuelto**

6 presente de subjuntivo

		13 perfecto de subjuntivo	
vuelva	**volvamos**	**haya vuelto**	**hayamos vuelto**
vuelvas	**volváis**	**hayas vuelto**	**hayáis vuelto**
vuelva	**vuelvan**	**haya vuelto**	**hayan vuelto**

7 imperfecto de subjuntivo

		14 pluscuamperfecto de subjuntivo	
volviera	**volviéramos**	**hubiera vuelto**	**hubiéramos vuelto**
volvieras	**volvierais**	**hubieras vuelto**	**hubierais vuelto**
volviera	**volvieran**	**hubiera vuelto**	**hubieran vuelto**
OR		OR	
volviese	**volviésemos**	**hubiese vuelto**	**hubiésemos vuelto**
volvieses	**volvieseis**	**hubieses vuelto**	**hubieseis vuelto**
volviese	**volviesen**	**hubiese vuelto**	**hubiesen vuelto**

imperativo

	volvamos
vuelve; no vuelvas	**volved; no volváis**
vuelva	**vuelvan**

Common idiomatic expressions using this verb

volver en sí to regain consciousness, to come to
volver sobre sus pasos to retrace one's steps
una vuelta turn, revolution, turning
dar una vuelta to take a stroll

un revólver revolver, pistol
revolver to revolve, to shake (up), to turn around
revolverse to turn around (oneself)

The subject pronouns are found in §68.66.

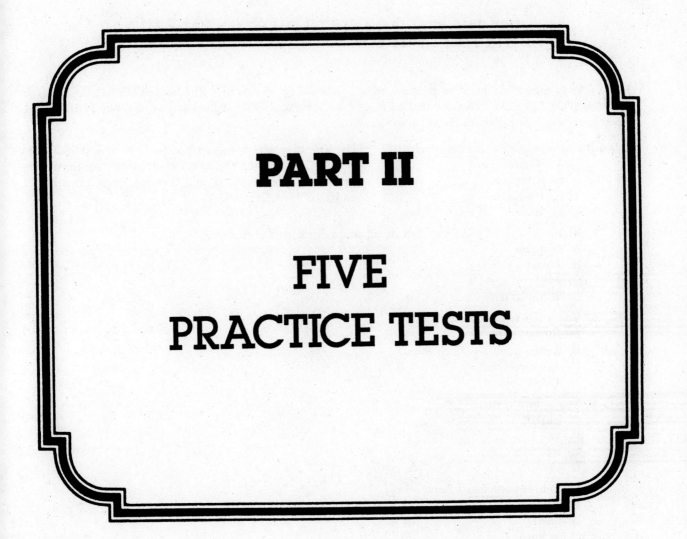

PART II

FIVE
PRACTICE TESTS

TEST 1

Each of the incomplete statements or questions below is followed by four choices. SELECT THE ONE CHOICE WHICH WOULD NOT FIT GRAMMATICALLY if substituted for the underlined word or words. The remaining three choices would fit grammatically and sensibly.

Example: José dice que está <u>comiendo</u>.
  A. lloviendo.
  B. hablando.
  C. leyendo.
  D. frío.

(The correct answer in this example is D because it WOULD NOT FIT GRAMMATICALLY if substituted for the underlined word. Choices A, B, and C would fit grammatically. See §53.27, §64.1, §68.63.)

1. María tiene que <u>buscar</u> un libro de español porque perdió el suyo.
  A. comprar
  B. limpia
  C. hallar
  D. reemplazar

2. <u>Voy</u> a tomar el tren esta mañana.
  A. Me apresuré
  B. Tengo que
  C. Me apresuraré
  D. Corrí

3. María <u>fue</u> a comer.
  A. gusta
  B. va
  C. irá
  D. iba

4. El hombre <u>comenzó</u> a llorar.
  A. empezó
  B. quería
  C. se puso
  D. volvió

5. <u>Nos acercamos</u> a la ciudad de México.
  A. Vamos
  B. Fuimos
  C. Vivimos
  D. Iremos

Read the following statements and choose the correct missing word or words that would fit grammatically and sensibly in each statement. Blacken the space under the letter of your choice on the special answer sheet.

Una residencia para escritores de . . . las nacionalidades se va . . .

6. A. todo
  B. todos
  C. toda
  D. todas

7. A. a
  B. de
  C. por
  D. para

construir en Aguilas, según . . . anunciado el novelista Angel María de Lera.

        8. A. he
               B. ha
               C. hemos
               D. han

Tendrá . . . jardines y será . . . preferentemente en los meses de verano.

  9. A. amplio   **10.** A. utilizado
       B. amplios   B. utilizados
       C. amplia   C. utilizada
       D. amplias   D. utilizadas

¿Podrán convivir en armonía personas de tan liberal profesión . . . es la de

        11. A. como
               B. que
               C. tanta
               D. cuando

escritor? Se espera que personas de . . . liberal profesión como los escritores

        12. A. tantos
               B. tantas
               C. tan
               D. como

. . . convivir en armonía.

13. A. pueden
     B. puedan
     C. podemos
     D. puede

Each of the incomplete statements or questions below is followed by four suggested completions. Select the most appropriate completion that would make the sentence grammatically correct and blacken the space under the letter of your choice on the special answer sheet.

  14. Cuento . . . tener éxito en este examen.
      A. con
      B. a
      C. de
      D. para

  15. Me contento . . . quedarme en casa hoy.
      A. con
      B. a
      C. de
      D. para

  16. José se casó . . . Ana.
      A. con
      B. a
      C. de
      D. para

17. Mis padres acaban . . . llegar.
    A. con
    B. a
    C. de
    D. para

18. Jaime dejó . . . escribir la composición.
    A. con
    B. a
    C. de
    D. por

19. Vamos a aprovecharnos . . . esta oportunidad.
    A. de
    B. a
    C. con
    D. en

20. La señora Pardo consintió . . . asistir a la conferencia.
    A. a
    B. en
    C. con
    D. de

Read the settings given below and select the best answer which is related to the situation described. Blacken the space under the letter of your choice on the special answer sheet.

21. Su maestro de español desea saber por qué Ud. no tiene su tarea.
Ud. le dice:
    A. ¡Se me olvidó!
    B. No tengo la tarea para hoy.
    C. Para bien aprender es necesario hacer las tareas.
    D. Ud. lo sabe bien, señor.

22. Un amigo viene a pasar unos días en su casa. Ud. lo encuentra en el aeropuerto.
Ud. le dice:
    A. Estoy aquí para encontrar a un amigo mío.
    B. Me gusta mirar los aviones.
    C. Voy a pasar unos días en su casa.
    D. ¡Hola! ¿Qué tal?

23. La señora Garrido dice:—El lunes vamos a tener un examen.
Ud. le pregunta:
    A. ¿En qué consistirá?
    B. ¿Qué vamos a tener el lunes?
    C. ¿Cuántos días hay en la semana?
    D. ¿Por qué tiene Ud. miedo?

24. Su compañera le dice que su hermano está en el hospital.
Ud. le contesta:
    A. ¡Con mucho gusto!
    B. ¿Por qué corres?
    C. ¡Ojalá que se mejore pronto!
    D. ¿En qué consistirá?

25. Un matrimonio está en el campo dando un paseo en coche cuando de repente se para el coche. Es la señora que conduce.

El señor dice:—¡Caramba! ¿Por qué se ha parado el motor?

La señora contesta:
A. Se ha parado el motor.
B. Se necesita gasolina.
C. Tengo que hablar contigo.
D. Acabo de saberlo.

26. El señor Robles, profesor de español, ha decidido retirarse. Roberto, el presidente del club de español, y Rosita, la secretaria, hablan sobre esto.

Roberto dice:
A. Le haremos un regalo.
B. Puedo tocar la guitarra.
C. Y tu puedes tocar el piano.
D. Vamos a clase ahora.

Select the antonym of the given word and blacken the space under the letter of your choice on the special answer sheet.

27. ancho
A. largo
B. corto
C. alto
D. estrecho

28. simpático
A. amable
B. antipático
C. lleno
D. limpio

29. aplicado
A. flojo
B. oscuro
C. valiente
D. fuerte

30. apresurarse
A. correr
B. andar
C. tardar
D. caminar

31. trágico
A. cómico
B. claro
C. descuido
D. culpable

32. cansar
A. descansar
B. saludar
C. despedir
D. cerrar

33. victoria
A. propina
B. silla
C. juguete
D. derrota

34. destruir
A. crear
B. creer
C. mentir
D. reír

35. desvanecerse
A. descubrir
B. recibir
C. aparecer
D. prestar

36. barato
A. costoso
B. religioso
C. delgado
D. distinto

37. este
A. norte
B. oeste
C. sur
D. central

38. feo
A. lejano
B. llenado
C. enano
D. bello

39. llenar
A. llegar
B. vaciar
C. contar
D. eliminar

40. llegada
A. mentira
B. partida
C. ida
D. vuelta

Read each of the following passages and select the best answer to each question by blackening the space under the letter of your choice on the special answer sheet.

41. Aunque nunca dio la impresión de estar agotado, Juan XXIII siempre encontró la forma de tener tiempo para todo y poder realizar una respetable cantidad de trabajo. Al tomar en cuenta la obra cumplida por Juan XXIII, se puede predecir que, en la historia de là Iglesia Católica, será recordado como un gran Papa.

¿De qué tenía fama el Papa Juan XXIII?
A. de ser muy enfermizo
B. de ser el primer historiador de la Iglesia
C. de organizar bien su trabajo
D. de poder predecir el futuro

42. El ministro de Asuntos Exteriores de la Argentina ha publicado una declaración conjunta de parte de Argentina y Bolivia. La declaración reconoce oficialmente un antiguo ofrecimiento de un puerto argentino, en el río Paraná, a Bolivia, para que este país tenga acceso al Océano Atlántico. Bolivia recibirá una zona marítima con capacidad para barcos de hasta dos mil toneladas.

¿Qué le proporciona a Bolivia el acuerdo?
A. una reexaminación de los asuntos militares argentinos
B. un puerto situado en territorio argentino
C. dos mil toneladas de carne argentina
D. unos barcos de la marina argentina

43. María Sánchez, una niñita peruana de dos meses y medio, tendrá una delicada operación al corazón en Boston. La pequeña será llevada en avión dentro de una cámara de oxígeno, ya que sufre de un defecto en el corazón que impide el normal recorrido de la sangre. Se espera que María pueda vivir normalmente y por largos años, ya que la operación en este caso es bastante común en los Estados Unidos.

¿Cuál es el motivo del optimismo de los padres de la niña?
A. El gobierno peruano va a pagar la operación.
B. El defecto físico desaparecerá sin necesidad de una operación.
C. Se puede conseguir la sangre necesaria en Lima.
D. Se ha ejecutado la operación muchas veces en los Estados Unidos.

44. El Caudillo de España tomó el micrófono y dijo:—"Señores Alcaldes: en estas batallas de la paz, uno de los problemas más importantes es unir a todos los pueblos con las capitales y hacer que lleguen a ellos todas las ventajas de la civilización y de la ténica moderna. Hoy llevamos a cabo uno de estos hechos con la inauguración de 200 centros telefónicos, que hacen aumentar más del ciento por ciento los que existían en la provincia."

¿En qué ocasión pronunció el Caudillo de España este discurso?
A. Se celebraba una gran victoria de la Guerra Civil.
B. Se les honraba a varios alcaldes caídos en una batalla.
C. Se inauguraba una expansión del servicio telefónico nacional.
D. Cien alcaldes de provincia se habían presentado pidiendo justicia.

45. Hace un año que el edificio donde funciona el Museo Provincial de Bellas Artes se encuentra en mal estado. A poco de iniciarse la renovación, los trabajos fueron interrumpidos y por eso continúan cerradas las salas. Los turistas no pueden conocer la obra de nuestros pintores y escultores. No sabemos si tiene la culpa el propietario del edificio o el gobierno que alquila el local, pero las autoridades deben resolver esta situación lamentable.

¿De qué situación se queja el escritor de este artículo?
A. El gobierno provincial tarda un año en construir un Museo de Bellas Artes.
B. Se les prohibe a los artistas alquilar salas en donde exhibir sus obras.
C. Hacen falta turistas que quieran comprar pinturas y esculturas provincianas.
D. Las autoridades no se dan prisa por completar la reparación del museo.

46. Algunos comerciantes se han dirigido a la Cámara de Comercio pidiendo que se impida que algunas tiendas tengan las puertas abiertas fuera del horario fijado por la ley y especialmente los domingos. Los dueños de estos establecimientos se aprovechan de las horas no permitidas por la ley para vender sus mercancías a los campesinos que vienen a la ciudad.

¿Qué es lo que quieren unos comerciantes?
A. que todos los comerciantes observen las horas legales
B. que no vengan a la ciudad los campesinos
C. que la Cámara de Comercio abra sus puertas los domingos
D. que se impida que los campesinos vendan sus productos en la ciudad

Hoy, que lloro amargamente la muerte de Mariano Benlliure, me voy a limitar a referir cómo y cuándo él ganó su primer dinero.

En nuestras charlas íntimas hubo de contármelo hace muchísimo tiempo. Habitaba la familia de Mariano en Valencia en el piso más alto de una casa, en cuya planta baja existía una tienda de comestibles, famosa por el buen chocolate que vendía. El dueño del establecimiento era un viejo carlista que había peleado en la primera guerra civil con fanático entusiasmo.

Benlliure, que tenía a la sazón nueve años, ya modelaba unas figurillas muy delicadas, y el chocolatero, que admiraba la habilidad del niño, le dijo un día:

—Mariano, si me copias estos dos retratos, te daré una peseta—y le entregó un retrato de San José otro del célebre caudillo carlista Pascual Cucala.

Mariano cumplió el encargo perfectamente, y gustó tanto su obra al veterano guerrillero, que le manifestó:

—Toma la peseta, que está bien ganada, y de propina, por lo parecido que están los retratos, te regalo una onza de chocolate.

Así obtuvo su primera ganancia quien en el curso de más de setenta años había de llenar el mundo entero de bustos, estatuas y monumentos, que han hecho célebre su nombre.

47. ¿Dónde vivía Benlliure en aquella época?
    A. en la planta baja de la casa
    B. en el despacho del chocolatero
    C. detrás de una tienda de comestibles
    D. en la parte superior de una casa

48. ¿A quién pertenecía la tienda?
    A. a la familia de Mariano
    B. a los Valencia
    C. a un antiguo soldado
    D. a Pascual Cucala

49. ¿Cómo estimuló el chocolatero la carrera de Benlliure?
    A. Le dio al muchacho una pequeña comisión.
    B. Le ofreció empleo en su tienda de comestibles.
    C. Le presentó a un gran artista.
    D. Le compró todas las figurillas que modelaba.

50. Para demostrar lo satisfecho que estaba, el chocolatero le
    A. regaló los retratos que había copiado.
    B. pagó lo prometido y le dio unos dulces.
    C. ofreció hacer el gasto de la carrera.
    D. dio otros tres retratos para copiar.

51. Benlliure era uno de los más famosos
    A. pintores de España.
    B. escultores del mundo.
    C. soldados españoles.
    D. arquitectos valencianos.

El extranjero llegó rendido a la estación desierta. Su gran maleta, que nadie quiso llevar, le había fatigado en extremo. Se limpió el rostro con un pañuelo, y miró los rieles del ferrocarril que se perdían en el horizonte. Desanimado y pensativo consultó su reloj: la hora justa en que el tren debía partir.

Alguien, salido de quién sabe dónde, le dio una palmada muy suave. Al volverse, el extranjero se halló ante un viejecillo de vago aspecto ferrocarrilero. Llevaba en la mano una linterna roja, pero tan pequeña, que parecía de juguete. Miró sonriendo al viajero, y éste le dijo ansioso su pregunta:

—Usted perdone, ¿ha salido ya el tren?

—¿Lleva usted poco tiempo en este país?

—Necesito salir inmediatamente. Debo hallarme en Toledo mañana mismo.

—Se ve que usted ignora por completo lo que ocurre. Lo que debe hacer ahora es buscar alojamiento en un hotel.

—Pero yo no quiero alojarme, sino salir en el tren.

—Alquile usted un cuarto inmediatamente, si es que lo hay. En caso de que pueda conseguirlo, contrátelo por mes, le resultará más barato y recibirá mejor atención.

—¿Está usted loco? Yo debo llegar a Toledo mañana mismo.

—Francamente, yo debería abandonarle a su suerte. Sin embargo, le daré unos informes.

—Por favor . . .

—Este país es famoso por sus ferrocarriles, como usted sabe. Falta solamente que los trenes cumplan las indicaciones contenidas en las guías y que pasen efectivamente por las estaciones. Los habitantes del país así lo esperan; mientras tanto, aceptan las irregularidades del servicio y su patriotismo les impide expresar cualquier manifestación de desagrado.

52. ¿Por qué llegó cansado el extranjero?
A. Se había perdido en el desierto.
B. Había viajado una gran distancia.
C. Lo que llevaba pesaba mucho.
D. La escalera de la estación era muy alta.

53. ¿Cuándo llegó el viajero a la estación?
A. dos horas antes de partir el tren
B. después de hallar un cuarto
C. a la hora exacta
D. momentos después de salir el tren

54. ¿Qué le recomendó el viejo al extranjero?
A. que buscase dónde vivir mientras esperaba
B. que alquilara un cuarto en otro pueblo
C. que consiguiese pasaje en el próximo tren
D. que echara ojo a su maleta

55. El viejo ofreció
A. llevarle al extranjero a su propia casa.
B. decirle por qué le hizo tal recomendación.
C. llevarle él mismo a Toledo.
D. servirle de guía.

56. El anciano acabó por decirle que
A. los trenes no llegaban ni partían a tiempo.
B. el servicio de ferrocarriles en Toledo era mejor.
C. se había suspendido la distribución de guías impresas.
D. todo español protestaba del servicio irregular.

Un salón de hotel absolutamente en silencio. Son las diez y media de la mañana. Hace unas horas, exactamente una noche, que Madrid ha sido espectadora de dos representaciones simultáneas; por un lado, vio la primera representación de la *Atlántida,* de Falla; por otro lado, vio debutar a Rafael Frühbeck como director oficial de la Orquesta Nacional. En un rincón del salón, Frühbeck y su señora. Sobre la mesa, los diarios de la mañana. Y en ellos, las críticas del doble debut. Nos hemos saludado y nos observamos. Frühbeck está tranquilo. Su esposa lee los periódicos.

—¿Los ha leído usted, Frühbeck?—le pregunté.

—Sí, todos.

—¿Qué piensa de esas críticas?

—No opino nunca sobre ellas. Profesionalmente, los críticos tienen una obligación. Y la cumplen. Si yo criticara las críticas, nunca se acabaría el asunto.

—¿Un director de orquesta puede ser crítico de sí mismo?

—No sólo puede, sino que debe serlo.

—Haga su crítica del concierto de ayer.

—No; públicamente, nunca lo hago.

—La Nacional, ¿es una gran orquesta?

—Sí.

—¿Qué es para usted?

—Como primera orquesta de España, ser su director supone haber realizado la ambición de todo director español.

—Y usted para la orquesta, ¿qué es usted?

—No lo sé.

—¿Qué le gustaría ser?

—Me gustaría ser para la Orquesta Nacional el director que la colocase en el punto más alto que jamás haya alcanzado.

—¿Esto es fácil o difícil?

—Muy difícil; tenga en cuenta que mis dos antecesores eran dos muy grandes maestros.

57. Esta conversación tuvo lugar entre dos hombres que estaban
   A. escuchando un concierto de música de Falla.
   B. escribiendo un artículo de crítica para los periódicos.
   C. preparándose para asistir a una función teatral.
   D. discutiendo las críticas sobre la función de la noche anterior.

58. ¿Por qué se negó Frühbeck a comentar sobre las críticas?
   A. No las había leído todavía.
   B. Tenía fama de nunca leer las críticas.
   C. Creía que sus comentarios causarían un debate interminable.
   D. Les tenía miedo a los críticos.

59. Frühbeck opina que un director de orquesta debe
   A. ser su propio crítico.
   B. hacer poco caso de la crítica.
   C. hacer su crítica públicamente.
   D. dedicarse también a la composición.

60. El llegar a ser director de la Orquesta Nacional le significaba haber
   A. alcanzado lo más alto del mundo musical español.
   B. dado el primer paso importante de su carrera.
   C. tenido éxito a pesar de los críticos.
   D. tenido mayor éxito que Manuel de Falla.

END OF TEST NO. 1

TEST 2

USE THE SPECIAL ANSWER SHEET ON PAGE 233.
THE TIME LIMIT FOR EACH TEST IS ONE HOUR.

Each of the incomplete statements or questions below is followed by four suggested completions. Select the most appropriate completion that would make the sentence grammatically correct and blacken the space under the letter of your choice on the special answer sheet.

1. Ahora tengo que . . . de usted.
   A. despedirme
   B. despedirse
   C. me despido
   D. despedir

2. Oí . . . de la boda de Anita.
   A. hablado
   B. hablando
   C. hablar
   D. hablo

3. ¿Qué piensa Ud. . . . nuestro profesor de español?
   A. de
   B. en
   C. a
   D. nothing needed

4. El avión tardó en
   A. llegando.
   B. llegado.
   C. llega.
   D. llegar.

5. El muchacho se empeñó . . . salir.
   A. en
   B. de
   C. a
   D. con

6. ¿ . . . qué piensa Ud.?
   A. De
   B. En
   C. A
   D. Con

7. Le agradecí . . . su paciencia.
   A. por
   B. para
   C. de
   D. no preposition needed.

8. ¿Qué buscas?—Busco . . . mis libros.
   A. para
   B. por
   C. de
   D. no preposition needed.

198

9. Se lo explico a ustedes a fin de que . . . comprenderlo.
   A. pueden
   B. poder
   C. puedan
   D. podrán

10. Le daré el dinero a Roberto cuando
    A. pedírmelo.
    B. me lo pida.
    C. me lo pide.
    D. me lo pedirá.

11. Le di el dinero a Roberto cuando
    A. me lo pidió.
    B. me lo pedirá.
    C. me lo pide.
    D. pedírmelo.

12. Trabajaré hasta que Ud.
    A. venga.
    B. viene.
    C. vendrá.
    D. venir.

13. Trabajé hasta que Ud.
    A. viene.
    B. venga.
    C. vino.
    D. vendrá.

14. Por más interesante que . . . , no quiero ver esa película.
    A. es
    B. será
    C. son
    D. sea

15. Por bien que . . . Roberto, no quiero jugar con él.
    A. juega
    B. juegue
    C. jugando
    D. jugar

16. No abriré la puerta, quienquiera que
    A. sea.
    B. es.
    C. será.
    D. fue.

17. Dondequiera que Ud. . . . , escríbame.
    A. está
    B. esté
    C. es
    D. sea

18. Adondequiera que Ud. . . . , dígamelo.
    A. va
    B. está
    C. irá
    D. vaya

19. Busco un libro que . . . interesante.
   A. es
   B. está
   C. esté
   D. sea

20. Tengo un libro que . . . bueno.
   A. es
   B. sea
   C. está
   D. esté

21. ¿Conoce Ud. a alguien que . . . paciencia?
   A. tiene
   B. tenga
   C. tendrá
   D. ten

22. No encontré a nadie que . . . la respuesta.
   A. sabe
   B. sepa
   C. supiera
   D. sabrá

23. No encuentro a nadie que . . . la respuesta.
   A. sabe
   B. sepa
   C. supiera
   D. sabido

24. Ayer encontré a alguien que . . . la respuesta.
   A. sabe
   B. sepa
   C. supiera
   D. sabido

Read the following statements and select the correct missing word or words that would fit grammatically and sensibly in each statement. Blacken the space under the letter of your choice on the special answer sheet.

En la sierra . . . Balcón de la Mancha, se va . . . levantar una monumental

25. A. llamado
   B. llamada
   C. llamados
   D. llamadas

26. A. a
   B. de
   C. con
   D. por

estatua al héroe creado . . . Cervantes: Don Quijote. La obra será . . .

27. A. para
   B. de
   C. por
   D. en

28. A. realizado
   B. realizados
   C. realizada
   D. realizadas

por el escultor Víctor de los Ríos. Tendrá la estatua treinta metros de alto y otros treinta de ancho. En el interior del caballo se hará un salón de recepciones, y en . . . cabeza de Don Quijote un punto de observación,

29. A. la
   B. el
   C. su
   D. nothing needed

desde . . . se podrán ver más de cincuenta pueblos de la región.

30. A. lo que
   B. cual
   C. el cual
   D. la cual

Read the settings given below and select the best answer which is related to the situation described. Blacken the space under the letter of your choice on the special answer sheet.

31. Jorge acaba de llegar a México donde lo está esperando en el aeropuerto su amigo mexicano, Raúl.

Raúl dice:—¡Qué bueno verte en México, por fin!

Jorge contesta:
A. No tuve ninguno.
B. Será un placer.
C. Vamos a recogerlas.
D. Me alegro mucho de estar aquí.

32. Es por la mañana y una señora habla por teléfono con su amiga Luisa. Hablan de las compras que cada una de ellas ha hecho el día anterior.

La señora dice: —¿A qué hora llegaste a casa ayer?

Luisa contesta:
A. Me compré un vestido rojo.
B. A eso de las cinco.
C. Me gustaría ir de compras.
D. Nos hablamos por teléfono.

33. Luis quiere comprar un coche y habla con su padre. El padre le dice: —Ya sé que sabes conducir pero me parece que eres muy joven para tener coche.

Luis contesta:
A. ¿No puedes prestarme algo?
B. Voy a buscar trabajo mañana.
C. Todos mis amigos tienen coche.
D. Es guapo y alto.

34. Bárbara y Lola están hablando acerca de un alumno nuevo de la clase de matemáticas. Hace una semana que él está en aquella clase y parece un poco tímido.

Bárbara dice: —No creo que ese chico haya hablado con nadie en la clase.

Lola contesta:
A. ¿Quieres invitarlo a nuestra fiesta?
B. ¿Quién va a invitarlo?
C. ¿Por qué estamos hablando acerca de él?
D. Vamos a clase ahora.

35. Usted entra en un banco de Madrid y el cajero dice: —Buenos días. ¿En qué puedo servirle a Ud.?

Usted contesta:
A. ¿Cuál es su dirección aquí?
B. Deseo cambiar dinero.
C. Vivo en el hotel Colón.
D. Me gusta mucho esta ciudad.

Read each of the following passages and select the best answer to each question by blackening the space under the letter of your choice on the special answer sheet.

Entre los regalos que la vida contemporánea nos ha dado está la obra de Walt Disney. Sus películas han duplicado el número de nuestros domingos, es decir, nuestros días de alegría. Todos estamos en deuda con él, porque nos ha regalado su genio a todos y no sólo a los niños. Gracias a Disney, principalmente, los chicos de todo el mundo han podido ir al cine sin que sus padres se sintieran avergonzados de comprar los billetes y entrar en el cine. He ahí quien siempre ha sabido algo muy sencillo, pero que sólo conoce una minoría de poetas: que en el viejo corazón del hombre respira todavía el niño que ese hombre fue.

Ante un film de Disney, el niño experimenta dos tipos de placer: el que proviene de la obra y el que le proporciona ver divertirse a los mayores tanto como él. Disney es, pues, universal en más de un sentido: le conocen todos, porque se dirige a todos. La violencia es una fuerza de atracción innegable, como el miedo o la risa; pero todavía por encima de ella existe una fuerza de atracción angélica que comunica algo que vale más: la alegría.

36. Lo que dice el autor de los domingos significa que
A. se dan regalos a todos los que van al cine los domingos.
B. con sólo comprar un billete pueden entrar dos niños.
C. se dan dos películas de Disney los domingos.
D. Disney nos ha proporcionado muchísimas horas alegres.

37. Los padres no se sienten avergonzados
A. de que no ganen tanto como Disney.
B. de que no les gusten las películas de Disney.
C. de acompañar a sus hijos al cine.
D. de prohibir que sus hijos vayan al cine.

38. Disney se da cuenta de que
A. a todos no les gustan sus películas.
B. todo hombre es un niño grande.
C. pocos poetas van al cine.
D. los niños prefieren películas policíacas.

39. ¿En qué consiste la universalidad de Disney?
A. Muchas de sus películas han sido premiadas.
B. Conoce a todos los actores del mundo cinematográfico.
C. Todo el mundo puede apreciar el arte de Disney.
D. No cuesta mucho la entrada en el cine donde se dan sus filmes.

40. La atracción más fuerte de las películas de Disney es
A. la alegría.
B. la violencia.
C. la vergüenza.
D. el miedo.

El viejo don Juan le presentó su huésped Osvaldo a su familia—mujer, hijos y un sinnúmero de parientes—y luego todos pasaron al comedor, sentándose en grandes sillas de madera ante una mesa muy pulida. Era un cuarto enorme que hacía eco a las palabras con sus desnudas paredes blancas. Leche fresca y pan moreno sirvió el mozo ante el anciano, que charlaba de esto y aquello, y un perrito que lo miraba dulcemente.

—Créame, mi señor don Osvaldo, que es un placer para mí recibirle en mi casa. El encuentro con un ser civilizado, por raro, hace el efecto de una revelación.

—Igual que a mí, don Juan. Esos campesinos son atentos, pero no hablan sino de lo suyo. Uno jamás podría conversar mano a mano con ellos: no nos entenderíamos.

El ingeniero da pedazos de pan mojados en leche al perrillo y luego ha de responder a todas las preguntas del dueño. ¿Y Lima? ¿Y la política? ¿Y el gobierno? ¿Habrá revolución? El joven Osvaldo no puede contestar satisfactoriamente porque ignora tales asuntos. Dice que le interesan otras cosas y termina por manifestar que él ha huido de la vida estéril de la capital y se encuentra de explorador.

—Conque vino usted a explorar la región ¿no? Entonces necesita guías—dice el viejo.

—Sí, claro.

41. El grupo en el comedor estaba compuesto de
   A. muchos niños y un perro.
   B. un anciano, su familia, y un invitado.
   C. un viejo y varios campesinos.
   D. un viejo y varios amigos suyos.

42. Mientras el criado servía la comida
   A. el anciano guardaba silencio.
   B. los niños jugaban con el perro.
   C. el viejo hablaba de distintos temas.
   D. la mujer hablaba de la revolución.

43. Al viejo le gustaba mucho
   A. estar solo.
   B. reunirse con los campesinos.
   C. conversar con los soldados del distrito.
   D. charlar con alguien venido de la ciudad.

44. El joven ingeniero se interesa sobre todo por
   A. la vida social de la ciudad.
   B. el trabajo de exploración.
   C. los problemas en el mundo.
   D. las cuestiones políticas.

45. El forastero había salido de Lima porque
   A. no se encontraba a gusto allí.
   B. deseaba estudiar la ingeniería.
   C. no había suficiente trabajo allí.
   D. los revolucionarios lo buscaban.

A los doce años, peleando Juan Peña con unos chicos, le tiraron una piedra en los dientes; la sangre corrió lavándole el sucio de la cara, y un diente se le quebró en forma de sierra. Desde ese día empieza la edad de oro de Juan Peña.

Con la punta de la lengua, Juan tocaba continuamente el diente roto; el cuerpo inmóvil, la mirada vaga sin pensar. Así, de malicioso y juguetón, se tornó en callado y tranquilo.

Los padres de Juan, cansados de escuchar quejas de los vecinos y las víctimas de las maldades del chico, y habiendo agotado toda clase de reprimendas y castigos, estaban ahora estupefactos y angustiados con la transformación de Juan.

—El niño no está, Pablo—decía la madre al marido. —Hay que llamar al médico.

Llegó el médico, grave y solemne, y procedió al diagnóstico: buen pulso, excelente apetito, ningún síntoma de enfermedad.

—Señora—terminó por decir el sabio, después de un largo examen—, su hijo está mejor que una manzana. Lo que sí es indiscutible—continuó con voz misteriosa—es que estamos en presencia de un caso fenomenal: su hijo, mi estimable señora, sufre de lo que llamamos hoy el mal de pensar. Su hijo es un filósofo precoz, un genio tal vez.

Parientes y amigos se hicieron eco de la opinión del médico, recibida con júbilo indecible por los padres de Juan. Pronto, en el pueblo se citó el caso admirable del "niño prodigio" y su fama se aumentó.

46. ¿Qué le pasó a Juan Peña a los doce años?
    A. Recibió un hermoso regalo de sus amigos.
    B. Se le rompió un diente en una pelea.
    C. Unos chicos le lavaron la cara con agua sucia.
    D. Halló un pedazo de oro en las montañas.

47. ¿Qué efecto produjo el incidente?
    A. Se puso reservado el niño.
    B. Juan se puso aun más malicioso.
    C. Siempre se miraba el diente en el espejo.
    D. Le quedó lastimada la lengua.

48. ¿Por qué quedaron sorprendidos los padres de Juan?
    A. Los vecinos se quejaron más que antes.
    B. Los severos castigos acabaron por corregirle.
    C. El niño había sufrido un cambio de genio.
    D. El niño se negó a hacer caso de las reprimendas.

49. ¿Cuál fue el diagnóstico del médico?
    A. Juan tenía varios síntomas de enfermedades graves.
    B. El niño se había comido muchas manzanas podridas.
    C. Había que estimularse su apetito.
    D. El estado de Juan era rarísimo.

50. ¿Qué ocurrió como resultado de la visita del doctor?
    A. Los parientes del prodigio lo desconocieron.
    B. Se vieron contrariados los padres del niño.
    C. Se extendió la celebridad del niño.
    D. Acudieron filósofos y genios de todas partes a verlo.

Para escribir la historia completa de la Vuelta a Colombia se necesitan noventa páginas y media. Sin embargo, para un periódico se puede hacer un relato breve de lo que es la competencia, la máxima del deporte colombiano, y lo que hacen los miembros de la llamada "familia de la Vuelta".

Cada año—durante la estación más fría del año—parten de Bogotá, generalmente, cincuenta, sesenta o más ciclistas en busca de un triunfo para los colores deportivos de sus regiones.

Muchos de ellos saben, de antemano, que sólo tendrán un éxito muy relativo en la carrera. Algunos llegan hasta adivinar las penalidades que van a pasar en las jornadas. Pero salen.

Otros, los biciclistas y "dedicados", tienen por lo menos las capacidades necesarias para luchar por los primeros lugares en la clasificación general.

Los ciclistas inician la Vuelta y con ellos cerca de seiscientas personas más. La "gran familia" está compuesta por unas setecientas en total.

Cuando ya han transcurrido cinco o seis fases, los ganadores usualmente se han identificado. En algunos casos—por ejemplo este año—el campeón de la Vuelta comenzó a tener nombre propio en Medellín.

51. La Vuelta a Colombia es una competencia deportiva de
    A. automóviles.
    B. caballos.
    C. bicicletas.
    D. motocicletas.

52. El autor dice que se necesitarían más de noventa páginas porque
    A. Colombia fue fundada en el siglo XV.
    B. hay tanto que contar sobre la Vuelta.
    C. los premios son ofrecidos por el periódico.
    D. el periodista era ciclista él mismo.

53. La Vuelta se efectúa
   A. en un club deportivo colombiano.
   B. en el Palacio de los Deportes de Medellín.
   C. por las calles de Bogotá.
   D. por las carreteras de Colombia.

54. ¿Quiénes son los "dedicados"?
   A. los que esperan ganar la Vuelta
   B. los que tienen el apellido de Medellín
   C. los que no saben qué penalidades van a pasar
   D. los dueños de las fábricas de bicicletas

55. Se sabe quienes serán los ganadores
   A. al formarse los ciclistas.
   B. al salir de Bogotá.
   C. después de un día.
   D. después de varias etapas.

56. Es muy conveniente guardar el mayor silencio posible durante la primera semana en todo trabajo nuevo. Sea usted cordial, amable; sonría y manténgase alerta, pero no charle. La mayor parte de las preguntas que formula el nuevo empleado provienen sólo de su nerviosidad, no de un verdadero deseo de aprender lo que desconoce.

   ¿Qué regla general debe observar un nuevo empleado?
   A. huir de la gente
   B. hablar lo menos posible
   C. hacer muchísimas preguntas
   D. llegar primero por la mañana

57. Los Presidentes de Venezuela y de Colombia se reunieron el mes pasado en un puente de la frontera que divide las dos repúblicas sudamericanas. Se encontraron allí para inaugurar un nuevo puente internacional que simboliza la amistad y la cooperación que une a los dos pueblos. El puente había sido pagado por las dos naciones respectivas.

   ¿Qué simboliza el nuevo puente internacional?
   A. las buenas relaciones entre las dos naciones
   B. el restablecimiento de relaciones políticas entre Venezuela y Colombia
   C. la elección de un nuevo presidente venezolano
   D. la construcción de un nuevo pueblo en la frontera

58. El joven pintor y caricaturista, David Carrillo, cuyo estilo en verdad es único, se apuntó un éxito más en su carrera profesional con su extraordinaria Exposición "20 retratos" efectuada en los salones del Club de Periodistas de México. El retrato que provocó más elogios fue el de José Clemente Orozco, cuya vigorosa expresión fue captada extraordinariamente por el pintor Carrillo.

   ¿Cuál fue la ocasión del más reciente éxito de Carrillo?
   A. un discurso pronunciado en el Club de Periodistas
   B. la publicación de un elogio escrito por José Clemente Orozco
   C. una exhibición de retratos
   D. la exhibición de un mural pintado en los salones del Club

59. Al dar la medianoche del 16 de abril, una fuerza de exilados cubanos desembarcó en una remota playa de su patria, en misión libertadora. Mucho se ha dicho y especulado sobre el desastroso fin que tuvo esa invasión, pero faltaba una relación completa de lo que realmente sucedió en la playa, es decir, el testimonio de los que allí lucharon. Léase la relación verdadera en ABC, revista preferida de los lectores españoles.

¿Por qué no se había escrito hasta ahora una relación definitiva de la invasión?

A. No hubo sobrevivientes entre los invasores.

B. La obscuridad de la noche dificultaba la observación.

C. Todos los libertadores fueron capturados por las tropas cubanas.

D. Los invasores mismos no habían contado su versión.

60. A bordo del buque HOPE, en el Perú, se ha auxiliado a más de 10,000 pacientes y alrededor de 1,000 operaciones en cuatro meses. Doctores y enfermeras peruanos han trabajado al lado de sus colegas de los Estados Unidos y se han perfeccionado en el uso de instrumentos y métodos modernos. Además del hospital, el buque tiene un circuito cerrado de televisión para los interesados en las técnicas más modernas de la cirugía.

¿Además de curar a los enfermos, ¿qué otro objetivo tiene este buque?

A. Se dan clases de televisión para los enfermos peruanos.

B. Se presentan divertidos programas norteamericanos de televisión.

C. Se les venden a los doctores peruanos instrumentos médicos norteamericanos.

D. Se les ofrece a los médicos peruanos la oportunidad de observar procedimientos avanzados.

END OF TEST NO. 2

USE THE SPECIAL ANSWER SHEET ON PAGE 234.
THE TIME LIMIT FOR EACH TEST IS ONE HOUR.

Each of the incomplete statements or questions below is followed by four suggested completions. Select the most appropriate completion that would make the sentence grammatically correct and blacken the space under the letter of your choice on the special answer sheet.

1. Es el mejor libro que . . . leído.
   A. he
   B. haya
   C. hube
   D. había

2. ¡Que lo . . . Juan!
   A. hace
   B. hizo
   C. hará
   D. haga

3. Los niños no están aquí. ¡Ojalá que
   A. vienen!
   B. vendrán!
   C. vengan!
   D. han venido!

4. ¿ . . . es este lápiz?
   A. Cuyo
   B. De quién
   C. Cuya
   D. El cual

5. Mamá, ¿ . . . sirven los anteojos?
   A. Porque
   B. Por qué
   C. Para qué
   D. Para

6. Ayer, . . . de entrar en la casa cuando el teléfono sonó.
   A. Acabo
   B. Acabamos
   C. Acaban
   D. Acabábamos

7. El soldado defendió a su
   A. campo.
   B. país.
   C. patria.
   D. nación.

8. ¿ . . . a María y a su hermano?
   A. Sabe Ud.
   B. Saben Uds.
   C. Conoce Ud.
   D. Supieran Uds.

9. ¿ . . . Ud. nadar bien?
  A. Sabe
  B. Saben
  C. Conoce
  D. Conocen

10. No puedo salir esta noche porque tengo . . . estudiar mis lecciones.
  A. a
  B. de
  C. que
  D. nothing needed

11. El alumno . . . sus libros en la sala de clase.
  A. dejó
  B. partió
  C. salió
  D. cayó

12. No me gusta . . . mucho dinero cuando voy de compras.
  A. gastar
  B. pasar
  C. gastando
  D. pasando

13. A Roberto y a María . . . gusta el helado.
  A. le
  B. lo
  C. los
  D. les

14. . . . chico le gusta bailar.
  A. El
  B. Al
  C. A
  D. nothing needed

15. A mi amigo le . . . los chocolates.
  A. gusta
  B. gustaron
  C. gustar
  D. gastar

16. Mis amigos han . . . traer sus discos.
  A. de
  B. a
  C. con
  D. nothing needed

17. Hay . . . estudiar para aprender.
  A. de
  B. que
  C. para
  D. nothing needed

18. ¿Cuánto tiempo . . . que Ud. estudia el español?
  A. hací
  B. hube
  C. hubo
  D. hace

19. ¿Cuánto tiempo hace que Ud. . . . el autobús?
  A. espera
  B. esperaba
  C. esperé
  D. esperó

20. Hace tres años que . . . el español.
  A. estudiaba
  B. estudiaré
  C. estudio
  D. estudió

Read the following letter and choose the correct missing word or words that would fit grammatically and sensibly in each statement. Blacken the space under the letter of your choice on the special answer sheet.

Muy señores . . . :
  21. A. mío
    B. míos
    C. mías
    D. mis

¿Cómo me llamo? . . . Pedro García y . . . diez y ocho años.
  22. A. Soy   **23.** A. tiene
    B. Estoy   B. tengo
    C. Voy   C. tienes
    D. Está   D. tuvo

Hace cuatro años que . . . el español y el francés y . . . hablar bien
  24. A. estudiaba   **25.** A. sé
    B. estudiaré   B. se
    C. estudió   C. sí
    D. estudio   D. supo

las dos lenguas. El verano pasado . . . en la tienda de Macy's. La señorita
  26. A. trabajo
    B. trabajaré
    C. trabajó
    D. trabajé

Smith es . . . profesora de español y de francés. Me . . . ganar . . .
  27. A. mía   **28.** A. gustaría   **29.** A. cientos
    B. la mía   B. gusto   B. cien
    C. mis   C. gustan   C. cientas
    D. mi   D. gustaron   D. ciento

dólares a la semana. Prefiero . . . en su tienda . . . la tarde.
  30. A. trabajando   **31.** A. en
    B. trabajó   B. por
    C. trabajé   C. de
    D. trabajar   D. para

Mi número de teléfono es 123–4567.

Atentamente,
Pedro García

Each of the incomplete statements or questions below is followed by four suggested completions. Choose the most appropriate completion and blacken the space under the letter of your choice on the special answer sheet.

32. Después de cenar, el señor colocó . . . sobre la mesa para el camarero.
    A. una propina
    B. un vaso de agua
    C. helado
    D. el sombrero

33. La mujer abrió la puerta y . . . a los invitados.
    A. despidió
    B. gritó
    C. ató
    D. saludó

34. Cuando una persona está muy triste generalmente
    A. se ríe.
    B. llora.
    C. llueve.
    D. lo celebra.

35. Luisa tiene mucha vergüenza y cuando habla con un muchacho guapo siempre
    A. se sonroja.
    B. habla en voz alta.
    C. pide una cita.
    D. pide el número de teléfono.

36. Generalmente, las mujeres se ponen . . . en las orejas.
    A. collares
    B. ojales
    C. ojeras
    D. pendientes

37. El vino se vende en
    A. cristales.
    B. botellas.
    C. cartones.
    D. latas.

38. Ayer era el cumpleaños de mi tía y le envié un ramillete de
    A. flores.
    B. chocolates.
    C. dulces.
    D. latas.

39. Este chico es huérfano; no tiene
    A. perrito.
    B. pájaro.
    C. periódico.
    D. padres.

40. Para leer las noticias del día, compro
    A. un abrigo.
    B. un periódico.
    C. un papel.
    D. una naranja.

Read each of the following passages and select the best answer to each question by blackening the space under the letter
of your choice on the special answer sheet.

Sin hacer ruido, llegó don Paco a la casilla y desde afuera vio la puerta que estaba cerrada con cerradura que había por dentro. La luz salía desde adentro por una ventana pequeña, donde, en vez de vidrios, se había puesto una tela sucia para protección contra la lluvia y el frío. Con el obstáculo de la tela no se podían ver los objetos de dentro; pero don Paco se aproximó y observó en la tela tres o cuatro agujeros. Aplicó el ojo al más cercano, que era bastante espacioso y lo que vio por dentro le llenó de susto. Imaginó que veía a Lucifer en persona, aunque vestido de campesino andaluz, con sombrero grande, chaqueta larga y pantalones amplios. La cara del así vestido era casi negra, inmóvil, con espantosa y ancha boca y con colosales narices en forma de pico de pájaro. Don Paco se tranquilizó, no obstante, al reconocer que aquello era una máscara de las que ponen en las procesiones religiosas.

En otra silla estaba otra persona, en quien reconoció al instante don Paco a don Ramón, el comerciante más importante de su lugar que era también el hombre más rico después de cierto don Andrés y el más enorme hablador que por entonces existía en nuestro planeta.

Notó don Paco que tenía don Ramón las manos atadas con una cuerda a las espaldas, y dedujo que le habían llevado allí y que le retenían por violencia.

41. Al acercarse a la casilla, Paco descubrió que
    A. no se podía entrar por la puerta.
    B. se le había olvidado la llave.
    C. la casilla no tenía puerta.
    D. la puerta no tenía cerradura.

42. ¿Por qué no podía ver bien lo que había en la casilla?
    A. Los vidrios estaban sucios.
    B. Una tela cubría la ventana.
    C. No había luz en la casilla.
    D. La ventana estaba cubierta de madera.

43. ¿Por qué se asustó don Paco?
    A. Oyó acercarse una procesión ruidosa.
    B. Oyó gritar a una persona.
    C. Vio unos pájaros muertos en la casilla.
    D. Vio una figura grotesca dentro de la casilla.

44. ¿A quién reconoció Paco sentado en una silla?
    A. don Andrés
    B. el sacerdote
    C. un hombre de negocios
    D. la mujer de don Ramón

45. Don Paco se dio cuenta de que una persona que estaba en el cuarto era
    A. prisionero.
    B. mendigo.
    C. astrónomo.
    D. el dueño de la casilla.

Las dos quintas partes de la población mundial adulta (más de quince años) están constituidas por analfabetos. Para remediar este defecto que padece la humanidad, la U.N.E.S.C.O. coordinará la Campaña Mundial de Alfabetización Universal, decretada por las Naciones Unidas, que se propone alfabetizar en diez años los dos tercios de los adultos analfabetos; estos dos tercios, 330 millones, representan aproximadamente el sector de población comprendido entre los quince y los cincuenta años de edad.

En una primera etapa de la campaña, los esfuerzos se concentrarán en ocho países del mundo, que vendrán a ser como un campo de experimentación de métodos, procedimientos de acción y evaluación de resultados.

Los esfuerzos de los países iberoamericanos por reducir el porcentaje de analfabetos existente en su población son notables. En casi todos los países se han emprendido campañas de alfabetización a escala nacional. Algunos países constituyen un ejemplo: Venezuela ha alfabetizado en los seis primeros meses de 1981 a 95,758 adultos, y no se ha limitado a esto, sino que ha dedicado esfuerzos y dinero a la ayuda bilateral, mostrando sus problemas, sus éxitos y soluciones, y también sus fracasos, a misiones de otros países y ha regalado material instructivo, como es ese lote de 165,000 libros de texto enviados a Bolivia, Panamá y Honduras.

46. De cada cinco adultos de quince años o más de edad, dos
   A. ignoran las actividades de la U.N.E.S.C.O.
   B. viven detrás del telón de acero.
   C. no tienen trabajo diario.
   D. no saben ni leer ni escribir.

47. ¿Qué se proponen las Naciones Unidas?
   A. educar a 330 millones de adultos entre 15 y 50 años de edad
   B. gastar 330 millones de dólares en su campaña de alfabetización
   C. enseñar inglés a todos los funcionarios de la Organización
   D. dar instrucción a los niños de diez a quince años de edad

48. La campaña se realizará de una manera experimental en
   A. media docena de países africanos.
   B. distintas partes del mundo.
   C. los países que quieran ser admitidos a las Naciones Unidas.
   D. los países de habla inglesa.

49. Las campañas de alfabetización iberoamericanas se desarrollan
   A. en grandes proporciones.
   B. en proporción limitada.
   C. en las grandes capitales.
   D. en las capitales de provincia.

50. Se espera que los países iberoamericanos
   A. se beneficien de las experiencias de Venezuela.
   B. se limiten a la alfabetización de niños escolares.
   C. fomenten el estudio del inglés.
   D. eviten los fracasos de Bolivia.

Si hay un momento emocionante en la historia americana, es el instante en que la lengua castellana, puesta en labios de los misioneros, se acerca al indio. ¡Qué aire de milagro y de drama envuelve al padre Gante, delgado y mal vestido, de blanca barba bíblica, que en la plaza mayor de Tenochtitlán, bajo un sol de justicia predica un sermón a grandes voces sin que nadie le comprenda aún!

Estos momentos los vivió el padre Gante, entre otros religiosos, de manera especial. Él se inquietó ante el abismo de incomprensión que le separaba del indio. Se acercó al niño, que tiene el alma pura y la memoria fresca. Palabra a palabra, gesto a gesto, un poco en castellano, otro poco en azteca recién conocido, va el padre hablando. Va cambiando las duras palabras largas del indio, los vocablos difíciles y guturales por el claro, sonoro castellano. Señala las cosas, pinta figuras, busca el gesto elocuente y traduce. Es una escena conmovedora: el padre suda explicando y se atormenta; el indiecito, serio, callado, le escucha, y a veces una luz de comprensión brilla en sus ojos oscuros. ¡Cuántos días así!

—Mira, Juan—ya casi todos los indios se llamaban Juan—. Ese que tú llamas Tloque Nahuaque es Dios, el Señor. Y no son muchos dioses, sino uno solo. Uno. Y aquello, no "mictlan", sino infierno. Y ésta— dibuja en la arena una mujer—es la Virgen.

51. El autor describe el primer encuentro entre
   A. religiosos e indios.
   B. padre e historiador.
   C. conquistador y misionero.
   D. misionero y universitario.

52. El sermón predicado por el misionero
    A. enojó a los indios.
    B. fue publicado en lengua indígena.
    C. fue dirigido a los españoles.
    D. no fue entendido por los indios.

53. Para poder hablar con el niño azteca, el padre Gante
    A. le enseñaba el latín.
    B. comunicaba con él mediante un jefe indio.
    C. había aprendido algo del idioma de los indios.
    D. había llevado un intérprete de España.

54. El misionero sabe que el niño le entiende
    A. por la expresión de la cara.
    B. por las palabras que pronuncia.
    C. por las señas que hace con las manos.
    D. por las figuras que dibuja.

55. Las lecciones dadas por el padre Gante tenían por objeto
    A. enseñar los misterios de la religión azteca.
    B. enseñar el arte del dibujo.
    C. enseñar la religión y la lengua de los españoles.
    D. instruir a los indios en el idioma latino.

María se lo estaba repitiendo siempre:

—No, Casimiro; esto no puede seguir así. Como tú comprenderás, hay que tomar una decisión. Después de todo, ese don Filomeno es un ladrón que te está robando el dinero pagándote lo menos posible; sí, no pongas esa cara; robando el dinero. Y si fuera por nosotros solos, mal estaría ya; pero piensa en la niña.

Casimiro Lobato no respondía nada. Demasiado sabía él que su mujer tenía toda la razón, que había que decidirse. Pero ¿cómo?, ¿cuándo? Ahí estaba el problema. Porque él no era de los que saben hablar alto, y hacerse valer, y ponerse cara a cara con el jefe. No; él tenía horror a las escenas, a las discusiones. Sobre todo a las discusiones materiales, de dinero. Lo malo era que—como decía María—, estaba la niña, esa criatura de cinco años, flaca, con unos ojos siempre asustados, bajo el pelo de color de paja. Le daba pena mirarla; y vergüenza. Vergüenza de ser un pobretón; de no haber conseguido (a pesar de que uno ha hecho también sus estudios) una posición más importante, y tener que depender todavía, a los treinta y seis años cumplidos, de los deseos extravagantes de don Filomeno. (Don Filomeno Porras, agente comercial; importación y exportación; automóvil; cincuenta y ocho años; noventa kilos; soltero; hombre de medios económicos, persona de orden.)

56. María insistía en que Casimiro tomara una decisión porque
    A. don Filomeno no le pagaba bastante.
    B. ella no tenía buena salud.
    C. ella no podía seguir trabajando.
    D. ella iba perdiendo la razón.

57. María le decía a su marido que
    A. pensara en el porvenir de su hija.
    B. confesara su crimen.
    C. denunciara a don Filomeno a la policía.
    D. pidiera ayuda a sus padres.

58. Casimiro no le respondía a su mujer porque
    A. fingía no oírla bien.
    B. era verdad lo que decía ella.
    C. no quería despertar a la niña.
    D. ella no comprendía el problema.

59. ¿De qué tenía vergüenza Casimiro?
    A. de ser dependiente en un almacén
    B. de no haber ayudado a los pobres
    C. de su poca instrucción
    D. de su condición humilde

60. Se le consideraría a don Filomeno un
    A. buen marido.
    B. buen profesor.
    C. hombre próspero.
    D. patrón benévolo.

END OF TEST NO. 3

USE THE SPECIAL ANSWER SHEET ON PAGE 235.
THE TIME LIMIT FOR EACH TEST IS ONE HOUR.

Each of the incomplete statements or questions below is followed by four suggested completions. Select the most appropriate completion that would make the sentence grammatically correct and blacken the space under the letter of your choice on the special answer sheet.

1. Llegaremos a Madrid . . . las tres de la tarde.
   A. eso
   B. a eso
   C. a eso de
   D. acerca de

2. Si Ud. . . . bien anoche, habría podido pasearse hoy.
   A. ha dormido
   B. hubiera dormido
   C. durmió
   D. duerme

3. Un fuego destruyó la casa
   A. hace una semana.
   B. hay una semana.
   C. hacía una semana.
   D. una semana hay.

4. . . . completar la tarea cuando el teléfono sonó.
   A. Acabo
   B. Acabo de
   C. Acababa
   D. Acababa de

5. Queríamos todos que el prisionero . . . la verdad.
   A. dijese
   B. dice
   C. diera
   D. diga

6. Busco un apartamento que . . . tres cuartos de baño.
   A. tenga
   B. tiene
   C. tenía
   D. tuviera

7. Pedro no quiere alquilar el automóvil . . . comprarlo.
   A. pero
   B. sino
   C. también
   D. cuando

8. Tenemos . . . trabajo hoy.
   A. poco
   B. pequeño
   C. mucha
   D. poca

9. Esta muchacha no . . . cantar.
   A. conoce
   B. sabe a
   C. sabe de
   D. sabe

10. ¿Quién te dio este dinero? —Mi madre
    A. me lo dio.
    B. me lo da.
    C. se lo da.
    D. se lo dio.

11. Se lo explico a Juan para que lo
    A. comprenda.
    B. comprende.
    C. comprenderá.
    D. comprendería.

12. Se lo explicaba a José para que lo
    A. comprendería.
    B. comprenda.
    C. comprenderá.
    D. comprendiese.

13. Después que . . . el profesor, salió.
    A. hubo hablado
    B. haber hablado
    C. hablando
    D. está hablando

14. Felipe llegará pasado mañana y yo . . . mis tareas.
    A. hube terminado
    B. habré terminado
    C. habría terminado
    D. habrá terminado

15. El padre . . . quitó a la niña el zapato.
    A. la
    B. lo
    C. le
    D. los

16. Los ladrones . . . robaron todo el dinero a él.
    A. le
    B. lo
    C. la
    D. los

17. Yo . . . compré mi automóvil a ellos.
    A. le
    B. lo
    C. la
    D. les

18. Ayer por la tarde, Elena y yo nos . . . en el cine.
    A. vimos
    B. vemos
    C. vieron
    D. vio

19. A las muchachas . . . faltan diez dólares.
    A. les
    B. los
    C. le
    D. las

20. A Guillermo . . . bastan cien dólares.
    A. le
    B. lo
    C. los
    D. les

Read the settings given below and select the best answer which is related to the situation described. Blacken the space under the letter of your choice on the special answer sheet.

21. Al salir de la escuela, Marcos y María pasan por delante de un cine que anuncia una película nueva.

    El muchacho dice:
    A. ¿Dónde están tus padres?
    B. ¿Te gustaría tomar algo?
    C. ¿Podemos llegar a tiempo?
    D. ¿Te gustaría ir a verla conmigo esta noche?

22. Ud. está en un restaurante con un amigo. El camarero tarda en venir y su amigo se pone muy impaciente.

    Le dice a Ud.:
    A. ¿Dónde está el camarero? Si no viene pronto, me voy a morir de hambre.
    B. Te invitaría para mañana porque hoy no tengo tiempo.
    C. ¿Por qué no vamos el sábado?
    D. La película que dan aquí me parece interesante.

23. Luis está en la estación de autobuses en Madrid y pide informes para ir a Toledo.

    El agente le dice a Luis:
    A. ¿A qué hora sale el autobús para Toledo?
    B. Buenos días, señor. ¿Qué desea?
    C. ¿Es un viaje muy largo?
    D. Buenos días, señor. Pido informes.

24. Durante una conversación, Ricardo y su amigo Esteban discuten planes para ofrecer una fiesta a Arturo, otro amigo.

    Esteban dice:
    A. Me gustaría organizar una fiesta en mi casa.
    B. Me acuerdo bien.
    C. Es el cumpleaños de Ricardo.
    D. Mis padres me darán permiso.

25. Elena y su madre quieren ir de compras. Pronto van a salir de casa. Su madre dice: ¿Qué me dijiste esta mañana? Necesitamos azúcar y ¿qué otra cosa?

    Elena contesta:
    A. Tenemos que quedarnos en casa.
    B. Tenemos que comprar pan.
    C. Estoy lista.
    D. Pues, vámonos.

Select the antonym of the given word and blacken the space under the letter of your choice on the special answer sheet.

26. alegre
A. contento
B. feliz
C. hermosa
D. triste

27. algo
A. nada
B. alguien
C. cosa
D. cualquier

28. alguien
A. algo
B. nadie
C. siempre
D. arriba

29. amigo
A. sobrino
B. prisa
C. enemigo
D. muchacho

30. después de
A. antes de
B. acercarse de
C. olvidarse de
D. lleno de

31. aquí
A. allí
B. acerca
C. cerca de
D. vacío

32. abajo
A. flaco
B. ojo
C. delante
D. arriba

33. caro
A. fuera
B. amargo
C. tren
D. barato

34. común
A. encima
B. raro
C. rostro
D. figura

35. vuelta
A. ida
B. vuelo
C. vuelva
D. idea

36. dulce
A. duro
B. dentro
C. amargo
D. abrigo

37. dejar caer
A. partir
B. recoger
C. recibir
D. hallar

38. peor
A. mejor
B. bajar
C. mal
D. bien

39. menor
A. joven
B. mayor
C. alcalde
D. más

40. hermosa
A. bella
B. linda
C. amable
D. fea

Read each of the following passages and select the best answer to each question by blackening the space under the letter of your choice on the special answer sheet.

No hace mucho, en una tertulia, un joven expresó su deseo de trabajar en determinado sitio, y preguntó qué posibilidades había de lograr su anhelo.

—Es sencillo—le contestaron—. Hazte amigo de don Crescencio.

—Bueno. Pero si interesa lo que yo puedo aportar a esa empresa, no es preciso hacerse amigo de don Crescencio.

—¡Oh, sí! Hay que ser amigo de don Crescencio. A ver si lo entiendes. Poco importa que tus proyectos valgan o no. Lo importante es que le caigas bien a don Crescencio.

En el café acababa de entrar un hombre, pálido el rostro, el cabello revuelto. Se acercó a nuestra tertulia y, cayendo en una silla, gimió desesperado:

—Creo que ya no soy amigo de don Crescencio.

Hubo un eco de lamentaciones. El recién llegado lloriqueó:

—Vosotros sabéis cómo lo he tratado, cómo le reía sus gracias, cómo asentía a sus opiniones, la de veces que acudí a sus comidas y le llevé flores a su esposa. Sabéis también que cuando él cogía odio a alguien, yo ejecutaba sus silenciosas órdenes y disponía el boicot contra el infeliz. ¡Pues hoy se ha negado a verme!

Corrieron los comentarios y consejos:

—Yo creo que si hablases con don Manuel, que manda en don Crescencio.

—Tendrías que hacerte amigo de don Manuel.

41. ¿Qué quería el joven?
A. encontrar empleo
B. conocer a una señorita
C. tomar un vaso de vino
D. ser invitado a una fiesta

42. ¿Qué le sugirieron los tertulianos?
   A. pagar la nota
   B. aportar dinero a un proyecto
   C. conseguir la amistad de cierto señor
   D. presentarse en persona en el Ministerio

43. ¿Por qué entró pálido el recién llegado?
   A. Temía que se le muriera su padre.
   B. Temía que don Crescencio se hubiera marchado.
   C. Temía haberle desagradado a don Crescencio.
   D. Temía haberle ofendido a don Manuel.

44. ¿Qué había hecho el recién llegado para complacer a don Crescencio?
   A. Le había invitado a comer.
   B. Había trabajado horas extraordinarias.
   C. Había trabajado en su jardín.
   D. Había hecho todo lo ordenado.

45. Los amigos quedaron en que sería mejor
   A. preparar un proyecto para la empresa.
   B. hacerse amigo del jefe de don Crescencio.
   C. dejar su cargo y buscar otro.
   D. guardar silencio y olvidar el asunto.

Hoy día el cine viene a ser casi un medio de diversión de todas las personas. En España, como ha sucedido en otros países, los espectáculos, así como la información y las distracciones en general, disponen de nuevos medios técnicos de transmisión, que orientan los gustos e inclinaciones de las grandes masas de habitantes. La televisión, que brinda el espectáculo en la propia casa, ha influido directamente en la evolución de la vida recreativa. En España, según las últimas estadísticas, existen 1,100,000 receptores de televisión; sin embargo, los españoles continúan siendo fervorosos espectadores del cine.

El número de salas de exhibición cinematográfica ha ido creciendo en estos años al mismo ritmo de expansión de las ciudades y pueblos. Actualmente se registran un total de 7,902 locales, en los que se incluyen 1,758 cines de verano al aire libre. Estos cines son típicos y característicos de nuestro país y se hallan en la parte sur de España, donde la benignidad del clima permite durante todo el verano la exhibición de películas al aire libre, una vez puesto el sol. Para estos cines descubiertos no se necesitan instalaciones costosas y se aprovecha el material de los cines de invierno, que en esta época permanecen cerrados. Este tipo de cine de verano se encuentra en los municipios menores de 10,000 habitantes. En las grandes poblaciones apenas si existen, y acaso uno de los motivos pueda ser el acondicionamiento de aire de las modernas salas cinematográficas.

46. ¿Qué influencia ejerce la tecnología moderna sobre las diversiones del público?
   A. Tiende a aburrir a los clientes.
   B. Limita los números de teatros.
   C. Repercute en los gustos de las masas.
   D. Reduce los ingresos de los empresarios.

47. En España ya asciende a más de un millón el número de
   A. cines de verano.
   B. aparatos de televisión.
   C. vendedores de radio.
   D. empresarios cinematográficos.

48. El número de cines en España crece de acuerdo con
   A. la expansión de la economía agrícola.
   B. la expansión de la población.
   C. el número de películas que llegan del extranjero.
   D. el número de turistas que acuden a España.

49. En el sur de España se han levantado
  A. cines de construcción modesta.
  B. teatros para dramas clásicos.
  C. varias escuelas para empresarios.
  D. dos fábricas de proyectores.

50. Se cree que el aire acondicionado en los cines de las grandes ciudades hace innecesaria la
  A. venta de entradas.
  B. fabricación de televisores.
  C. construcción de cines de verano.
  D. instalación de nuevas butacas.

Quizá fuera José Clará el único artista español residente en París que no vivía en Montmartre; estaba en París desde 1903, con su hermano Juan, también escultor. Pocas veces le encontrábamos en la ciudad, recluido en su laboratorio, tan laborioso siempre. Trabajador ilusionado, discípulo entonces de Augusto Rodín y, más tarde, de la Escuela de Bellas Artes en el barrio latino. Amigo del famoso escultor Bourdelle, nos encontrábamos en el estudio del maestro las tardes de domingo, en que Bourdelle solía recibir a sus amigos.

Por esta época realizó una numerosa serie de dibujos, actitudes fugaces de la famosa danzarina Isidora Duncan, llenos de gracia y movimiento, divulgados hoy en la Prensa y revistas de arte.

En 1920 viene Clará a Madrid para realizar una gran estatua en bronce a gran tamaño destinada al monumento de Alfonso XII, en el Retiro de Madrid. Siempre que fui a su estudio en la calle Lista le encontraba en pleno labor; podía encontrarle de improviso, seguro de hallarle trabajando.

51. Entre los artistas españoles residentes en París a principios del siglo, era posible que sólo Clará
  A. viviera fuera de Montmartre.
  B. viviera con su madre.
  C. cobrara una pensión.
  D. tuviera un empleo.

52. Clará se dedicaba principalmente
  A. a la música.
  B. a la cerámica.
  C. a la escultura.
  D. a la pintura.

53. Los artistas solían reunirse en
  A. el barrio latino.
  B. la casa de Rodín.
  C. una galería en Montmartre.
  D. el estudio de Bourdelle.

54. ¿A qué le llamaron a Clará a Madrid en 1920?
  A. a pintarle un retrato a Alfonso XII
  B. a ver a su hermano Juan
  C. a labrar una gran obra artística
  D. a asistir a una reunión de artistas

Hoy, tarde de domingo, estoy sola en casa. Ha tenido que producirse una serie de circunstancias extrañas para que esto ocurra, porque otros domingos, como muchos habitantes de Madrid, yo salgo disparada del núcleo urbano de la ciudad hacia lugares quietos, quizá desolados, los mismos sitios que antes abandonamos atraídos por las luces lejanas de la ciudad.

Nadie se queda en casa los domingos ahora. Nadie puede quedarse en casa los domingos porque todo el mundo tiene coche o moto o bicicleta. Recuerdo que hace algún tiempo me encontré en la calle con un amigo al que no veía desde años atrás. Me saludó con aire tan abatido que, temiendo que le hubiera ocurrido alguna desgracia, le pregunté:

—¿Te sucede algo, Antonio?

Me contestó aún más entristecido:

—Estoy hecho polvo. Me han concedido un coche hace un mes.

Pero ése no es motivo, hombre.

—¿Qué no es motivo? Mira, yo antes, los domingos me los pasaba en casa, pero desde que tengo el coche . . . que si Cuenca, que si Avila, que si El Escorial. No puedo convencer a la familia que donde mejor descanso es en un sillón de la casa.

55. Era poco corriente que la señora
    A. se encontrara en casa el domingo.
    B. se marchara de Madrid el domingo.
    C. cenara con su hermano los domingos.
    D. fuera al cine con una amiga los domingos.

56. ¿Qué se comprende por "luces lejanas"?
    A. lugares de recreo en el campo
    B. la vida universitaria de las provincias
    C. la vida de la metrópoli
    D. sitios tranquilos de las montañas

57. Según esta señora, todo el mundo ya dispone de
    A. un chalet en el campo.
    B. luz eléctrica en su domicilio.
    C. televisor y radio de transistores.
    D. su propio modo de transporte.

58. ¿Qué temía esta señora?
    A. tener que mudarse de casa
    B. tener que vender su coche
    C. que algo le hubiera sucedido a su amigo
    D. que su amigo no la conociera

59. ¿Qué le informó el amigo?
    A. que le iban a operar
    B. que ya disponía de un coche
    C. que había sacado mil pesetas en la lotería
    D. que le habían concedido un premio literario

60. ¿En dónde prefiere pasar el amigo los domingos?
    A. en un sitio de interés turístico
    B. en el cine o el teatro
    C. en el café
    D. en su hogar

END OF TEST NO. 4

USE THE SPECIAL ANSWER SHEET ON PAGE 236.
THE TIME LIMIT FOR EACH TEST IS ONE HOUR.

Each of the incomplete statements or questions below is followed by four suggested completions. Select the most appropriate completion that would make the sentence grammatically correct and blacken the space under the letter of your choice on the special answer sheet.

1. ¿Desde cuándo . . . Ud. el español?
A. estudia
B. estudié
C. estudió
D. estudiará

2. Estudio el español desde . . . tres años.
A. cuando
B. hace
C. hay
D. nothing needed

3. ¿Cuánto tiempo . . . que Ud. hablaba cuando entré en la sala de clase?
A. hace
B. hacía
C. hubo
D. hice

4. Hacía una hora que yo . . . cuando Ud. entró en la sala.
A. hablaba
B. hablo
C. hablaré
D. hablaría

5. Yo hablaba desde . . . una hora cuando Ud. entró.
A. hace
B. hacía
C. hubo
D. nothing needed

6. ¿A qué . . . vamos al baile?
A. tiempo
B. vez
C. hora
D. veces

7. ¿Juega Ud. . . . ?
A. el piano
B. al tenis
C. la guitarra
D. el violín

8. Carmen . . . muy bien el piano.
A. juega
B. toca
C. conoce
D. llena

9. ¿A quién . . . toca?
  A. lo
  B. la
  C. los
  D. le

10. Mi hermano quiere llegar . . . ser doctor.
  A. de
  B. por
  C. para
  D. a

11. Cuando vi el accidente, . . . pálido.
  A. me puse
  B. me hice
  C. seré
  D. me pondré

12. José . . . la silla de la cocina al comedor.
  A. tomé
  B. llevó
  C. vendió
  D. compró

13. La profesora . . . el libro y comenzó a leer a la clase.
  A. llevó
  B. tomó
  C. tomé
  D. vendió

14. Necesito . . . docena de huevos.
  A. medio
  B. media
  C. mitad
  D. mediodía

15. El alumno estudió . . . de la lección de español.
  A. la mitad
  B. el medio
  C. el mediodía
  D. la mediana

16. La alumna . . . un lápiz al profesor.
  A. preguntó
  B. pidió
  C. pedí
  D. pregunté

17. Los alumnos . . . a la profesora cómo estaba.
  A. preguntaron
  B. pidieron
  C. pediremos
  D. preguntamos

18. ¿Qué piensa Ud. . . . este libro?
  A. de
  B. en
  C. a
  D. no preposition needed

19. María, no hablas mucho; ¿ . . . qué piensas?
   A. de
   B. en
   C. a
   D. no preposition needed

20. Pienso . . . las vacaciones de verano.
   A. de
   B. en
   C. a
   D. no preposition needed

Read the following paragraphs and choose the correct missing word or words that would fit grammatically and sensibly in each statement. Blacken the space under the letter of your choice on the special answer sheet. Read each paragraph first entirely before selecting answers.

La Estación del año que prefiero

De . . . las estaciones del año, yo prefiero . . . porque no hay

21. A. todos   **22.** A. la primavera
   B. toda   B. el invierno
   C. todas   C. el otoño
   D. todo   D. el verano

clases en julio y agosto. Por . . . general, . . . buen tiempo. . . . a

23. A. lo   **24.** A. está   **25.** A. Toco
   B. el   B. es   B. Juego
   C. la   C. hay   C. Toqué
   D. los   D. hace   D. Jugué

mis deportes favoritos y . . . frecuencia, voy a la playa con mis amigos.

26. A. a
   B. de
   C. por
   D. con

Por supuesto, cuando . . . me . . . en casa mirando la televisión o escuchando

27. A. llueve   **28.** A. queja
   B. llovía   B. quedo
   C. llovió   C. quiero
   D. lloverá   D. quiebro

mis discos . . . . No llevo mucha . . . porque hace calor. El cuatro de . . .

29. A. favoritas   **30.** A. ropa   **31.** A. junio
   B. favores   B. dinero   B. julio
   C. favoritos   C. ropería   C. agosto
   D. favorezco   D. ropero   D. mayo

celebramos nuestra fiesta nacional. Mi cumpleaños cae en agosto. Por desgracia, muchos de mis amigos están de vacaciones y no pueden venir. El verano que viene, según mi papá, toda la familia va a . . . un viaje a México.

32. A. tener
   B. haber
   C. tomar
   D. hacer

La Ciudad en que vivo

Vivo en la ciudad de Nueva York. . . . ciudad está en el sur . . .

33. A. Este   **34.** A. de
      B. Esta   B. de la
      C. Aquel   C. del
      D. Ese   D. al

estado de Nueva York. Se encuentra cerca . . . Océano Atlántico. Es una

35. A. de
      B. de la
      C. del
      D. el

ciudad de unos ocho millones de habitantes. Hay varios medios de transporte,
como el ómnibus, el metro, y el automóvil. Es el centro comercial . . . industrial

36. A. y
      B. e
      C. de
      D. del

más grande del mundo. También es un centro cultural y tiene muchos teatros
y cines. . . . ciudad es famosa . . . sus rascacielos, como el Empire State

37. A. Esta   **38.** A. por
      B. Este   B. para
      C. Aquel   C. de
      D. Ese   D. a

Building. Es mejor visitar a Nueva York en el otoño porque . . . es muy

39. A. la hora
      B. la vez
      C. el tiempo
      D. hace

agradable. En mi opinión, Nueva York es la ciudad más interesante . . . mundo.

40. A. en el
      B. de
      C. al
      D. del

Read each of the following passages and select the best answer to each question by blackening the space under the letter of your choice on the special answer sheet.

Lorenzo el Vagabundo creía que su hermano Ignacio, la mujer Hilda, y los hijos de éstos le odiaban, y por eso no iba a visitarlos más que de vez en cuando; pero pronto vio que su hermano e Hilda le estimaban, y sólo le hacían reproches porque él no iba a verlos. Lorenzo comenzó a ir a casa de su hermano con más frecuencia.

Cuando Lorenzo fue a casa de su hermano, y con más confianza, Hilda e Ignacio, que era farmacéutico, seguidos de todos los chicos, le enseñaron la casa, limpia, clara y bien ordenada; después fueron a ver el jardín, y aquí Lorenzo vio por primera vez a Conchita, que con la cabeza cubierta con un sombrero de paja, estaba recogiendo flores. Lorenzo y ella se saludaron fríamente.

—Vamos hacia el río—le dijo Hilda a su hermana Conchita. —Diles a las criadas que lleven el chocolate allí.

Conchita se fue hacia la casa y los demás bajaron a una plazoleta que estaba junto al río, entre árboles, en donde había una mesa rústica y un banco de piedra. El sol, al penetrar entre el follaje, iluminaba el fondo del río, y se veían las piedras redondas y los peces que pasaban lentamente brillando como si fueran de plata. El tiempo era de una tranquilidad admirable; el cielo azul, puro y sereno.

Antes del caer de la tarde, las dos criadas del farmacéutico vinieron con platos en la mano trayendo chocolate caliente y pasteles. Los chicos se pusieron a comer los pasteles como animales. Lorenzo el Vagabundo habló de sus viajes, contó algunas aventuras, y tuvo suspensos de sus labios a todos. Sólo ella, Conchita, pareció no entusiasmarse gran cosa con aquellas narraciones.

41. Al principio, Lorenzo visitaba a su hermano con muy poca frecuencia porque
    A. pensaba que el hermano no lo quería.
    B. éste vivía a gran distancia.
    C. los niños le molestaban mucho a Lorenzo.
    D. Conchita no estaba allí.

42. Lorenzo y Conchita se encontraron por primera vez en
    A. la casa de Lorenzo.
    B. el jardín de la casa de Ignacio.
    C. una farmacia antigua.
    D. un barco de viaje a Sudamérica.

43. Hilda pidió que se sirvieran los refrescos en
    A. el comedor de su casa.
    B. el jardín detrás de la casa.
    C. un sitio cerca del río.
    D. la farmacia del esposo.

44. Cuando las sirvientas trajeron los refrescos, ¿qué hicieron los niños?
    A. Volvieron a la casa.
    B. Se fueron a pescar en el río.
    C. Sirvieron a todos con mucho decoro.
    D. Empezaron a consumirlo todo.

45. Todos escuchaban a Lorenzo con entusiasmo menos
    A. Conchita.
    B. los chicos.
    C. Ignacio.
    D. Hilda.

Cuando levanté los ojos, ¡horror!, vi una persona que me hizo temblar de espanto. Mientras estaba yo absorto en la interesante lectura del periódico, el tranvía se había detenido varias veces para tomar o dejar algún viajero. En una de estas ocasiones había entrado aquel hombre, cuya súbita presencia me produjo tan grande impresión. Era él, Mudarra, sentado frente de mí, con sus rodillas casi tocando mis rodillas. En un segundo le examiné de pies a cabeza y reconocí las facciones cuya descripción había leído. No podía ser otro: hasta los más insignificantes de su vestido indicaban claramente que era él. Era el mismo hombre en el aspecto, en el traje, en el respirar, en el sonreír, hasta en el modo de meterse la mano en el bolsillo para pagar.

De pronto le vi sacar una cartera y observé que ésta tenía una gran "M" dorada, la inicial de su apellido.

46. El narrador está en
    A. una biblioteca.
    B. un vehículo.
    C. una tienda.
    D. casa con un amigo.

47. El narrador había estado ocupado
    A. admirando el paisaje.
    B. hablando con Mudarra.
    C. leyendo el diario.
    D. admitiendo a los huéspedes.

48. El escritor tuvo miedo porque
    A. hubo un accidente automovilístico.
    B. se encontró de repente en la oficina del médico.
    C. el tranvía se paró sin avisar.
    D. reconoció a un sentado cerca de él.

49. El autor había conocido a Mudarra por haber
    A. recorrido el país en su compañía.
    B. estado en el mismo hospital.
    C. pasado su niñez con él.
    D. leído de él en el periódico.

50. El autor estaba seguro de la identidad del hombre porque
    A. vio una carta que llevaba el nombre de él.
    B. el hombre sacó del bolsillo algo con una "M".
    C. el hombre le dijo su nombre.
    D. ellos habían trabajado juntos.

Los días jueves y domingos son los días de mercado en Chichicastenango. Llega multitud de indígenas hacia la plaza. Esta se llena de ruido y colorido. Los trajes de los indios perturban la vista con sus extravagantes colores y con sus curiosos dibujos que representan mitos y leyendas.

La plaza ofrece un espectáculo confuso. La multitud de compradores y de vendedores conversa, discute, regatea y hace sus negocios en lengua indígena. Se anda con dificultad entre los comerciantes que se quedan cerca de sus mercancías.

En uno de los extremos de la plaza está la iglesia; se levanta al final de una escalera en forma de anfiteatro y de angostos pasos de piedra. Aquí es donde rezan los chichicastecos, unos de rodillas, otros de pie. Sus incensarios lanzan al viento enormes nubes de humo. Los indígenas queman lo que se llama "pom." El ambiente es agradable. El aroma del "pom" invade la escalera y el pórtico de la iglesia. En el interior del templo, entre la penumbra y el humo, los indios rezan arrodillados sobre el piso cubierto de pétalos de flores y entre centenares de velas encendidas. Los indios elevan sus oraciones y lamentos, piden a Dios que les ayude en sus cosechas y en sus problemas. Con un gesto solemne y conmovedor alzan su voz pidiendo justicia.

El espectáculo nos deja estupefactos.

Hace ya cinco años que visitamos, por primera vez, Chichicastenango. Entonces vivimos momentos verdaderamente intensos. Nos sentimos trasladados a otro mundo, a otra época; sin embargo, estábamos en nuestra propia tierra, en el siglo XX. Frente a nosotros teníamos una expresión de la religiosidad y fervor indígenas con un profundo sabor legendario, y también el espectáculo de una época que avanza rápidamente: por el cielo cruzaban aviones, y veloces automóviles llegaban con visitantes a contemplar las costumbres tradicionales de un pueblo en el corazón de Guatemala.

51. ¿Cómo eran los trajes de los indios?
    A. Eran coloridos y simbólicos.
    B. Parecían poco atractivos.
    C. Eran muy sencillos.
    D. Eran todos del mismo color.

52. ¿Qué problema causaron tantos chichicastecos en la plaza?
    A. Al público le fue casi imposible circular.
    B. No era posible rezar como de costumbre.
    C. No se pudo más que mirar las mercancías desde la escalera.
    D. La gente abandonó temprano la plaza y regresó a casa.

53. El "pom" que quemaban los indios es una clase de
    A. papel.
    B. madera.
    C. incienso.
    D. vela.

54. ¿Cuál fue el objeto de los rezos de los indios guatemaltecos?
    A. Pedían descanso tranquilo para los muertos.
    B. Pedían cosechas generosas en sus campos.
    C. Le daban las gracias a Dios por su bondad pasada.
    D. Expresaban su agradecimiento por las lluvias recientes.

55. El autor quedó impresionado sobre todo por
    A. los aviones que cruzaban por el cielo.
    B. los coches rápidos que llegaban.
    C. la mezcla de dos épocas distintas.
    D. la irreligiosidad de los indios.

Un catalán que visitaba Sevilla pidió un guía para que le enseñara los monumentos más importantes de la ciudad. El hotel donde se quedaba no tenía esta clase de empleado especializado, pero el dueño, un verdadero sevillano, era muy amable y simpático y se ofreció para enseñar al extranjero todo lo mejor de la ciudad.

Primero fueron a las murallas y puertas de la ciudad, que datan de la época romana.

—¿No son maravillosas? —preguntó el sevillano.

—Sí, son hermosas—dijo el otro—, pero en Cataluña las hay más grandes.

Desde allí fueron a ver la Torre del Oro y luego el Alcázar y sus maravillosos jardines. Pasaron después al barrio de Santa Cruz y de allí le llevó a la inmensa y magnífica catedral de Sevilla. El extranjero, aunque los admiró, dijo que en su provincia había monumentos más grandes.

Mostró el sevillano a su huésped la Giralda, orgullo de todo el que haya nacido en esta ciudad. Visitaron luego la iglesia de San Gil, donde se venera la famosa imagen de la Virgen de la Macarena. Vieron después el Palacio de las Dueñas, la Universidad, el Museo de Bellas Artes con todos sus tesoros, pero el catalán tenía la misma respuesta para todo.

Fuera de Sevilla le enseñó las ruinas de la primera ciudad que los romanos construyeron en España. Pero ni con esto logró impresionar al visitante.

Todo fue inútil; todo aquí era chiquitico. En Cataluña todo era más grande.

Más tarde, el catalán se dirigió al patio y al poco rato se le oyó gritar.

—¿Qué animal es éste? —exclamó el extranjero señalando al hotelero un tigre en una jaula.

—Este, amigo, es un gato de Sevilla.

56. El dueño del hotel acompañó al catalán porque
    A. era muy amigo del catalán.
    B. no tenía nada que hacer.
    C. aquel servicio no existía allí y él se ofreció.
    D. quería salir del hotel un rato a dar un paseo.

57. ¿Cuál fue la reacción del catalán al ver las murallas?
    A. Quedó sin poder hablar.
    B. Mencionó las de Cataluña.
    C. Preguntó acerca de la edad.
    D. Quería regresar al hotel.

58. ¿Qué comparación hacía el catalán entre Sevilla y Cataluña?
    A. Insistía en que todo era más grande en Cataluña.
    B. Decía que Cataluña tenía pocas cosas buenas.
    C. Le gustaba más la ciudad de Sevilla.
    D. Lo consideraba todo muy insignificante en ambos lugares.

59. ¿Por qué gritó el catalán después de irse al patio?
    A. Había oído unas voces extrañas.
    B. Lo atacó un gato.
    C. Vio un animal salvaje.
    D. Se dio cuenta de que alguien lo había robado.

60. ¿Qué insinuó el hotelero cuando salió al patio y le habló al catalán?
    A. que el patio era el mejor de Sevilla
    B. que se oía demasiado ruido y los vecinos se quejaban
    C. que los gatos de Sevilla eran los más grandes
    D. que Cataluña tenía los mejores hoteles

END OF TEST NO. 5

ANSWER SHEETS FOR TESTS 1 TO 5

ANSWER SHEET ■ TEST 1

Use a soft lead pencil to blacken the space under the letter which you choose as your answer. If you finish the test before the time limit has expired, go over the questions and your answers again and, if necessary, be sure that you erase completely before you blacken another space. The time limit is one hour.

	A	B	C	D			A	B	C	D			A	B	C	D
1	‖	‖	‖	‖		21	‖	‖	‖	‖		41	‖	‖	‖	‖
2	‖	‖	‖	‖		22	‖	‖	‖	‖		42	‖	‖	‖	‖
3	‖	‖	‖	‖		23	‖	‖	‖	‖		43	‖	‖	‖	‖
4	‖	‖	‖	‖		24	‖	‖	‖	‖		44	‖	‖	‖	‖
5	‖	‖	‖	‖		25	‖	‖	‖	‖		45	‖	‖	‖	‖
6	‖	‖	‖	‖		26	‖	‖	‖	‖		46	‖	‖	‖	‖
7	‖	‖	‖	‖		27	‖	‖	‖	‖		47	‖	‖	‖	‖
8	‖	‖	‖	‖		28	‖	‖	‖	‖		48	‖	‖	‖	‖
9	‖	‖	‖	‖		29	‖	‖	‖	‖		49	‖	‖	‖	‖
10	‖	‖	‖	‖		30	‖	‖	‖	‖		50	‖	‖	‖	‖
11	‖	‖	‖	‖		31	‖	‖	‖	‖		51	‖	‖	‖	‖
12	‖	‖	‖	‖		32	‖	‖	‖	‖		52	‖	‖	‖	‖
13	‖	‖	‖	‖		33	‖	‖	‖	‖		53	‖	‖	‖	‖
14	‖	‖	‖	‖		34	‖	‖	‖	‖		54	‖	‖	‖	‖
15	‖	‖	‖	‖		35	‖	‖	‖	‖		55	‖	‖	‖	‖
16	‖	‖	‖	‖		36	‖	‖	‖	‖		56	‖	‖	‖	‖
17	‖	‖	‖	‖		37	‖	‖	‖	‖		57	‖	‖	‖	‖
18	‖	‖	‖	‖		38	‖	‖	‖	‖		58	‖	‖	‖	‖
19	‖	‖	‖	‖		39	‖	‖	‖	‖		59	‖	‖	‖	‖
20	‖	‖	‖	‖		40	‖	‖	‖	‖		60	‖	‖	‖	‖

ANSWER SHEET ■ TEST 2

Use a soft lead pencil to blacken the space under the letter which you choose as your answer. If you finish the test before the time limit has expired, go over the questions and your answers again and, if necessary, be sure that you erase completely before you blacken another space. The time limit is one hour.

	A	B	C	D			A	B	C	D			A	B	C	D
1	‖	‖	‖	‖		21	‖	‖	‖	‖		41	‖	‖	‖	‖
2	‖	‖	‖	‖		22	‖	‖	‖	‖		42	‖	‖	‖	‖
3	‖	‖	‖	‖		23	‖	‖	‖	‖		43	‖	‖	‖	‖
4	‖	‖	‖	‖		24	‖	‖	‖	‖		44	‖	‖	‖	‖
5	‖	‖	‖	‖		25	‖	‖	‖	‖		45	‖	‖	‖	‖
6	‖	‖	‖	‖		26	‖	‖	‖	‖		46	‖	‖	‖	‖
7	‖	‖	‖	‖		27	‖	‖	‖	‖		47	‖	‖	‖	‖
8	‖	‖	‖	‖		28	‖	‖	‖	‖		48	‖	‖	‖	‖
9	‖	‖	‖	‖		29	‖	‖	‖	‖		49	‖	‖	‖	‖
10	‖	‖	‖	‖		30	‖	‖	‖	‖		50	‖	‖	‖	‖
11	‖	‖	‖	‖		31	‖	‖	‖	‖		51	‖	‖	‖	‖
12	‖	‖	‖	‖		32	‖	‖	‖	‖		52	‖	‖	‖	‖
13	‖	‖	‖	‖		33	‖	‖	‖	‖		53	‖	‖	‖	‖
14	‖	‖	‖	‖		34	‖	‖	‖	‖		54	‖	‖	‖	‖
15	‖	‖	‖	‖		35	‖	‖	‖	‖		55	‖	‖	‖	‖
16	‖	‖	‖	‖		36	‖	‖	‖	‖		56	‖	‖	‖	‖
17	‖	‖	‖	‖		37	‖	‖	‖	‖		57	‖	‖	‖	‖
18	‖	‖	‖	‖		38	‖	‖	‖	‖		58	‖	‖	‖	‖
19	‖	‖	‖	‖		39	‖	‖	‖	‖		59	‖	‖	‖	‖
20	‖	‖	‖	‖		40	‖	‖	‖	‖		60	‖	‖	‖	‖

ANSWER SHEET ■ TEST 3

Use a soft lead pencil to blacken the space under the letter which you choose as your answer. If you finish the test before the time limit has expired, go over the questions and your answers again and, if necessary, be sure that you erase completely before you blacken another space. The time limit is one hour.

	A B C D		A B C D		A B C D
1	‖ ‖ ‖ ‖	21	‖ ‖ ‖ ‖	41	‖ ‖ ‖ ‖
2	‖ ‖ ‖ ‖	22	‖ ‖ ‖ ‖	42	‖ ‖ ‖ ‖
3	‖ ‖ ‖ ‖	23	‖ ‖ ‖ ‖	43	‖ ‖ ‖ ‖
4	‖ ‖ ‖ ‖	24	‖ ‖ ‖ ‖	44	‖ ‖ ‖ ‖
5	‖ ‖ ‖ ‖	25	‖ ‖ ‖ ‖	45	‖ ‖ ‖ ‖
6	‖ ‖ ‖ ‖	26	‖ ‖ ‖ ‖	46	‖ ‖ ‖ ‖
7	‖ ‖ ‖ ‖	27	‖ ‖ ‖ ‖	47	‖ ‖ ‖ ‖
8	‖ ‖ ‖ ‖	28	‖ ‖ ‖ ‖	48	‖ ‖ ‖ ‖
9	‖ ‖ ‖ ‖	29	‖ ‖ ‖ ‖	49	‖ ‖ ‖ ‖
10	‖ ‖ ‖ ‖	30	‖ ‖ ‖ ‖	50	‖ ‖ ‖ ‖
11	‖ ‖ ‖ ‖	31	‖ ‖ ‖ ‖	51	‖ ‖ ‖ ‖
12	‖ ‖ ‖ ‖	32	‖ ‖ ‖ ‖	52	‖ ‖ ‖ ‖
13	‖ ‖ ‖ ‖	33	‖ ‖ ‖ ‖	53	‖ ‖ ‖ ‖
14	‖ ‖ ‖ ‖	34	‖ ‖ ‖ ‖	54	‖ ‖ ‖ ‖
15	‖ ‖ ‖ ‖	35	‖ ‖ ‖ ‖	55	‖ ‖ ‖ ‖
16	‖ ‖ ‖ ‖	36	‖ ‖ ‖ ‖	56	‖ ‖ ‖ ‖
17	‖ ‖ ‖ ‖	37	‖ ‖ ‖ ‖	57	‖ ‖ ‖ ‖
18	‖ ‖ ‖ ‖	38	‖ ‖ ‖ ‖	58	‖ ‖ ‖ ‖
19	‖ ‖ ‖ ‖	39	‖ ‖ ‖ ‖	59	‖ ‖ ‖ ‖
20	‖ ‖ ‖ ‖	40	‖ ‖ ‖ ‖	60	‖ ‖ ‖ ‖

ANSWER SHEET ■ TEST 4

Use a soft lead pencil to blacken the space under the letter which you choose as your answer. If you finish the test before the time limit has expired, go over the questions and your answers again and, if necessary, be sure that you erase completely before you blacken another space. The time limit is one hour.

	A B C D		A B C D		A B C D
1	‖ ‖ ‖ ‖	21	‖ ‖ ‖ ‖	41	‖ ‖ ‖ ‖
2	‖ ‖ ‖ ‖	22	‖ ‖ ‖ ‖	42	‖ ‖ ‖ ‖
3	‖ ‖ ‖ ‖	23	‖ ‖ ‖ ‖	43	‖ ‖ ‖ ‖
4	‖ ‖ ‖ ‖	24	‖ ‖ ‖ ‖	44	‖ ‖ ‖ ‖
5	‖ ‖ ‖ ‖	25	‖ ‖ ‖ ‖	45	‖ ‖ ‖ ‖
6	‖ ‖ ‖ ‖	26	‖ ‖ ‖ ‖	46	‖ ‖ ‖ ‖
7	‖ ‖ ‖ ‖	27	‖ ‖ ‖ ‖	47	‖ ‖ ‖ ‖
8	‖ ‖ ‖ ‖	28	‖ ‖ ‖ ‖	48	‖ ‖ ‖ ‖
9	‖ ‖ ‖ ‖	29	‖ ‖ ‖ ‖	49	‖ ‖ ‖ ‖
10	‖ ‖ ‖ ‖	30	‖ ‖ ‖ ‖	50	‖ ‖ ‖ ‖
11	‖ ‖ ‖ ‖	31	‖ ‖ ‖ ‖	51	‖ ‖ ‖ ‖
12	‖ ‖ ‖ ‖	32	‖ ‖ ‖ ‖	52	‖ ‖ ‖ ‖
13	‖ ‖ ‖ ‖	33	‖ ‖ ‖ ‖	53	‖ ‖ ‖ ‖
14	‖ ‖ ‖ ‖	34	‖ ‖ ‖ ‖	54	‖ ‖ ‖ ‖
15	‖ ‖ ‖ ‖	35	‖ ‖ ‖ ‖	55	‖ ‖ ‖ ‖
16	‖ ‖ ‖ ‖	36	‖ ‖ ‖ ‖	56	‖ ‖ ‖ ‖
17	‖ ‖ ‖ ‖	37	‖ ‖ ‖ ‖	57	‖ ‖ ‖ ‖
18	‖ ‖ ‖ ‖	38	‖ ‖ ‖ ‖	58	‖ ‖ ‖ ‖
19	‖ ‖ ‖ ‖	39	‖ ‖ ‖ ‖	59	‖ ‖ ‖ ‖
20	‖ ‖ ‖ ‖	40	‖ ‖ ‖ ‖	60	‖ ‖ ‖ ‖

ANSWER SHEET ▪ TEST 5

Use a soft lead pencil to blacken the space under the letter which you choose as your answer. If you finish the test before the time limit has expired, go over the questions and your answers again and, if necessary, be sure that you erase completely before you blacken another space. The time limit is one hour.

	A	B	C	D		A	B	C	D		A	B	C	D
1	‖	‖	‖	‖	21	‖	‖	‖	‖	41	‖	‖	‖	‖
2	‖	‖	‖	‖	22	‖	‖	‖	‖	42	‖	‖	‖	‖
3	‖	‖	‖	‖	23	‖	‖	‖	‖	43	‖	‖	‖	‖
4	‖	‖	‖	‖	24	‖	‖	‖	‖	44	‖	‖	‖	‖
5	‖	‖	‖	‖	25	‖	‖	‖	‖	45	‖	‖	‖	‖
6	‖	‖	‖	‖	26	‖	‖	‖	‖	46	‖	‖	‖	‖
7	‖	‖	‖	‖	27	‖	‖	‖	‖	47	‖	‖	‖	‖
8	‖	‖	‖	‖	28	‖	‖	‖	‖	48	‖	‖	‖	‖
9	‖	‖	‖	‖	29	‖	‖	‖	‖	49	‖	‖	‖	‖
10	‖	‖	‖	‖	30	‖	‖	‖	‖	50	‖	‖	‖	‖
11	‖	‖	‖	‖	31	‖	‖	‖	‖	51	‖	‖	‖	‖
12	‖	‖	‖	‖	32	‖	‖	‖	‖	52	‖	‖	‖	‖
13	‖	‖	‖	‖	33	‖	‖	‖	‖	53	‖	‖	‖	‖
14	‖	‖	‖	‖	34	‖	‖	‖	‖	54	‖	‖	‖	‖
15	‖	‖	‖	‖	35	‖	‖	‖	‖	55	‖	‖	‖	‖
16	‖	‖	‖	‖	36	‖	‖	‖	‖	56	‖	‖	‖	‖
17	‖	‖	‖	‖	37	‖	‖	‖	‖	57	‖	‖	‖	‖
18	‖	‖	‖	‖	38	‖	‖	‖	‖	58	‖	‖	‖	‖
19	‖	‖	‖	‖	39	‖	‖	‖	‖	59	‖	‖	‖	‖
20	‖	‖	‖	‖	40	‖	‖	‖	‖	60	‖	‖	‖	‖

ANSWER KEYS TO TESTS 1 TO 5

#	A	B	C	D
1		B		
2		B		
3	A			
4		B		
5			C	
6				D
7	A			
8		B		
9		B		
10			C	
11	A			
12			C	
13		B		
14	A			
15	A			
16	A			
17			C	
18			C	
19	A			
20		B		

#	A	B	C	D
21	A			
22				D
23	A			
24			C	
25	A			
26	A			
27				D
28		B		
29	A			
30			C	
31	A			
32	A			
33				D
34	A			
35			C	
36	A			
37		B		
38				D
39		B		
40		B		

#	A	B	C	D
41			C	
42		B		
43				D
44			C	
45				D
46	A			
47				D
48			C	
49	A			
50		B		
51	A			
52			C	
53				D
54	A			
55	A			
56	A			
57				D
58			C	
59	A			
60	A			

#	A	B	C	D		#	A	B	C	D		#	A	B	C	D
1	●					21		●				41			●	
2	●					22			●			42			●	
3	●					23		●				43				●
4	●					24	●					44	●			
5	●					25			●			45	●			
6		●				26	●					46		●		
7				●		27				●		47	●			
8				●		28			●			48			●	
9			●			29	●					49				●
10		●				30			●			50		●		
11	●					31				●		51			●	
12	●					32		●				52	●			
13			●			33			●			53				●
14				●		34	●					54	●			
15		●				35				●		55				●
16	●					36			●			56			●	
17		●				37			●			57	●			
18				●		38		●				58			●	
19			●			39			●			59				●
20	●					40	●					60				●

#	A	B	C	D		#	A	B	C	D		#	A	B	C	D
1		■				21		■				41	■			
2				■		22	■					42		■		
3			■			23			■			43				■
4		■				24				■		44			■	
5			■			25	■					45	■			
6				■		26	■					46				■
7			■			27				■		47	■			
8			■			28	■					48	■			
9	■					29	■					49	■			
10			■			30			■			50	■			
11	■					31		■				51	■			
12	■					32	■					52				■
13				■		33				■		53			■	
14		■				34		■				54	■			
15		■				35	■					55			■	
16	■					36				■		56	■			
17						37		■				57				
18				■		38	■					58				
19	■					39				■		59				■
20			■			40			■			60			■	

240

	A	B	C	D		A	B	C	D		A	B	C	D
1			C		21	A				41	A			
2		B			22	A				42			C	
3	A				23		B			43			C	
4				D	24	A				44				D
5	A				25		B			45		B		
6	A				26				D	46			C	
7		B			27	A				47	A			
8	A				28		B			48		B		
9				D	29			C		49	A			
10	A				30	A				50			C	
11	A				31	A				51	A			
12				D	32				D	52			C	
13	A				33	A				53			C	
14		B			34		B			54			C	
15			C		35	A				55	A			
16	A				36			C		56			C	
17				D	37	A				57	A			
18	A				38	A				58	A			
19	A				39	A				59	A			
20	A				40		B			60				D

#	Ans	#	Ans	#	Ans
1	A	21	C	41	A
2	B	22	D	42	B
3	B	23	A	43	C
4	A	24	C	44	D
5	B	25	B	45	A
6	C	26	A	46	A
7	B	27	A	47	C
8	B	28	B	48	D
9	D	29	C	49	D
10	D	30	A	50	C
11	A	31	B	51	A
12	B	32	D	52	A
13	B	33	B	53	C
14	B	34	C	54	C
15	A	35	C	55	B
16	B	36	A	56	C
17	A	37	A	57	A
18	A	38	A	58	A
19	B	39	C	59	C
20	B	40	D	60	C

ANSWERS EXPLAINED TO TESTS 1 TO 5

ANSWERS EXPLAINED ■ TEST 1

Students, please note: Throughout the *Answers Explained* section, question numbers that are omitted are those that do not require grammatical explanations because they test a knowledge of Spanish vocabulary, idioms, and skill in general reading comprehension. If you had an incorrect answer because you did not recognize the meaning of a Spanish word or idiom, look it up in the Spanish-English vocabulary at the end of this book, in the Index, or in §53.ff. If it is not there, consult a standard Spanish-English dictionary.

1. See §20.3 and §53.27 (where **tener que + inf.** is listed).

2. See §67.19, §68.25ff and §68.31ff. **Tener que** does not take the prep. **a.**

3. See §25., §67.19, §68.14ff, §68.20ff, §68.25ff, and §68.31ff.

4. See §67.20 and §67.29. You must account for the prep. **a** which follows the verb.

5. See §67.21. You must account for the prep. **a** which follows the verb. Here, **vivimos** requires **en,** not **a.**

6. See §1.2.

7. See §67.19.

8. See §67.2 and §68.55.

9 & 10. See §1.2.

11 & 12. See §1.39.

13. See §67.87 (where **esperar** is listed) and §68.41.

14 & 15. See §67.22.

16. See §67.23.

17 & 18. See §67.24.

19 & 20. See §67.25 and §67.26.

27 to 40. See §3.

ANSWERS EXPLAINED ■ TEST 2

1 to 3. See §67.25 where the following are listed alphabetically: **despedirse de, oír hablar de, pensar de,** and the examples.

4 & 5. See §67.26 where **tardar en** and **empeñarse en** are listed, and the examples.

6. See §67.27 where **pensar en** is listed and the examples.

7 & 8. See §67.30.

9. See §67.33—§67.35.

10 & 11. See §67.37 and the examples, §68.25—§68.30, where **pedir** is listed.

12. See §67.33—§67.42.

13. See §67.43, §68.25, and §68.30 where **venir** is listed.

14. See §67.33, §67.47, and §67.48.

15. See §67.33 and §67.49.

16. See §67.33, §67.50, §67.51, and §68.41ff.

17. See §67.33, §67.50, §67.52, and §68.41ff.

18. See §67.33, §67.50, §67.53, and §68.41ff.

19. See §67.33, §67.54, §67.56, and §68.41ff.

20. See §67.57 and §68.14ff.

21. See §67.58 and §68.41ff.

22. See §67.60 and §68.50ff.

23. See §67.61, §68.41ff, and §68.45.

24. See §67.62.

25. See §1.—§1.2.

26. See §67.16—§67.19.

27. See §60.—§60.3.

28. See §1.—§1.2.

29. See §4.—§4.3.

30. See §66.88—§66.92ff; **el cual** refers to *un punto* (de observación).

ANSWERS EXPLAINED ■ TEST 3

1. See §67.33, §67.63, §67.34, §68.41ff.

2. See §67.33, §67.66, §68.41ff.

3. See §67.33, §67.67—§67.70, §68.41ff.

4. See §9.

5. See §11.

6. See §15.—§15.5.

7. See §18.

8 & 9. See §19.

10. See §20.—§20.3.

11. See §21.—§22.1.

12. See §24., §25.

13. See §25.

14 & 15. See §25.(g).

16. See §26.—§26.4.

17. See §27.—§27.2.

18 & 19. See §28.

20. See §29.

21. See §1.60ff.

22. See §48.

23. See §53.27, §68.14, §68.19 **(tener).**

24. See §29.

25. See §68.14 and §68.19 **(saber).**

26. See §68.25—§68.27ff.
27. See §1.57—§1.58.
28. See §25., §68.36.
29. See §1.23.
30. See §67.29 (**preferir** + inf.).
31. See §53.22, §60.

ANSWERS EXPLAINED ■ TEST 4

1. See §53.1.
2. See §67.111 (3).
3. See §53.13.
4. See §68.20 (b).
5. See §67.33, §67.87, §68.50—§68.54.
6. See §67.54—§67.57ff, §68.41—§68.44.
7. See §44.—§44.6, §51.
8. See §46.—§46.2.
9. See §19., §47.2, §67.29 (**saber**).
10. See §66.7—§66.20, §66.43—§66.45.
11. See §67.33—§67.36, §68.41—§68.49, in particular §68.41 (i).
12. See §67.33—§67.36, §68.50—§68.54, in particular §68.50 (2).
13. See §68.57.
14. See §68.58.
15, 16, 17. See §66.19.
18. See §67.2, §68.25ff, §68.30 (**ver**).
19, 20. See §66.20.
26 to 40. See §14.

ANSWERS EXPLAINED ■ TEST 5

1. See §30.
2. See §31.
3. See §32. (b).
4. See §33. (b).
5. See §35. (b).

6. See §36.—§36.3.

7, 8. See §37.—§37.2.

9. See §37.2.

10, 11. See §38.—§38.2.

12. See §39.—§39.2.

13. See §39.2.

14, 15. See §40.—§40.2.

16, 17. See §41.—§41.2.

18 to 20. See §42.—§42.2.

21. See §1.—§1.15.

22. See §6.4. Your choice here depends on the content of the rest of the sentence. Read the entire paragraph first to see what it's all about.

23. See §53.15, §53.22.

24. See §64.—§64.3.

25. See §37.—§37.2.

26. See §53.4.

27. See §68.14, §68.19 **(llover).** You have to understand the sense of the entire paragraph to know that the present indicative is needed here. Consult my *301 (or 501) Spanish verbs fully conjugated in all the tenses in a new easy to learn format* for review of verb forms, in addition to consulting §68.12—§68.66 in this book.

28. See §68.65 and consult the Spanish-English vocabulary in the back pages.

29. See §1.—§1.15.

30. Consult the Spanish-English vocabulary in the back pages.

31. See §6.3. Your choice here depends on the content of the rest of the sentence. Did you read the entire paragraph first before selecting answers?

32. See §53.13.

33. See §1.54ff.

34. See §4.7, §4.8.

35. See §4.7, §4.8, §53.7.

36. See §1.65, §51., §59.4.

37. See §1.54ff.

38. See §52.—§52.19.

39. See §36.—§36.3, §64.ff.

40. See §1.42—§1.46.

END TO ANSWERS EXPLAINED

SPANISH-ENGLISH VOCABULARY

If you look up a Spanish word and it is not listed in the pages that follow, consult the Vocabularies beginning with §1. In particular, consult the Comprehensive Index under the entry **Vocabulary** where you will find § references to such topics as the following: adjectives, adverbs, antonyms, cognates, conjunctions, indefinite and negative words, nouns, prepositions and prepositional phrases, common irregular present participles, pronouns, proverbs, synonyms, tricky words, and verbs with prepositions. For the most part, I have tried not to repeat in the following Vocabulary Spanish words and meanings in English already given in those § numbers.

To find certain categories and types of words, especially needed for a mastery of grammatical control and idioms, including verbal, idiomatic, common and useful expressions, you must consult the Comprehensive Index. For other Spanish words of interest to you, which are not given in this book, consult your Spanish-English dictionary.

The Spanish alphabet contains the letters **ch, ll, ñ,** and **rr** which are considered separately. A Spanish word that contains **ch** is alphabetized *after* the letter **c; ll** is alphabetized after the letter **l;** and **ñ** is alphabetized after the letter **n.** Therefore, in the following alphabetical listing of words, you will find **falla** listed after **falta, mañana** after **manzana, ochenta** after **ocupar.** This rule does not apply to the double consonant **rr.**

A

a *prep.* at, to; *see also* **a** in idioms **§53.1**
abajo *adv.* below, downstairs, down below
abandonar *v.* to abandon, leave
abandono *n.m.* abandonment
abarcar *v.* to encompass, embrace, take in
abatido *adj.* dejected, unhappy
abatir *v.* to knock down, throw down
abeja *n.f.* bee
abierto *past part.* of **abrir**
abismo *n.m.* abyss
abogado *n.m.* lawyer
abolir *v.* to abolish, repeal
aborigen *adj.* aboriginal
aborrecer *v.* to abhor, hate
abracé *v.* form of **abrazar**
abrasar *v.* to burn, fire
abrazar *v.* to embrace, clamp, hug; **abrazarse** *v.* to hug (embrace) each other
abrazo *n.m.* embrace, hug
abrigar *v.* to cherish, harbor, hold
abrigo *n.m.* coat, overcoat
abril *n.m.* April
abrir *v.* to open
absolutamente *adv.* absolutely
absoluto *adj.* absolute

absolver *v.* to absolve, acquit
absorber *v.* to absorb
absorto *adj.* absorbed
abstenerse *v.* to abstain
abuelo *n.m.* grandfather; **abuela** *n.f.* grandmother; **los abuelos**/grandparents
abundancia *n.f.* abundance
abundar *v.* to abound, be abundant
aburrir *v.* to annoy, bore, vex; **aburrirse** *v.* to become bored, grow tired, grow weary
abuso *n.m.* abuse
acá *adv.* here; **por acá**/this way, through here, around here
acabar *v.* to achieve, complete, end, finish; **acabar de**/to have just; **acabar con**/to end up by (with); **acabarse** *v.* to be used up; *see also* **§15.ff** & **§53.7, por** in idioms **§53.22,** and **§67.28**
academia *n.f.* academy; **académico** *n.m.* academician, professor, teacher
acariciar *v.* to caress
acaso *adv.* maybe, perhaps
acceso *n.m.* access
accidente *n.m.* accident
acción *n.f.* action
aceite *n.m.* oil
acelerar *v.* to accelerate

acento *n.m.* accent
aceptar *v.* to accept
acera *n.f.* sidewalk
acerca de/about, concerning
acercar *v.* to bring near, place near; **acercarse** *v.* to approach, come (draw) near
acero *n.m.* steel
acertar *v.* to hit the mark, hit upon, do (something) right, succeed (in)
aclamar *v.* to acclaim, applaud, shout
aclarar *v.* to explain, clarify, make clear, rinse
acompañar *v.* to accompany, escort, go with
acondicionado *adj.* conditioned; **aire acondicionado**/air conditioned
acondicionamiento *n.m.* conditioning; **acondicionamiento de aire**/air conditioning
aconsejable *adj.* advisable; **aconsejar** *v.* to advise, counsel
acontecer *v.* to happen
acordar *v.* to accord, agree; **acordarse**/to remember
acostar *v.* to put to bed; **acostarse** *v.* to go to bed, lie down
acostumbrados *adj.* accustomed; **acostumbrar** *v.* to accustom, be accustomed, be in the habit of;

Consult the Comprehensive Index for additional § references.

acostumbrarse *v.* to be accustomed

acróbata *n.m.f.* acrobat; *n.f.* acrobatics

actitud *n.f.* attitude, position

actividad *n.f.* activity

activo, activa *adj.* active

acto *n.m.* act

actor, actriz *n.m.f.* actor, actress

actual *adj.* actual, present, present-day

actualidad *n.f.* actuality, present time

actualmente *adv.* at present

actuar *v.* to act

acuchillar *v.* to knife, cut, slash, cut open

acudir *v.* to attend, be present at, respond (to a call), come to the rescue

acueducto *n.m.* aqueduct

acuerdo *v. form of* **acordar;** *n.m.* agreement; **de acuerdo con**/in accord with, according to; *see also* §53.11

acumulación *n.f.* accumulation

acusar *v.* to accuse

acústica *n.f.* acoustics; **acústico** *adj.* acoustic

adaptarse *v.* to adapt oneself (itself)

adecuada *adj.* adequate

adelantar(se) *v.* to advance, keep on, progress, go ahead, go forward

adelante *adv.* forward, ahead; **de hoy en adelante**/from now on

ademán *n.m.* attitude, gesture; **ademanes** *n.m.pl.* manners

además *adv.* furthermore; **además de**/in addition to

adentro *adv.* inside, within

adicional *adj.* additional

adiós *interj.* good-bye

adivinando *pres. part. of* **adivinar** *v.* to guess, divine, foretell

administración *n.f.* administration; **administrador, administradora** *n.m.f.* administrator

admiración *n.f.* admiration; **admirador, admiradora** *n.m.f.* admirer; **admirar** *v.* to admire

admitir *v.* to admit, allow, permit

adonde *adv.* to where; **adondequiera**/to wherever; *see* §67.50ff

adoptar *v.* to adopt

adorar *v.* to adore, worship

adornar *v.* to adorn; **adorno** *n.m.* adornment

adquiere *v. form of* **adquirir** *v.* to acquire, get, obtain

aduana *n.f.* customs, customs office; **aduanero** *n.m.* customs officer

adular *v.* to flatter

adulta *adj.* adult

adversario *n.m.* adversary, foe, opponent

advertir *v.* to advise, give notice (warning), take notice of, warn, notify

aeroplano *n.m.* airplane, plane

aeropuerto *n.m.* airport

afable *adj.* affable, friendly

afán *n.m.* anxiety, eagerness

afecto *n.m.* affection; **afectuosamente** *adv.* affectionately

afeitarse *v.* to shave oneself; **¡aféitatela!**/shave it off!

afición *n.f.* fondness; **aficionado, aficionada** *n.m.f.* amateur, fan (fond of)

afirmación *n.f.* affirmation; **afirmar** *v.* to affirm, assert

afligir *v.* to afflict, affect, grieve

afortunado *adj.* fortunate

africano, africana *n.m.f., adj.* African

afuera *adv.* outside

agarrar *v.* to grasp, get hold of, obtain, come upon, seize, clutch

agencia *n.f.* agency; **agencia de viajes**/tourist agency

agente *n.m.* agent; **agente de policía**/police officer

agitado *adj.* busy; **agitar** *v.* to agitate, wave, shake up, stir; **agitarse** *v.* to become excited

agosto *n.m.* August

agotado *adj.* exhausted, used up; **agotar** *v.* to exhaust, use up

agradable *adj.* pleasant, agreeable; **agradar** *v.* to please, be pleasing

agradecer *v.* to be thankful, grateful, to show gratitude, to thank; **agradecido** *adj.* grateful, thankful; **agradecimiento** *n.m.* thankfulness

agrado *n.m.* appreciation

agrandar *v.* to enlarge, grow larger, increase

agravar *v.* to aggravate, make worse

agregar *v.* to add, collect, gather

agrícola *adj.* agricultural; **agricultura** *n.f.* agriculture

agrupar *v.* to group

agua *n.f.* water **(el agua)**

aguantar *v.* to tolerate, endure, bear

aguardar *v.* to wait, await, wait for, expect

agudo *adj.* acute, sharp

agüero *n.m.* omen, augury

águila *n.f.* eagle (el aguila)

aguja *n.f.* needle

agujero *n.m.* hole

ahí *adv.* here, there; *see also* §16.

ahogado *adj.* drowned; **ahogar** *v.* to choke; **ahogarse** *v.* to drown

ahora *adv.* now; **ahora mismo**/right now, right away

ahorrar *v.* to save, economize

aire *n.m.* air; **al aire libre**/in the open air, outdoors; **el acondicionamiento de aire**/air conditioning

aislado *adj.* isolated; **aislamiento** *n.m.* isolation; **aislarse** *v.* to isolate oneself

ajedrez *n.m.* chess

ajeno *adj.* foreign, alien, other, different, belonging to another

ajustar *v.* to adjust

al *contraction of* **a** + **el;** *see also* §53.3

al + *inf.*/on, upon + *pres. part.;* **al llegar**/on (upon) arriving; **al partir**/on (upon) leaving; *see also* §53.3, §56.12, §58.13

ala *n.f.* wing, brim of a hat

alabar *v.* to praise

álamo *n.m.* poplar tree

alargar *v.* to lengthen, make longer; **¡alárguemela!**/lengthen it!

alarma *n.f.* alarm

alba *n.f.* dawn **(el alba)**

alcalde *n.m.* mayor

alcanzar *v.* to arrive, reach, attain, overtake

alcoba *n.f.* bedroom

aldea *n.f.* village

alegrarse *v.* to be glad, rejoice; **alegre** *adj.* happy; **alegremente** *adv.* happily; **alegría** *n.f.* joy, happiness

alejar *v.* to move away, to be distant, separate, draw away; **alejarse** *v.* to go away

alemán *n.m., adj.* German; **alemanes, alemanas** *adj.* German; **Alemania** *n.f.* Germany

alentar *v.* to encourage

alerto, alerta *adj.* alert

alfabetizar *v.* to teach reading and writing, to alphabetize; **alfabeto** *n.m.* alphabet

alfiler *n.m.* brooch, pin

alfombra *n.f.* carpet, rug

algo *indef. pron.* something

algodón *n.m.* cotton

alguien *indef. pron.* somebody, someone; *see also* §55., §62.2ff

algún, alguno, alguna *adj., pron.* some, any, something; *see also* §1.20, §55; **alguna vez**/some time

alhaja *n.f.* jewel, gem

alianza *n.f.* alliance

aliento *n.m.* breath, encouragement

alimento *n.m.* food

aliviar *v.* to lighten, relieve

alma *n.f.* soul, spirit **(el alma)**

almacén *n.m.* department store, general store

almohada *n.f.* pillow

almorzar *v.* to lunch, have lunch; **almuerzo** *n.m.* lunch; *also v. form of* **almorzar**

alojamiento *n.m.* lodging; **alojarse** *v.* to find lodging

alquilar *v.* to rent

alrededor *adv.* around

altar *n.m.* altar (church)

alteración *n.f.* alteration; **alteraciones**/alterations, changes; **alterar** *v.* to alter, change; **alterado**/changed, disturbed, upset

alternativamente *adv.* alternately

altísimo *adj.* very tall, very high

altitud *n.f.* altitude

altivo *adj.* proud, haughty

alto, alta *adj.* high, tall; *n.m.* height; **lo alto**/the top; **los altos**/top floor; **las altas, los altos**/tall women, tall men, tall people; **más alto**/higher, highest

altura *n.f.* height

alumbrado, alumbrada *adj.* lighted; **alumbrar** *v.* shine, illuminate, light, enlighten; **alumbrarse** *v.* to be (get) high, get tipsy, become lively

alumna, alumno *n.f.m.* pupil, student

alzar *v.* to heave, lift, pick up, raise

allá *adv.* over there; **por allá**/that way; *see also* §16.

allí *adv.* there; **he allí**/here you have; *see also* §16.

amable *adj.* pleasant, nice; **amablemente** *adv.* in a friendly way

amado *adj.* loved, beloved

amanecer *v.* to dawn; *n.m.* dawn

amante *n.m.* lover; *n.f.* mistress

amar *v.* to love

amargamente *adv.* bitterly; **amargo** *adj.* bitter; **amargura** *n.f.* bitterness

amarillo *n.m., adj.* yellow

ámbar *n.m.* amber

ambas, ambos *adj.* both

ambición *n.f.* ambition

ambiente *n.m.* surroundings, atmosphere

ambulante *adj.* ambulatory; **vendedor ambulante**/traveling salesman

amenazar *v.* to menace, threaten

ameno *adj.* pleasant, pleasing

América latina *n.f.* Latin America

americano *n.m., adj.* American

ametralladora *n.f.* machine gun

amiga, amigo *n.f.m.* friend; *see also* **§1.60ff**

amigote *n.m.* chum, pal; **amiguitos** *n.m.pl.* little friends

amistad *n.f.* friendship, friend, amnesty; **amistoso** *adj.* friendly

amo, ama *n.m.f.* owner, master, head of household

amor *n.m.* love; **amoroso** *adj.* affectionate, loving

amotinarse *v.* to mutiny, riot, rebel

amplia, amplio, amplios *adj.* ample, full

amueblar *v.* to furnish

analfabeto *n.m., adj.* illiterate

análisis *n.m.* analysis

anciana, anciano *n.m.f.* old woman, old man; *adj.* old

ancho *n.m.* width; **ancho, ancha,** *adj.* wide

andaluz *adj.* of or pertaining to Andalucía

andar *v.* to walk, to run (machine); **se anda**/one walks, a person walks; *see also* §58.10

anduve *v. form of* **andar**

anfiteatro *n.m.* amphitheater

ángel *n.m.* angel; **angélico** *adj.* angelic

angosto *adj.* narrow

ángulo *n.m.* angle, corner

angustia *n.f.* anguish; **angustiado** *adj.* distressed, in anguish; **angustiar** *v.* to distress, anguish

anhelo *n.m.* eagerness, desire, yearning, longing

anillo *n.m.* ring (finger)

animado *adj.* animated, alive, lively

animalito *n.m.* little animal

animar *v.* to animate, enliven, cheer up

aniversario *n.m.* anniversary

anoche *adv.* last night, yesterday evening

anochecer *n.m.* nightfall

ansiedad *n.f.* anxiety; **ansioso** *adj.* anxious, eager, anxiously

ante *prep.* before, in front, in the presence of

anteayer *adv.* day before yesterday

antecesor *n.m.* ancestor, predecessor

antemano *adv.* **de antemano**/beforehand, previously

anteojo *n.m.* spyglass, telescope; **anteojos**/eye glasses, binoculars

anterior *adj.* previous

antes *adv.* formerly, first, before; **antes (de)**/before, in front of; **antes (de) que** *conj.* before; **cuanto antes**/as soon as possible; *see also* **§1.64, §7.3, §53.7**

anticipar *v.* to anticipate

anticuada *adj.* antiquated, old

antigüedad *n.f.* antiquity

antiguo, antigua *adj.* former, ancient, old

antipatía *n.m.* dislike, antipathy; **antipático** *adj.* unfriendly

anual *adj.* annual; **anualmente** *adv.* annually

anular *v.* to annul, make void

anunciar *v.* to announce, foretell, proclaim; **anuncio** *n.m.* announcement

anzuelo *n.m.* fishhook

añadir *v.* to add

año *n.m.* year

apagar *v.* to extinguish, put out a light (flame)

aparato *n.m.* apparatus, appliance

aparecer *v.* to appear, show up

apariencia *n.f.* appearance

apartamento (apartamiento) *n.m.* apartment

apartar *v.* to separate; **apartarse de** *v.* to withdraw from, separate from

aparte *adj.* aside, apart

apasionado *adj.* impassioned person

apellido *n.m.* family name

apenas *adv.* hardly, scarcely; **apenas si**/hardly; **apenas . . . cuando**/hardly, scarcely . . . when

apetito *n.m.* appetite

apetitoso *adj.* appetizing, tasty

apiadarse de *v.* to have pity on

aplaudir *v.* to applaud

aplazar *v.* to postpone

aplicaciones *n.f.pl.* applications

aplicado *adj.* hard-working, diligent; **aplicar** *v.* to apply

apoderarse de *v.* to take power, take possession

aportar *v.* to contribute

apóstol *n.m.* apostle

apoyados *adj.* leaning

apoyar(se) *v.* to aid, support, lean on; **apoyo** *n.m.* support

apreciar *v.* to appreciate; **aprecio** *n.m.* esteem

aprender *v.* to learn; **lo aprendido**/what was learned; **se aprende**/is learned

apresurarse *v.* to rush, hurry, hasten

apretar(se) *v.* to clench, squeeze, tighten

aprovechar(se) *v.* to make use of; take advantage of, avail oneself

aproximadamente *adv.* approximately; **aproximarse** *v.* to approach, draw near

apuesta *n.f.* bet, wager

apuntar *v.* to begin to show, appear

apurarse *v.* to fret, grieve, worry; **apuro** *n.m.* distress, predicament, worry, concern

aquel *adj.* that; *see also* §1.54, §66.56ff

aquí *adv.* here; **por aquí**/this way, around here; **he aquí**/here you have; *see also* §17.

árbol *n.m.* tree

arbusto *n.m.* shrub

arder *v.* to blaze, burn

ardía *v. form of* **arder**

ardiente *adj.* ardent

ardoroso *adj.* fiery

arena *n.f.* sand, arena

argentino *adj.* of or pertaining to Argentina

argumento *n.m.* argument, premise

arma *n.f.* arm, weapon

armada *n.f.* fleet

armado *adj.* armed

armar *v.* to arm

armario *n.m.* closet

armonía *n.f.* harmony

arqueólogo *n.m.* archaeologist

arquitecto *n.m.* architect

arquitectónico *adj.* architectural

arquitectura *n.f.* architecture

arrancar *v.* to pull out, tear off

arrasar *v.* to level, raze

arrastrar *v.* to drag

arrebatar *v.* to snatch, captivate

arreglar *v.* to repair, arrange, adjust, regulate, settle, put in order, put back in working condition

arreglarse *v.* to come to an agreement, compromise, conform, settle

arreglo *n.m.* arrangement; **con arreglo a**/according to

arrepentirse de *v.* to repent

arriba *adv.* upstairs, up, high, above

arrodillados *adj.* kneeling; **arrodillarse** *v.* to kneel

arrojar *v.* to fling, hurl, throw; **arrojarse** *v.* to throw oneself, rush

arroyo *n.m.* gutter

arroz *n.m.* rice; **arroz con pollo**/chicken with rice

arruga *n.f.* wrinkle (on skin)

arruinado *adj.* in ruins

arte *n.m. or f.* art; **las bellas artes**/fine arts

artefacto *n.m.* artifact, device

articular *v.* to articulate

artículo *n.m.* article

artista *n.m.f.* artist

artístico *adj.* artistic

asaltar *v.* to assail, assault

ascender *v.* to ascend, lift, raise, go up, promote

ascenso *n.m.* ascent, rise, promotion

ascensor *n.m.* elevator

asciende *v. form of* **ascender**

asegurar *v.* to assure, affirm, assert, insure

asentir *v.* to assent, agree

así *adv.* thus, so, like this, like that; **así que**/as soon as, so that; **así como**/as well as, just as; **así . . . como**/both . . . and; not only . . . but also

asiento *n.m.* seat

asignatura *n.f.* subject, course (of study)

asir *v.* to grasp, seize

asistencia *n.f.* assistance

asistir *v.* to attend

asno *n.m.* ass, donkey

asomarse a *v.* to look out of

asombrar *v.* to amaze, astonish, frighten; **asombrarse** *v.* to be amazed

asombro *n.m.* amazement

aspecto *n.m.* aspect, appearance

aspiración *n.f.* aspiration

aspirar *v.* to aspire

aspirina *n.f.* aspirin

astro *n.m.* star

astronauta *n.m.f.* astronaut

astronomía *n.f.* astronomy

astrónomo *n.m.* astronomer

asturiano, asturianas *n., adj.* of or pertaining to Asturias

asumir *v.* to assume, take upon oneself

asunto *n.m.* affair, matter, subject

asustado *adj.* frightened, afraid

asustar *v.* to frighten, scare

asustarse *v.* to be (become) frightened, scared

atacar *v.* to attack

atadas *adj.* tied

ataque *n.m.* attack

atar *v.* to bind, tie

atención *n.f.* attention; **prestar atención**/to pay attention

atender *v.* to pay attention, to attend to

atendiendo *pres. part. of* **atender**

atenerse *v.* to rely on, depend on

atentamente *adv.* courteously

atento *adj.* attentive, helpful

aterrizar *v.* to land (airplane)

aterrorizada *adj.* full of terror, frightened

Atlántico *adj.* Atlantic

atleta *n.m.f.* athlete

atmósfera *n.f.* atmosphere

ató *v. form of* **atar**

atormentado *adj.* tormented

atormentarse *v.* to torment (distress) oneself

atracción *n.f.* attraction

atractivo *adj.* attractive

atraer *v.* to attract, allure, charm

atraído *past part. of* **atraer**

atrás *adv.* back, behind, to the rear

atrasarse *v.* to lag behind, be slow, late

atravesar *v.* to cross, go (run) through

atreverse *v.* to dare, venture

atrevido *adj.* bold, daring

atropellar *v.* to run over, trample

atropello *n.m.* car accident

auditorio *n.m.* audience

aula *n.f.* classroom (**el aula**)

aúlla *v. form of* **aullar** *v.* to howl

aumentar *v.* to increase, augment

aun, aún *adv.* also, as well, even

aunque *conj.* although

aureola *n.f.* halo

ausencia *n.f.* absence

ausente *adj.* absent

auténtica *adj.* authentic

autobús *n.m.* bus

automóvil *n.m.* automobile, car

automovilístico *adj.* automobile

autor, autora *n.m.f.* author

autoridad *n.f.* authority

autorizar *v.* to authorize

auxiliar *v.* to aid, assist, help

auxilio *n.m.* help

avalancha *n.f.* avalanche

avanzados *adj.* advanced

avanzar *v.* to advance

avaro *n.m., adj.* stingy, avaricious

ave *n.f.* bird

avenida *n.f.* avenue

aventura *n.f.* adventure

aventurarse *v.* to take a chance, take a risk

avergonzado *adj.* ashamed

avergonzarse *v.* to be (feel) ashamed

averiguar *v.* to find out, inquire, investigate

avión *n.m.* airplane, plane

avisar *v.* to warn

aviso *n.m.* notice, warning, word

avivar *v.* to inflame, enliven

ayer *adv.* yesterday

ayuda *n.f.* help, assistance, aid

ayudante *n.m.f.* aid, assistant, helper

ayudar *v.* to help, aid, assist; **¡ayúdeme!**/help me!

ayuntamiento *n.m.* municipal government

azteca *n., adj.* Aztec

azúcar *n.m.* sugar; **la caña de azúcar**/sugar cane

azul *n.m., adj.* blue

azur *n.m., adj.* azure

B

bachillerato *n.m.* baccalaureate

bahía *n.f.* bay, harbor

bailar *v.* to dance; **bailarín** *n.m.* dancer

bailarina *n.f.* dancer

baile *n.m.* dance

bajar *v.* to go (come) down, descend, lower, get off a moving vehicle

bajo *adj., adv., prep.* under, below, beneath, short

bala *n.f.* bullet, ball, shot

balazo *n.m.* bullet wound

balbucear *v.* to stammer, hesitate (in speech)

balsa *n.f.* raft, barge

banco *n.m.* bank, bench

banda *n.f.* band, scarf, ribbon, sash

bandeja *n.f.* tray

bandera *n.f.* banner, flag, standard

banderilla *n.f.* banderilla (ornamental dart that a banderillo uses to stick in the neck or shoulder of a bull)

bandido *n.m.* bandit

banquero *n.m.* banker

banquete *n.m.* banquet, dinner

bañar *v.* to bathe

bañarse *v.* to bathe oneself, take a bath, bathe

baño *n.m.* bath; **el cuarto de baño**/bathroom

barato *adj.* cheap

barba *n.f.* beard

bárbaro *n.m., adj.* barbarian, rude, barbarous

barbero *n.m.* barber

barco *n.m.* boat

barrile *n.m.* barrel

barrio *n.m.* section, quarter

base *n.f.* basis

bastante *adj., adv.* enough, sufficient

bastar *v.* to suffice, be enough, sufficient; *see also* §66.20

basura *n.f.* trash, garbage, refuse, sweepings

batalla *n.f.* battle

batallar *v.* to battle, fight, struggle

batallón *n.m.* battalion

batir *v.* to beat, strike

batirse *v.* to fight

baúl *n.m.* trunk (baggage)

bautizar *v.* to baptize, christen

beber *v.* to drink; **se bebe**/one drinks; **bebida** *n.f.* drink; *see also* §53.6

béisbol *n.m.* baseball

bella, bello *adj.* beautiful; **bellas artes**/fine arts

belleza *n.f.* beauty

bendecir *v.* to bless, consecrate

bendición *n.f.* blessing

bendigo *v. form of* **bendecir**

beneficiar *v.* to benefit

benévolo *adj.* benevolent

benignidad *n.f.* mildness, kindness

besar *v.* to kiss; **beso** *n.m.* kiss

bestia *n.f.* beast, animal

biblioteca *n.f.* library

bibliotecario, bibliotecaria *n.m.f.* librarian

bicicleta *n.f.* bicycle

biciclista *n.m.f.* bicycle rider, cyclist

bien *adv.* well; *n.m.* good, benefit, welfare; *see also* §2.7

bienestar *n.m.* well-being

bienvenida *n.f., adj.* welcome

billete *n.m.* ticket; **billete ida y vuelta**/round-trip ticket

biología *n.f.* biology

bizarro *adj.* brave, gallant

bizcocho *n.m.* cake, biscuit

blanco *n.m., adj.* white

blando *adj.* bland, soft, weak

blusa *n.f.* blouse

boca *n.f.* mouth

boda(s) *n.f. (pl.)* wedding

boicot *n.m.* boycott

boliviano *n., adj.* of or pertaining to Bolivia

bolsa *n.f.* purse, stock market

bolsillo *n.m.* pocket

bombilla *n.f.* bulb (electric light)

bondad *n.f.* goodness, kindness

bondadoso *adj.* kind

bonita, bonito *adj.,* pretty

borde *n.m.* border, brim, brink, edge

bordear *v.* to border

bordo *n.m.* board; **a bordo**/on board, aboard

borrador *n.m.* eraser

borrar *v.* to erase, obliterate, cross out

bosque *n.m.* forest, woods

bostezar *v.* to yawn, gape

botella *n.f.* bottle

botica *n.f.* drugstore

botón *n.m.* button

bracero *n.m.* laborer

bracito *n.m.* little arm

bravo, brava *adj.* brave

brazalete *n.m.* bracelet

brazo *n.m.* arm

breve *adj.* brief

brevedad *n.f.* brevity

brillando *adj., pres. part. of* **brillar** shining

brillar *v.* to shine, glitter, sparkle

brindar *v.* to invite, offer

brisa *n.f.* breeze

británico *adj.* British

broma *n.f.* joke

bronce *n.m.* bronze

brotar *v.* to sprout, bud

brújula *n.f.* compass

buen, bueno, buena, buenos, buenas *adj.* good; **buenos días**/hello, good day; **el visto bueno**/approval; *see also* §1.12, §1.20

bufanda *n.f.* muffler, scarf

búlgaro *adj.* of or pertaining to Bulgaria

bullir *v.* to boil

buque *n.m.* boat, ship

burla *n.f.* jest, mockery, trick

burlarse (de) *v.* to make fun (of), poke fun (at), ridicule

burrito *n.m.* little burro, donkey; **burro** *n.m.* donkey

busca *n.f.* search

buscar *v.* to look for, seek

buscase *v. form of* **buscar**

busto *n.m.* bust (sculptured work of art)

butaca *n.f.* armchair, orchestra seat

C

caballería *n.f.* cavalry; **caballero** *n.m.* gentleman, knight

caballito *n.m.* small (little) horse

caballo *n.m.* horse

cabello *n.m.* hair

caber *v.* to be contained, fit into

cabeza *n.f.* head

cabo *n.m.* end; **llevar a cabo**/to bring about, succeed in, accomplish; **al cabo de**/at the end of; **al fin y al cabo**/in the long run

cabra *n.f.* goat

cada *adj.* each

cadena *n.f.* chain

caer(se) *v.* to fall, knock down (over), to fell; **dejar caer**/to drop

café *n.f.* coffee, café

cafetería *n.f.* cafeteria

caída *n.f.* fall

caído *past part. of* **caer**

caja *n.f.* box

cajero, cajera *n.m.f.* bank teller

cajón *n.m.* box, carton

calcetín *n.m.* sock

calentar *v.* to heat, warm (up)

calentarse *v.* to warm oneself, to become (get) excited (angry)

calidad *n.f.* quality

caliente *adj.* warm, hot

californiano, californiana *n.m.f., adj.* of or pertaining to California

calma *n.f.* calmness, composure

calmar *v.* to calm

calor *n.m.* heat; *see also* **hacer** in idioms §53.13 and **tener** §53.27

calorcito *n.m.* warmth

caluroso *adj.* warm

calvo *adj.* bald

calzar *v.* to shoe, wear (shoes), put on shoes

calzas *n.f.pl.* stockings, hose

callado *adj.* quiet, silent, in silence (silently)

callarse *v.* to keep quiet (still), to be quiet (still, silent)

calle *n.f.* street; **calle abajo**/down the street

calló *v. form of* **callar(se)**

cama *n.f.* bed; **guardar cama**/to remain (stay) in bed

cámara *n.f.* chamber, room

camarero *n.m.* waiter; **camarera** *n.f.* waitress

cambiar(se) *v.* to change; **cambiarse de ropa**/to change clothing

cambio *n.m.* change, exchange; **en cambio**/on the other hand; **a cambio de**/in exchange for

caminar *v.* to walk, move along

camino *n.m.* road, way, walk, walking; **camino de**/on the way to; **en camino**/on the road

camión *n.m.* truck

camisa *n.f.* shirt; **camisa de seda**/silk shirt

campana *n.f.* bell

campanada *n.f.* striking (peal) of a bell

campanario *n.m.* belfry, bell tower

campanilla *n.f.* small hand bell

campaña *n.f.* campaign, field

campeón *n.m.* champion

campesina *n.f.* farmer's wife; **campesino, campesina** *n.m.f.* farmer; *adj.* country

campo *n.m.* field, campus, country (opposite of city), countryside

canal *n.m.* canal, channel

canario *n.m.* canary; **las Islas Canarias**/Canary Islands

canción *n.f.* song

candidato, candidata *n.m.f.* candidate

cansado, cansada, cansados, cansadas *adj.* tired

cansancio *n.m.* fatigue, tiredness, weariness

cansar *v.* to tire, fatigue, weary

cansarse *v.* to become tired, become weary, get tired (weary)

cantando *pres. part. of* **cantar**; **cantando a grito pelado**/singing at the top of one's lungs

cantante *n.m.f.* singer

cantar *v.* to sing

cantatriz *n.f.* singer

cantidad *n.f.* quantity

canto *n.m.* canto, epic poem, song, singing

caña *n.f.* pole, stick, cane, reed, rod; **caña de pescar**/fishing rod

cañón *n.m.* cannon

caos *n.m.* chaos

capa *n.f.* cape, cloak

capaces *pl. of* **capaz**

capacidad *n.f.* capacity

capaz *adj.* capable, competent

capilla *n.f.* chapel

capital *n.m.* capital (money, finances); **la capital**/capital city

capitán *n.m.* captain

capítulo *n.m.* chapter

capricho *n.m.* caprice, desire, whim

captada, capturados *adj.* captured

cara *n.f.* face

carácter *n.m.* character

caracteres *n.m.pl.* character; **caracteres históricos**/historical characters

características *n.f.pl.* characteristics

característico *adj.* characteristic

caracterizar *v.* to characterize

¡caramba! *interj.* Darn it! Oh, nuts!

carbón *n.m.* coal

carcajada *n.f.* guffaw, loud laughter

cárcel *n.m.* jail

carecer (de) *v.* to be in need, lack, need

cargado, cargada *adj.* loaded, heavy

cargar *v.* to charge, load, burden

cargo *n.m.* burden, task, charge, load, position, post; **hacer(se) cargo de**/to realize, take over, take charge of

Caribe *n., adj.* Caribbean

caricaturista *n.m.f.* caricaturist, cartoonist

caridad *n.f.* charity

cariño *n.m.* affection, warmth

cariñoso *adj.* affectionate, loving

carlismo *n.m.* Carlism

carlista *n.m.f.* Carlist

carnaval *n.m.* carnival

carne *n.f.* meat; **carnicería** *n.f.* butcher shop; **carnicero** *n.m.* butcher

caro *adj.* expensive

carpintero *n.m.* carpenter

carrera *n.f.* career, race, course, run

carretera *n.f.* highway

carrito *n.m.* little wagon, cart

carta *n.f.* letter, card; **una partida de cartas**/game of cards

cartera *n.f.* wallet

cartero *n.m.* mailman, postman

casa *n.f.* house; **en casa**/at home, home; **casa de correos**/post office

casados *adj.* married; **recién casados**/newlyweds; **casamiento** *n.m.* marriage, wedding

casarse *v.* to get married, marry; **casarse con**/to marry someone; **Juan se casó con María**/John married Mary

casi *adv.* almost, nearly

casilla *n.f.* hut

casita *n.f.* little house

caso *n.m.* case, matter; **caso que**/in case that; **hacer caso a** *or* **de**/to pay attention to; **en caso de que**/in case; **en todo caso**/in any case

castañuelas *n.f.* castanets

castellano *n.m., adj.* Castilian

castigar *v.* to punish

castigo *n.m.* punishment

castillo *n.m.* castle, fortress

casualidad *n.f.* chance, coincidence; **por casualidad**/by chance

catalán *n., adj.* of or pertaining to Catalan

catástrofe *n.f.* catastrophe

catedral *n.f.* cathedral

catedrático, catedrática *n.m.f.* professor

categoría *n.f.* category

Católica *adj.* Catholic

catorce *n.m., adj.* fourteen

caucho *n.m.* rubber

caudillo *n.m.* commander, leader

causa *n.f.* cause; **a causa de**/because of, on account of

causar *v.* to cause

caverna *n.f.* cave, cavern

cayéndose *pres. part. of* **caerse**

cayó *v. form of* **caer**

caza *n.f.* hunting, hunt

ceder *v.* to cede, give in, give up, yield

celda *n.f.* cell

celebrar *v.* to celebrate

célebre *adj.* famous, celebrated

celebridad *n.f.* celebrity, fame

cementerio *n.m.* cemetery

cemento *n.m.* cement

cenar *v.* to dine, have dinner, have supper, eat supper; **cena** *n.f.* supper

cenicero *n.m.* ash tray

cenit *n.m.* zenith

cenizas *n.f.pl.* ashes

censurar *v.* to censure

centavo *n.m.* cent, penny

centenar *n.m.* hundred; **centenares**/hundreds

centenario *n.m.* centenary

centro *n.m.* center, downtown

ceñir *v.* to surround

cepillar *v.* to brush; **cepillo** *n.m.*

brush

cerámica *n.f.* ceramics

cerca *adv.* close, near; **cerca de**/near; **de cerca**/close by, at close hand

cercanía *n.f.* proximity; **las cercanías**/surroundings

cercano, cercana *adj.* near, nearby; **más cercano**/closest, nearest

cereal *n.m.* cereal

cerebro *n.m.* brain

ceremonia *n.f.* ceremony

cereza *n.f.* cherry

cero *n.m.* zero

ceroso, cerosa *adj.* waxy, waxen

cerradera *n.f.* clasp, lock

cerrado *adj.* closed ·

cerradura *n.f.* lock

cerrar(se) *v.* to close

certificar *v.* to certify, register (a letter), attest

cerveza *n.f.* beer

cesar *v.* to cease, stop

cesta *n.f.* basket

cestillo *n.m.* little basket

cesto *n.m.* basket

ciclista *n.m.f.* cyclist

ciclo *n.m.* cycle

ciego, ciega *adj.* blind; *n.*, blind person

cielo *n.m.* sky; **por el cielo**/in (through) the sky

cien, ciento *n.m., adj.* (one, a) hundred; *see also* §1.23ff, §4.19(a)

ciencia *n.f.* science

científico *adj.* scientific

científicos *n.m.pl.* scientists

ciento *n.m., adj.* (one, a) hundred; **ciento por ciento**/one hundred per cent

ciertamente *adv.* certainly

cierto, cierta *n.m.f., adj.* (a) certain; *adv.*, surely, certainly; *see also* §4.19(b)

cigarrillo *n.m.* cigarette; **cigarro** *n.m.* cigar

cinco *n.m., adj.* five

cincuenta *n.m., adj.* fifty

cine *n.m.* movies

cinematográfico *adj.* cinematographic

circo *n.m.* circus

circuito *n.m.* circuit

circular *v.* to circulate, move about

círculo *n.m.* club, circle

circunstancias *n.f.pl.* circumstances

cirugía *n.f.* surgery

cita *n.f.* date, appointment

citar *v.* to cite, quote

ciudad *n.f.* city

ciudadano *adj.* city

cívicamente *adv.* civically

civiles *adj.* civil

civilización *n.f.* civilization

civilizado, civilizada *adj.* civilized

claridad *n.f.* clarity

claro *adj.* clear; **¡claro!** *interj.* of course!

clase *n.f.* class, type, kind

clásica *adj.* classic, classical

clasificación *n.f.* classification

clavel *n.m.* carnation

cliente *n.m.f.* customer, client

clientela *n.f.* clientele, customers

clima *n.m.* climate

cobarde *adj.* cowardly, coward

cobijar *v.* to cover, shelter, protect

cobrar *v.* to charge, collect; **se cobra**/is charged, collected

cobre *n.m.* copper

cocer *v.* to cook, bake, boil

cocina *n.f.* kitchen, cooking

cocinar *v.* to cook

cocinera, cocinero *n.f.m.* cook

coche *n.m.* car, auto; **cochero** *n.m.* driver, coachman

codo *n.m.* elbow

coger *v.* to grab, grasp, get, catch, take, seize

cola *n.f.* tail, line; **hacer cola**/to stand in line

colaboración *n.f.* collaboration

colaborar *v.* to collaborate

colchón *n.m.* mattress

colega *n.m.f.* colleague

colegio *n.m.* college, school; **colegio interno**/boarding school

colegir *v.* to collect

cólera *n.f.* anger, wrath

colgar *v.* to hang (up)

colina *n.f.* hill

colocación *n.f.* job

colocar *v.* to place, put

colocase *v. form of* **colocar**

colombiano, colombiana *n.m.f., adj.* of or pertaining to Colombia

Colón *n.m.* Columbus

colonia *n.f.* colony

colonización *n.f.* colonization

colonizador *n.m.* colonizer

color, colores *n.m.s.pl.* color

colorido *n.m.* color, coloring

colosal *adj.* colossal, enormous

columna *n.f.* column

collar *n.m.* collar, necklace

comandante *n.m.* commandant, commander, major

combate *n.m.* combat, fight, struggle

combatiente *n.m.f.* fighter, combatant

combatir *v.* to combat, fight

combinación *n.f.* combination

combinar(se) *v.* to combine

comedia *n.f.* comedy

comedor *n.m.* dining room

comentar *v.* to comment (on)

comentario *n.m.* comment, commentary

comenzar *v.* to begin, start, commence

comer *v.* to eat; **se come**/one eats; **comerse** *v.* to eat up

comercial *n.m., adj.* commercial

comerciante *n.m.f.* merchant, business person

comercio *n.m.* commerce

comerse *v.* to eat up

comestible *adj.* edible, eatable; **comestibles** *n.m.* provisions; **una tienda de comestibles**/grocery store

cometer *v.* to commit

comía *v. form of* **comer**

cómico *n.m.* comedian; *adj.* comic, comical, funny

comida *n.f.* meal

comience *v. form of* **comenzar**

comiendo *pres. part. of* **comer**

comieron *v. form of* **comer**

comisión *n.f.* commission

comisionado *adj.* commissioned

como *conj., adv.* how, as, like, as if; **como si**/as if; **¿cómo?** *adv.* how? what?; **tan pronto como**/as soon as; *see also* §7.ff

comodidad *n.f.* commodity, comfort

cómodo *adj.* comfortable

compadecer *v.* to pity

compañero, compañera *n.m.f.* companion, friend

compañía *n.f.* company

comparación *n.f.* comparison

comparar *v.* to compare

compasivo *adj.* compassionate, merciful

competencia *n.f.* competition, competency

compilar *v.* to compile

complacer *v.* to please, accommodate

completamente *adv.* completely

completar *v.* to complete

completo *adj.* complete; **por completo**/completely

componer *v.* to compose

comportamiento *n.m.* comportment, behavior, conduct

composición *n.f.* composition

compositor *n.m.* composer

compra *n.f.* purchase; **ir de compras**/to go shopping

comprador, compradora *n.m.f.* buyer, customer
comprar *v.* to buy, purchase
comprender *v.* to understand, comprehend, comprise; **comprendido**/comprising, comprised of; **se comprende**/is understood
comprensión *n.f.* comprehension, understanding
comprensivo *adj.* comprehensive
compuesto *past part. of* componer
común *n.m., adj.* common, usual; **por lo común**/ordinarily, commonly; *n.* community, public
comunicación *n.f.* communication
comunicar *v.* to communicate
comunidad *n.f.* community
comunión *n.f.* communion
con *prep.* with; **para con**/toward, with; *see also* **con** *in idioms* §53.4
conceder *v.* to concede, grant
concentrado, concentrada *adj.* concentrated
concentrar *v.* to concentrate; **se concentrarán**/will concentrate
concepto *n.m.* concept
conciencia *n.f.* conscience
concierto *n.m.* concert
concluir *v.* to conclude
concretamente *adv.* concretely
conde *n.m.* count
condecoración *n.f.* decoration, medal
condenar *v.* to condemn
condesa *n.f.* countess
condición *n.f.* condition; **condicional**/conditional
conducir *v.* to drive, conduct, lead, take (a person somewhere)
condujo *v. form of* **conducir**
conejo *n.m.* rabbit
conferencia *n.f.* conference, lecture, meeting; **conferenciante** *n.m.f.* lecturer
conferenciar *v.* to confer, hold a conference
conferir *v.* to confer
confesar *v.* to confess
confianza *n.f.* confidence, trust
confiar *v.* to confide, entrust
confinamiento *n.m.* confinement
confirmar *v.* to confirm, verify
confortable *adj.* comfortable
confundido *adj.* confused
confundir *v.* to confuse, confound
confusos *adj. pl.* confused
congreso *n.m.* congress, meeting, convention
conjunto *n.m.* ensemble, group; *adj.* joint, united
conmigo/with me; *see also* §66.33

conmovedora *adj.* moving, stirring, touching
conmover(se) *v.* to stir, affect, fill with emotion, touch, disturb, rouse
conocedor, conocedora *n.m.f.* connoisseur
conocer *v.* to know, be acquainted with, to meet (a person for the first time); *see also* §62.10
conocido *adj.* known
conocimiento *n.m.* knowledge
conozco, conozca *v. forms of* **conocer**
conque *conj., adv.* now then, so then
conquista *n.f.* conquest
conquistador *n.m.* conqueror
conquistar *v.* to conquer, vanquish
conseguir *v.* to attain, get, obtain
consejo *n.m.* advice, counsel
consentir *v.* to consent
consequencia *n.f.* consequence
consideración *n.f.* consideration, magnitude
considerar *v.* to consider, look intently at, examine, think over; **se considera**/is considered
consignar *v.* to consign, assign
consigo/*see* §66.33
consiguiente *adj.* consequent, consequential; **por consiguiente**/therefore, consequently
consiguiese *v. form of* **conseguir**
consintió *v. form of* **consentir**
consistir *v.* to consist
consolar *v.* to console, comfort
constancia *n.f.* constancy, certainty
constantemente *adv.* constantly
constituir *v.* to constitute, make up
constituyeron *v. form of* **constituir**
construcción *n.f.* construction
construir *v.* to construct, build
construyeron *v. form of* **construir**
consuela *v. form of* consolar; **consuela ver . . .**/it is comforting to see . . .
consuelo *n.m.* consolation; *also v. form of* **consolar**
consulado *n.m.* consulate
consultar *v.* to consult
consumir *v.* to consume, eat
consumo *n.m.* consumption
contacto *n.m.* contact
contado *see* **contar**
contaminar *v.* to contaminate
contar *v.* to count, relate, tell about; **contar con**/to count on, rely on; **al contado**/cash payment
contemplar *v.* to contemplate
contemporáneo *adj.* contemporary
contener *v.* to contain, hold

contenido *n.m.* content, contents; *also adj. & past part. of* **contener**
contentarse *v.* to content oneself, be content
contento *n.m.* contentment, joy; *adj.* pleased, content, happy
contestación *n.f.* response, reply
contestar *v.* to answer, reply (to)
contigo/with you (*familiar*)
continente *n.m.* continent
continuamente *adv.* continually
continuar *v.* to continue
contra *prep.* against
contradecir *v.* to contradict
contrariado *adj.* upset, troubled, annoyed
contrario *n.m., adj.* contrary, opposite; **por el contrario**/on the contrary
contraste *n.m.* contrast
contratar *v.* to agree, engage, contract for
contribuir *v.* to contribute
convaleciente *adj., n.* convalescing, convalescent
convencer *v.* to convince; **convencerse** *v.* to convince oneself
conveniente *adj.* proper, fitting
convenir *v.* to agree, be fitting, suitable
conversación *n.f.* conversation
conversar *v.* to converse, talk
convertir *v.* to convert; **convertirse** *v.* to convert oneself (itself), to be converted
convidar *v.* to invite
conviene *v. form of* **convenir**
convirtió *v. form of* **convertir**
convivir *v.* to live together
convocar *v.* to convoke, call (a meeting), call together, convene, summon
cooperación *n.f.* cooperation
coordinar *v.* to coordinate
copa *n.f.* tree top, glass, cup, goblet
copiar *v.* to copy
coqueta *adj., n.f.* coquette, flirt
corazón *n.m.* heart
corbata *n.f.* tie, necktie
corderito *n.m.* little lamb
cordialidad *n.f.* cordiality
cordillera *n.f.* mountain range
Corea *n.f.* Korea
corona *n.f.* crown, wreath
coronel *n.m.* colonel
corporación *n.f.* corporation
corral *n.m.* corral, barnyard
corrección *n.f.* correction
corregir *v.* to correct

correo *n.m.* mail; **echar al correo/** to mail

correr *v.* to run, flow, race

correspondencia *n.f.* correspondence

corresponder *v.* to correspond; **correspondiente/**corresponding

corresponsal *n.m.f.* correspondent (of a newspaper)

corría *v. form of* **correr**

corrida *n.f.* race, course, bullfight

corriendo *pres. part. of* **correr**

corriente *n.f., adj.* draft, current, present, common, flowing; **lo corriente/**present; **era poco corriente/**not long ago

corrientemente *adv.* fluently

corrió *v. form of* **correr**

cortar *v.* to cut; **se corta/**is cut; **cortarse el pelo/**to have one's hair cut; **córtemela/**cut it for me

cortés, corteses *adj.* courteous

cortesía *n.f.* courtesy

corteza *n.f.* crust, bark, rind, peel

cortina *n.f.* curtain

corto *adj.* short; *see also* §1.ff

cosa *n.f.* thing; **no es gran cosa**/it's not very much

cosecha *n.f.* crop, harvest

coser *v.* to sew

cosiendo *pres. part. of* **coser**

cosmopolito *adj.* cosmopolitan

costa *n.f.* coast

costar *v.* to cost

costarricense *adj., n.* of or pertaining to Costa Rica

costear *v.* to defray

costoso *adj.* costly

costumbre *n.f.* custom, habit; **de costumbre/**customarily, usually

costura *n.f.* sewing

creación *n.f.* creation

creado *adj.* created

créame/believe me

crear *v.* to create

crecer *v.* to increase, grow

creciendo *pres. part. of* **crecer**

creciente *adj.* increasing

crecimiento *n.m.* increase

credo *n.m.* belief, creed

creer *v.* to believe; **creerse** *v.* to think oneself, consider (believe) oneself; **se cree/**it is believed

creo *v. form of* **creer**

creó *v. form of* **crear**

creyó *v. form of* **creer**

criada *n.f.* maid, servant; **los criados/**servants

criar *v.* to breed, raise, bring up (rear a child)

criatura *n.f.* creature, infant

crimen *n.m.* crime

cristal *n.m.* crystal, glass window pane

cristiana *adj., n.* Christian

cristiandad *n.f.* Christendom

cristianismo *n.m.* Christianity

cristiano, cristiana *n.m.f., adj.* Christian

Cristo *n.m.* Christ

crítica *n.f.* critique, criticism, review; *n.m.* **crítico/**critic

criticar *v.* to criticize

criticara *v. form of* **criticar**

crítico *n.m., adj.* critic, critical

cruce *n.m.* crossing

crueles *adj. pl. of* **cruel**

cruz *n.f.* cross

cruzada *n.f.* crusade

cruzar *v.* to cross

cuaderno *n.m.* notebook

cuadra *n.f.* city block

cuadradas *adj.* square

cuadro *n.m.* picture, painting

cual *pron.* which (one); **tal o cual/** such and such; *see also* §6.1, §9., §61.ff

cualidad *n.f.* quality

cualquier *indef. adj. & pron.* whichever, whatever, any

cuando *adv.* when; **de vez en cuando/**from time to time; **de cuando en cuando/**from time to time; **cuando menos/**at least; ¡ **cuán . . . !/how . . . !**

cuanto *pron. rel. adj.* all that, as many as, as much as; **unos cuantos/**some; **en cuanto a/**as for, as soon as; **cuánto, cuánta, cuántos, cuántas** *adj.* how much, how many; **cuanto antes/**as soon as possible

cuarenta *n., adj.* forty; **cuarenta y siete/**forty-seven

cuartel *n.m.* barracks, quarters

cuarto *n.m.* room, quarter(s); **el cuarto de baño/**bathroom

cuatro *n.m., adj.* four

cubano, cubana *n.m.f., adj.* of or pertaining to Cuba

cubierta *n.f.* cover, bedspread; *n.m.* deck (of a boat); **cubierto** *past part. of* **cubrir; cubierto, cubierta** *adj.* covered

cubo *n.m.* cube, bucket

cubrir *v.* to cover

cuchara *n.f.* spoon

cuchillo *n.m.* knife

cuello *n.m.* neck, collar

cuenta *n.f.* account, bill, tab; **darse cuenta de/**to realize

cuento *n.m.* story, tale

cuerda *n.f.* cord, rope

cuero *n.m.* leather

cuerpo *n.m.* body

cuestión *n.f.* question, problem, matter

cueva *n.f.* cave, cellar

cuidado *n.m.* care; **perder cuidado/** not to care, not to worry; **cuidar** *v.* to take care of

culpa *n.f.* blame, fault, guilt; **echar la culpa a/**to blame

culpable *adj.* guilty

cultivo *n.m.* cultivation

culto *n.m.* cult, worship; *adj.* cultured, cultivated, learned

cultura *n.f.* culture

cumbre *n.f.* peak, top, summit

cumpleañero *n.m.* birthday boy

cumpleaños *n.m.* birthday

cumplida *adj.* completed, fulfilled

cumplimiento *n.m.* fulfillment, compliance, completion

cumplir *v.* to fulfill, accomplish, keep (a promise), reach one's birthday (use with **años**)

cura *n.m.* priest; **la cura/**cure

curar *v.* to cure

curiosidad *n.f.* curiosity

curioso *adj.* curious; **los curiosos/** curious people

curso *n.m.* course, race, progress

curva *n.f.* curve, bend

cuyo, cuya, cuyos, cuyas *rel. pron.* whose

CH

chafar *v.* to crease, flatten, crumple

chaleco *n.m.* vest

chaqueta *n.f.* jacket

charla *n.f.* chatting, talking

charlar *v.* to chat, prattle

cheque *n.m.* check

Chianti *n.m.* name of an Italian wine

chicle *n.m.* chewing gum

chico, chica *n.m.f.* boy, girl; *adj.* small, little; **el chico, la chica/**little boy, little girl; **los chicos/**children

chichicastecos *n.m., adj.* of or pertaining to Chichicastenango, Guatemala

chiflar *v.* to whistle

chillar *v.* to scream, shriek

chimenea *n.f.* chimney, fireplace

chiquillo, chiquilla *n.m.f.* little boy, little girl

chiquitico *adj.* tiny, very small

chistar *v.* to mumble, mutter
chiste *n.m.* joke
chistoso *adj.* humorous, witty, funny
chocar *v.* to collide, to be shocking, surprising
chocolate *n.m.* chocolate
chocolatero *n.m.* chocolate maker
chofer, chófer *n.m.* chauffeur, driver
choque *v. form of* **chocar**; *n.m.* shock
choza *n.f.* hut
chupar *v.* to suck, sip
chupete *n.m.* teething ring, pacifier
chusco *adj.* amusing, droll, funny

D

da, daba *v. forms of* **dar**
dama *n.f.* lady
dan, dando *v. forms of* **dar**
danzarina *n.f.* dancer
daño *n.m.* harm, hurt, damage; **hacer daño**/to harm, hurt; **hacerse daño**/to harm, hurt oneself
dar *v.* to give, hit, strike; **dar a**/to look out upon, face; **dar con**/to find, come upon (across); **dar contra**/to hit against; **dar las diez**/to strike ten o'clock; **dar un paseo**/to take a walk; *see also* **dar** *in idioms* §53.6
dará *v. form of* **dar**
darse *v.* to give oneself (itself); **darse cuenta de**/to realize; *see also* **darse** *in idioms* §53.6
datar *v.* to date (calendar)
dato *n.m.* datum, fact
de *prep.* of, from, by, about; *see also* **de** *in idioms* §53.7
dé *v. form of* **dar**
debajo *adv.* below, under, underneath; **debajo de**/under
debatida *adj.* debated
debatir *v.* to debate, argue
deber *v.* to owe, have to, must, ought, should, supposed to; **deber de**/must, probably; **se debe**/is due, is owed; **debido a**/due to; *n.m.* duty; **los deberes**/homework; *see also* §20.1, §20.2, §53.25
debía *v. form of* **deber**; **se debía**/was due, was owed
debido *past part. of* **deber**; *adj.* exact
débil *adj.* weak
debilidad *n.f.* weakness
debutar *v.* to make a debut
década *n.f.* decade
decadencia *n.f.* decadence
decidir *v.* to decide; **decidirse** *v.* to decide, make up one's mind; **decidirse a**/to decide to
decir *v.* to say, tell; **es decir**/that is,

that is to say; **querer decir**/to mean; **se puede decir**/it can be said; *n.m.* a saying; **decir la buenaventura**/to tell one's fortune; *see also* **decir** *in idioms* §53.8
decisión *n.f.* decision
decisivo, decisiva *adj.* decisive
declaración *n.f.* declaration
declarar *v.* to declare; **declararse** *v.* to declare oneself
decorar *v.* to decorate
decoro *n.m.* decorum, respect
decretada *adj.* decreed
decretar *v.* to resolve, decree
dedicación *n.f.* dedication
dedicado *adj.* dedicated, devoted; *also past part. of* **dedicar** *v.* to dedicate, devote; **dedicarse** *v.* to dedicate, devote oneself (itself)
dediqué *v. form of* **dedicar**
dedo *n.m.* finger, toe
deducir(se) *v.* to deduce
dedujo *v. form of* **deducir**
defecto *n.m.* defect
defender *v.* to defend
defensa *n.f.* defense
defensor *n.m.* defender
definido *adj.* definite
definitivo *adj.* definitive, definite
dejar *v.* to leave, quit, let, allow, permit; **dejar caer**/to drop; **dejar de**/to stop, fail to, neglect to; *see also* §21.2, §22, §22.1, §56.8
del *contraction of* **de** + **el**/from the, of the
delante *adv.* ahead, before, in front; **delante de**/in front of, before
delgado *adj.* delicate, thin, slender
delicado *adj.* delicate, frail
delinquir *v.* to be guilty, offend
delito *n.m.* crime, offense
demanda *n.f.* demand
demás *adj., adv.* besides, moreover; **los (las) demás**/the others, the rest, the remaining; **por lo demás**/as for the rest
demasiado *adj., adv.* too much, too many, too
déme/give me
demonio *n.m.* demon, devil
demostrar *v.* to show, demonstrate; **demostrativo** *adj.* demonstrative
den *v. form of* **dar**
denotar *v.* to denote
dentista *n.m.f.* dentist
dentro *adv.* inside, within; **dentro de**/inside of; **dentro de poco**/in (within) a short while
denunciar *v.* to denounce
depender *v.* to depend
dependiente *n.m.f.* employee, clerk

deporte *n.m.* sport; **una tienda de deportes**/sporting goods store
deportivo *adj.* sport, sporting
depósito *n.m.* deposit, depository, storehouse, warehouse
derecho *n.m.* right, privilege; **derecho, derecha** *adj.* straight, right (opposite of left); **a la derecha**/at (to) the right
derramar *v.* to scatter, shed, spill
derribar *v.* to knock down, overthrow, tear down, throw down
derrota *n.f.* defeat; **derrotar** *v.* to defeat
desagradable *adj.* unpleasant, disagreeable
desagradar *v.* to displease
desagrado *n.m.* displeasure
desaire *n.m.* disdain, rebuff
desanimado *adj.* discouraged, disheartened
desaparecer *v.* to disappear
desaparición *n.f.* disappearance
desarrollar(se) *v.* to develop, expand, unfold
desastre *n.m.* disaster
desastroso *adj.* disastrous
desatar *v.* to untie
desayunar(se) *v.* to breakfast, have breakfast
desayuno *n.m.* breakfast
descansado *adj.* rested
descansar(se) *v.* to rest
descanso *n.m.* rest
descender *v.* to descend, go down
descendiente *n.m.* descendant
descolorido *adj.* discolored
desconectar *v.* to disconnect
desconocer *v.* to be unaware of, not to know, not to recognize
desconocido *adj.* unknown, unrecognizable (person or thing)
descontento *n.m.* displeasure; *adj.* unhappy, discontented
descortés *adj.* discourteous
describir *v.* to describe, sketch, delineate
descripción *n.f.* description
descubierto *past part. of* **descubrir**; **descubiertos** *adj.* discovered, uncovered, open
descubrimiento *n.m.* discovery
descubrir *v.* to discover, disclose
descuento *n.m.* discount
descuido *n.m.* carelessness, neglect
desde *prep.* from, since; **desde luego**/since then, of course, at once; **desde que**/ever since; **desde hace mucho tiempo**/for a long time; *see also* §30.—35.ff
desear *v.* to desire, want, wish

desembarcar *v.* to disembark, unload

desempeñar *v.* to play (a part), act (a part), discharge, perform (a duty), take out of pawn

deseo *n.m.* desire, wish; *also v. form of* **desear**

desesperación *n.f.* desperation, despair, hopelessness

desesperado *adj.* desperate

desesperante *adj.* discouraged, in despair

desesperar *v.* to despair

desfile *n.m.* parade

desgracia *n.f.* misfortune, mishap, something terrible; **por desgracia**/unfortunately

desgraciadamente *adv.* unfortunately

desgraciado *adj.* unfortunate

deshacer *v.* to undo

desierto *n.m.* desert; *adj.* deserted

designar *v.* to designate

desilusionado *adj.* disillusioned

desistir *v.* to desist

deslizar(se) *v.* to slide, slip, glide

deslumbrar *v.* to daze, dazzle

desmayar(se) *v.* to dismay, faint

desmayo *n.m.* faint

desmentir *v.* to belie, disprove

desnuda *adj.* naked, nude

desnudar *v.* to undress; **desnudarse**/to undress oneself

desobedecer *v.* to disobey

desolados *adj.* desolate

desorden *n.m.* disorder

desordenada *adj.* disorganized, in disarray, disordered, disorderly

desorientado *adj.* confused

desorientarse *v.* to become confused, get lost

despacio *adv.* slowly

despacho *n.m.* dispatch, office

despedazar *v.* to tear to pieces

despedir *v.* to dismiss; **despedirse**/to take leave, say good-bye

despertar *v.* to awaken, wake up (someone)

despertarse *v.* to wake up, awaken oneself

despidieron, despidió *v. forms of* **despedir**

despierto *v. form of* **despertar**; *adj.* awake

despreciar *v.* to despise, disdain, scorn

·después *adv.* after, then, afterwards, later

destacado *adj.* outstanding

destacar(se) *v.* to emphasize, excel, stand out

desterrar *v.* to banish, drive out, exile

destinación *n.f.* destination

destinar *v.* to destine

destino *n.m.* destiny, destination, fate

destrozar *v.* to destroy, shatter

destruir *v.* to destroy

desvanecerse *v.* to faint, disappear, vanish

desvestirse *v.* to undress, get undressed

detalle *n.m.* detail

detención *n.f.* detention

detener *v.* to stop, detain (someone or something)

detenerse *v.* to stop (oneself)

determinado *adj.* definite, specific, determined

determinar *v.* to determine, decide

detestar *v.* to detest

detrás *prep.* behind, in back; **detrás de**/behind, in back of

detuvo *v. form of* detener

deuda *n.f.* debt

devastar *v.* to devastate

devoción *n.f.* devotion; **devocionario** *n.m.* prayer book

devolver *v.* to return (an object), refund, give back; *see also* §49.ff

devuelva *v. form of* **devolver**

di *v. form of* **decir, dar**

día *n.m.* day; **a los pocos días**/in a few days; **al día siguiente**/on the following day; **buenos días**/hello, good day; **hoy día**/nowadays; **todos los días**/every day; *see also* **día, días** *in idioms* §53.9

diablo *n.m.* devil

diagnóstico *n.m.* diagnosis

dialéctico *adj.* dialectical

diálogo *n.m.* dialogue

diariamente *adv.* daily

diario *n.m.* diary, newspaper; *adj.* daily

dibujar *v.* to draw, sketch

dibujo *n.m.* drawing, sketch

diccionario *n.m.* dictionary

dice *v. form of* **decir; se dice**/it is said

diciembre *n.m.* December

diciendo *pres. part. of* **decir**

dictado *n.m.* dictation; **dictados**/dictates, maxims, dictations

dictador *n.m.* dictator

dictadura *n.f.* dictatorship

dicha *n.f.* happiness; *adj.* aforementioned, above-mentioned, said, stated; *see also* §43.5

dicho *past part. of* **decir**; *see also* §43.ff

dichoso *adj.* happy, lucky, fortunate, blessed; *see also* §43.4

dieciséis *n.m., adj.* sixteen

diente *n.m.* tooth

diera, dieron *v. forms of* **dar**

diferencia *n.f.* difference

diferenciar *v.* to differentiate, distinguish

diferente *adj.* different

difícil *adj.* difficult

dificultad *n.f.* difficulty

dificultar *v.* to make difficult

dificultoso *adj.* difficult

difunto *adj.* dead

diga *v. form of* **decir**; **¡diga!**/say! hello! (on the telephone); **dígamelo**/tell me it, tell it to me, tell me so

dignidad *n.f.* dignity

digno *adj.* worthy

digo *v. form of* **decir**

dije, dijiste, dijo *v. forms of* **decir**

diles/tell them

diligente *adj.* diligent

dime/tell me

Dinamarca *n.f.* Denmark

dinamarqués *n.m., adj.* Danish, Dane; of or pertaining to Denmark

dinamita *n.f.* dynamite

dinero *n.m.* money

dio *v. form of* **dar**

Dios *n.m.* God; **dioses** *n.m.pl.* gods

diplomático *adj.* diplomatic

diré *v. form of* **decir**

dirección *n.f.* address, direction

directamente *adv.* directly

directo *adj.* direct

director, directora *n.m.f.* director, principal

diría *v. form of* **decir**

dirigido *adj.* directed

dirigir *v.* to direct, manage; **dirigirse** *v.* to go toward, go into a direction, direct oneself, address oneself, make one's way (toward)

dirija *v. form of* **dirigir**

disciplina *n.f.* discipline

discípulo *n.m.* disciple, student

disco *n.m.* phonograph record, recording

disconforme *adj.* unconforming

discreto *adj.* discreet

disculpa *n.f.* apology, excuse

discúlpame/excuse me, pardon me

disculpar *v.* to excuse, exculpate

discurrir *v.* to speak, ramble, discourse

discurso *n.m.* speech, discourse, lecture

discusión *n.f.* discussion

discutir *v.* to discuss

diseminados *adj.* disseminated, scattered

diseminar *v.* to disseminate

disfrutar *v.* to enjoy

disgustado *adj.* displeased

disgustar *v.* to displease

disgusto *n.m.* displeasure

disminuir *v.* to diminish, decrease

disparada *adj.* in a hurry

disparar *v.* to fire, shoot, discharge

dispensar *v.* to excuse, dispense, distribute, exempt

disperso *adj.* dispersed, scattered

disponer *v.* to dispose, arrange; **disponer de**/to have available, have at one's disposal; **disponerse a**/to get ready to

disposición *n.f.* disposition, arrangement

dispuesto *adj.* ready, disposed

disputa *n.f.* dispute, quarrel

distancia *n.f.* distance

distante *adj.* far, distant

distar *v.* to be distant

distinguir *v.* to distinguish; **distinguirse** *v.* to distinguish oneself (itself)

distinto *adj.* distinct, different

distracción *n.f.* distraction, amusement

distribución *n.f.* distribution

distribuir *v.* to distribute

distrito *n.m.* district

diversión *n.f.* amusement, diversion

diversiones *n.f.pl.* amusements, diversions

diverso *adj.* diverse, different, various; **diversos**/several

divertido *adj.* diverting, amusing

divertir *v.* to amuse, entertain; **divertirse** *v.* to have a good time, enjoy oneself

divididos *adj.* divided

dividir *v.* to divide

divierte *v. form of* **divertir**

divinidad *n.f.* divinity

divulgado *adj.* divulged

doblar *v.* to double, fold; **doblarse** *v.* to double itself; **doblar la esquina**/to turn the corner

doble *n.m., adj.* double

doce *n.m., adj.* twelve

docena *n.f.* dozen

doctor *n.m.* doctor; **doctorado** *n.m.* doctorate

documento *n.m.* document

dólar *n.m.* dollar

doler *v.* to ache, pain, hurt, cause grief, cause regret; **dolerle a uno la cabeza**/to have a headache; **un dolor de cabeza**/headache; **tener dolor**/to have an ache, pain

doliesen *v. form of* **doler**

dolor *n.m.* ache, pain, sorrow

doméstica *adj.* domestic

domicilio *n.m.* domicile, residence

dominar *v.* to dominate, command, have a command

domingo *n.m.* Sunday

dominio *n.m.* domination, command; **dominio del español, del inglés, del francés**/command of Spanish, English, French

don, Don *n.m.* title used before a gentleman's first name, *e.g.,* **Don José**

donde *adv.* where; **¿dónde?**/where?; *see also* §2.10, §9.

dondequiera *indef. & rel. adv.* wherever, anywhere; *see also* §67.50

doña *n.f.* title used before a lady's first name, *e.g.,* **Doña Ana**

dorar *v.* to gild

dormido *adj.* asleep

dormir *v.* to sleep; **dormirse** *v.* to fall asleep

dormitar *v.* to nap, doze

dormitorio *n.m.* dormitory, sleeping quarters, bedroom

dos *n.m., adj.* two; **los dos**/both

doscientos *n.m., adj.* two hundred

doy *v. form of* **dar**

drama *n.m.* drama

dramaturgo *n.m.* dramatist

duda *n.f.* doubt; **sin duda**/without a doubt, doubtless; **no cabe duda**/no room for doubt, no doubt about it

dudar *v.* to doubt

dudoso *adj.* doubtful

duele *v. form of* **doler**

dueña *n.f.* owner, proprietress

dueño *n.m.* master, owner, landlord

duerme, duermen *v. forms of* **dormir**

dulce *n.m.* candy; *adj.* sweet; **dulces**/candy; **dulcemente** *adv.* sweetly

dulzura *n.f.* sweetness, gentleness, tenderness

duplicar *v.* to duplicate

dura *adj.* hard

durante *prep.* during

durar *v.* to last, endure

dureza *n.f.* harshness

durmiendo *pres. part. of* **dormir**

duro *adj.* hard; *n.m.* **duro** (Spanish coin)

E

e *conj.* and; *see also* §1.65, §51., §59.4, §7.ff

eco *n.m.* echo

economía *n.f.* economy, economics; **economía doméstica**/home economics

económico *adj.* economic, economical

economista *n.m.f.* economist

economizar *v.* to economize, save (money)

ecuatoriano *n.m., adj.* of or pertaining to Ecuador

echar *v.* to cast, fling, hurl, pitch, throw; **echar al correo**/to mail; **echar de menos**/to miss; **echar la culpa**/to blame; **echar ojo a**/to glance at, keep an eye on; **echar una carta al correo**/to mail (post) a letter; **echarse a + inf.**/to begin to, start to; *see also* §53.7

edad *n.f.* age; **la Edad Media**/the Middle Ages

edición *n.f.* edition

edificar *v.* to build erect; **se edificó**/was built

edificio *n.m.* edifice, building

editar *v.* to publish; to edit: **redactar**

educación *n.f.* education

educador, educadora *n.m.f.* educator

educados *adj.* educated

educativo *adj.* educational

efectivamente *adv.* effectively

efecto *n.m.* effect; **en efecto**/in fact, as a matter of fact

efectuado *adj.* carried out

efectuar *v.* to accomplish, carry out, put into effect, to effect

egoísta *adj.* egotistical, egoistic, selfish

ejecutar *v.* to execute, carry out, perform

ejemplar *n.m.* sample, copy; *adj.* exemplary

ejemplo *n.m.* example; **por ejemplo**/for example

ejercer *v.* to exert, exercise

ejercicio *n.m.* exercise, practice

ejército *n.m.* army

el *def. art. m.s.* the; **el que**/he (she) who; *see also* §4.ff, §66.60, §66.66, §66.82ff, §66.88ff, §66.90ff

elección *n.f.* election

electricidad *n.f.* electricity

eléctrico *adj.* electric, electrical

elefante *n.m.* elephant

elegancia *n.f.* elegance; **elegante** *adj.* elegant

elegir *v.* to elect

elemental *adj.* elementary

elemento *n.m.* element

elevar *v.* to exalt, raise, elevate

eliminar *v.* to eliminate
elocuente *adj.* eloquent
elogiar *v.* to praise, eulogize
elogio *n.m.* praise
embajada *n.f.* embassy
embajador, embajadora *n.m.f.* ambassador
embarcación *n.f.* embarkation
embarcarse *v.* to embark
embargo *n.m.* embargo, seizure; **sin embargo**/nevertheless, however
embeber *v.* to soak in, soak up, suck in
emergencia *n.f.* emergency
emoción *n.f.* emotion
emocionante *adj.* moving, touching
emocionar *v.* to move, touch, thrill
emocionarse *v.* to feel emotion
empecé *v. form of* **empezar**
empeñarse *v.* to insist, persist
emperador *n.m.* emperor; **emperatriz** *n.f.* empress
empezar *v.* to begin, start
empieza *v. form of* **empezar**
empleado, empleada *n.m.f.* employee
emplear *v.* to employ, use
empleo *n.m.* job, employment
emprender *v.* to undertake, begin
empresa *n.f.* enterprise, undertaking, purpose
empresario *n.m.* impresario
empujar *v.* to push
empujón *n.m.* push, shove
en *prep.* in, on, at; *see also* **en** in idioms §53.10; in prepositional phrases §62.3
enamorado de/in love with
enamorar *v.* to enamor, court, woo; **enamorarse de**/to fall in love with
enano *n.m.* dwarf
encabezar *v.* to head, lead
encaminarse *v.* to walk (toward)
encantado *adj.* enchanted, delighted
encantador, encantadora *adj.* charming
encantar *v.* to enchant, charm
encanto *n.m.* charm, enchantment
encarcelar *v.* to jail, imprison, incarcerate
encargar *v.* to put in charge
encargarse de *v.* to take charge of
encargo *n.m.* task, charge, trust
encender *v.* to incite, inflame, kindle, light, ignite
encendidas *adj.* lighted, lit, burning
encendieron *v. form of* **encender**
encerrar *v.* to enclose, lock up, confine
enciclopedia *n.f.* encyclopedia
encima *adv.* above, over, over and above; **por encima de**/in spite of; **encima de**/above, on top of
encogerse de hombros/to shrug one's shoulders
encontrar *v.* to meet, encounter, find
encontrarse *v.* to be located, to be found, to meet each other, to find oneself; **se encuentra**/is found, is located; **encontrarse con**/to meet, come across, find, come upon
encuentro *v. form of* **encontrar**; *n.m.* encounter, meeting
enemigo, enemiga *n.m.f.* enemy
energía *n.f.* energy
enero *n.m.* January
enfadar *v.* anger; **enfadarse** *v.* to become (get) angry, upset, annoyed
enfado *n.m.* annoyance
enfermarse *v.* to become sick
enfermedad *n.f.* illness, sickness
enfermera *n.f.* nurse
enfermita *n.f.* sick little girl
enfermizo *adj.* sickly
enfermo *n.m.* sick man; *adj.* sick, ill; **los enfermos**/the sick persons
enfrente de/in front of, opposite
engaño *n.m.* deceit
engañar *v.* to deceive, cheat, fool
engañarse *v.* to be mistaken, deceived
enojado *adj.* angry, annoyed, irritated
enojar *v.* to annoy, irritate, make angry, vex, anger
enojarse *v.* to become angry, annoyed
enojo *n.m.* anger, trouble, annoyance, bother
enorme *adj.* enormous, big, huge
enormemente *adv.* enormously
enriquecerse *v.* to become rich, enrich oneself
enrollar *v.* to roll
ensalada *n.f.* salad
ensayar *v.* to test, try, rehearse
ensayista *n.m.f.* essayist
ensayo *n.m.* essay, test
enseñanza *n.f.* teaching
enseñar *v.* to teach, show, point out
entablar *v.* to start
entender *v.* to understand, hear; **se entiende**/is understood
entenderse *v.* to understand each other, get along with each other
enterar *v.* to inform; **enterarse de**/to find out about, become aware of
enternecidamente *adv.* with compassion

entero *adj.* entire
entiende *v. form of* **entender**
entierro *n.m.* burial
entonces *adj.* well, then, at that time
entrada *n.f.* entrance, admission ticket, arrival
entrar (en) *v.* to enter (into), go (in), come (in)
entre *prep.* between, among
entrega *n.f.* delivery, handing over, giving over
entregado *adj.* delivered
entregar *v.* to deliver, hand over, give
entregarse *v.* to devote oneself
entretenerse *v.* to amuse oneself
entrevista *n.f.* interview
entristecerse *v.* to become saddened, grow sad, grieve
entristecido *adj.* saddened
entusiasmarse *v.* to feel enthusiasm
entusiasmo *n.m.* enthusiasm
enunciar *v.* to enunciate
enviado *adj., past part. of* **enviar**
enviar *v.* to send
envolver *v.* to wrap
episodio *n.m.* episode
época *n.f.* epoch, era, age; **por esta época**/at that period of time
equipaje *n.m.* equipment, luggage, baggage
equipo *n.m.* team
equivocarse *v.* to be mistaken
era, eres *v. forms of* **ser**
erguir *v.* to erect, set up straight; **erguirse** *v.* to straighten up, sit up straight, stand erect
erigir *v.* to erect, found, establish, elevate, raise
ermita *n.f.* hermitage
errante *adj.* errant, roving, wandering
errar *v.* to err, wander, roam, miss
error *n.m.* error, mistake
erudito *n.m.* scholar
esa *demons. adj., f.s.* that; **ésa** *dem. pron.* that one; *see also* §1.54, §66.56
esbelta *adj.* lithe, svelte, slender
escala *n.f.* scale
escalera *n.f.* stairs, stairway, staircase
escaparse *v.* to escape
escasez *n.f.* scarcity
escaso *adj.* scarce
escena *n.f.* scene
esclavo *n.m.* slave
escoba *n.f.* broom
escoger *v.* to choose, select
escolar *n.m.f.* school child; **escolares**/students, school children
esconder(se) *v.* to hide

escribiente *n.m.f.* clerk

escribir *v.* to write

escrito *past part. of* **escribir; por escrito**/in writing; *see also* §4.11(b), §58.17, §67.5, §67.31

escritor, escritora *n.m.f.* writer, author

escritorio *n.m.* desk

escuadrón *n.m.* squadron

escuchadas *adj.* listen to, heard

escuchar *v.* to listen (to)

escudero *n.m.* attendant, squire

escuela *n.f.* school

escultor, escultora *n.m.f.* sculptor

escultura *n.f.* sculpture

ese *demons. adj., m.s.* that; **ése** *dem. pron.* that one; *see also* §1.54, §66.56

esencial *adj.* essential

esforzar *v.* to strengthen; **esforzarse** *v.* to force oneself, make an effort

esfuerzo *n.m.* effort

eso *neuter pron.* that; **por eso**/therefore; **a eso de las tres**/at about three o'clock; *see also* §1.54, §66.56, §66.58

espacio *n.m.* space

espacioso *adj.* spacious, large

espada *n.f.* sword

espalda *n.f.* back (of shoulders)

espantar *v.* to drive away, chase away, frighten away, scare

espantarse *v.* to become frightened

espanto *n.m.* terror, shock, dread

espantosa *adj.* dreadful

España *n.f.* Spain

español, español *adj.* Spanish, Spaniard; *n.m.* Spanish language; **todo español**/all Spanish people; **a la española**/Spanish style

esparcir *v.* to scatter, spread

especial *adj.* special

especializado *adj.* specialized; **especialista** *n.m.f.* specialist

especialmente *adv.* especially

específico *adj.* specific

espectáculo *n.m.* spectacle, theatrical presentation, show

espectador, espectadora *n.m.f.* spectator

especular *v.* to speculate

espejo *n.m.* mirror

espera *n.f.* expectation, waiting, hope

esperanza *n.f.* hope

esperar *v.* to wait (for), hope, await, expect; **la sala de espera**/waiting room; **se espera**/it is hoped

espeso *adj.* thick, dense

espiar *v.* to spy (on)

espíritu *n.m.* spirit

espontaneidad *n.f.* spontaneity

espontáneo *adj.* spontaneous

esposa *n.f.* wife; **esposo** *n.m.* husband; **esposos** *n.m.pl.* husband and wife, couple, Mr. and Mrs.

esquimal *n.m.f., adj.* Eskimo

esquina *n.f.* corner (outside, as a street corner); **el rincón**/corner (inside, as in a room)

esta *dem. adj. f.s.* this; **ésta** *dem. pron.* this one; *see also* §1.54, §66.56, §66.59

está, están *v. forms of* **estar; el niño no está**/the child is not all there (there is something wrong with this child)

estable *adj.* stable

establecer *v.* to establish; **establecerse** *v.* to settle down

establecimiento *n.m.* establishment

establo *n.m.* stable (for animals)

estación *n.f.* station, season

estadio *n.m.* stadium

estadísticas *n.f. pl.* statistics

estado *n.m.* state, condition; *also past part. of* **estar; los Estados Unidos**/the United States

estadounidense *adj.* of or pertaining to the United States (American)

estallar *v.* to break out

estamos *v. form of* **estar**

estancia *n.f.* stay, sojourn

estante *n.m.* shelf, bookcase

estaño *n.m.* tin

estar *v.* to be; *see also* **estar** in idioms §53.11; also consult the general index

estatua *n.f.* statue

este *n.m.* East; *also dem. adj. m.s.* this; **éste** *dem. pron. m.s.* this one; *see also* §1.54, §66.56ff, §66.58ff

esté *v. form of* **estar**

estéril *adj.* sterile

estilo *n.m.* style

estimable, estimado *adj.* esteemed

estimar *v.* to estimate, esteem, respect, value; **se estimó**/it was estimated

estimular *v.* to stimulate

esto *neuter pron.* this; **por esto**/for this reason; *see also* §1.54, §66.56ff, §66.58ff

estómago *n.m.* stomach

estoy *v. form of* **estar**

estrechar *v.* to press, tighten, squeeze

estrecharse *v.* to become friendlier, more understanding, more intimate

estrecho *adj.* narrow, tight; *n.m.* strait

estrella *n.f.* star

estremecer *v.* to shake, tremble; **estremecerse** *v.* to shudder

estremecido *adj.* shaken, trembling

estridente *adj.* strident

estructura *n.f.* structure

estuco *n.m.* stucco

estudiante *n.m.f.* student

estudiar *v.* to study

estudio *n.m.* study; **estudioso** *adj.* studious

estupefactos *adj.* stupefied

estupendo *adj.* stupendous

estuve, estuvieron *v. forms of* **estar**

etapa *n.f.* phase, stage

eterno *adj.* eternal

Europa *n.f.* Europe

europea, europeo *adj.* European, of or pertaining to Europe

evaluación *n.f.* evaluation

evidente *adj.* evident

evitar *v.* to avoid

evolución *n.f.* evolution

exactamente *adv.* exactly

exacto *adj.* exact

examen *n.m.* exam, examination, test

examinar *v.* to examine

exangüe *adj.* lifeless, bloodless

exasperado *adj.* exasperated

excelente *adj.* excellent

excepto *adv.* except, excepting

excitante *adj.* exciting

exclamación *n.f.* exclamation

exclamar *v.* to exclaim

exclusivo *adj.* exclusive

excursión *n.f.* excursion

excusarse *v.* to excuse oneself

exhibición *n.f.* exhibit, exhibition

exhibir *v.* to exhibit

exigir *v.* to demand, insist, require, urge

exilado *adj.* exiled

existencia *n.f.* existence

existente *adj.* existent, existing, extant

existir *v.* to exist

éxito *n.m.* success; **tener éxito**/to be successful

expansión *n.f.* expansion

expectación *n.f.* expectation

expedición *n.f.* expedition

experiencia *n.f.* experience

experimentación *n.f.* experimentation

experimentar *v.* to experiment, experience

explicación *n.f.* explanation

explicar *v.* to explain

exploración *n.f.* exploration

explorador, exploradora *n.m.f.* explorer

explosión *n.f.* explosion

explotación *n.f.* exploitation

exponer *v.* to expose, expound
exportar *v.* to export
exposición *n.f.* exposition, exhibit
expresar *v.* to express
expresión *n.f.* expression
expresivamente *adv.* expressively, affectionately, warmly
expreso *n.m.* express (train)
expulsar *v.* to expel
extender *v.* to extend; **extenderse** *v.* to extend, spread
extensión *n.f.* extension, extent, expanse, area, space
extenso *adj.* extensive
exterior *adj.* external; *n.m.* exterior
extinguir *v.* to extinguish, put out (light, flame)
extracción *n.f.* extraction
extracto *n.m.* extract
extranjero, extranjera *n.m.f.* foreigner, stranger; *adj.* foreign
extrañar *v.* to be strange
extrañarse *v.* to be amazed at, to wonder at
extraño *adj.* strange, foreign; **lo extraño**/the strange thing
extraordinariamente *adv.* extraordinarily
extraordinario *adj.* extraordinary
extravagante *adj.* extravagant
extremo *adj.* extreme; *n.m.* end, tip, extremity; **en extremo**/extremely
exudar *v.* to exude
exultar *v.* to exult

F

fábrica *n.f.* factory
fabricación *n.f.* manufacture
fabricar *v.* to manufacture, make
facción *n.f.* faction, opposing group
facciones *n.f.pl.* facial features
fácil *adj.* easy; *see also* §65
fácilmente *adv.* easily
facturar *v.* to bill, invoice
facultad *n.f.* faculty
fachada *n.f.* façade
falda *n.f.* skirt
falso, falsa *adj.* false
falta *n.f.* error, mistake, fault, lack; **sin falta**/without fail; **hacer falta**/to be lacking
faltar *v.* to be lacking, wanting, to need, lack, miss, need; *see also* §63.25, §66.20
falte *v. form of* **faltar**
falla *n.f.* defect, flaw
fallecer *v.* to die
fama *n.f.* fame, reputation
familia *n.f.* family

familiares *n.m.pl.* familiar persons
famoso *adj.* famous
fanático *adj.* fanatic, fanatical
fantásticas *adj.* fantastic
farmacéutico, farmacéutica *n.m.f.* pharmacist
farmacia *n.f.* pharmacy, drug store
faro *n.m.* lighthouse, headlight; **farol** *n.m.* lantern
fase *n.f.* phase
fatiga *n.f.* fatigue
fatigar *v.* to fatigue, tire
favor *n.m.* favor; **por favor**/please
favorecer *v.* to favor
favorito, favorita *adj.* favorite
fe *n.f.* faith
fea *adj.* ugly
febrero *n.m.* February
fecha *n.f.* date; **fechado** *adj.* dated
felices *pl. of* **feliz**
felicidad *n.f.* felicity, happiness
felicitaciones *n.f.pl.* congratulations
felicitar *v.* to congratulate; **felicitarse**/to congratulate oneself
feliz *adj.* happy
femenino, femenina *adj.* feminine
fenomenal *adj.* phenomenal
feo *adj.* ugly
feria *n.f.* fair
feroz *adj.* ferocious
ferrocarril *n.m.* railroad
ferrocarrilero, ferroviario *n.m.* railroad worker
fervoroso *adj.* fervent
festejar *v.* to feast, entertain, celebrate
fiar *v.* to confide, intrust; **fiarse de**/to trust
fiebre *n.f.* fever
fiel *adj.* faithful
fiesta *n.f.* party, festival, holiday, celebration; **un día de fiesta**/holiday
fiestecita *n.f.* small party
figura *n.f.* figure, shape
figurar *v.* to figure
figurarse *v.* to figure out, to imagine, picture
figurilla *n.f.* figurine
fijado *adj.* fixed, set
fijar *v.* to fix, settle, set, clinch, fasten
fijarse *v.* to fix itself (oneself), take notice, pay attention, note, notice; **fijarse en**/to notice, stare
fijo, fija *adj.* fixed, firm, set
fila *n.f.* row
filipino *n.m., adj.* of or pertaining to the Philippines
filósofo *n.m.* philosopher
fin *n.m.* end; **a fin de**/in order to; **a**

fin de que/so that, in order that; **a fines de**/at the end of; **al fin**/finally, at last; **al fin y al cabo**/in the long run; **por fin**/finally, at last
final *adj.* end, final; **al final de**/at the end of
finalmente *adv.* finally
financiera *adj.* financial
finca *n.f.* farm, ranch
fingir *v.* to pretend, feign
finísima *adj.* very fine
fino, fina *adj.* delicate, fine
firmamento *n.m.* firmament, sky
firmar *v.* to sign
firme *adj.* firm
firmemente *adv.* firmly
físico, física *adj.* physical
flaco *adj.* skinny, thin, weak
flagelar *v.* to flagellate, whip
flojo *adj.* lazy, indolent
flor *n.f.* flower
florecer *v.* to flourish
florería *n.f.* flower shop
florista *n.m.f.* florist
flota *n.f.* fleet
fluir *v.* to flow
folklórico *adj.* folkloristic
follaje *n.m.* foliage
fomentar *v.* to foment, foster, promote
fonda *n.f.* inn, small restaurant
fondo *n.m.* depth, bottom; **a fondo**/thoroughly
fondos *n.m.pl.* funds
forastero *n.m.* stranger, foreigner
forma *n.f.* form
formal *adj.* formal, polite
formar *v.* to form, constitute, shape, develop; **se forma**/is formed
formular *v.* to formulate
fortaleza *n.f.* fortress, fort
fortificadas *adj.* fortified
fortificarse *v.* to fortify oneself (itself)
fortuna *n.f.* fortune
forzado *adj.* forced
forzar *v.* to force
forzoso *adj.* inevitable, necessary
fósforo *n.m.* match
foto *n.f.* photo, picture; **sacar fotos**/to take pictures
fotografía *n.f.* photograph, photography
fracaso *n.m.* failure
franca *adj.* frank
francamente *adv.* frankly
francés, francesa *adj.* French; *n.m.* French language
Francia *n.f.* France
franqueo *n.m.* postage
frase *n.f.* sentence, phrase

frazada *n.f.* blanket
frecuencia *n.f.* frequency; **con frecuencia**/frequently; *see also* idioms with **con** §53.4
frecuente *adj.* frequent
freír(se) *v.* to fry
frente *n.m.* front, forehead; **al frente**/in front, out front; **frente a, frente de, en frente**/opposite, across; **frente a frente**/face to face; **hacer frente a**/to confront, to face
fresa *n.f.* strawberry
fresco, fresca *adj.* fresh, cool; *n.m.* fresco painting; **hacer fresco**/to be cool weather; *see also* weather expressions §36.2, §64.ff
fría *adj.* cold
frialdad *n.f.* coldness, coolness
fríamente *adv.* coldly
frío *n.m.* cold; **hacer frío**/to be cold weather; **tener frío**/to feel cold (person); *see also* **tener** in idioms §53.27 and weather expressions §36.2, §64.ff
frontera *n.f.* frontier
fruta *n.f.* fruit
fruto *n.m.* benefit, consequence
fue *v. form of* **ser, ir**
fuego *n.m.* fire
fuente *n.f.* fountain
fuera *v. form of* **ir, ser;** *also adv.* outside, out
fuere, fueres, fueron *v. forms of* **ser, ir**
fuerte *adj.* strong
fuertemente *adv.* vigorously
fuerza *n.f.* force, strength
fugaces *pl. of* **fugaz** *adj.* fleeting
fui, fuimos *v. forms of* **ser, ir**
fumar *v.* to smoke
función *n.f.* function, performance (theatrical)
funcionar *v.* to function, (mechanical)
funcionario *n.m.* official
fundación *n.f.* foundation
fundador *n.m.* founder
fundar *v.* to found, establish
furia *n.f.* fury
fusil *n.m.* gun, rifle
fusilar *v.* to shoot
fútbol *n.m.* football, soccer
fútil *adj.* futile
futilidad *n.f.* futility
futuro *n.m., adj.* future

G

gala *n.f., adj.* finery, gala, festal, festive
galería *n.f.* gallery

gallego *n.m., adj.* of or pertaining to Galicia
gallina *n.f.* hen
gallo *n.m.* rooster
gana *n.f.* desire, inclination, appetite; **de buena gana**/willingly, with pleasure; **de mala gana**/unwillingly; **tener ganas de + inf.**/to feel like, have a desire to
ganada *adj.* earned; **ganado** *past part. of* **ganar**
ganadería *n.f.* cattle raising, animal husbandry
ganadero *n.m.* rancher
ganado *n.m.* cattle; *also past part. of* **ganar**
ganador, ganadora *n.m.f.* winner
ganancia *n.f.* profit, gain
ganar(se) *v.* to earn, gain, win; **ganada**/earned
gangas *n.f.* bargains
garantizar *v.* to guarantee
gaseosa *n.f.* soda pop, carbonated drink
gasolina *n.f.* gasoline
gastar *v.* to spend (money); *see also* §24.2
gasto *n.m.* cost, expense, expenditure
gatito *n.m.* kitten
gato *n.m.* cat
gemir *v.* to grumble, moan, groan, howl, grieve
generación *n.f.* generation
general *n.m., adj.* general; **por lo general**/generally, usually; *see also* **por** in idioms §53.22
generalmente *adv.* generally
género *n.m.* merchandise, textile, goods, gender, kind, class, type
generosidad *n.f.* generosity
generoso *adj.* generous
genio *n.m.* genius, temperament, mood
gente *n.f.* people; **las gentes**/the people, inhabitants, persons
genuino *adj.* genuine
geografía *n.f.* geography
gerente *n.m.* manager
gesto *n.m.* gesture; **gesto a gesto**/gesture by gesture
gimen, gimió *v. forms of* **gemir**
girar *v.* to rotate, turn
gitano, gitana *n.m.f.* gypsy
gloria *n.f.* glory
gloriosamente *adv.* gloriously
glorioso *adj.* glorious
gobernador *n.m.* governor
gobernar *v.* to govern, rule
gobierno *n.m.* government
gocé *v. form of* **gozar**

golpe *n.m.* blow, hit, attack, stroke
golpear *v.* to strike, hit, beat
golpetazo *n.m.* knock, knocking, blow
gordito *adj.* chubby
gordo, gorda *adj.* fat, plump, stout; **el premio gordo**/first prize
gorila *n.m.* gorilla
gorra *n.f.* cap (hat)
gota *n.f.* drop (of liquid)
góticas *adj.* Gothic
gozar de *v.* to enjoy
gozo *n.m.* joy; *also v. form of* **gozar**
grabar *v.* to engrave
gracia *n.f.* grace, favor, joke; **no estar para gracias**/not to be in the mood for jokes; **hacer gracia**/to be funny; **gracias**/thanks; **muchas gracias**/many thanks, thank you very much; **gracias a**/thanks to; **dar las gracias**/to thank
grado *n.m.* degree, grade, rank
graduado, graduada *adj.* graduate, graduated
gramática *n.f.* grammar
gran, grande *adj.* large, big, great; **gran cosa**/much, very much; **no es gran cosa**/it's not very much; *see also* §1.15, §1.22
grandemente *adv.* largely, grandly
grandeza *n.f.* size, greatness
granero *n.m.* granary, barn, haystack
gratificación *n.f.* gratification, bonus
gratis *adv.* free, gratis
gratitud *n.f.* gratitude
gratuitamente *adv.* gratuitously, free of charge
grave *adj.* grave, serious
gravedad *n.f.* gravity, seriousness
griego, griega *n.m.f., adj.* Greek; **el griego**/Greek language
gris *n.m., adj.* gray
gritar *v.* to shout, scream, shriek, cry out
grito *n.m.* cry, shouting; **a grito pelado**/at the top of one's lungs; **dar gritos**/to shout; *see also* **dar** in idioms §53.6
Groenlandia *n.f.* Greenland
grotesca *adj.* grotesque
grueso *adj.* stout, thick
gruñir *v.* to grumble, grunt, growl, creak
grupito *n.m.* little group
grupo *n.m.* group
guante *n.m.* glove
guapo, guapa *adj.* handsome, pretty
guardar *v.* to keep, guard; **guardar cama**/to stay in bed
guardarse de *v.* to guard against

Consult the Comprehensive Index for additional § references.

guardia *n.f.* guard; *n.m.* policeman
guatemalteco *n.m.*, *adj.* of or pertaining to Guatemala
guerra *n.f.* war
guerrillero *n.m.* guerrilla fighter
guía *n.m.* guide; *n.f.* guide book
guiar *v.* to guide, lead, drive
guisante *n.m.* pea
guisar *v.* to cook
guitarra *n.f.* guitar
guitarrista *n.m.f.* guitarist
gustar *v.* to be pleasing to, like, taste; *see also* §24.2ff, §25
gusto *n.m.* pleasure, taste; **con mucho gusto**/with much pleasure, gladly
gustoso *adj.* tasty, enjoyable
gutural *adj.* guttural

H

ha *v. form of* **haber;** for words beginning with stressed **ha** or **a** see §4.6
haber *v.* to have (as a helping verb); see **haber** in idioms §53.12
había *v. form of* **haber**
hábil *adj.* skillful
habilidad *n.f.* skill
habitación *n.f.* room, dwelling
habitante *n.m.f.* inhabitant
habitar *v.* to inhabit, live, dwell, reside
hábito *n.m.* habit, clothing, attire
hablador, habladora *n.m.f.* talker; *adj.* talkative
hablar *v.* to speak, talk
habrá *v. form of* **haber**
hace *v. form of* **hacer; hace algún tiempo**/some time ago; **no hace mucho**/not long ago; **hace un año**/one year ago; **hace muchísimo tiempo**/a long time ago; **desde hace mucho tiempo**/for a long time
hacer *v.* to do, make; **se hace**/is made; **hacer falta**/to be lacking; **hacer compras**/to do shopping, **hacerse** *v.* to become, make oneself (itself); **hacerse cargo de**/to realize, take over, take charge; *see also* **hacer** and **hacerse** in idioms §53.13
hacia *prep.* toward; **hacía** *v. form of* **hacer**
hacienda *n.f.* estate, large ranch, home
hacha *n.f.* ax **(el hacha)**; see §4.6
haga *v. form of* **hacer**
halagar *v.* to flatter

hallar *v.* to find; **hallarse** *v.* to be found, located, to find oneself, to be; **se halla**/is found
hambre *n.f.* hunger **(el hambre)**; *see* §4.6; *see also* idioms with **tener** §53.27
han *v. form of* **haber; han de**/they have to; *see* **haber** in idioms §53.12
haré, *v. form of* **hacer**
has *v. form of* **haber**
hasta *adv.* until, up to, even; **hasta que** *conj.* until; *see also* §7.ff, §53.14
hay *idiomatic v. form of* **haber;** there is, there are; **hay que**/it is necessary; *see also* §8., §27.ff, §64.2
haz *v. form of* **hacer**
hazaña *n.f.* good deed, feat, exploit
hazlo/do it
hazte/become; *v. form of* **hacerse**
he *v. form of* **haber;** also, *interj.* behold; **he allí**/here you have
hecho *n.m.* deed, fact; **de hecho**/in fact; also, *past part. of* **hacer; hechos** *adj.* made
helado *n.m.* ice cream
helar *v.* to freeze
hembra *n.f.* female
hemos *v. form of* **haber**
heraldo *n.m.* herald
heredar *v.* to inherit
herencia *n.f.* inheritance
herida *n.f.* wound; **herido** *adj.* wounded
herir *v.* to wound, harm, hurt
hermano, hermana *n.m.f.* brother, sister; **los hermanos**/brothers, brothers and sisters
hermosísimo *adj.* very handsome
hermoso, hermosa *adj.* beautiful
hermosura *n.f.* beauty
héroe *n.m.* hero
heroico, heroica *adj.* heroic
heroína *n.f.* heroine
heroísmo *n.m.* heroism
hervir *v.* to boil
hice, hiciera, hicieron, hiciste *v. forms of* **hacer**
hidráulica *adj.* hydraulic
hielo *n.m.* ice
hierba *n.f.* grass
hierro *n.m.* iron
hija *n.f.* daughter
hijo *n.m.* son; **hijos**/children, sons, sons and daughters
hilo *n.m.* thread
hispánico *adj.* Hispanic
Hispanoamérica *n.f.* Spanish America
hispanoamericano *adj.* Spanish American
historia *n.f.* history, story

historiador *n.m.* historian
histórico *adj.* historic, historical
hizo *v. form of* **hacer**
hogar *n.m.* home, house, hearth, fireplace
hoja *n.f.* leaf, sheet of paper
¡hola! *interj.* Hi! Hello!
holandeses *adj.* Dutch
holgazán *n.m.* idler, loafer
hombre *n.m.* man
hombro *n.m.* shoulder; **encogerse de hombros**/to shrug one's shoulders
homenaje *n.m.* homage
hondo *n.m.* depth, bottom; *adj.* deep
honorario *adj.* honorary
honrado *adj.* honorable, honored, honest
honrar *v.* to honor
hora *n.f.* hour, time; *see also* §36.1
horario *n.m.* timetable, schedule
horizonte *n.m.* horizon
horóscopo *n.m.* horoscope
horroroso *adj.* horrible, horrid
hospedería *n.f.* hostel, inn
hotelero *n.m.* hotel manager
hoy *adv.* today; **hoy día**/nowadays; **de hoy en adelante**/from now on; **hoy mismo**/this very day
huaracino *n.m.*, *adj.* of or pertaining to Huaraz
hubiera, hubo *v. forms of* **haber;** *see also* §53.12, §68.65
huelga *n.f.* labor strike
huérfano, huérfana *n.m.f.* orphan
huerta *n.f.* vegetable garden
hueso *n.m.* bone, stone, pit (of fruit)
huésped *n.m.* guest
huevo *n.m.* egg
huido *past part. of* **huir** *v.* to flee, escape, run away, slip away; **huir de** *v.* to shun, avoid
humanidad *n.f.* humanity
humano *adj.* human
humedecer *v.* to moisten, dampen, lick
húmedo *adj.* humid
humilde *adj.* humble
humo *n.m.* smoke, fume, vapor
humor *n.m.* disposition, humor
hundir(se) *v.* to sink, plunge
huyeron *v. form of* **huir**

I

iba *v. form of* **ir**
iberoamericano *n.m.*, *adj.* Latin American
ida *n.f.* departure, going; **ida y vuelta**/round trip
idea *n.f.* idea

identidad *n.f.* identity
identificación *n.f.* identification
identificarse *v.* to identify oneself (itself)
idioma *n.m.* language; **un modismo**/an idiom, idiomatic expression
idiota *n.m.f.* idiot
iglesia *n.f.* church
ignorar *v.* to ignore, to be ignorant of, not to know
igual *adj.* equal, similar; **igual que a mí**/same with me
igualmente *adv.* equally, likewise
iluminado *adj.* illuminated, lighted
iluminar *v.* to light, illuminate
ilusión *n.f.* illusion
ilusionada *adj.* deluded, given to false hopes
ilustración *n.f.* illustration
ilustre *adj.* famous, illustrious
imagen *n.f.* image, statue
imaginación *n.f.* imagination
imaginar(se) *v.* to imagine
imaginario *adj.* imaginary
imitar *v.* to imitate
impaciencia *n.f.* impatience
impacientarse *v.* to become impatient
impaciente *adj.* impatient
impedir *v.* to hinder, impede, prevent
imperativo *n.m., adj.* imperative
imperio *n.m.* empire
impermeable *n.m.* raincoat
impide *v. form of* **impedir**
implorar *v.* to beg, entreat, implore
imponer(se) *v.* to impose; **se impone**/is imposed
importado *adj.* imported
importancia *n.f.* importance
importante *adj.* important; **lo importante**/the important thing
importar *v.* to import, to be important, to matter; **no importa**/it doesn't matter; **no me importa**/it's not important to me, I don't care; **poco importa**/it's of little importance
importunar *v.* to disturb
impresas *adj.* printed
impresionado *adj.* impressed; also *past part. of* **impresionar** *v.* to impress, make an impression
imprimir *v.* to imprint, impress, print, fix in the mind
improviso, improvisto *adj.* unforeseen; **de improviso, a la improvista**/suddenly, unexpectedly
impuesto *n.m.* tax; also *past part. of* **imponer**

impulso *n.m.* impulse
impusieron *v. form of* **imponer**
inauguración *n.f.* inauguration
inaugurar *v.* to inaugurate
incendiar *v.* to set on fire
incendio *n.m.* fire
incensario *n.m.* censer (which burns incense)
incidente *n.m.* incident
incienso *n.m.* incense (for burning in a censer)
incierto *adj.* uncertain
inclinación *n.f.* inclination
inclinar *v.* to bow, incline, tilt
incluir *v.* to enclose, include; **incluirse** *v.* to be included; **incluso**/included
incomodidad *n.f.* inconvenience, discomfort
incómodos *adj.* uncomfortable
incomprensión *n.f.* lack of understanding
increíble *adj.* incredible
indecible *adj.* inexpressible
indefinidamente *adv.* indefinitely
independencia *n.f.* independence
indiada *n.f.* multitude of Indians
indicación *n.f.* indication
indicado *adj.* indicated
indicar *v.* to indicate, point out
indicativo *n.m., adj.* indicative
indiecito *n.m.* little Indian boy
indiferencia *n.f.* indifference
indiferente *adj.* indifferent
indígena *n.m.f., adj.* indigenous, native
indio *n.m.* Indian
indiscutible *adj.* unquestionable
individuo *n.m.* individual, person
índole *n.f.* kind, nature, disposition
inducir *v.* to induce, influence, persuade
indudablemente *adv.* undoubtedly, indubitably
industria *n.f.* industry
inesperado *adj.* unexpected
inestabilidad *n.f.* instability
infancia *n.f.* infancy
infeliz *n.m.* wretch; *adj.* unhappy, unfortunate
infierno *n.m.* hell, inferno
infinitivo *n.m.* infinitive
infinito *adj.* infinite
inflexión *n.f.* inflection
influencia *n.f.* influence
influir *v.* to influence
informar *v.* to inform; **informarse** *v.* to find out, inform oneself
informe *n.m.* report; **informes** *n.m.pl.* information
infracción *n.f.* infraction

ingeniería *n.f.* engineering
ingeniero *n.m.* engineer
ingenio *n.m.* wit, talent
Inglaterra *n.f.* England
inglés, inglesa *adj.* English; **el inglés**/English language
ingrato *adj.* ungrateful
ingresos *n.m.pl.* income, revenue
inhabitable *adj.* uninhabitable
inhumano *adj.* inhuman
iniciación *n.f.* initiation, beginning
iniciar *v.* to initiate, begin, start
injusticia *n.f.* injustice
injustos *adj.* unjust
inmediatamente *adv.* immediately
inmediato *adj.* immediate
inmemorial *adj.* immemorial
inmensidad *n.f.* immensity
inmenso *adj.* immense, large
inmigración *n.f.* immigration
inmigrante *n.m.f.* immigrant
inmortal *adj.* immortal
inmóvil *adj.* motionless, still
innecesario *adj.* unnecessary
innegable *adj.* undeniable
innovación *n.f.* innovation
inocente *adj.* innocent
inolvidable *adj.* unforgettable
inquietante *adj.* disturbing
inquietarse *v.* to worry, feel disturbed
inquieto *adj.* uneasy, restless
inquietud *n.f.* restlessness, uneasiness
inscribir *v.* to inscribe, record; **inscribirse** *v.* to register, enroll
insignificante *adj.* insignificant
insinuar *v.* to insinuate
insistencia *n.f.* insistence
insistir (en) *v.* to insist (on, upon)
insoportable *adj.* unbearable
inspirar *v.* to inspire
instalación *n.f.* installation
instalar *v.* to install
instante *n.m.* instant; **al instante**/instantly, at once
instituto *n.m.* institute
instrucción *n.f.* instruction, learning
instructivo *adj.* instructional
instruir *v.* to instruct
instrumento *n.m.* instrument
integrar *v.* to integrate
inteligencia *n.f.* intelligence
inteligente *adj.* intelligent
intención *n.f.* intention
intensos *adj.* intense
intentar *v.* to attempt, try, intend
intercambio *n.m.* interchange
interés *n.m.* interest
interesados *adj.* interested; **los interesados**/those interested

interesante *adj.* interesting
interesar *v.* to interest; **interesarse** *v.* to be interested, interest oneself
interno *adj.* internal; **un colegio interno**/boarding school
interpretar *v.* to interpret; **intérprete** *n.m.f.* interpreter
interrogante *adj., adv.* in a questioning way
interrumpir *v.* to interrupt; **interrumpido**/interrupted
íntimo *adj., adv.* intimate, intimately
introducir *v.* to introduce
inundar *v.* to flood, inundate
inútil *adj.* useless
invadir *v.* to invade
inválido, inválida *n.m.f.* invalid (person)
invasión *n.f.* invasion
invasores *n.m.* invaders
inventar *v.* to invent
invento *n.m.* invention
investigación *n.f.* investigation, research
investigador, investigadora *n.m.f.* investigator, researcher
invierno *n.m.* winter
invitado, invitada *n.m.f.* guest
invitar *v.* to invite
involuntario *adj.* involuntary
inyección *n.f.* injection
ir *v.* to go; *see also* §23.1, §53.7, §66.38, §66.49, §68.14, §68.24, §68.30
ira *n.f.* anger, ire
iré, iremos *v. forms of* **ir**
irregularidad *n.f.* irregularity
irreligiosidad *n.f.* irreligiousness
irresponsable *adj.* irresponsible
irritar *v.* to irritate
irse *v.* to go away; *see also* §23.2, §68.14
isla *n.f.* island; **las Islas Canarias**/Canary Islands
isleño *n.m.* islander
Istanbul *n.m.* Istanbul (formerly Constantinople)
Italia *n.f.* Italy
italiano, italiana *adj.* Italian; **el italiano**/Italian language
itinerario *n.m.* itinerary
izquierdo, izquierda *adj.* left (opposite of right); **a la izquierda**/at (on, to) the left; **la izquierda**/left, left side, left hand

J

jabón *n.m.* soap
jamás *adv.* ever, never

jamón *n.m.* ham
jardín *n.m.* garden
jarrón *n.m.* vase
jaula *n.f.* cage
jefe *n.m.* chief, boss; **jefe del estado**/chief of state
jinete *n.m.* horseman
jornada *n.f.* journey, day's journey
joven *adj.* young; *n.m.f.* young person, young man, young woman
joya *n.f.* jewel
júbilo *n.m.* jubilation, joy
jubiloso *adj.* jubilant
juega, juego *v. forms of* **jugar; se juega**/one plays; **un juego**/a game
jueves *n.m.* Thursday
juez *n.m.* judge
jugador, jugadora *n.m.f.* player
jugar *v.* to play, play a game; *see also* §37.1
jugo *n.m.* juice
juguete *n.m.* toy
juguetón *adj.* playful
juicio *n.m.* judgment
julio *n.m.* July
junio *n.m.* June
juntar *v.* to join, unite, connect; **juntarse (con)** *v.* to assemble, join, get together with
junto *adj.* together, joined; **junto a**/next to, beside; **junto con**/together with
juntos, juntas *adj.* together
jurado *n.m.* jury
jurar *v.* to swear, vow, take an oath
justicia *n.f.* justice
justo *adj.* just, exact, right
juventud *n.f.* youth
juzgar *v.* to judge

K

kilogramo *n.m.* kilogram
kilómetro *n.m.* kilometer
klaxson *n.m.* automobile horn

L

la *def. art. f.s.* the; also, *pron.; see* §4.ff, §66.—§66.105
labio *n.m.* lip
laboratorio *n.m.* laboratory
laborioso *adj.* laborious, hard-working
labrador *n.m.* farmer
labrar *v.* to work on, build, carve
lado *n.m.* side; **al lado de**/next to, beside; **por un lado**/on the one hand; **por otro lado**/on the other hand

ladrar *v.* to bark (dog)
ladrillo *n.m.* brick
ladrón *n.m.* thief
lago *n.m.* lake
lágrima *n.f.* tear, tear drop
lamentación *n.f.* sorrow, lamentation
lamento *n.m.* lament
lámpara *n.f.* lamp
lana *n.f.* wool
lancha *n.f.* boat, launch
lanzar *v.* to throw, cast, hurl, fling; **lanzarse a**/to rush upon
lápiz *n.m.* pencil; **lápices**/pencils
largarse *v.* to go away, go far away
largo, larga, largos, largas *adj.* long
larguísima *adj.* very long
lástima *n.f.* pity, compassion; **¡Qué lástima!**/What a pity! What a shame!
lastimar *v.* to hurt, injure
lastimarse *v.* to hurt oneself, be sorry for, complain, regret
lata *n.f.* tin can
latín *n.m.* Latin
latinoamericano *adj.* Latin American
latitud *n.f.* latitude
lavar *v.* to wash; **lavarse** *v.* to wash oneself
léase/read
lección *n.f.* lesson
lector, lectora *n.m.f.* reader (person)
lectura *n.f.* reading
leche *n.f.* milk
lechero *n.m.* milkman
leer *v.* to read
legales *adj.* legal
legendario *adj.* legendary
legión *n.f.* legion
legumbre *n.f.* vegetable
leía, leímos *v. forms of* **leer; leído** *past part. of* **leer**
lejano *adj.* distant
lejos *adv.* far; **a lo lejos**/in the distance; **lejos de**/far from
lengua *n.f.* language, tongue; **sacar la lengua**/to stick out one's tongue
lenguaje *n.m.* language, speech
lentamente *adv.*, slowly
lente *n.m.f.* lens; **los lentes**/eyeglasses
lento *adj.* slow
leña *n.f.* firewood, kindling
leñador, leñadora *n.m.f.* woodcutter
león *n.m.* lion
letra *n.f.* letter (alphabet)
levantado *adj.* raised
levantándose *pres. part. of* **levantarse**

levantar v. to lift, raise, build, erect
levantarse v. to get up, stand up, rise; **se levanta**/it rises
ley n.f. law
leyenda n.f. legend, story
leyendo pres. part. of **leer**
leyó v. form of **leer**
liberadas adj. liberated; **liberar** v. to free, liberate
libertad n.f. liberty, freedom
libertador, libertadora n. liberator
libra n.f. pound
librar v. to free, liberate; **librarse** v. to escape
libre adj. free; **al aire libre**/in the open air, outdoors
librería n.f. bookstore
libro n.m. book
licencia n.f. license
líder n.m. leader
liga n.f. league
ligero adj. light (not heavy)
limitación n.f. limitation
limitado adj. limited
limitar v. to limit, restrict
límite n.m. border, boundary, limit
limón n.m. lemon
limonada n.f. lemonade
limosna n.f. alms, charity
limpiar v. to clean, wipe, cleanse, clear
limpiarse v. to clean oneself
límpiela/clean it
limpieza n.f. cleanliness
limpio adj. clean
linda, lindo adj. pretty
línea n.f. line
lingüístico adj. linguistic
linterna n.f. lantern, flashlight
líquido n.m. liquid
lista n.f. list
listo, lista adj. ready, clever; **estar listo**/to be ready; **ser listo**/to be clever
literario adj. literary
literatura n.f. literature
litro n.m. liter
lo pron. him, it; see §66.—§66.105; **lo que**/that which; see §66.93
lobo n.m. wolf
local n.m. location, place, premises
localidad n.f. locality
loco, loca n.m.f., adj. crazy, mad, fool, insane
lodo n.m. mud; see **hay** in weather expressions §64.ff
lograr v. to attain, get, obtain, procure, achieve; **lograr + inf.**/succeed in
lomo n.m. back of an animal
longitud n.f. length, longitude

lote n.m. lot, share
lotería n.f. lottery
luces pl. of **luz**
lucientes adj. lucid, shining
lucir v. to shine
lucha n.f. battle, struggle, fight, combat
luchar v. to fight, combat, struggle, strive, wrestle
luego adv. then, soon; **hasta luego**/see you later; **desde luego**/since then; **luego como, luego que**/as soon as; see also **luego** in idioms §53.16
lugar n.m. place, small village; **tener lugar**/to take place
lujo n.m. luxury
lujoso adj. luxurious
lumbre n.f. fire; brightness, light (from a burning fire)
luna n.f. moon; see also **hay** in weather expressions §64.ff
lunes n.m. Monday
luz n.f. light
luzco v. form of **lucir**

LL

llama n.f. flame, llama (animal)
llamada n.f. call; **llamado, llamada** adj. called, so-called
llamar v. to call, name; **llamar a la puerta**/to knock on the door
llamarse v. to be called, named
llano adj. smooth, flat; n.m. plain
llanta n.f. rim, tire, wheel (auto)
llanto n.m. crying, weeping, sobbing
llanura n.f. prairie, plain
llave n.f. key
llegada n.f. arrival
llegar v. to arrive; **llegar a**/to reach; **llegar a ser**/to become; **el llegar a ser**/becoming; see also §38.1
llena n.f. flood, overflow; adj. full, filled
llenado adj. full
llenar v. to fill; **llenarse** v. to be filled
lleno adj. filled, full; **llenos de**/full of, filled with
llevado adj. carried, taken, brought
llevar v. to bring, carry, carry away, take away, wear, bear, to take (a person somewhere); **llevar a cabo**/to succeed in, accomplish, carry out, bring about; **llevarse** v. to carry away; **llevarse bien con**/to get along well with; see also §39
llorar v. to cry, weep, whine; also n.m. crying, weeping

lloriquear v. to whine, whimper
lloro v. form of **llorar**; also n.m. weeping, crying
llorón n.m. weeper, whiner
llover v. to rain
lloviendo pres. part. of **llover**
lluvia n.f. rain; see also weather expressions §36.2, §64.ff

M

machete n.m. knife, machete
macho n.m., adj. male, he-man, macho, manly
madera n.f. wood
madre n.f. mother
madrileño adj. of or pertaining to Madrid
madrugada n.f. dawn, daybreak
madrugar v. to get up very early in the morning
maduro adj. mature, ripe
maestro, maestra n.m.f. master, teacher
magistrado n.m. magistrate
magnífico adj. magnificent
mago n.m. magician, wizard
maíz n.m. corn
majestad n.f. majesty
majestuoso adj. majestic
mal n.m. evil, grief, harm, illness; adv. badly, poorly; **mal vestido**/poorly dressed; see also §1.12, §1.20, §2.7
maldad n.f. wickedness
maldecir v. to curse
maldición n.f. curse
maldito adj. cursed
maleta n.f. suitcase, valise
maletón n.m. large, heavy suitcase
malgastar v. to waste, misuse
malhumorado adj. ill humored, in a bad mood, bad temper
malicioso adj. malicious
malo, mala adj. bad, evil, sick; n.m. bad one, bad, evil (person); **lo malo**/the bad thing; see also §1.12, §1.20, §2.7
maltratar v. to mistreat
mallorquino, mallorquina adj. of or pertaining to Mallorca
mamá n.f. mom, mother
manco adj. maimed, crippled
mancha n.f., spot, stain
mandado adj. sent; past part. of **mandar** v. to order, command, send
manejar v. to drive (a vehicle), to manage
manera n.f. manner; **de manera**

que/so that; **de todas maneras**/in any case, anyway, by all means; **de esta manera**/in this way

manga *n.f.* sleeve

manifestación *n.f.* manifestation

manifestar *v.* to manifest, show, declare

mano *n.f.* hand; **¡manos a la obra!** to work!

mansión *n.f.* mansion

manta *n.f.* blanket

mantel *n.m.* tablecloth

mantener *v.* to maintain, keep up, support, provide for

manténgase/maintain yourself

mantequilla *n.f.* butter

manzana *n.f.* apple; **manzano** *n.m.* apple tree

mañana *n.f.* morning; *adv.* tomorrow; **mañana por la mañana**/tomorrow morning; **por la mañana**/in the morning; **pasado mañana**/the day after tomorrow; *see also* **mañana** in idioms **§53.17**

mapa *n.m.* map

maquillarse *v.* to make up one's face, put make up on, put on cosmetics

máquina *n.f.* machine; **máquina de coser**/sewing machine; **máquina de escribir**/typewriter

maquinaria *n.f.* machinery

mar *n.m. or f.* sea

maravilla *n.f.* marvel, wonder

maravilloso *adj.* marvelous

marcar *v.* to mark, note, observe, designate

marcha *n.f.* march, course, progress; **ponerse en marcha**/to start (set) out

marchar *v.* to march, walk; **marcharse** *v.* to leave, go away, walk away

marido *n.m.* husband

marina *n.f.* marine, navy

marinero *n.m.* sailor

mariposa *n.f.* butterfly

marítima *adj.* maritime

mármol *n.m.* marble

marqués *n.m.* marquis

marquesa *n.f.* marchioness

Marte *n.m.* Mars

martes *n.m.* Tuesday

marzo *n.m.* March

mas *conj.* but

más *adv.* more, most; **lo más**/the more; **más bien**/moreover; **más tarde**/later; **cada vez más**/more and more; **más vale tarde que nunca**/better late than never; **lo más pronto posible**/as soon as

possible; *see also* **§1.40ff.**, **§45.**, and see this word in the general index

masa *n.f.* mass

mascar *v.* to chew

máscara *n.f.* mask

¡Mátala!/Kill it!

matar *v.* to kill

matemáticas *n.f.* mathematics

materia *n.f.* matter

matrimonio *n.m.* married couple, marriage

máxima *adj.* maximum

mayo *n.m.* May

mayor *adj.* major, important, greater, older, larger, main

mayordomo *n.m.* steward, major-domo, servant

mayores *n.m.pl.* grown-ups

mayoría *n.f.* majority

mazo *n.m.* mallet

me *pron.* me, to me, myself; *see also* **§66.—§66.105**

mecánica *n.f.* mechanics

mecánico *n.m.* mechanic

mecha *n.f.* wick

medalla *n.f.* medal

media *n.f.* stocking, sock; *adj.* half; **la Edad Media**/Middle Ages; *see also* **§63.7**

mediano *adj.* medium size

medianoche *n.f.* midnight

mediante *adj.* mediating; *prep.* by means of, through, with the help of

medicina *n.f.* medicine

médico *n.m.* doctor, physician; **médicos** *adj.* medical

medida *n.f.* measure

medio *n.m.* middle, method, way, means; **medios literarios**/literary circles; *adj.* half; *see also* **§40.1**

mediodía *n.m.* noon

medir *v.* to measure, compare, judge, weigh, scan (verses)

meditar *v.* to meditate, think

mejicano *n.m., adj.* of or pertaining to Mexico

mejilla *n.f.* cheek

mejor *adj., adv.* better, best; **todo lo mejor**/all the best; *see also* **§2.7**

mejorar *v.* to improve, become better

melocotón *n.m.* peach

memoria *n.f.* memory, recollection; **de memoria**/by heart, from memory

mencionar *v.* to mention

mendigo *n.m.* beggar

menester *n.m.* need; **ser menester**/to be necessary

menor *adj.* younger, youngest,

smaller, minor; **al por menor**/retail sale

menos *adv.* less, least; **cuando menos**/at least; **lo menos**/the least; **por lo menos**/at least; **a menos que**/unless; **echar de menos**/to miss; *see also* **§1.40ff** and this word in the general index

mensaje *n.m.* message

mensajero *n.m.* messenger

mentir *v.* to lie, tell a lie

mentira *n.f.* lie, falsehood

menudo *adj.* little, small, minute, petty; *n.m.* small change; **a menudo**/often

mercado *n.m.* market

mercancía, mercancías *n.f.* merchandise

merecer *v.* to deserve, merit

mérito *n.m.* merit

mes *n.m.* month; **al mes**/a month; **el mes próximo**/next month; **por mes**/by the month; *see also* **§6.3(d)**

mesa *n.f.* table

mesero *n.m.* waiter

meses *n.m.pl.* of **mes**

meseta *n.f.* plateau

mesón *n.m.* inn, tavern

mestizo *n.m., adj.* mestizo (a person of mixed blood)

meter *v.* to put, place, insert

metió *v. form of* **meter**

método *n.m.* method

metro *n.m.* meter, subway

metrópoli *n.f.* metropolis

mexicano *n.m., adj.* of or pertaining to Mexico

mezcla *n.f.* mixture

mezclar *v.* to mix

mi *poss. adj.* my; *see also* **§1.58**

micrófono *n.m.* microphone

miedo *n.m.* fear; **tener miedo**/to be afraid

miedosa *adj.* fearful, scary

miembro *n.m.* member, limb

mientras *adv., conj.* while, meanwhile, as, whereas; **mientras que**/while; **mientras tanto**/meanwhile, in the meantime; *see also* **§2.ff**, **§7.ff**

miércoles *n.m.* Wednesday

mil *n.m., adj.* one thousand; **miles**/thousands; *see also* **§4.19(a)**

milagro *n.m.* miracle

militar *n.m., adj.* military, soldier

milla *n.f.* mile

millares/thousands

millón *n.m.* million

mina *n.f.* mine

mínimo *n.m.* minimum

ministerio *n.m.* ministry

ministro *n.m.* minister

minoría *n.m.* minority

minuto *n.m.* minute

¡Mira!/Look!

mirada *n.f.* glance, look, facial expression

mirar *v.* to look (at), watch; **mirarse** *v.* to look at oneself

mire *v. form of* **mirar**

miseria *n.f.* misery, poverty

misericordia *n.f.* mercy, pity

misión *n.f.* mission

misionero *n.m.* missionary

mismo *adj.* same, very; **el mismo día**/the same day; **el día mismo**/the very day; **él mismo**/he himself; **lo mismo**/the same thing; *see also* **mismo** in idioms §53.18

misterio *n.m.* mystery

misterioso *adj.* mysterious

mitad *n.f.* half, middle; *see also* §40.2

mitin *n.m.* meeting

mito *n.m.* myth

moda *n.f.* fashion, style; **de última moda**/latest style

modal *n.m.* modal; **modales**/manners

modelar *v.* to model

modelo *n.m.* model, pattern

modesta *adj.* modest

modismo *n.m.* idiom, idiomatic expression

modo *n.m.* mode, manner, way, means; **de modo que**/so that, in order that, in such a way that; **de otro modo**/otherwise; **de ningún modo**/by no means, no way; **de este modo**/in this way; *see also* §7.ff

moho *n.m.* mildew, mold, must, rust

mojado *adj.* wet, drenched

mojar *v.* to wet

molestar *v.* to molest, bother, annoy, disturb

molestia *n.f.* bother, annoyance, trouble

monarca *n.m.* monarch, king

monasterio *n.m.* monastery

moneda *n.f.* coin, money

mono *n.m.* monkey

montaña *n.f.* mountain

montañoso *adj.* mountainous

montar *v.* to mount, get on

monte *v.* mountain

monumento *n.m.* monument

morder *v.* to bite, gnaw

moreno *adj.* dark hair, brunette, dark skin, brown

morir(se) *v.* to die

moro, mora *n., adj.* Moor, Moorish

mosca *n.f.* fly

mostrar *v.* to show, point out, appear

motivo *n.m.* motive, reason

moto *n.f.* short for **motocicleta**/motorcycle

movedizo, movediza *adj.* moving

mover *f.* to move, persuade, induce, shake, excite

moviendo *pres. part. of* **mover**

movimiento *n.m.* movement

movió *v. form of* **mover**

moza *n.f.* maid, girl

mozo *n.m.* young man, waiter, boy

muchacha *n.f.* girl

muchacho *n.m.* boy

muchedumbre *n.f.* crowd

muchísimo *adj.* many, very many, very much; *see also* §1.47ff

mucho, mucha *adj.* much, many, a great deal; *see also* §1.49, §2.5, §2.7

mudar *v.* to change; **mudarse** *v.* to move (from one place to another), change one's clothes, change one's place of residence

mudo *adj.* mute, silent, dumb

mueble *n.m.* piece (article) of furniture; **muebles**/furniture

muerde *v. form of* **morder**

muero *v. form of* **morir**

muerte *n.f.* death

muerto *past part. of* **morir**; died; *n.* dead man, **los muertos**/dead persons

muestra *v. form of* **mostrar**; *n.f.* show, presentation, sample

mujer *n.f.* woman

mula *n.f.* female mule; **mulo** *n.m.* male mule

muleta *n.f.* cape

multa *n.f.* penalty, fine

multiplicar *v.* to multiply

multitud *n.f.* multitude, crowd

mundial *adj.* world, world-wide

mundo *n.m.* world; **todo el mundo**/everybody, everyone

municiones *n.f.pl.* munitions

municipios *n.m.* municipalities

muñeco *n.m.*, **muñeca** *n.f.* doll

muralla *n.f.* wall, rampart

murieron *v. form of* **morir**

murmurar *v.* to murmur

muro *n.m.* thick, supporting wall

musa *n.f.* muse

museo *n.m.* museum

música *n.f.* music

músico *n.m.* musician; *adj.* musical

muslo *n.m.* thigh

musulmanas *adj.* Moslem

muy *adv.* very; *see also* §1.49, §2.5

N

nacer *v.* to be born

nacido *past part. of* **nacer**; born

nacimiento *n.m.* birth

nación *n.f.* nation, country; *see also* §18.

nacional *adj.* national

nacionalidad *n.f.* nationality

nacionalizar *v.* to nationalize

Naciones Unidas *n.f.* United Nations

nada *indef. pron.* nothing, not anything; *see also* §55.ff, §62.ff; also *v. form of* **nadar**

nadando *v. form of* **nadar**

nadar *v.* to swim

nadie *indef. pron.* no one, nobody, not anyone; *see also* §55.ff, §62.ff

naranja *n.f.* orange (fruit)

narices *n.f.pl.* nostrils

nariz *n.f.* nose

narración *n.f.* narration, story

narrador *n.m.* narrator

narrar *v.* to narrate

natal *adj.* native

naturaleza *n.f.* nature

naturalmente *adv.* naturally

navaja *n.f.* razor, folding blade, jacknife, razor clam

naval *adj.* naval, navy

nave *n.f.* ship, vessel

navegante *n.m.* navigator

navegar *v.* to sail, navigate

Navidad *n.f.* Nativity; **el día de Navidad**/Christmas Day

neblina *n.f.* fog; *see also* weather expressions §36.2ff, §64.ff

necesario *adj.* necessary, required

necesidad *n.f.* necessity, need

necesitar *v.* to need, necessitate, be necessary; **se necesita**/it is necessary

negar *v.* to deny; **negarse a** *v.* to refuse to, deny

negociante *n.m.* business person, merchant

negociar *v.* to negotiate

negocio *n.m.* business, business deal, transaction; **negocios** *n.m.pl.* business, businesses; **un hombre de negocios**/businessman

negro *n.m.*, *adj.* black

nena, nene *n.m.f.* baby, child

neoyorquino *n.m.*, *adj.* of or pertaining to New York

nerviosidad *n.f.* nervousness

nervioso *adj.* nervous

nevar *v.* to snow

ni *conj.* neither, nor, not (one); **ni . . . ni**/neither . . . nor; **ni si-**

quiera *adv.* not even; *see also* **§7.ff, §55.ff**

nicaragüense *adj.* of or pertaining to Nicaragua

nieto *n.m.* grandson; **nieta** *n.f.* granddaughter

nieva *v. form of* **nevar; nieve** *n.f.* snow

ningún, ninguno, ninguna *indef. pron., adj.* not any, not one, none; *see also* **§1.20ff, §55.ff**

niñez *n.f.* childhood

niñita *n.f.* little girl

niño, niña *n.m.f.* child; **niños/**children

nivel *n.m.* level

no *adv.* no, not; **no obstante/**notwithstanding; *see also* **no** in idioms **§53.19**

nobles *adj.* noble

noche *n.f.* night, evening; **esta noche/**tonight, this evening; *see also* **de** in idioms **§53.7** and **por** in idioms **§53.22**

nombrar *v.* to name

nombre *n.m.* name; **nombre de pila/**given name (first name)

normalizar *v.* to normalize

normalmente *adv.* normally

norte *n.m.* North

norteamericano *n.m., adj.* American, North American

nota *n.f.* note, bill, grade, mark

notable *adj.* noteworthy, notable

notar *v.* to note, notice, mark, remark, observe

noticia *n.f.* news, notice; **noticias** *n.f.pl.* news

novedad *n.f.* novelty, new thing

novela *n.f.* novel; **novela policíaca/**detective story, novel

novelista *n.m.f.* novelist

noventa *n.m., adj.* ninety

novicio *n.m.* novice, learner, beginner

noviembre *n.m.* November

novio, novia *n.m.* sweetheart, fiancé(e), bride, bridegroom; **novios/**sweethearts

nube *n.f.* cloud; *see also* weather expressions **§36.2ff, §64.ff**

núcleo *n.m.* nucleus

nudo *n.m.* knot

nueces *n.f.pl.* nuts, walnuts; *pl. of* **nuez**

nuestro, nuestra *poss. adj.* our; *see also* **§1.58ff, §66.64ff**

Nueva York/New York

nuevamente *adv.* again

nueve *n.m., adj.* nine

nuevo, nueva *adj.* new; **de nuevo/**again

nuez *n.f.* nut, walnut

número *n.m.* number; *see also* **§57.ff**

numeroso *adj.* numerous

nunca *adv.* never; **nunca jamás/**nevermore

nupcias *n.f.pl.* nuptials, wedding

nutrir *v.* to nourish, nurture

O

o *conj.* or; **o . . . o/**either . . . or; *see also* **§7., §50.**

obedecer *v.* to obey

objetivo *n.m.* objective, purpose; **objeto** *n.m.* object

obligación *n.f.* obligation

obligado *adj.* obligated

obligar *v.* to obligate, compel

obra *n.f.* work; **obra maestra/**masterpiece; **¡manos a la obra!** to work!

obrero *n.m.* worker

obscurecer *v.* to obscure, darken, cloud

obscuridad *n.f.* obscurity, darkness

obscuro *adj.* obscure, dark

observación *n.f.* observation

observar *v.* to observe; **observarse** *v.* to observe oneself (each other)

obstáculo *n.m.* obstacle

obstante *adv.* **no obstante/**nevertheless

obstruir *v.* to obstruct

obstruyeron *v. form of* obstruir

obtener *v.* to obtain, get

obtuvo *v. form of* **obtener**

ocasión *n.f.* occasion, opportunity

occidental *adj.* western

ocasionar *v.* to occasion, provoke

océano *n.m.* ocean

octava *adj.* eighth

octubre *n.m.* October

ocultar *v.* to hide

ocupación *n.f.* trade, occupation

ocupado *adj.* busy, occupied

ocupar *v.* to occupy; **ocuparse de/**to take care of, look after, be busy with

ocurrir *v.* to occur, happen

ochenta *n.m., adj.* eighty

ocho *n.m., adj.* eight

ochocientos *n.m., adj.* eight hundred

odiar *v.* to hate

odio *n.m.* hate, hatred

oeste *n.m.* West

ofender *v.* to offend

oferta *n.f.* offer

oficial *n.m.* official, officer

oficialmente *adv.* officially

oficina *n.f.* office

oficio *n.m.* craft, occupation, trade, job

ofrecer *v.* to offer; **ofreciéndole/**offering to him

ofrecimiento *n.m.* offer

oía *v. form of* **oír; oído** *past part. of* **oír**

oído *n.m.* hearing, ear; **de oídas/**hearsay

oír *v.* to hear; *see also* **§56.11**

ojal *n.m.* buttonhole

¡ojalá! *interj.* May God grant . . . ! I hope, I hope to God . . . ! *see also* **§67.67**

ojera *n.f.* eyecup

ojo *n.m.* eye

ola *n.f.* wave

oler *v.* to smell, scent

olor *n.m.* odor, smell

oloroso *adj.* fragrant, odorous

olvidado *adj.* forgotten

olvidar(se) *v.* to forget

omitir *v.* to omit; **omitido** *past part. and adj.* omitted

ómnibus *n.m.* bus

onza *n.f.* ounce

operación *n.f.* operation

operar *v.* to operate

opinar *v.* to have an opinion, think, opine

opinión *n.f.* opinion

oponer(se) *v.* oppose, be opposed, object

oportunidad *n.f.* opportunity, occasion

oportuno *adj.* opportune

optimismo *n.m.* optimism

opuesto *adj.* opposite, opposed

oración *n.f.* prayer, oration, speech, sentence

orador *n.m.* orator, speaker

orales *adj.pl.* oral

orar *v.* to pray

orden *n.m.* order, group; *n.f.* order, command; **órdenes/**orders

ordenar *v.* to order, command, put in order, arrange; **lo ordenado/**what was ordered

ordinario *adj.* ordinary

oreja *n.f.* ear

organizador, organizadora *n.m.f.* organizer

organizar *v.* to organize, set up

órgano *n.m.* organ

orgullo *n.m.* pride

orgulloso *adj.* proud

orientar *v.* to inform, orient, brief

orientarse *v.* to become informed

origen *n.m.* origin

Consult the Comprehensive Index for additional § references.

orilla *n.f.* bank, shore, edge (of a river)
oro *n.m.* gold
orquesta *n.f.* orchestra
osar *v.* to dare, venture
oscurecer *v.* to obscure, darken, cloud
oscuridad *n.f.* obscurity, darkness
oscuro *adj.* dark
oso *n.m.* bear
otoño *n.m.* autumn, fall
otro, otra *adj.* other, another; **otra vez**/again; **de otro modo**/otherwise; **otra cosa**/something else; *see also* §4.19(c)
oveja *n.f.* ewe, sheep
oxígeno *n.m.* oxygen
oye, oyen oyó *v. forms of* **oír**

P

pabellón *n.m.* pavilion
paciencia *n.f.* patience
paciente *n.m.f.* patient
pacto *n.m.* pact
padecer *v.* to suffer
padre *n.m.* father; **los padres**/mother and father, parents
paella *n.f.* rice with seafood, meat or chicken
pagar *v.* to pay (for); **se paga**/is paid
página *n.f.* page
país *n.m.* country, nation; *see also* §18.
paisaje *n.m.* countryside
paisanaje *n.m.* countryfolk, peasantry
paja *n.f.* straw
pajarito *n.m.* little bird
pájaro *n.m.* bird
palabra *n.f.* word; **palabra a palabra**/word by word
palacio *n.m.* palace
paleta *n.f.* palette
pálido *adj.* pale; **ponerse pálido**/to turn pale
paliza *n.f.* spanking
palmada *n.f.* handclap, slap
palo *n.m.* pole, stick
paloma *n.f.* dove, pigeon
pan *n.m.* bread
panadería *n.f.* bakery
panadero *n.m.* baker
panamericano *n.m., adj.* of or pertaining to Pan-America
pantalón *n.m.,* **pantalones**/pants, trousers
panza *n.f.* belly, paunch
paño *n.m.* cloth
pañuelo *n.m.* handkerchief
papá *n.m.* dad, papa

Papa *n.m.* Pope
papel *n.m.* paper; **hacer el papel de**/to play the role of; **papel secante**/blotter
paquete *n.m.* package, parcel
par *n.m.* pair, couple; **de par en par**/wide open
para *prep.* for, in order to, by; **para con**/toward, with, to; *see also* §62.15; **para que**/so that, in order that; *see also* §7., §52.ff, para in idioms §3.20 and this word in the general index
parado *adj.* stopped
paraguas *n.m.* umbrella
paralítica *adj.* paralyzed, paralytic
parar *v.* to stop (someone or something)
pararse *v.* to stop oneself
pardo *n.m., adj.* brown
parecer *v.* to seem, appear; **parecerse** *v.* to resemble each other, look alike, resemble; **al parecer**/apparently; **a mi parecer**/in my opinion; *see also* §66.12, §66.20
parecido *n.m.* likeness, resemblance; **bien parecido**/good-looking; *adj.* similar, like
pared *n.f.* wall
pareja *n.f.* couple
pariente *n.m.* relative
parque *n.m.* park
párrafo *n.m.* paragraph
parte *n.f.* part; **por todas partes**/everywhere; **de todas partes**/from everywhere
participación *n.f.* participation
participar *v.* to participate
particular *adj.* particular, private
partida *n.f.* departure
partidario *n.m.* partisan
partido *n.m.* game, political party
partir *v.* to leave, depart, divide, split
pasada *n.f.* passing, passage, pass; *adj.* past, last; **la semana pasada**/last week
pasado *n.m.* past; *adj.* past, last; **pasado mañana**/the day after tomorrow
pasaje *n.m.* passage
pasajero *adj.* fleeting, temporary, passing
pasajero, pasajera *n.m.f.* passenger
pasar *v.* to pass (spend time), pass by, go by, send, happen; **¡Que lo pases bien!**/Have a good time! *see also* §24.3
pasear(se) *v.* to stroll, promenade, take a walk, parade; **pasear en automóvil**/to go for a drive

paseo *n.m.* boulevard, avenue, walk, promenade; **dar un paseo**/to take a walk
paso *n.m.* step, way, lane, path, pace, pass
pasó *v. form of* **pasar**
pastel *n.m.* pie, pastry
pata *n.f.* paw
patata *n.f.* potato
patio *n.m.* patio, courtyard
patria *n.f.* native land; *see also* §18.
patriota *n.m.f.* patriot
patriótico *adj.* patriotic
patriotismo *n.m.* patriotism
patrón *n.m.* boss, employer, patron saint
pausadamente *adv.* in a pause, pausingly
pavo *n.m.* turkey
paz *n.f.* peace
pecado *n.m.* sin
peces *pl. of* **pez**
pecho *n.m.* chest, breast
pedazo *n.m.* piece
pedía *v. form of* **pedir; pedido** *past part. of* **pedir; lo pedido**/what was requested
pedir *v.* to request, ask for; **pedir prestado**/to borrow; *see also* §41.1, §66.12
pegar *v.* to beat, hit, slap, spank, attach, glue, stick
¡Péinala!/Comb it!
peinar *v.* to comb
peinarse *v.* to comb one's hair
peine *n.m.* comb
pelado *past part. of* **pelar** *v.* to pluck; **a grito pelado**/at the top of one's lungs
pelea *n.f.* fight, quarrel; **pelear** *v.* to fight, combat
película *n.f.* film, movie
peligro *n.m.* danger, peril
peligroso *adj.* dangerous, perilous
pelo *n.m.* hair
pelota *n.f.* ball; **jugar a la pelota**/to play ball
peluca *n.f.* wig
peluquería *n.f.* beauty salon, barber shop
peluquero *n.m.* barber, hairdresser
pena *n.f.* pain, sorrow, grief, trouble; **valer la pena**/to be worthwhile
penalidad *n.f.* penalty
pendiente *n.m.* earring
penetrar *v.* to penetrare
penetrente *adj.* penetrating
peninsulares *n.m.pl.* inhabitants of a peninsula
penoso *adj.* painful

pensamiento *n.m.* thought

pensar *v.* to think; **pensar en**/to think about; **se ha pensado**/it has been thought; **pensar de**/to think (have an opinion) of

pensativo *adj.* pensive, thoughtful

penumbra *n.f.* twilight

peor *adj., adv.* worse, worst; *see also* §2.7

pequeño *adj.* small, little; **pequeño, pequeña** *n.m.f.* little one, little boy, little girl; *see also* §46.2

pequeñito *adj.* tiny

pera *n.f.* pear

peral *n.m.* pear tree

percibir *v.* to perceive

perder *v.* to lose; **perder cuidado**/not to care, not to worry

perderse *v.* to be lost, become lost

pérdida *n.f.* loss; **perdido**/lost

perdón *n.m.* pardon

perdonar *v.* to pardon, excuse, forgive

peregrinación *n.f.* pilgrimage

peregrina, peregrino *n.f.m.* pilgrim

pereza *n.f.* laziness, sloth

perezoso *adj.* lazy

perfeccionar *v.* to perfect

perfeccionarse *v.* to perfect oneself

perfectamente *adv.* perfectly

perfecto, perfecta *adj.* perfect

pérfido *adj.* perfidious

periódico *n.m.* newspaper; *adj.* periodic, periodical

periodismo *n.m.* journalism

periodista *n.m.f.* journalist, newspaperman, newspaperwoman

periodístico *adj.* journalistic

período *n.m.* period

perla *n.f.* pearl

permanecer *v.* to remain, stay

permanencia *n.f.* sojourn, stay, permanence

permanentemente *adv.* permanently

permiso *n.m.* permit, permission

permitir *v.* to permit, admit, allow, grant; *see also* §56.8

pero *conj.* but; *see also* §7., §44.ff, §45.

perplejo *adj.* perplexed

perrillo, perrito *n.m.* little dog, doggie

perro *n.m.* dog

perseguido *adj.* persecuted

perseguir *v.* to persecute, pursue

persiga, persiguió *v. forms of* **perseguir**

persona *n.f.* person

personaje *n.m.* personage, character (in literature)

personal *n.m.* personnel, staff; *adj.* personal

personalidades *n.f.* personalities

personalmente *adv.* personally

perspectiva *n.f.* perspective

pertenecer *v.* to pertain, belong, appertain

perturbar *v.* to perturb, upset, disturb

peruano *n.m., adj.* of or pertaining to Peru

pesado *adj.* heavy

pesar *v.* to weigh, be heavy; **a pesar de**/in spite of; *n.m.* grief

pesca *n.f.* fishing

pescado *n.m.* fish

pescador *n.m.* fisherman

pescar *v.* to fish

peseta *n.f.* peseta (monetary unit of Spain)

peso *n.m.* weight, peso (monetary unit)

pestilente *adj.* pestilent

pétalo *n.m.* petal

petróleo *n.m.* petroleum

pez *n.m.* fish

pianista *n.m.f.* pianist

picaresco *adj.* picaresque

pícaro *n.m.* rascal, rogue

pico *n.m.* beak, peak

pide, pidiendo, pidiera, pido *v. forms of* **pedir**

pie *n.m.* foot; **a pie**/on foot; **de pie**/standing

piedad *n.f.* piety, mercy, pity

piedra *n.f.* stone

piel *n.f.* fur, skin, hide

piensa *v. form of* **pensar**

pierda *v. form of* **perder**

pierna *n.f.* leg

pieza *n.f.* room, piece, part

pila *n.f.* font (baptismal); **nombre de pila**/given (first) name of a person

pimienta *n.f.* black pepper; **pimiento** *n.m.* red pepper

pincel *n.m.* brush, paint brush (artist's)

pintar *v.* to paint

pintarse *v.* to make up (one's face), tint, color (one's hair, lips, *etc.*)

pinte *v. form of* **pintar**

pintor, pintora *n.m.f.* painter

pintoresco *adj.* picturesque

pintura *n.f.* painting

piña *n.f.* pineapple

pipa *n.f.* pipe (smoking)

pirámide *n.f.* pyramid

pisar *v.* to tread on, step on

piscina *n.f.* swimming pool

piso *n.m.* floor, story (of a building); **piso bajo**/ground floor

pizarra *n.f.* chalkboard

placer *v.* to gratify, humor, please, be pleasing; *n.m.* pleasure; *see also* §66.20

plácidamente *adv.* placidly, calmly

planchar *v.* to iron, press

planear *v.* to plan

planeta *n.m.* planet

planta *n.f.* plant; **planta baja**/ground floor

plata *n.f.* silver

plátano *n.m.* plane tree, plantain tree, banana

platicar *v.* to talk informally, chat

plato *n.m.* plate, dish

playa *n.f.* beach, seashore

plaza *n.f.* plaza, square

plazo *n.m.* term, installment

plazoleta *n.f.* small plaza

pleno *adj.* full; **en pleno**/right in the middle of; **en pleno día**/in broad daylight; **en pleno labor**/right in the middle of work

pluma *n.f.* feather, pen

pluscuamperfecto *n.m.* pluperfect

población *n.f.* population

pobre *adj.* poor; *n.m.f.* poor person, poor man, poor woman

pobrecillo, pobrecilla *n.m.f.* poor little person

pobrecito, pobrecita *n.m.f.* poor little child

pobretón *n.m.* poor wretch

pobreza *n.f.* poverty

poco, poca *adj.* small, little; *n.m.* a little bit; **a poco**/shortly, soon, in a little while; **a poco de**/soon after; **poco a poco**/little by little; **poco**/some; **pocos**/a few; **por poco**/almost; *see also* §2.7, §46.1, and **poco** in idioms §53.21

poder *v.* to be able, can; *n.m.* power; *see also* §47.ff

poderoso *adj.* powerful

podido, podrá *v. form of* **poder**

podrida *adj.* rotten

poema *n.m.* poem

poesía *n.f.* poetry, poem

poeta *n.m., poetisa* *n.f.* poet

poética *adj.* poetic

policía *n.m.* policeman; *n.f.* police

policíaco *adj.* police, mystery

política *n.f.* politics, policy; politician, woman of politics; *n.m.* **político**/man of politics, politician; *adj.* political

polvo *n.m.* dust, powder; **hay polvo**/it is dusty; **Estoy hecho polvo**/I've been beaten to a pulp

pollo *n.m.* chicken
pon *v. form of* **poner; ponte**/put on (**ponerse**)
poner *v.* to put, place; **poner la mesa**/to set the table; **ponerse** *v.* to wear, put on, become, set (of sun), begin, become, place oneself; **ponerse en marcha**/to start (set) out; **se pone**/is worn; **al ponerse el sol**/at sunset; **ponerse pálido**/to turn (become) pale; *see also* §38.2
ponga *v. form of* **poner; póngase**/put on (**ponerse**)
poquito *adj.* very little; **a poquitos**/bit by bit; **poquito a poco, poquito a poquito**/little by little
por *prep.* for, by, through, because of, on account of; **tres por cinco**/three times five; *see also* **por** in idioms §53.22 and **por** in the index for other uses
por qué *interrog. adv.* why
porcentaje *n.m.* percentage
porque *conj.* because; *see also* §7.ff
portal *n.m.* porch, gateway
portar *v.* to carry, bear arms
portarse *v.* to behave, conduct oneself
portero *n.m.* porter, gatekeeper
portón *n.m.* gate, large door
portugués, portuguesa *adj.* Portuguese; **el portugués**/Portuguese language
porvenir *n.m.* future
posada *n.f.* inn, tavern, lodging
poseer *v.* to possess, own
posesión *n.f.* possession
posibilidad *n.f.* possibility
posibilitar *v.* to make possible
posible *adj.* possible; **lo más pronto posible**/as soon as possible
posición *n.f.* position
positivo *adj.* positive
poste *n.m.* post, pole
posteriores *adj.* posterior
postre *n.m.* dessert
postura *n.f.* position
práctica *n.f.* practice; *adj.* practical
practicar *v.* to practice
precio *n.m.* price
precioso *adj.* precious
precisamente *adv.* precisely
preciso *adj.* precise, exact, necessary; **es preciso**/it is necessary
predecir *v.* to predict, forecast, foretell
predicar *v.* to make public, to make known publicly, preach
prefecto *n.m.* prefect, director
preferencia *n.f.* preference
preferentemente *adv.* preferably

preferida *adj.* preferred
preferir *v.* to prefer
pregunta *n.f.* question, query; **hacer una pregunta**/to ask a question
preguntar *v.* to ask, inquire, question; *see also* this verb in the index
preguntarse *v.* to ask oneself, to wonder
premiar *v.* to reward, decorate, give an award to
premio *n.m.* prize, reward; **el premio gordo**/first prize
prenda *n.f.* pledge
prendar *v.* to pledge, charm, please
prendarse *v.* to become enamored
prender *v.* to seize, arrest
prensa *n.f.* press (newspaper)
preocuparse *v.* to be concerned, to worry; **no te preocupes**/don't worry
preparar *v.* to prepare
prepararse *v.* to be prepared, get ready, prepare oneself
preparativos *n.m.* preparations
presencia *n.f.* presence
presenciar *v.* to witness, be present
presentar *v.* to present, introduce, display, show
presentarse *v.* to introduce oneself, present oneself (itself), appear
presente *n.m.* present
presidencia *n.f.* presidency
presidente *n.m.* president
presidir *v.* to preside, preside over
preso *adj.* caught up in, taken by, imprisoned
prestado *adj.* on loan; **dar prestado**/to lend; **pedir prestado**/to borrow, ask for a loan of
prestador *n.m.* lender
prestar *v.* to lend; **prestar atención**/to pay attention
presteza *n.f.* haste, promptness
pretérito *n.m.* preterit
primario *adj.* primary
primavera *n.f.* spring, springtime
primer, primero, primera *adj.* first; *see also* §1.20, §6.1
primo, prima *n.m.f.* cousin
princesa *n.f.* princess
principal *adj.* principal, main
principalmente *adv.* principally
príncipe *n.m.* prince
principiar *v.* to begin
principio *n.m.* beginning, principle; **a principios**/in (at) the beginning
prisa *n.f.* haste; **tener prisa**/to be in a hurry; **darse prisa**/to hurry; **tan de prisa**/in such a hurry
prisión *n.f.* prison
prisionero *n.m.* prisoner

privada *adj.* private
privar *v.* to deprive
pro *prefix* pro, in favor of
probar(se) *v.* to try, test, prove, try (on)
problema *n.m.* problem
procedente *adj.* originating, coming from
proceder *v.* to proceed
procedimiento *n.m.* proceeding, procedure
procesión *n.f.* procession
proceso *n.m.* process, proceedings, trial
proclamar *v.* to proclaim, promulgate
procurar *v.* to procure, secure, attempt, try, endeavor
prodigio *n.m.* prodigy
prodigioso *adj.* prodigious
producción *n.f.* production
producir *v.* to produce, cause
producto *n.m.* product
productora *adj.* productive
produjo *v. form of* **producir**
profesión *n.f.* profession
profesional *n.m.f., adj.* professional
profesionalmente *adv.* professionally
profesor, profesora *n.m.f.* professor, teacher
profesorado *n.m.* professorate, professorship
profundo *adj.* profound, deep
programar *v.* to program
progresar *v.* to progress, make progress
progreso *n.m.* progress
prohibir *v.* to prohibit, forbid
prolongación *n.f.* prolongation, extension
prolongar *v.* to prolong
promesa *n.f.* promise
prometer *v.* to promise
prometido *past part. of* **prometer; lo prometido**/what was promised
pronombre *n.m.* pronoun
pronóstico *n.m.* weather forecast
pronto *adv.* quickly, soon, right away; *adj.* fast, quick; **tan pronto como**/as soon as; **de pronto**/suddenly; *see also* **pronto** in idioms §53.23
pronunciar *v.* to pronounce, deliver a speech, make a speech, state, say
propia *adj.* own, proper
propiedad *n.f.* property
propietario, propietaria *n.m.f.* owner, proprietor
propina *n.f.* tip
propio *adj.* own, proper

proponer(se) *v.* to propose, resolve, determine, suggest
proporción *n.f.* proportion
proporcionar *v.* to provide, proportion, furnish
propósito *n.m.* proposal
proseguir *v.* to continue, prosecute
próspero *adj.* prosperous
protección *n.f.* protection
proteger *v.* to protect
protestar *v.* to protest
provecho *n.m.* profit, advantage
provenir *v.* to originate, come from
proverbio *n.m.* proverb
proviene *v. form of* **provenir**
provincia *n.f.* province
provinciana *adj.* provincial
provocar *v.* to provoke
próxima *adj.* close, near, nearby, next; **el mes próximo**/next month
proyecto *n.m.* plan, project
proyector *n.m.* projector
prudente *n.m.* prudent, wise
prueba *v. form of* **probar**; *n.f.* proof, trial, test
psicológico *adj.* psychological
publicación *n.f.* publication
públicamente *adv.* publicly
publicar *v.* to publish
público *adj.* public; *n.m.* public, audience
pudo *v. form of* **poder**
pueblecito *n.m.* small town
pueblo *n.m.* town, people
puede *v. form of* **poder**; **se puede decir**/it can be said; **se puede**/it can be, it is possible; *see also* §68.65
puente *n.m.* bridge
puerta *n.f.* door
puerto *n.m.* port
puertorriqueño *n.m., adj.* of or pertaining to Puerto Rico
pues *adv., conj.* well, since, then; **pues bueno**/well now, well then
puesta *n.f.* setting; *adj.* placed, wearing of a garment; **puesta del sol**/sunset
puesto *adj.* placed, put; *past part. of* **poner**; *n.m.* post, station, position, place, job; **puesto que** *conj.*/since, although, inasmuch as, as long as; *see also* §7.ff
pugnar *v.* to strive, struggle, persist, be obstinate
pulida *adj.* polished
pulir *v.* to polish
pulmón *n.m.* lung
pulsera *n.f.* bracelet, wristlet; **un reloj pulsera**/wrist watch
pulso *n.m.* pulse
punta *n.f.* tip, edge

punto *n.m.* period, point, dot; **en punto**/sharp; **estar a punto de**/to be about to; *see also* **estar** in idioms §53.11
puntualidad *n.f.* punctuality
puño *n.m.* fist
pupitre *n.m.* student's desk
pusiera, puso *v. forms of* **poner**

Q

que *conj.* than; *rel. pron.* which, who, what, whom, that; *interrog. pron.* **qué**/what; **sí que**/certainly; **que** is sometimes used for **porque**; *see also* §7.ff and **que** in the index
quebrar *v.* to break
quedar(se) *v.* to remain, stay; **quedar en**/to agree; **quedarle algo a alguien**/to have something remaining to someone; **quedarse con**/to keep; *see also* §58.23, §66.20
queja *n.f.* complaint
quejarse *v.* to complain, grumble
quemar *v.* to burn, fire
querer *v.* to wish, want, love; **querer decir**/to mean; *see also* **querer** in the index
quería *v. form of* **querer**
querido *adj.* dear, beloved
queso *n.m.* cheese
quiebro *v. form of* **quebrar**; *see also* §68.65
quien *pron.* who, he (she) who, whom, someone who; *see also* **quien** in the index
quienquiera, quienesquiera *indef. pron.* whoever, whomever, whosoever; *see also* §67.50ff
quiere, quieren, quiero *v. forms of* **querer**; *see* §68.65
quietos *adj.* quiet
química *n.f.* chemistry
químico *n.m.* chemist
quince *n.m., adj.* fifteen; **quince días**/two weeks
quinientos *n.m., adj.* five hundred
quinqué *n.m.* kerosene (hurricane) lamp
quinto *n.m., adj.* fifth; **dos quintos (quintas)**/two fifths
quise, quiso *v. forms of* **querer**; *see* §68.65
quisiera *v. form of* **querer**/I should like
quitar *v.* to leave, let go (of), remove
quitarse *v.* to take off, remove (clothing), remove oneself, withdraw

quiteños *n.m.pl., adj.* of or pertaining to Quito (Ecuador)
quizá(s) *adv.* maybe, perhaps

R

raer *v.* to scrape, rub off, erase, wipe out
ramillete *n.m.* bouquet
ramo *n.m.* sprig, small branch
rampa *n.f.* ramp
rápidamente *adv.* rapidly
rapidez *n.f.* rapidity, speed, swiftness
rápido *adj.* rapid, fast, swift
raqueta *n.f.* racket
rarísimo *adj.* very rare; *see also* §1.47ff, §2.5
raro *adj.* rare; **raras veces**/rarely, seldom; **por raro**/rarely
rascacielos *n.m.s. & pl.* skyscraper(s)
rascar *v.* to scrape, scratch
rata *n.f.* rat
rato *n.m.* moment, time, free time; **al poco rato**/in a short (little) while
ratón *n.m.* **ratones** *pl.* mouse, mice
rayo *n.m.* ray
raza *n.f.* race (people)
razón *n.f.* reason; **tener razón**/to be right; **no tener razón**/to be wrong
reacción *n.f.* reaction
real *adj.* royal, real
realidad *n.f.* reality
realizar *v.* to fulfill, realize (come true), carry out
realmente *adv.* really, actually
rebajar *v.* to bring down, reduce
rebelarse *v.* to rebel, revolt
recepción *n.f.* reception
receptor *n.m.* receiver
receta *n.f.* recipe, prescription
recibir *v.* to receive, get
recibo *n.m.* receipt; *also v. form of* **recibir**
recién, reciente, recientemente *adj., adv.* recent, recently; **recién casados**/newlyweds
recitar *v.* to recite
reclamador, reclamadora *n.m.f.* protester
reclamar *v.* to claim, demand
recluido *adj.* secluded
recluir *v.* to seclude, confine, shut in
recobrar *v.* to regain, recover
recoger *v.* to gather, reap, pick up, collect, pick
recomendación *n.f.* recommendation

recomendar *v.* to recommend, commend

recompensa *n.f.* reward, recompense

reconocer *v.* to recognize, acknowledge, be grateful for

recordado *adj.* recorded, remembered

recordar *v.* to remember, remind, recall

recorrer *v.* to run through, go through, visit here and there, travel through

recorrido *n.m.* flow, run, course, route

recreativa *adj.* recreational, recreative

recreo *n.m.* recreation

recuerdo *v. form of* **recordar**; *n.m.* memory, recollection, remembrance; **recuerdos**/regards

recurso *n.m.* recourse, means, resource

rechazar *v.* to reject, repel

redacción *n.f.* editing, writing, editorial work, newspaper writing

redactar *v.* to edit

redondo *adj.* round

reducido *adj.* reduced, small, little, confined

reducir *v.* to reduce

reemplazado *adj.* replaced

reemplazar *v.* to replace

reexaminación *n.f.* reexamination

referir *v.* to refer, relate, tell about, narrate

refiere *v. form of* **referir**

reflejar *v.* to reflect

reflexivo *adj.* reflexive

reforma *n.f.* reform

reformar *v.* to reform, straighten out, alter, reshape

refresco *n.m.* refreshment

refugiarse *v.* to take refuge

refugio *n.m.* refuge, shelter

regalar *v.* to present (give) as a gift, present, make a present of

regalo *n.m.* gift, present

regatear *v.* to dicker, haggle (over a price)

región *n.f.* region

registrar(se) *v.* to register

regla *n.f.* rule, ruler

reglamento *n.m.* regulation, rule

regocijado *adj.* gladdened, rejoiced

regocijar *v.* to gladden, rejoice

regresar *v.* to return, go back; *see also* §49.1

regreso *n.m.* return; **el viaje de regreso**/trip (drive) back

regular *adj.* regular; **por lo regular**/ordinarily, usually; *v.* to regulate

rehacer *v.* to redo

reina *n.f.* queen

reinar *v.* to reign

reino *n.m.* kingdom

reír(se) *v.* to laugh; **reír a carcajadas**/to burst out laughing

relación *n.f.* relation

relámpago *n.m.* streak of lightning

relativo *adj.* relative, related

relato *n.m.* account, statement, report

religiosidad *n.f.* religiousness, religiosity

religioso *adj.* religious; *n.m.* member of a religious order

reloj *n.m.* watch, clock; **reloj pulsera**/wrist watch

relucir *v.* to shine, sparkle, glow

remediar *v.* to correct, remedy

remedio *n.m.* remedy

remitir *v.* to forward, remit, transmit

remo *n.m.* oar, paddle

remota *adj.* remote

rendido *adj.* exhausted

rendir(se) *v.* to surrender, submit, overcome

renombrados *adj.* renowned

renovación *n.f.* renovation

renovar *v.* to renew, restore, renovate, remodel

renunciar *v.* to renounce, resign

reñir *v.* to scold, quarrel

reparación *n.f.* repair

reparar *v.* to repair

repartir *v.* to distribute, divide

repente *n.m.* sudden movement; **de repente**/suddenly

repentinamente *adv.* suddenly, abruptly

repentino *adj.* abrupt, sudden

repercusión *n.f.* repercussion

repercutir *v.* to resound, rebound, have repercussions

repetir *v.* to repeat

repite, repitiéndose *v. forms of* **repetir(se)**

replicar *v.* to reply

reposar *v.* to repose, rest

reposo *n.m.* rest

representación *n.f.* representation, performance, show

representante *n.m.f.* representative

representar *v.* to represent, perform (in theater)

reprimenda *n.f.* reprimand

reprochar *v.* to reproach

reproche *n.m.* reproach

reproducir *v.* to reproduce

república *n.f.* republic, government

repudiar *v.* to repudiate

repugnancia *n.f.* repugnance

requerimiento *n.m.* request, demand

resbalar *v.* to slip, slide

resentimiento *n.m.* resentment

resfiarse *v.* to catch cold

resfriado *n.m.* cold (sick)

residencia *n.f.* residence

residir *v.* to reside, live

resignado *adj.* resigned

resignarse *v.* to resign oneself

resistir *v.* to resist

resolución *n.f.* resolution

resolver *v.* to resolve, solve

respecto *n.m.* concern, relation; **respecto a**/with respect to

respetable *adj.* respectable

respetada *adj.* respected

respetar *v.* to respect

respeto *n.m.* respect, regard

respirar *v.* to breathe; *n.m.* breathing

responder *v.* to respond, answer, reply

respuesta *n.f.* reply, answer

restablecimiento *n.m.* reestablishment

restauración *n.f.* restoration

restaurante *n.m.* restaurant

restaurar *v.* to restore

resto *n.m.* rest, remainder, remaining

restricción *n.f.* restriction

resucitar *v.* to resuscitate, revive, resurrect

resultado *n.m.* result

resultar *v.* to result

retener *v.* to retain, keep, confine

retirados *adj.* withdrawn

retirar *v.* to withdraw; **retirarse** *v.* to retire, withdraw

Retiro *n.m.* retirement, retreat; name of a park in Madrid

retraso *n.m.* retard, delay, slowness

retrato *n.m.* likeness, picture, portrait

retroceder *v.* to recede, turn back

reunidos *adj.* gathered together

reunión *n.f.* meeting, reunion

reunir *v.* to bring together, accumulate, gather, join, unite

reunirse *v.* to get together, assemble, meet, gather

revelación *n.f.* revelation

revelar *v.* to reveal

revista *n.f.* magazine

revocar *v.* to revoke, repeal

revolución *n.f.* revolution

revolucionario *n.m., adj.* revolutionist, revolutionary

revolver *v.* to mix, turn over, mix up, rummage through; revolve, turn around, turn upside down, scramble (eggs)

revuelto *past part. of* **revolver; el cabello revuelto**/hair not combed; **huevos revueltos**/scrambled eggs

rey *n.m.* king; **Los Reyes Magos**/ The Three Wise Men, the Magi

reyes *n.m.pl.* king and queen, royalty

rezar *v.* to pray, recite a prayer

ría *v. form of* **reír(se)**

rico, rica *adj.* rich; **los ricos, las ricas**/rich men, rich women, rich people; **más rico**/richer, richest

ridículo *adj.* ridiculous

ríe *v. form of* **reír(se)**

riel *n.m.* rail; **rieles**/rails

riendo *pres. part. of* **reír(se)**

riesgo *n.m.* risk

rigor *n.m.* rigor, strictness

rincón *n.m.* corner (inside, as in a room); **la esquina**/corner (outside, as a street corner)

río *n.m.* river

rió *v. form of* **reír**

riqueza *n.f.* wealth, riches

risa *n.f.* laughter, laugh

risueño *adj.* smiling, laughing

ritmo *n.m.* rhythm

robar *v.* to rob, steal

robustez *n.f.* robustness

roca *n.f.* rock

rodar *v.* to roll, spin

rodeada *adj.* surrounded

rodear *v.* to go round, surround

rodilla *n.f.* knee; **de rodillas**/kneeling

rogar *v.* to pray, beg, ask, request

rojo *n.m., adj.* red; *pron.* red one

rol *n.m.* catalogue, list, roll

Roma *n.f.* Rome

románico *adj.* Romanesque

romano *adj.* Roman

romántico *adj.* romantic

¡Rómpamela!/Break it for me!

romper *v.* to break, tear, shatter, wear out

ropa *n.f.* clothing, clothes

ropería *n.f.* clothing store, wardrobe

ropero *n.m.* clothes dealer, clothier, clothes closet, wardrobe

rosa *n.f.* rose

rostro *n.m.* face

roto *past part. of* **romper;** *see* §68.65; *adj.* torn, broken

rubio *adj.* blond

rudo *adj.* rude

rueda *n.f.* wheel

ruego *v. form of* **rogar;** *n.m.* request

ruido *n.m.* noise

ruidoso *adj.* noisy

ruina *n.f.* ruin

rumbo *n.m.* direction, course

rumor *n.m.* murmur, sound, rumor

Rusia *n.f.* Russia

ruso *n.m., adj.* Russian

rústico *n.m., adj.* rustic

ruta *n.f.* route

rutina *n.f.* routine

S

sábado *n.m.* Saturday

saber *v.* to know (how); **se sabe**/it is known; *see also* **saber** in the index

sabio *n.m.* wise man, sage, learned; *adj.* wise

sabor *n.m.* savor, taste, flavor

sabré, sabrá *v. forms of* **saber;** *see* §68.65

sacar *v.* to take out, get; **sacar fotos, sacar fotografías**/to take pictures; **sacar la lengua**/to stick out one's tongue

sacerdote *n.m.* priest

saco *n.m.* bag, sack, jacket

sacrificar(se) *v.* to sacrifice (oneself)

sacrificio *n.m.* sacrifice

sacudir *v.* to shake, jerk, jolt

sagrado *adj.* sacred, holy

sal *n.f.* salt; also, *verb form of* **salir**

sala *n.f.* large room, living room; **sala de espera**/waiting room; **sala de clase**/classroom; **sala de recibo**/reception, waiting room

salario *n.m.* salary

saldré, sale, salga, salgo *v. forms of* **salir**

salida *n.f.* departure, exit; **salida del sol**/sunrise

salir *v.* to go out, to come out, leave; **salir de**/to go out of, leave from; **salir bien**/to come out well, to pass; **salir mal**/to come out badly, to fail; **salir el sol**/to rise (sun); *see also* §21.3

salón *n.m.* room, hall, living room

saltar *v.* to jump, leap, hop, spring

salud *n.f.* health

saludar *v.* to greet, salute; **saludarse** *v.* to greet each other

saludos *n.m.pl.* greetings

salvaje *adj.* savage, wild

salvar *v.* to rescue, save

salvo *adj.* safe; **sano y salvo**/safe and sound; *prep.* save, except

sangre *n.f.* blood

sanitario *adj.* sanitary

sano *adj.* healthy, sound; **sano y salvo**/safe and sound

santo, santa *n.m., f. adj.* saint, holy; *see also* §1.21

sartén *n.m.* frying pan

sastre *n.m.* tailor

sastrería *n.f.* tailor shop

satisfacción *n.f.* satisfaction

satisfacer *v.* to satisfy

satisfactoriamente *adv.* satisfactorily

satisfecho *adj.* satisfied; **lo satisfecho**/how much satisfied

sazón *n.f.* maturity; **a la sázon**/at the time, then

sea, sean *v. forms of* **ser**

secamente *adv.* dryly

secar *v.* to dry, wipe dry

secarse *v.* to dry oneself

seco *adj.* dry

secretario, secretaria *n.m.f.* secretary

secreto *n.m.* secret; *adj.* secret

secundario *adj.* secondary

sed *n.f.* thirst; **tener sed**/to be thirsty

seda *n.f.* silk

seguida *n.f.* pursuit, continuation; **en seguida**/immediately, at once

seguir *v.* to follow, continue, pursue; **seguir un curso**/to take a course; *see also* **seguir** in the index

según *prep.* according to

segundo *n.m., adj.* second

seguramente *adv.* surely

seguridad *n.f.* security, certainty

seguro *adj.* certain, secure, sure

seis *n.m., adj.* six

seiscientos *n.m., adj.* six hundred

selección *n.f.* selection

selva *n.f.* forest, jungle

sello *n.m.* postage stamp, seal

semana *n.f.* week; **la semana que viene**/next week; **la semana pasada**/last week; **el fin de semana** / weekend

sembrar *v.* to sow, seed, plant

semejante *adj.* similar, like, alike

semejanza *n.f.* similarity

semestral *adj.* semi-annual

sencillamente *adv.* simply

sencillez *n.f.* simplicity

sencillo *adj.* simple, plain

seno *n.m.* bosom, breast

sentado *adj.* seated

sentar *v.* to seat; **sentarse** *v.* to sit down

sentencia *n.f.* sentence, punishment

sentido *n.m.* meaning, sense; **sentido común**/common sense

sentimiento *n.m.* feeling, sentiment

sentir *v.* to feel sorry, regret, feel

sentirse *v.* to feel (well, not well, ill, sick)

seña *n.f.* sign, mark; **las señas**/address

señal *n.f.* signal, mark, sign

señalar *v.* to signal, mark, point out, indicate, show

Señor *n.m.* Lord; **señor** *n.m.* Mr. sir, mister, gentleman

señora *n.f.* Mrs. madam, lady (wife, woman)

señores *n.m.* gentlemen, Mr. and Mrs.

señorita *n.f.* Miss, young lady

señorito *n.m.* young gentleman, master, little gentleman

sepa *v. form of* **saber**; *see* §68.65

separación *n.f.* separation

separado *adj.* separated

separar *v.* to separate

separarse *v.* to draw away, withdraw

septiembre *n.m.* September

sepulcro *n.m.* sepulcher

ser *v.* to be; *n.m.* being, human being; **a no ser que**/unless; *see also* **ser** in idioms §53.25 and **ser** in the general index

será *v. form of* **ser**

serenidad *n.f.* serenity

sereno *adj.* calm, serene; *n.m.* night watchman

seria, serio *adj.* serious

sería *v. form of* **ser**

serie *n.f.* series

serio *adj.* serious

sermón *n.m.* sermon

servicio *n.m.* service

servidor *n.m.* servant

servilleta *n.f.* napkin

servir *v.* to serve; **servirle**/to serve you; **¿En qué puedo servirle?**/ May I help you? How may I be of some help to you? **servir de**/to serve as; **servir para**/to be used for; *see* §11.

servirse *v.* to help oneself (itself), to serve oneself

sesenta *n.m., adj.* sixty

sesión *n.f.* session

setecientos *n.m., adj.* seven hundred

setenta *n.m., adj.* seventy

seudónimo *n.m.* pseudonym

severo *adj.* severe

sevillano *n.m., adj.* of or pertaining to Sevilla

si *conj.* if, whether; *see also* §67.111

sí *adv.* yes, indeed; **creo que sí**/I think so; **digo que sí**/I say so; **sí**

que/certainly; *pron.* **sí**/oneself, yourself, yourselves, himself, *etc.*; **para sí**/to himself, herself, *etc.*; **volver en sí**/to come to, regain consciousness

siamés *n.m., adj.* Siamese

sido *past part. of* **ser**; *see* §68.65

siembra *v. form of* **sembrar**

siempre *adv.* always; **siempre que fui**/whenever I went, at all times when I went

siendo, *v. form of* **ser**

siente, siento *v. forms of* **sentar, sentir; siento**/I'm sorry; **se siente**/it is felt

sierra *n.f.* saw, mountain range

siesta *n.f.* afternoon rest, nap; **tomar la siesta**/to take an afternoon nap

siete *n.m., adj.* seven

siga *v. form of* **seguir**

siglo *n.m.* century

significado *n.m.* meaning

significar *v.* to signify, mean

siguen *v. form of* **seguir**

siguiente *adj.* next, following; **al día siguiente**/on the following day

siguiera, siguieron, siguió *v. forms of* **seguir**

silbar *v.* to whistle

silencio *n.m.* silence

silencioso *adj.* silent

silla *n.f.* chair

sillón *n.m.* armchair

simbólicos *adj.* symbolic

simbolizar *v.* to symbolize, signify

simpatía *n.f.* sympathy, congeniality

simpático *adj.* sympathetic, pleasant, congenial, nice

simular *v.* to simulate, feign, pretend, sham

simultánea *adj.* simultaneous

sin *prep.* without; **sin embargo**/ nevertheless, however; *see also* conjunctions with **sin** §7.ff, **sin** in idioms §53.26, and **sin** in the index

sincero *adj.* sincere

sinfónica *adj.* symphonic

sinfonía *n.f.* symphony

singular *adj.* singular, unique

sinnúmero *n.m.* countless number

sino *conj.* but (rather, on the contrary); **sino que**/but rather; *see also* §44.2ff

sinónimo *n.m.* synonym

sintiendo, sintieran, sintió *v. forms of* **sentir**

síntoma *n.m.* symptom

siquiera *adv.* at least; *conj.* though, although; **ni siquiera**/not even

sírvase *v. form of* **servirse;** be good enough to

sirve, sirven *v. forms of* **servir**

sirvienta, sirviente *n.f.m.* servant

sirvió *v. form of* **servir**

sistema *n.m.* system

sitio *n.m.* place, site, spot, siege

situación *n.f.* situation

situado *adj.* situated

situar *v.* to situate, place

soberano *n.m., adj.* sovereign

sobrar *v.* to exceed, be more than sufficient, be left over

sobre *prep.* on, upon, about, over; **sobre todo**/above all, especially; *n.m.* envelope

sobresaliente *adj.* outstanding

sobretodo *n.m.* overcoat

sobreviviente *n.m.f.* survivor

sobrina *n.f.* niece

sobrino *n.m.* nephew

sociedad *n.f.* society

socio *n.m.* member, partner

sociológico *adj.* sociological

socorrer *v.* to aid, assist, help, succor

socorro *n.m.* help, succor

sofocar *v.* to suffocate, choke, smother, stifle

sol *n.m.* sun; **la puesta del sol**/sunset; **la salida del sol**/sunrise; *see also* weather expressions with **sol** §36.2, §64.ff

sola *adj.* alone, single

solamente *adv.* only

solar *adj.* solar

solariego *adj.* ancestral; **la casa solariega**/family home, homestead

soldado *n.m.* soldier

soledad *n.f.* solitude

solemne *adj.* solemn

soler + *inf. v.* to have the custom of, be in the habit of, be accustomed to; *see* §68.14

soles *pl. of* **sol**

solicitar *v.* to solicit, request, apply for

sólidas *adj.* solid

solitario *n.m.* solitary person; *adj.* solitary

solo *adj.* alone, only, single, sole; **sólo** *adv.* only

soltar *v.* to unfasten, untie, loosen, let go, let loose

soltero *n.m.* bachelor; *adj.* unmarried

solterona *n.f.* old maid, unmarried woman

solución *n.f.* solution; **soluciones** *n.f.pl.*

sollozar *v.* to sob

sombra *n.f.* shade, shadow

sombrero *n.m.* hat

someter *v.* to subdue, subject, surrender, submit

somos, son *v. forms of* **ser**; *see* §68.65

sonar *v.* to sound, ring, echo, resound

sonido *n.m.* sound

sonoro *adj.* sonorous, pleasant sounding

sonreír(se) *v.* to smile

sonriendo, sonrió *v. forms of* **sonreír**

sonriente *adj.* smiling

sonrisa *n.f.* smile

sonrojarse *v.* to blush

soñar *v.* to dream; **soñar con**/to dream of

sopa *n.f.* soup

soplar *v.* to blow, blow out

soportar *v.* to endure

sordo *adj.* deaf

sorprendentes *adj.* surprising, amazing

sorprender *v.* to surprise, astonish; **sorprenderse de**/to be surprised at

sorprendidos *adj.* surprised

sorpresa *n.f.* surprise

sortija *f.* ring (finger)

sospecha *n.f.* suspicion

sospechar *v.* to suspect

sostener *v.* to sustain, maintain, support, uphold

soviético *adj.* Soviet

soy *v. form of* **ser**; *see* §68.65

su, sus *poss. adj.* your, his, her, its, their; *see* §1.58

suave *adj.* gentle, mild, soft

suavidad *n.f.* gentleness, softness

suavizar *v.* to smooth, soften, ease, temper

subir *v.* to go up, come up, climb, rise, mount, ascend, get in (a vehicle)

súbitamente *adv.* suddenly

súbito *adj.* sudden

subjetivo *adj.* subjective

subjuntivo *n.m.* subjunctive

subrayar *v.* to underline, underscore, emphasize

subscribir *v.* to subscribe, agree to, sign

subscriptor *n.m.* subscriber

subsistencia *n.f.* subsistence

subterráneo *n.m.* subway; *adj.* subterranean

suceder *v.* to happen, occur, follow, succeed

suceso *n.m.* happening, event, occurrence; (success: **éxito**)

sucio *adj.* dirty

sud *see* **sur**

sudamericano *n.m., adj.* South American

sudar *v.* to sweat, perspire

sudoeste *n.m.* southwest

sudor *n.m.* perspiration, sweat

sueldo *n.m.* salary

suele *v. form of* **soler**

suelo *n.m.* floor, ground; also *v. form of* **soler**; *see* §68.65

suelto *n.m.* change, small change, coins; **sueltos** *adj.* loose

sueño *n.m.* dream, sleep; **tener sueño**/to be sleepy

suerte *n.f.* luck, fate; **buena suerte**/good luck; **tener suerte**/to be lucky

suficiente *adj., adv.* enough, sufficient

sufre *v. form of* **sufrir**

sufrido *adj.* undergone, suffered

sufrimiento *n.m.* suffering

sufrir *v.* to suffer, endure, bear up, undergo

sugerir *v.* to suggest, hint, insinuate

sugirieron *v. form of* **sugerir**

sujetar *v.* to grasp, hold, secure, subject, hold fast, overcome, subdue

suma *n.f.* sum

sumamente *adv.* extremely

sumar *v.* to add, sum up

sumergir *v.* to submerge, plunge, immerse, sink

suntuoso *adj.* sumptuous

supe *v. form of* **saber**

superior *n.m., adj.* upper, superior

supiesen *v. form of* **saber**

suplicar *v.* to beg, implore

supo *v. form of* **saber**; found out, learned; **se supo**/it was found out, it was learned

suponer *v.* to suppose, assume

supremacía *n.f.* supremacy

suprimir *v.* to suppress, abolish, cut out, cancel (in math), eliminate

supuesto *past part. of* **suponer**; supposed; **por supuesto**/of course, certainly

supuse *v. form of* **suponer**

sur *n.m.* South

surgir *v.* to surge, appear, spout, spurt

suspender *v.* to suspend; **suspensos** *adj.* suspended

suspirar *v.* to sigh

suspiro *n.m.* sigh

sustantivo *n.m.* noun

sustituir *v.* to substitute

sustituto *n.m.* substitute

susto *n.m.* fright

suyo, suya, suyos, suyas, *poss. pron.* yours, his, hers, *etc.*; *see* §1.60ff, §66.64ff; **los suyos**/one's relatives

T

taberna *n.f.* bar, pub, tavern

tabernero *n.m.* tavern keeper

tabla *n.f.* board

tal *adj.* such, such a; **¿Qué tal?**/What's up? How goes it? **tal o cual**/such and such; **tal vez**/perhaps; **con tal que**/provided that; *see* **tal** in the index

tales *pl. of* **tal**

tamaño *n.m.* size

también *adv.* also, too

tampoco *adv.* neither, nor, not either

tan *adv.* so; **tan como**/as . . . as; **tan pronto como**/as soon as; *see* **tan** in the index

tanque *n.m.* tank

tanta, tanto *adj., pron.* so (as) much, so (as) many; **por lo tanto**/therefore; **tanto . . . como**/as much . . . as; **mientras tanto**/meanwhile; *see also* §1.53

tantísimos *adj.* so many, so much; *see also* §1.47ff, §2.5

tañer *v.* to play, pluck a string instrument

tapar *v.* to cover, cover up, hide, stop up, plug up

taquígrafa, taquígrafo *n.f.m.* stenographer

tardanza *n.f.* delay, tardiness, lateness

tardar (en) + inf. to be late (in), to take long (in), to delay (in)

tarde *adv.* late; **más tarde**/later; *n.f.* afternoon; **(de) por la tarde**/in the afternoon

tarea *n.f.* duty, homework, task

tarjeta *n.f.* card

taxi, taxímetro *n.m.* taxi

taza *n.f.* cup

té *n.m.* tea

te *pron.* you, to you, yourself; *see* pronouns §66.ff

teatral *adj.* theatrical

teatro *n.m.* theater

técnica *n.f.* technique; **técnico** *adj.* technical

tecnología *n.f.* technology

techo *n.m.* roof

tejado *n.m.* tiled roof

tela *n.f.* fabric, cloth

telefonear *v.* to telephone

telefónico *adj.* telephonic

telefonista *n.m.f.* telephone operator

teléfono *n.m.* telephone; **por teléfono**/on the telephone

telegrafiar *v.* to telegraph, cable

telegrafista *n.m.f.* telegraph operator

telegrama *n.m.* telegram

televisión *n.f.* television
televisor *n.m.* television set
telón *n.m.* curtain (stage)
tema *n.m.* theme, subject, topic, plot
temblar *v.* to tremble, quake, quiver, shake, shiver
temer *v.* to fear, dread
temor n.m. dread, fear
temperatura *n.f.* temperature
tempestad *n.f.* tempest, storm
templado *adj.* temperate
templo *n.m.* temple (house of prayer)
temporada *n.f.* period of time
tempranito *adv.* very early
temprano *adv.* early
ten *v. form of* **tener**
tender *v.* to hold out, tend, extend, offer, stretch, spread out, hang out (washing)
tenderos *n.m.* storekeepers
tendido *n.m.* laying out, installation
tendrá *v. form of* **tener**
tenedor *n.m.* fork, holder, keeper; **tenedor de libros** *n.m.* bookkeeper
tener *v.* to have, hold; *see also* **tener** in idioms §53.27 and **tener** in the index
tener que + inf. to have to, must; *see also* §20.3
tengo, tenía, tenido *v. forms of* **tener;** *see* §68.65
tenis *n.m.* tennis
tensión *n.f.* tension
tentar *v.* to examine by touch, feel with the fingers, attempt, tempt, try
teñir(se) *v.* to dye, stain, tint, color
tercer, tercero, tercera *adj., pron.* third; *see also* §1.20
tercio *n.m.* third; **dos tercios**/two thirds
terminar *v.* to terminate, end, finish
término *n.m.* end, boundary, term, limit, terminal
terreno *n.m.* terrain, ground, land
territorio *n.m.* territory
tertulia *n.f.* party, social gathering
tertulianos *n.m.* participants in a **tertulia**
tesis *n.m.* thesis
tesoro *n.m.* treasure
testigo *n.m.* witness
testimonio *n.m.* testimony
tiempo *n.m.* time, weather; **a tiempo**/on time; **desde hace mucho tiempo**/for a long time; **hace muchísimo tiempo**/a long time ago; *see also* §36.2, §64.ff
tienda *n.f.* tent, store, shop; **tienda de comestibles**/grocery store;

tienda de deportes/sporting goods store
tiende *v. form of* **tender**
tiendecita *n.f.* small store
tienden *v. form of* **tender**
tiene *v. form of* **tener**
tierra *n.f.* earth, ground, land
tigre *n.m.* tiger
tímido *adj.* timid, shy
tinta *n.f.* ink
tiña *v. form of* **teñir**
¡Tíñela!/Tint it! Color it!
tío, tía *n.m.f.* aunt, uncle; **tíos** *n.m.* aunt and uncle, aunts and uncles
típico *adj.* typical
tipo *n.m.* type
tirano *n.m.* tyrant
tirar *v.* to throw, pull, draw, pitch (a ball), shoot (a gun), fling
titulado *adj.* entitled, titled
título *n.m.* title
tiza *n.f.* chalk
toalla *n.f.* towel
tocar *v.* to touch, play (a musical instrument); **tocar las campanas**/to ring the bells; **tocarle a uno**/to be someone's turn; *see also* §37.2, §66.20
tocino *n.m.* bacon
todavía *adv.* yet, still, even
todo *adj.* all; *pron.* all; **sobre todo**/above all, especially; **todo español**/all Spanish people; **todo**/everything; **todo el mundo**/everybody; *see also* §53.28, §66.96
tomar *v.* to take, have (something to eat or drink); **se toma**/one takes, it is taken, is being taken; *see also* §39.
tomé *v. form of* **tomar**
tonelada *n.f.* ton
tono *n.m.* tone, voice
tontería *n.f.* foolishness, nonsense
tonto *adj., n.* stupid, fool, foolish
torcer *v.* to twist
torero *n.m.* bullfighter
tormenta *n.f.* torment, storm
tornarse *v.* to become, to change into
torno *n.m.* turnstile, wheel; **en torno**/around
toro *n.m.* bull; **la corrida de toros**/bullfight
toronja *n.f.* grapefruit
torre *n.f.* tower
tortilla *n.f.* omelet, tortilla
tortuoso *adj.* tortuous
tortura *n.f.* torture
tostar *v.* to toast
trabajador, trabajadora *n.m.f.* worker

trabajar *v.* to work
trabajo *n.m.* work
tradicional *adj.* traditional
traducción *n.f.* translation
traducir *v.* to translate
traduzca *v. form of* **traducir**
traer *v.* to bring
tragedia *n.f.* tragedy
trágico *adj.* tragic
traidor *adj., n.* traitor, treacherous
tráigame . . . /bring me . . .
traigo *v. form of* **traer**
traje *n.m.* suit, outfit; **traje de baño**/bathing suit; also *v. form of* **traer**
trajeron, trajo *v. forms of* **traer**
tranquilidad *n.f.* tranquility
tranquilizar *v.* to calm, calm down, quiet down, tranquilize
tranquilo *adj.* quiet, tranquil, calm
transacción *n.f.* transaction
transcurrir *v.* to elapse, pass
transformar *v.* to transform
transgresor *n.m.* offender, transgressor
transmisión *n.f.* transmission
transporte *n.m.* transportation
tranvía *n.m.* streetcar, trolley
tras *prep.* after, behind, beyond; **tras (de)**/after, behind
trascendental *adj.* important, momentous, transcendental
trasladar *v.* to transport, transfer, convey, move
tratamiento *n.m.* treatment
tratar *v.* to try, treat (a subject), deal with; **tratar de**/to try, be concerned with; **tratarse de**/to be a question of, a matter of
trato *n.m.* trade, business transaction, business deal; **trato cerrado**/deal closed
través *n.m.* slant, diagonal; **a través**/through, across
travieso *adj.* mischievous, naughty
trayendo *pres. part. of* **traer**
treinta *n.m., adj.* thirty; **treinta y cinco**/thirty-five; **treinta y tres**/thirty-three
tremendo *adj.* tremendous
trémulo *adj.* trembling
tren *n.m.* train
trenza *n.f.* braid, tress
tres *n.m., adj.* three
tribu *n.f.* tribe
trigo *n.m.* wheat
triplicar *v.* to triple
triste *adj.* sad
tristeza *n.f.* sadness
triunfar *v.* to triumph, to win
triunfo *n.m.* triumph
trofeo *n.m.* trophy

trompo *n.m.* top (spin)
tronar *v.* to thunder
tronco *n.m.* trunk (of body, tree, etc.)
trono *n.m.* throne
tropa *n.f.* troop
tropezar *v.* to stumble, blunder, trip; **tropezar con**/to stumble upon, meet, come across, come upon
trotar *v.* to trot
trozo *n.m.* selection, piece
trueno *n.m.* thunder
tu, tus *poss. adj. see* §1.57ff
tubo *n.m.* tube, pipe (smoking pipe: **una pipa**)
turbar *v.* to disturb, trouble; **turbarse** *v.* to feel disturbed, upset
turco *n.m., adj.* Turk, Turkish
turismo *n.m.* tourism
turista *n.m.f.* tourist
turno *n.m.* turn
Turquía *n.f.* Turkey
tuviera, tuvo *v. forms of* **tener**
tuyo, tuya, *etc.,* **el tuyo, la tuya,** *etc. poss. pron.* yours; *see* §1.60ff, §66.64ff

U

u *conj.* or; *see* §50.
últimamente *adv.* lately, ultimately
último *adj.* latest, final, last
un, uno *see* §1.18ff
une *v. form of* **unir**
U.N.E.S.C.O. United Nations Educational, Scientific, and Cultural Organization
único *adj.* only, single, sole, unique
unidad *n.f.* unity
unidas *adj.* united
uniforme *n.m.* uniform
unión *n.f.* union, uniting, combination
unir(se) *v.* to unite, join, bind, attach, connect
universalidad *n.f.* universality
universidad *n.f.* university
universitario *n.m., adj.* university, university student
uno, una *pron.* a person, someone, somebody; **unos, unas** *adj., pron.* some, several; **unos cuantos**/some, a few, several
untar *v.* to grease, moisten, anoint, oil
uña *n.f.* fingernail
urbano *adj.* urban
urgente *adj.* urgent
urgir *v.* to urge, to be urgent

usada *adj.* used
usar *v.* to use, employ, wear
uso *n.m.* use, usage
usualmente *adv.* usually
útil *adj.* useful
utilización *n.f.* utilization
utilizar *v.* to utilize, use
uva *n.f.* grape

V

va *v. form of* **ir**
vaca *n.f.* cow
vacaciones *n.f.pl.* vacation, vacations
vaciar *v.* to empty, vacate
vacilar *v.* to hesitate, vacillate, waver, fluctuate, stagger
vacío *adj.* empty
vagabundo *n.m.* vagabond
vago *adj.* vague
vaguedad *n.f.* vagueness
vale *v. form of* **valer**
valenciano *n.m., adj.* of or pertaining to Valencia
valer *v.* to be worth, to value; **valer la pena**/to be worthwhile; **más vale**/it is better (worth more); **más vale tarde que nunca**/better late than never
valerosamente *adv.* bravely, courageously
valgan *v. form of* **valer**
valiente *adj.* brave, valiant, courageous
valor *n.m.* valor, value
valle *n.m.* valley
¡Vámonos! Let's leave! Let's go away! *v. form of* **irse**; *see also* **vámonos** in the index
vamos, van *v. forms of* **ir**
vanidad *n.f.* vanity
vano *n.m.* vain; **en vano**/in vain
vapor *n.m.* steam, steamship, steamboat, vapor, boat
variado *adj.* varied
variar *v.* to vary, change
variedad *n.f.* variety
varios *adj.* several, various
varón *n.m.* male, man, male person
vaso *n.m.* glass (drinking)
vasto *adj.* vast
vaya *v. form of* **ir**; **¡Vaya un . . . !** **¡Vaya una . . . !**/What a . . . ! What an . . . !
ve *v. form of* **ir, ver**; **se ve**/it is seen, it can be seen
veces *pl. of* **vez**; **a veces**/at times; **la de veces**/how many times; **pocas veces**/seldom, few times; *see also* §36.3 and **veces** in idioms §53.29

vecindad *n.f.* vicinity
vecino, vecina *n.m.f.* neighbor; *adj.* neighboring
vehículo *n.m.* vehicle
veinte *n.m., adj.* twenty; **veinticinco**/twenty-five; **veintidós**/twenty-two; **veintiocho**/twenty-eight; **veintiún**/twenty-one
vejez *n.f.* old age
vela *n.f.* candle, vigil
velar *v.* to stay awake, guard, watch (over)
veloces *adj., pl. of* **veloz** *adj.* swift, fast, speedy
vencer *v.* to conquer, vanquish, overcome
vendedor, vendedora *n.m.f.* seller, salesman, saleslady
vender *v.* to sell; **se vende**/is sold; **se venden**/are sold
veneno *n.m.* poison
venerar *v.* to venerate, to honor; **se venera**/is venerated
venezolano *n.m., adj.* of or pertaining to Venezuela
venganza *n.f.* revenge, vengeance
vengo *v. form of* **venir**
venidera *adj.* coming, future, those to come
venir *v.* to come; **hacer venir**/to send for
venta *n.f.* sale, inn
ventaja *n.f.* advantage
ventana *n.f.* window; **ventanuco** *n.m.* small opening
ver *v.* to see; **a ver**/let's see; *see also* §56.11
veraneante *n.m.f.* summer vacationer
veranear *v.* to summer, to spend the summer
veraneo *adj.* summer, summer vacation
verano *n.m.* summer
veras *n.f. pl.* fact; **de veras**/truly, really
verbo *n.m.* verb
verdad *n.f.* truth; **¿No es verdad? ¿Verdad?**/Isn't it so?
verdaderamente *adv.* truly
verdadero *adj.* real, true
verde *n.m., adj.* green
veré *v. form of* **ver**
vergüenza *n.f.* shame
vería *v. form of* **ver**
verificarse *v.* to be verified, to prove true, to take place
verso *n.m.* verse
vestíbulo *n.m.* vestibule, waiting room, lobby
vestido *past part. of* **vestir;** dressed;

also *n.m.* dress, robe, suit; **mal vestido**/poorly, badly dressed

vestir *v.* to dress, clothe; also *n.m.* dressing

vestirse *v.* to get dressed, dress oneself

vete *v. form of* **irse**; go away

veterano *n.m.* veteran

veterinario *n.m., adj.* veterinarian, veterinary

vez *n.f.* time, occasion; **una vez**/once, one time; **dos veces**/twice, two times, *etc.;* **en vez de**/instead of; **de vez en cuando**/from time to time; **una vez**/the moment when; **de una vez**/all at once; **otra vez**/again, once more; **a la vez**/at the same time, at once, at one time; **tal vez**/perhaps, maybe; *see also* §36.3, §53.29

vi *v. form of* **ver**

vía *n.f.* way, road

viajar *v.* to travel

viaje *n.m.* trip, voyage, journey; **hacer un viaje**/to take a trip

viajero, viajera *n.m.f.* passenger, traveler

vibrar *v.* to vibrate

vicio *n.m.* vice

víctima *n.f.* victim (refers to male or female person)

victoria *n.f.* victory

vid *n.f.* vine, grapevine

vida *n.f.* life

vidrio *n.m.* glass window pane

viejecillo *n.m.* little old man

viejo, vieja *n.m.f., adj.* old, old man, old woman; **los viejos**/old people

viendo *pres. part. of* **ver**

viene, vienen *v. forms of* **venir**; **la semana que viene**/next week

viento *n.m.* wind; *see also* weather expressions §36.2, §64.ff

vientre *n.m.* abdomen, belly

viera, viéramos *v. forms of* **ver**

vieres *fut. subj. of* **ver**; *see* §54., §54.18, §68.64

viernes *n.m.* Friday

vieron, viesen *v. forms of* **ver**

vigilar *v.* to watch (over), guard, keep guard, look out (for)

vigoroso *adj.* vigorous

vinagre *n.m.* vinegar

vine, viniera *v. forms of* **venir**

vino *n.m.* wine; also *v. form of* **venir**; *see* §68.65

vio *v. form of* **ver**

violación *n.f.* violation

violencia *n.f.* violence

violenta *adj.* violent

violentamente *adv.* violently

violeta *n.f.* violet

virgen *n.f., adj.* virgin

virtud *n.f.* virtue

visibilidad *n.f.* visibility

visita *n.f.* visit; **hacer una visita**/to pay a visit

visitante *n.m.f.* visitor

visitar *v.* to visit

víspera *n.f.* eve

vista *n.f.* view, sight; **un punto de vista**/a point of view

viste *v. form of* **ver, vestir**

vistiendo, vistiese *v. forms of* **vestir(se)**; **vistiéndome**/dressing myself

visto *past part. of* **ver**; **dar el visto bueno**/to approve; **por lo visto**/apparently

viuda *n.f.* widow

viudo *n.m.* widower

vivienda *n.f.* home, house

vivir *v.* to live, reside

vivísimo, vivísima *adj.* very lively, bright; *see* §1.47ff, §2.5

vivo *adj.* alive, living

vocablo *n.m.* term, word

vocacional *adj.* vocational

voces *n.f.pl. of* **voz**; **grandes voces**/loud voice

volando *pres. part. of* **volar** *v.* to fly; **volarse**/to fly away

voltear *v.* to overturn, revolve, turn, turn around

volúmen *n.m.* volume

voluntad *n.f.* will

volver *v.* to return, go back, come back; **volverse**/to turn around; **al volverse**/upon turning around; *see also* §49.ff

volviese *v. form of* **volver**

votante *n.m.f.* voter

votar *v.* to vote, vow

voto *n.m.* vote, vow

voy *v. form of* **ir**

voz *n.f.* voice; **en voz alta**/in a loud voice; **dar voces**/to shout

vuela, vuelan *v. forms of* **volar**

vuelo *n.m.* flight

vuelta *n.f.* stroll, walk, tour, return, turn; **dar una vuelta**/to go for a stroll; **ida y vuelta**/round trip

vuelto *past part. of* **volver**

vulgar *adj.* common, ordinary, vulgar

Y

y *conj.* and; *see* §1.65, §51., §59.4; *see also* **y** in idioms §53.30 and in telling time §63.5

ya *adv.* now, already, indeed; **ya que**/as long as, since, inasmuch as, because; **ya no**/no longer; **¡Ya lo creo!** I should say so! Of course! *see also* §53.31

yacer *v.* to lie down, be lying down

yendo *pres. part. of* **ir**; **yéndose** *v. form of* **irse**

yugo *n.m.* yoke

Z

zapateado *n.m.* Spanish clog dance, tap dance

zapatería *n.f.* shoe store, bootery, shoe repair shop

zapatero *n.m.* shoe repair worker, shoemaker

zapatilla *n.f.* slipper

zapato *n.m.* shoe

zona *n.f.* zone

zopenco *n.m.* blockhead; *adj.* stupid

zorra *n.f.* she-fox, vixen

zorrillo *n.m.* skunk

zorro *n.m.* fox

zumbar *v.* to buzz, hum, flutter around

zumo *n.m.* juice; **zumoso** *adj.* juicy

zurcir *v.* to mend, darn

zurdo *adj.* left-handed

Verbs Used in Idiomatic Expressions

On the pages containing 50 verbs fully conjugated in all the tenses, I offer simple sentences, idiomatic expressions, or words and expressions related to verbs. They can help build your Spanish vocabulary and knowledge of Spanish idioms.

When you look up the verb forms of a particular verb in this book, consult the following list so that you may learn some common idiomatic expressions. Consulting this list will save you time because you will not have to use a standard Spanish-English word dictionary to find out what the verbal idiom means. Also, if you do this, you will learn two things at the same time: the verb forms for a particular verb and verbal idioms.

Remember that not all verbs in the Spanish language are used in idioms. Those given below are used very frequently in Spanish readings and in conversation. Some of the following entries contain words, usually nouns, that are related to the verb entry. This, too, will help build your vocabulary. I also include a few proverbs containing verbs because they are interesting, colorful, useful, and they help build your knowledge of Spanish words and idiomatic expressions.

acabar de + inf.

The Spanish idiomatic expression **acabar de + inf.** is expressed in English as *to have just* + past participle.

In the present indicative:
María acaba de llegar.   Mary has just arrived.
Acabo de comer.   I have just eaten.
Acabamos de terminar la lección.   We have just finished the lesson.

In the imperfect indicative:
María acababa de llegar.   Mary had just arrived.
Acababa de comer.   I had just eaten.
Acabábamos de terminar la lección.   We had just finished the lesson.

Note:
(a) When you use **acabar** in the present tense, it indicates that the action of the main verb (+ inf.) has just occurred now in the present. In English, we express this by using *have just* + the past participle of the main verb: *Acabo de llegar/*I have just arrived. (See the other examples above under present indicative.)

(b) When you use **acabar** in the imperfect indicative, it indicates that the action of the main verb (+ inf.) had occurred at some time in the past when another action occurred in the past. In English, we express this by using *had just* + the past participle of the main verb: *Acabábamos de entrar en la casa cuando el teléfono sonó/*We had just entered the house when the telephone rang. (See the other examples above under imperfect indicative.)

Note also that when **acabar** is used in the imperfect indicative + the inf. of the main verb being expressed, the verb in the other clause is usually in the preterit.

conocer and **saber** (See also **poder** and **saber**)

These two verbs mean *to know* but they are each used in a distinct sense:

(a) Generally speaking, **conocer** means to know in the sense of *being acquainted* with a person, a place, or a thing: *¿Conoce Ud. a María?*/Do you know Mary? *¿Conoce Ud. bien los Estados Unidos?*/Do you know the United States well? *¿Conoce Ud. este libro?*/Do you know (Are you acquainted with) this book?

In the preterit tense, **conocer** means *met* in the sense of *first met, first became acquainted with someone*: *¿Conoce Ud. a Elena?*/Do you know Helen? *Sí, (yo) la conocí anoche en casa de un amigo mío*/Yes, I met her (for the first time) last night at the home of one of my friends.

(b) Generally speaking, **saber** means to know a fact, to know something thoroughly: *¿Sabe Ud. qué hora es?*/Do you know what time it is? *¿Sabe Ud. la lección?*/Do you know the lesson?

When you use **saber** + **inf.**, it means *to know how*: *¿Sabe Ud. nadar?*/Do you know how to swim? *Sí, (yo) sé nadar*/Yes, I know how to swim.

In the preterit tense, **saber** means *found out*: *¿Lo sabe Ud.?*/Do you know it? *Sí, lo supe ayer*/Yes, I found it out yesterday.

dar and **darse**

dar a   to face (*El comedor da al jardín*/The dining room faces the garden.)

dar con algo   to find something, to come upon something (*Esta mañana di con dinero en la calle*/This morning I found money in the street.)

dar con alguien   to meet someone, to run into someone, to come across someone, to find someone (*Anoche, di con mi amiga Elena en el cine*/Last night I met my friend Helen at the movies.)

dar cuerda al reloj   to wind a watch

dar de beber a   to give something to drink to

dar de comer a   to feed, to give something to eat to (*Me gusta dar de comer a los pájaros en el parque*/I like to feed the birds in the park.)

dar en   to hit against, to strike against

dar en el blanco   to hit the target, to hit it right

dar gritos   to shout

dar la bienvenida   to welcome

dar la hora   to strike the hour

dar la mano a alguien   to shake hands with someone

dar las buenas noches a alguien   to say good evening (good night) to someone

dar las gracias a alguien   to thank someone

dar los buenos días a alguien   to say good morning (hello) to someone

dar por + past part.   to consider (*Lo doy por perdido*/I consider it lost.)

dar recuerdos a   to give one's regards (best wishes) to

dar un abrazo   to embrace

dar un paseo   to take a walk

dar un paseo a caballo   to go horseback riding

dar un paseo en automóvil   to go for a drive

dar una vuelta   to go for a short walk, to go for a stroll

dar unas palmadas   to clap one's hands

dar voces   to shout

darse cuenta de   to realize, to be aware of, to take into account

darse la mano   to shake hands with each other

darse por + past part.   to consider oneself (*Me doy por insultado*/I consider myself insulted.)

darse prisa   to hurry

deber, deber de and tener que

Generally speaking, use **deber** when you want to express a moral obligation, something you ought to do but that you may or may not actually do: *Debo estudiar esta noche pero estoy cansado y no me siento bien*/I ought to study tonight but I am tired and I do not feel well.

Generally speaking, **deber de + inf.** is used to express a supposition, something that is probable: *La señora Gómez debe de estar enferma porque sale de casa raramente*/Mrs. Gómez must be sick (is probably sick) because she goes out of the house rarely.

Generally speaking, use **tener que** when you want to say that you *have to* do something: *No puedo salir esta noche porque tengo que estudiar*/I cannot go out tonight because I have to study.

decir

decirle al oído   to whisper in one's ear

dicho y hecho   no sooner said than done

Es decir   That is to say . . .

querer decir   to mean (*¿Qué quiere decir este muchacho?*/What does this boy mean?)

dejar, salir, and salir de

These verbs mean *to leave*, but notice the difference in use:

Use **dejar** when you leave someone or when you leave something behind you: *El alumno dejó sus libros en la sala de clase*/The pupil left his books in the classroom.

Dejar also means *to let* or *to allow* or *to let go*: *Déjelo!*/Let it! (Leave it!)

Use **salir de** when you mean *to leave* in the sense of *to go out of* (a place): *El alumno salió de la sala de clase*/The pupil left the classroom; *¿Dónde está su madre? Mi madre salió*/Where is your mother? My mother went out.

dejar de + inf. and dejar caer

Use **dejar de + inf.** when you mean *to stop* or *to fail to*: *Los alumnos dejaron de hablar cuando la profesora entró en la sala de clase*/The students stopped talking when the teacher came into the classroom; *¡No deje Ud. de llamarme!*/Don't fail to call me!

Dejar caer means *to drop*: *Luis dejó caer sus libros*/Louis dropped his books.

estar (See also ser and estar beginning on p. 293)

está bien   all right, okay

estar a punto de + inf.   to be about + inf. (*Estoy a punto de salir*/I am about to go out.)

estar a sus anchas   to be comfortable

estar aburrido (aburrida)   to be bored

estar al día   to be up to date

estar bien   to be well

estar conforme con   to be in agreement with

estar de acuerdo   to agree

estar de acuerdo con   to be in agreement with

estar de boga   to be in fashion, to be fashionable

estar de buenas   to be in a good mood

estar de más   to be unnecessary

estar de pie   to be standing

estar de vuelta   to be back

estar en boga   to be in fashion, to be fashionable

estar listo (lista)   to be ready

estar mal   to be ill

estar para + inf.   to be about to (*Estoy para salir*/I am about to go out.)

estar por   to be in favor of

no estar para bromas   not to be in the mood for jokes

gastar and pasar

These two verbs mean *to spend*, but notice the difference in use:

Use **gastar** when you spend money: *No me gusta gastar mucho dinero*/I do not like to spend much money.

Use **pasar** when you spend time: *Me gustaría pasar un año en España*/I would like to spend a year in Spain.

gustar

(a) Essentially, the verb **gustar** means *to be pleasing to* . . .

(b) In English, we say, for example, *I like ice cream*. In Spanish, we say *Me gusta el helado*; that is to say, "Ice cream is pleasing to me (To me ice cream is pleasing)."

(c) In English, the thing that you like is the direct object. In Spanish, the thing that you like is the subject. Also, in Spanish, the person who likes the thing is the indirect object: to me, to you, etc.: *A Roberto le gusta el helado*/Robert likes ice cream; in other words, "To Robert, ice cream is pleasing to him."

(d) In Spanish, therefore, the verb **gustar** is used in the third person, either in the singular or plural, when you talk about something that you like — something that is pleasing to you. Therefore, the verb form must agree with the subject; if the thing liked is singular, the verb is third person singular; if the thing liked is plural, the verb **gustar** is third person plural: *Me gusta el café/* I like coffee; *Me gustan el café y la leche/* I like coffee and milk (Coffee and milk are pleasing to me).

(e) When you mention the person or the persons who like something, you must use the preposition **a** in front of the person; you must also use the indirect object pronoun of the noun which is the person: *A los muchachos y a las muchachas les gusta jugar*/Boys and girls like to play; that is to say, "To play is pleasing to them, to boys and girls."

(f) Other examples:

Me gusta leer.   I like to read.

Te gusta leer.   You (*familiar*) like to read.

A Felipe le gusta el helado.   Philip likes ice cream.

Al chico le gusta la leche.   The boy likes milk.

A Carlota le gusta bailar.   Charlotte likes to dance.

A las chicas les gustó el libro.   The girls liked the book.

Nos gustó el cuento.   We liked the story.

¿Le gusta a Ud. el español?   Do you like Spanish?

A Pedro y a Ana les gustó la película.   Peter and Anna liked the film.

A mi amigo le gustaron los chocolates.   My friend liked the chocolates; that is to say, "The chocolates were pleasing (pleased) to him (to my friend)."

haber

ha habido . . .   there has been . . . , there have been . . .

había . . .   there was . . . , there were . . .

habrá . . .   there will be . . .

habría . . .   there would be . . .

hubo . . .   there was . . . , there were . . .

haber, haber de + inf., and tener

The verb **haber** (to have) is used as an auxiliary verb (or helping verb) in order to form the seven compound tenses, which are as follows:

Compound Tenses	Example (in the 1st person sing.)
Present Perfect (or Perfect) Indicative	**he hablado** (I have spoken)
Pluperfect (or Past Perfect) Indicative	**había hablado** (I had spoken)
Preterit Perfect (or Past Anterior)	**hube hablado** (I had spoken)
Future Perfect (or Future Anterior)	**habré hablado** (I will have spoken)
Conditional Perfect	**habría hablado** (I would have spoken)
Present Perfect (or Past) Subjunctive	**haya hablado** (I may have spoken)
Pluperfect (or Past Perfect) Subjunctive	**hubiera hablado** *or* **hubiese hablado** (I might have spoken)

For an explanation of the formation of these tenses, see §68.55—§68.61.

The verb **haber** is also used to form the perfect (or past) infinitive: *haber hablado* (to have spoken). As you can see, this is formed by using the infinitive form of haber + the past participle of the main verb.

The verb **haber** is also used to form the perfect participle: *habiendo hablado* (having spoken). As you can see, this is formed by using the present participle of haber + the past participle of the main verb.

The verb **haber + de + inf.** is equivalent to the English use of "to be supposed to . . ." or "to be to . . .": *María ha de traer un pastel, yo he de traer el helado, y mis amigos han de traer sus discos*/Mary is supposed to bring a pie, I am supposed to bring the ice cream, and my friends are to bring their records.

The verb **tener** is used to mean *to have* in the sense of *to possess* or *to hold*: *Tengo un perro y un gato*/I have a dog and a cat; *Tengo un lápiz en la mano*/I have (am holding) a pencil in my hand.

In the preterit tense, **tener** can mean *received*: *Ayer mi padre tuvo un cheque*/Yesterday my father received a check.

hay and hay que + inf.

The word **hay** is not a verb. You might regard it as an impersonal irregular form of **haber.** Actually, the word is composed of **ha** + the archaic **y,** meaning *there.* It is generally regarded as an adverbial expression because it points out that something or someone "is there." Its English equivalent is *There is . . .* or *There are . . .*, for example: *Hay muchos libros en la mesa*/There are many books on the table; *Hay una mosca en la sopa*/There is a fly in the soup; *Hay veinte alumnos en esta clase*/There are twenty students in this class.

Hay que + inf. is an impersonal expression that denotes an obligation and it is commonly translated into English as: *One must . . .* or *It is necessary to . . .* Examples: *Hay que estudiar para aprender*/It is necessary to study in order to learn; *Hay que comer para vivir*/One must eat in order to live.

hacer and **hacerse** (See also **Weather Expressions Using Verbs** in §64. — §64.3)

hace poco   a little while ago

hace un año   a year ago

Hace un mes que partió el señor Molina.   Mr. Molina left one month ago.

hace una hora   an hour ago

hacer caso de   to pay attention to

hacer daño a algo   to harm something

hacer daño a alguien   to harm someone

hacer de   to act as (*El señor González siempre hace de jefe/*Mr. González always acts as a boss.)

hacer el baúl   to pack one's trunk

hacer el favor de + inf.   please (*Haga Ud. el favor de entrar/*Please come in.)

hacer el papel de   to play the role of

hacer la maleta   to pack one's suitcase

hacer pedazos   to smash, to break, to tear into pieces

hacer un viaje   to take a trip

hacer una broma   to play a joke

hacer una pregunta   to ask a question

hacer una visita   to pay a visit

hacerle falta   to need (*A Juan le hace falta un lápiz/*John needs a pencil.)

hacerse   to become (*Elena se hizo dentista/*Helen became a dentist.)

hacerse daño   to hurt oneself, to harm oneself

hacerse tarde   to be getting late (*Vámonos; se hace tarde/*Let's leave; it's getting late.)

¿Cuánto tiempo hace que + present tense . . . ?

(a) Use this formula when you want to ask *How long + the present perfect tense* in English:

¿Cuánto tiempo hace que Ud. estudia el español?   How long have you been studying Spanish?

¿Cuánto tiempo hace que Ud. espera el autobús?   How long have you been waiting for the bus?

(b) When this formula is used, you generally expect the person to tell you how long a time it has been, e.g., one year, two months, a few minutes.

(c) This is used when the action began at some time in the past and continues up to the present moment. That is why you must use the present tense of the verb — the action of studying, waiting, etc. is still going on at the present.

Hace + length of time + que + present tense

(a) This formula is the usual answer to the question **¿Cuánto tiempo hace que + present tense . . . ?**

(b) Since the question is asked in terms of *how long*, the usual answer is in terms of time: a year, two years, a few days, months, minutes, etc.:

Hace tres años que estudio el español. I have been studying Spanish for three years.

Hace veinte minutos que espero el autobús. I have been waiting for the bus for twenty minutes.

(c) The same formula is used if you want to ask *how many weeks, how many months, how many minutes*, etc.:

¿Cuántos años hace que Ud. estudia el español? How many years have you been studying Spanish?

¿Cuántas horas hace que Ud. mira la televisión? How many hours have you been watching television?

¿Desde cuándo + present tense . . . ?

¿Desde cuándo estudia Ud. el español? How long have you been studying Spanish?

Present tense + desde hace + length of time

Estudio el español desde hace tres años. I have been studying Spanish for three years.

¿Cuánto tiempo hacía que + imperfect tense

·a) If the action of the verb began in the past and ended in the past, use the imperfect tense.

(b) This formula is equivalent to the English: *How long + past perfect tense*:

¿Cuánto tiempo hacía que Ud. hablaba cuando entré en la sala de clase? How long had you been talking when I entered into the classroom?

(c) Note that the action of talking in this example began in the past and ended in the past when I entered the classroom.

Hacía + length of time + que + imperfect tense

The imperfect tense of the verb is used here because the action began in the past and ended in the past; it is not going on at the present moment.

Hacía una hora que yo hablaba cuando Ud. entró en la sala de clase. I had been talking for one hour when you entered the classroom.

¿Desde cuándo + imperfect tense . . . ?

¿Desde cuándo hablaba Ud. cuando yo entré en la sala de clase?   How long had you been talking when I entered into the classroom?

Imperfect tense + desde hacía + length of time

(Yo) hablaba desde hacía una hora cuando Ud. entró en la sala de clase.
I had been talking for one hour when you entered into the classroom.

ir, irse

Use **ir** when you simply mean *to go*: *Voy al cine*/I am going to the movies.

Use **irse** when you mean *to leave* in the sense of *to go away*: *Mis padres se fueron al campo para visitar a mis abuelos*/My parents left for (went away to) the country to visit my grandparents.

ir a caballo   to ride horseback
ir a medias   to go halves
ir a pie   to walk (to go on foot)
ir bien   to get along well
ir con tiento   to go quietly, softly
ir delante   to go ahead
ir por   to go for, to go ahead
irse de prisa   to rush away
¡Qué va!   Nonsense! Rubbish!
¡Vaya!   You don't say!
Vaya con Dios.   God be with you.

jugar and tocar

Both these verbs mean *to play* but they have different uses. **Jugar a** means to play a sport, a game: *¿Juega Ud. al tenis?*/Do you play tennis? *Me gusta jugar a la pelota*/I like to play ball.

The verb **tocar** means to play a musical instrument: *Carmen toca muy bien el piano*/Carmen plays the piano very well.

The verb **tocar** has other meanings, too. It is commonly used as follows:
to be one's turn, in which case it takes an indirect object: *¿A quién le toca?*/Whose turn is it? *Le toca a Juan*/It is John's turn.
to knock on a door (tocar a la puerta): *Alguien toca a la puerta*/Someone is knocking on (at) the door.

Essentially, **tocar** means *to touch*.

llegar a ser, hacerse and ponerse

These three verbs mean *to become*. Note the difference in use:

Use **llegar a ser** + **a noun**, e.g., *to become a doctor, to become a teacher*; in other words, the noun indicates the goal that you are striving for: *Quiero llegar a ser doctor*/I want to become a doctor. **Hacerse** is used similarly: *Juan se hizo abogado*/John became a lawyer.

Use **ponerse** + **an adj.**, e.g., *to become pale, to become sick*; in other words, the adj. indicates the state or condition (physical or mental) that you have become: *Cuando vi el accidente, me puse pálido*/When I saw the accident, I became pale; *Mi madre se puso triste al oír la noticia desgraciada*/My mother became sad upon hearing the unfortunate news.

llevar and tomar

These two verbs mean *to take* but note the difference in use:

Llevar means *to take* in the sense of carry or transport from place to place: *José llevó la silla de la cocina al comedor*/Joseph took the chair from the kitchen to the dining room.

The verb **llevar** is also used when you *take someone somewhere*: *Pedro llevó a María al baile anoche*/Peter took Mary to the dance last night.

As you probably know, **llevar** also means *to wear*: *María, ¿por qué llevas la falda nueva?*/Mary, why are you wearing your new skirt?

Tomar means *to take* in the sense of grab or catch: *La profesora tomó el libro y comenzó a leer a la clase*/The teacher took the book and began to read to the class; *Mi amigo tomó el tren esta mañana a las siete*/My friend took the train this morning at seven o'clock.

pedir and preguntar

Both these verbs mean *to ask* but note the difference:

Pedir means *to ask for something* or *to request*: *El alumno pidió un lápiz al profesor*/The pupil asked the teacher for a pencil.

Preguntar means *to inquire, to ask a question*: *La alumna preguntó a la profesora cómo estaba*/The pupil asked the teacher how she was.

pensar de and pensar en

Both these verbs mean *to think of* but note the difference:

Pensar is used with the prep. **de** when you ask someone what he/she thinks of someone or something, when you ask for someone's opinion: *¿Qué piensa Ud. de este libro?*/What do you think of this book? *Pienso que es bueno*/I think that it is good.

Pensar is used with the prep. **en** when you ask someone what or whom he/she is thinking about: *Miguel, no hablas mucho; ¿en qué piensas?*/Michael, you are not talking much; of what are you thinking? (what are you thinking of?); *Pienso en las vacaciones de verano*/I'm thinking of summer vacation.

poder and **saber** (See also **conocer** and **saber**)

Both these verbs mean *can* but the difference in use is as follows:

Poder means *can* in the sense of *ability*: *No puedo ayudarle; lo siento*/I cannot (am unable to) help you; I'm sorry.

Saber means *can* in the sense of *to know how*: *Este niño no sabe contar*/This child can't (does not know how to) count.

In the preterit tense **poder** has the special meaning of *succeeded*: *Después de algunos minutos, Juan pudo abrir la puerta*/After a few minutes, John succeeded in opening the door.

In the preterit tense, **saber** has the special meaning of *found out*: *Lo supe ayer*/I found it out yesterday.

no poder más   to be exhausted, to be all in
No puede ser.   It's impossible. (It can't be.)

poner and **ponerse**

al poner del sol   at sunset
poner coto a   to put a stop to
poner el dedo en la llaga   to hit the nail right on the head
poner en claro   to explain simply and clearly
poner en duda   to doubt, to question
poner en marcha   to set in motion
poner en ridículo   to ridicule
poner los puntos sobre las íes   to mind one's p's and q's; to mind one's own business; to dot the i's
poner por escrito   to put in writing
ponerse de acuerdo   to reach an agreement
ponerse cómodo   to make oneself at home
ponerse en marcha   to start (out)
ponerse mal   to get sick

ser

Debe de ser . . .   It is probably . . .
Debe ser . . .   It ought to be . . .

Es de lamentar.   It's too bad.

Es de mi agrado.   It's to my liking.

Es hora de . . .   It is time to . . .

Es lástima or **Es una lástima.**   It's a pity; It's too bad.

Es que . . .   The fact is . . .

para ser   in spite of being (*Para ser tan viejo, él es muy ágil*/In spite of being so old, he is very nimble.)

sea lo que sea   whatever it may be

ser aficionado a   to be a fan of (*Soy aficionado al béisbol*/I'm a baseball fan.)

ser amable con   to be kind to (*Mi profesora de español es amable conmigo*/My Spanish teacher is kind to me.)⌐

ser todo oídos   to be all ears (*Te escucho; soy todo oídos*/I'm listening to you; I'm all ears.)

si no fuera por . . .   if it were not for . . .

ser and **estar** (See also **estar** on p. 285)

These two verbs mean *to be* but note the differences in use:

Generally speaking, use **ser** when you want to express *to be*.

Use **estar** when *to be* is used in the following ways:

(a) Health:
    (1) *¿Cómo está Ud.?*   How are you?
    (2) *Estoy bien.*   I am well.
    (3) *Estoy enfermo (enferma).*   I am sick.

(b) Location: persons, places, things
    (1) *Estoy en la sala de clase.*   I am in the classroom.
    (2) *La escuela está lejos.*   The school is far.
    (3) *Barcelona está en España.*   Barcelona is (located) in Spain.
    (4) *Los libros están en la mesa.*   The books are on the table.

(c) State or condition: persons
    (1) *Estoy contento (contenta).*   I am happy.
    (2) *Los alumnos están cansados. (Las alumnas están cansadas.)*
    The students are tired.
    (3) *María está triste hoy.*   Mary is sad today.
    (4) *Estoy listo (lista).*   I am ready.
    (5) *Estoy pálido (pálida).*   I am pale.
    (6) *Estoy ocupado (ocupada).*   I am busy.
    (7) *Estoy seguro (segura).*   I am sure.
    (8) *Este hombre está vivo.*   This man is alive.

(9) *Ese hombre está muerto.*   That man is dead.

(10) *Este hombre está borracho.*   This man is drunk.

(d) State or condition: things and places

(1) *La ventana está abierta.*   The window is open.

(2) *La taza está llena.*   The cup is full.

(3) *El té está caliente.*   The tea is hot.

(4) *La limonada está fría.*   The lemonade is cold.

(5) *La biblioteca está cerrada los domingos.*   The library is closed on Sundays.

(e) To form the progressive present of a verb, use the present tense of **estar** + the present part. of the main verb:

Estoy estudiando en mi cuarto y no puedo salir esta noche.
I am studying in my room and I cannot go out tonight.

(f) To form the progressive past of a verb, use the imperfect tense of **estar** + the present part. of the main verb:

Mi hermano estaba leyendo cuando (yo) entré en el cuarto.
My brother was reading when I entered (came into) the room.

ser aburrido   to be boring

ser de   to belong to; **Este libro es de María.**   This book is Mary's.

ser de rigor   to be indispensable

ser de ver   to be worth seeing

ser listo (lista)   to be clever

estar aburrido (aburrida)   to be bored

estar de buenas   to be lucky

estar de buen humor   to be in good spirits, a good mood

estar listo (lista)   to be ready

See also the verbs **ser** and **estar** among the 50 verbs arranged alphabetically in §68.66 in this book.

tener and **tenerse**

¿Cuántos años tienes?   ¿Cuántos años tiene Ud.?   How old are you?
Tengo diez y seis años.   I am sixteen years old.

¿Qué tienes?   ¿Qué tiene Ud.?   What's the matter?   What's the matter with you?   **No tengo nada.**   There's nothing wrong; There's nothing the matter (with me).

tener algo que hacer   to have something to do

tener apetito   to have an appetite

tener calor   to feel (to be) warm (persons)

tener cuidado   to be careful

tener dolor de cabeza   to have a headache

tener dolor de estómago   to have a stomach ache

tener en cuenta   to take into account

tener éxito   to be successful

tener frío   to feel (to be) cold (persons)

tener ganas de + inf.   to feel like + pres. part. (*Tengo ganas de tomar un helado/*I feel like having an ice cream.)

tener gusto en + inf.   to be glad + inf. (*Tengo mucho gusto en conocerle/* I am very glad to meet you.)

tener hambre   to feel (to be) hungry

tener la bondad de   please, please be good enough to . . . (*Tenga la bondad de cerrar la puerta/*Please close the door.)

tener la culpa de algo   to take the blame for something, to be to blame for something (*Tengo la culpa de eso/*I am to blame for that.)

tener lugar   to take place (*El accidente tuvo lugar anoche/*The accident took place last night.)

tener miedo de   to be afraid of

tener mucha sed   to feel (to be) very thirsty (persons)

tener mucho calor   to feel (to be) very warm (persons)

tener mucho frío   to feel (to be) very cold (persons)

tener mucho que hacer   to have a lot to do

tener poco que hacer   to have little to do

tener por   to consider as

tener prisa   to be in a hurry

tener que + inf.   to have + inf. (*Tengo que estudiar/*I have to study.)

tener que ver con   to have to do with (*No tengo nada que ver con él/*I have nothing to do with him.)

tener razón   to be right (*Usted tiene razón/*You are right.) **no tener razón** to be wrong (*Usted no tiene razón/*You are wrong.)

tener sed   to feel (to be) thirsty (persons)

tener sueño   to feel (to be) sleepy

tener suerte   to be lucky

tener vergüenza de   to be ashamed of

tenerse en pie   to stand

volver and devolver

These two verbs mean *to return* but note the difference:

Volver means *to return* in the sense of *to come back*: *Voy a volver a casa/*I am going to return home. A synonym of **volver** is **regresar**: *Los muchachos* *regresaron a las ocho de la noche/*The boys came back (returned) at eight o'clock.

Devolver means *to return* in the sense of *to give back*: *Voy a devolver el libro a la biblioteca/*I am going to return the book to the library.

See also the section on verbs with prepositions in §67.16 — §67.30.

COMPREHENSIVE INDEX

References in this Index are to sections in the book indicated by the symbol § in front of a numerical decimal system. Read my introductory note at the beginning of §1. The abbreviation **ff** means *and the following*. In this Index, find the p. number of Abbreviations used in this book. Other references are to page numbers, and these are cited as p. and the number.